Common Sense, The Crisis
& Other Writings from the
American Revolution

Thomas Paine

Common Sense, The Crisis & Other Writings from the American Revolution

EDITED AND WITH AN INTRODUCTION BY

Eric Foner

LIBRARY OF AMERICA PAPERBACK CLASSICS

Contents

INTRODUCTION

by Eric Foner

Of the men who made the American Revolution, none had a more remarkable career, or suffered a more peculiar fate, than Thomas Paine. While his friends Thomas Jefferson and George Washington, and his ideological antagonist John Adams, came from middle- and upper-class families long established on American soil, Paine's origins lay among the lower orders of eighteenth-century England, and he did not even arrive in the American colonies until the very eve of the War of Independence. Unlike Alexander Hamilton, another leader of the Revolution born abroad, Paine always remained something of an outsider in America, never developing true local roots. His preoccupation was promoting social change. When Benjamin Franklin remarked to Paine, "Where liberty is, there is my country," Paine replied, "Where liberty is not, there is my country."

Paine's profound influence on American events was acknowledged by friends and opponents alike, but after his death he was excluded from the group of revolutionary leaders canonized in American popular culture. His assault upon revealed religion and institutionalized Christianity in *The Age of Reason*, first published in Paris in 1794, cut him off from the evangelical fervor that would play so powerful a role in nineteenth-century American life. His memory would be kept alive primarily by succeeding generations of radicals, who rediscovered him again and again as a symbol of revolutionary internationalism, free thinking, and defiance of existing institutions.

Paine took part in military campaigns and held a number of public offices. But his greatest contribution to the cause of American independence lay in his writings. Through them, he played a pivotal role in the expansion of what scholars call the "public sphere"—the arena of political debate outside the direct control of government. Paine was the pioneer of a new mode of political discourse. In *Common Sense*, his clarion call for American independence published in January 1776, he

employed language carefully crafted to appeal to a mass audience
of ordinary readers, assuming knowledge of no authority but
the Bible and avoiding the florid wording and obscure classical
references typical of pamphlets addressed to educated readers.
His literary style powerfully embodied the democratic thrust of
his political arguments: anyone could grasp the nature of politics
and government. All that was required was common sense.

In his writings both in America and Europe, Paine helped
to create the language of revolution of the late eighteenth
century, and he transformed the meaning of the key words
of political debate. In *Common Sense* he was among the first
writers to use "republic" in a positive rather than a derogatory
sense, as a government representing the will of the people.
In *The Rights of Man*, published in the early 1790s after his
return to England, he abandoned the old classical definition
of "democracy" as a state where each citizen participated
directly in government, and gave it its far broader, far more
favorable modern meaning. Even the word "revolution" was
transformed in his writing from a term deriving from the motion of the planets and implying a cyclical view of history, to
one signifying vast and irreversible social and political change.

But it was *Common Sense*, that remarkable pamphlet advocating the independence of the American colonies from
Britain, which more than any other document impressed
Paine's language on the American political tradition. More
than an argument for independence, the pamphlet rejected
the entire principle of hereditary rule and aristocratic privilege.
Paine's savage attack on "the so much boasted constitution of
England" contained the pamphlet's most striking passages. His
description of the accession of William the Conqueror would
become one of his most frequently quoted passages: "A French
bastard landing with an armed banditti and establishing himself king of England against the consent of the natives, is in
plain terms a very paltry rascally original. . . . The plain truth
is, that the antiquity of English monarchy will not bear looking
into." Or, again, his assault on the principle of hereditary rule:
"Of more worth is one honest man to society . . . than all the
crowned ruffians that ever lived."

Instead of the debased constitution of England, Paine proposed the establishment of republican government in America,

based on new state legislatures with broad suffrage, popular representation through frequent elections, and a written constitution guaranteeing the rights of person and property. He offered a picture of an independent America, trading freely with the entire world, pursuing a policy of friendship with all nations, promoted by a strong continental government. In lyrical rhetoric, he outlined a breathtaking vision of the meaning of American independence: "We have it in our power to begin the world over again. . . . The birthday of a new world is at hand." Paine transformed the struggle over the rights of Englishmen into a contest with meaning for all mankind: "O ye that love mankind! Ye that dare oppose, not only tyranny, but the tyrant, stand forth! Every spot of the old world is overrun with oppression. Freedom hath been hunted round the globe. Asia, and Africa, have long expelled her.—Europe regards her like a stranger, and England hath given her warning to depart. O! receive the fugitive, and prepare in time an asylum for mankind." Paine articulated a vision of the world-historical significance of the American Revolution, identifying the new nation as a beacon of liberty in a world of tyrannies.

Common Sense was an astonishing success. It went through twenty-five editions and reached literally hundreds of thousands of readers in 1776. Paine then threw himself into the dual struggle for independence and democratic reform. In the spring of 1776, under the pseudonym "The Forester," he published a series of articles in the Philadelphia press responding to critics of Common Sense. Shortly after Congress adopted the Declaration of Independence, Paine joined a Philadelphia militia company. In September 1776 he became aide-de-camp to General Nathanael Greene. After the evacuation of Fort Lee, Paine joined the forces of George Washington retreating across New Jersey. To help revive American morale, that December Paine published *The American Crisis*, which began with the famous words, "These are the times that try men's souls." Between 1777 and 1783, Paine published twelve more *Crisis* essays commenting on political and military events as they happened and arousing support for the war.

Paine was also deeply involved in the internal affairs of Pennsylvania, where a popular movement in 1776 inspired the drafting of a new democratic constitution that eliminated the office of governor, abolished imprisonment for debt, called for the establishment of schools with low fees, and allowed all men who paid taxes to vote. In 1777, Paine was elected to the Committee of Correspondence of the Whig Society, an organization established to defend the new constitution against conservative attacks, and in a series of letters in the Pennsylvania press he praised the new frame of government and gave voice to the egalitarian impulse unleashed by the War for Independence. "Wherever I use the words *freedom or rights*," Paine wrote, "I desire to be understood to mean a perfect equality of them." All men, he insisted, should vote, except those who had "voluntarily" surrendered their independence by working as personal servants (a definition of democracy even broader than that in the constitution he was defending).

Beginning with *Common Sense*, Paine outlined in his writings a social and political vision that had a profound impact on the American tradition. For Paine, a republic was simply a government devoted to the public good. Among its hallmarks was equality among its citizens, rather than the ascendancy of any particular social interest. Class conflict was, in a sense, incompatible with the essence of republicanism that, Paine believed, "does not admit of an interest distinct to that of the nation." Paine saw society as divided between the people—a homogenous body with a definable common interest—and a narrow, parasitic aristocracy.

Because of its relatively equal distribution of wealth (always excepting of course slavery, which Paine condemned and played a role in abolishing in Pennsylvania), America, Paine believed, was uniquely fitted to possess a republican government. In such a circumstance, governmental structure need be extremely simple. A central axiom of his outlook was the distinction between society and government. In the opening section of *Common Sense*, Paine explained: "Some writers have so confounded society with government, as to leave little or no distinction between them; whereas they are not only different, but have different origins. Society is produced by our wants, and government by our wickedness. . . . The first is a patron, the last a punisher. Society in every state is a blessing, but government even in its best state is but a necessary evil."

This distinction between society and government helps to explain Paine's vision of a nation without class conflict or economic oppression. Paine was, to be sure, an eloquent and scathing critic of the social order of Europe. He had lived in poverty in England and, working for some years as an excise tax collector, had witnessed the burden of taxation on the poor. He could comment in moving terms on the "mass of wretchedness" lying "hidden from the eye of common observation," which had "scarcely any other chance, than to expire in poverty or infamy." But the cause of this wretchedness, in his view, was political, not economic: the existence of poverty implied that "something must be wrong in the system of government," most notably an aristocratic system that pursued innumerable wars and then burdened the society with excessive taxation to pay for them. Only in *Agrarian Justice*, written in 1796 in France, did Paine suggest that economic inequality might have a deeper origin outside the political system. In that pamphlet, Paine noted that private property in land deprived millions of men their natural right to a portion of the soil.

Paine returned to England in 1787, and subsequently played a role in the French Revolution. In Europe, he produced works that circulated even more widely than his American writings, especially *The Rights of Man* and *The Age of Reason*. This volume, however, focuses on Paine's American career. In these works, Paine enunciated themes which would have a powerful impact on nineteenth-century American political thought: a commitment to social and political equality, a division of society into producing and non-producing classes, hostility to monarchy and hereditary privilege, and an American nationalism coupled with a concern for the fate of liberty overseas. Yet within Paine's American writings lay a crucial tension. On the one hand, Paine exalted the common good and rejected the notion of a society divided into competing social classes. James Madison, more attuned to the reality of class conflict, even in a republic, was in this sense more realistic than Paine. Madison helped to write into the Constitution an elaborate system of checks and balances to prevent a propertyless majority using their democratic power to seize control of the reins of government in order to despoil the rich.

Yet in other respects Paine was no less attuned than Madison to modern currents of economic thought of the late eighteenth century. He exalted commerce as the cement of the natural order of society, and was generally optimistic about economic change. It is instructive that during the crisis in Philadelphia in 1779 over the high price of the necessities of life, Paine first favored public regulation of prices and then switched positions and advocated laissez-faire. In his writings in the 1780s on the Bank of North America, Paine insisted that a central financial institution was essential for promoting the roads, bridges, and other improvements necessary for American economic development. There was a natural affinity between the new political economy of Adam Smith and the politics of Thomas Paine—both arose from belief in the harmonious workings of society.

Recent works on the transformation of American society and social thought during the era of the Revolution have emphasized the shift from a world based on hierarchy and patronage to a more democratic, egalitarian, and competitive culture. These works highlight Paine's role in articulating an egalitarian ideology for a mass audience. In rejecting the crown, as well as the principle of hereditary aristocracy, many Americans also rejected the very idea of human inequality and the society of privileged and fixed status that these traditions embodied. If, as Gordon S. Wood has written, "equality was in fact the most radical and most powerful ideological force let loose in the Revolution," Paine, more than any other individual, championed and explained equality to a mass audience. And unlike many of his contemporaries, Paine recognized the liberating implications of market ideology in a society where status traditionally rested not on individual merit but on one's place in a complex web of privilege and patronage.

In other words, Paine's political philosophy contained within it the common origins of streams of thought—egalitarian democratic politics and laissez-faire economics—that would often diverge in the nineteenth century. Indeed, because his outlook does not fit neatly with modern political alignments, Paine has been claimed as a forebear by individuals and movements with very different political purposes. His democratic ideas, his disdain for established authority, his participation in the American and French Revolutions, make him a hero of the political left; his identification of government as a source of evil, adherence to laissez-faire economics, and call for lowered taxes appeal to the modern right. While American radicals from the abolitionist William Lloyd Garrison to the socialist Eugene V. Debs have been inspired by Paine's writings, many conservatives have recently laid claim to Paine. Beginning with his speech accepting the Republican nomination in 1980, for example, Ronald Reagan frequently quoted Paine's words about the possibility of radical change in human affairs: "we have it in our power to begin the world over again."

As a political writer and as an amateur scientist (he helped design an early iron bridge) Paine helped to usher in the modern world. Yet at the same time he provided a body of ideas and a personal example that would continue to inspire those who believed that the modern world had betrayed, not fulfilled, the high hopes for a just social order raised during Paine's Age of Revolution.

"I know not," John Adams observed in 1806, "whether any man in the world has had more influence on its inhabitants or affairs for the last thirty years than Thomas Paine." Paine's protean intellect and far-reaching vision of political and social change ensure that, like every generation since his death, Americans of the twenty-first century will continue to find him relevant, challenging, and inspiring.

COMMON SENSE,
THE CRISIS
& OTHER WRITINGS FROM
THE AMERICAN REVOLUTION

❦

PAMPHLETS
ARTICLES
LETTERS

Contents

Common Sense

Addressed to the
Inhabitants of America

Man knows no Master save creating HEAVEN,
Or those whom Choice and common Good ordain.
THOMSON.

February 14, 1776

INTRODUCTION.

PERHAPS the sentiments contained in the following pages, are not *yet* sufficiently fashionable to procure them general favor; a long habit of not thinking a thing *wrong*, gives it a superficial appearance of being *right*, and raises at first a formidable outcry in defence of custom. But the tumult soon subsides. Time makes more converts than reason.

As a long and violent abuse of power, is generally the Means of calling the right of it in question (and in Matters too which might never have been thought of, had not the Sufferers been aggravated into the inquiry) and as the King of England hath undertaken in his *own Right*, to support the Parliament in what he calls *Theirs*, and as the good people of this country are grievously oppressed by the combination, they have an undoubted privilege to inquire into the pretensions of both, and equally to reject the usurpation of either.

In the following sheets, the author hath studiously avoided every thing which is personal among ourselves. Compliments as well as censure to individuals make no part thereof. The wise, and the worthy, need not the triumph of a pamphlet; and those whose sentiments are injudicious, or unfriendly, will cease of themselves unless too much pains are bestowed upon their conversion.

The cause of America is in a great measure the cause of all mankind. Many circumstances hath, and will arise, which are not local, but universal, and through which the principles of all Lovers of Mankind are affected, and in the Event of which, their Affections are interested. The laying a Country desolate with Fire and Sword, declaring War against the natural rights of all Mankind, and extirpating the Defenders thereof from the Face of the Earth, is the Concern of every Man to whom Nature hath given the Power of feeling; of which Class, regardless of Party Censure, is the

AUTHOR.

P. S. The Publication of this new Edition hath been delayed, with a View of taking notice (had it been necessary) of any Attempt to refute the Doctrine of Independance: As no Answer hath yet appeared, it is now presumed that none will, the Time needful for getting such a Performance ready for the Public being considerably past.

Who the Author of this Production is, is wholly unnecessary to the Public, as the Object for Attention is the *Doctrine itself*, not the *Man*. Yet it may not be unnecessary to say, That he is unconnected with any Party, and under no sort of Influence public or private, but the influence of reason and principle.

Philadelphia, February 14, 1776.

COMMON SENSE.

OF THE ORIGIN AND DESIGN OF GOVERNMENT IN GENERAL. WITH CONCISE REMARKS ON THE ENGLISH CONSTITUTION.

SOME writers have so confounded society with government, as to leave little or no distinction between them; whereas they are not only different, but have different origins. Society is produced by our wants, and government by our wickedness; the former promotes our happiness *positively* by uniting our affections, the latter *negatively* by restraining our vices. The one encourages intercourse, the other creates distinctions. The first is a patron, the last a punisher.

Society in every state is a blessing, but government even in its best state is but a necessary evil; in its worst state an intolerable one; for when we suffer, or are exposed to the same miseries *by a government*, which we might expect in a country *without government*, our calamity is heightened by reflecting that we furnish the means by which we suffer. Government, like dress, is the badge of lost innocence; the palaces of kings are built on the ruins of the bowers of paradise. For were the impulses of conscience clear, uniform, and irresistably obeyed, man would need no other lawgiver; but that not being the case, he finds it necessary to surrender up a part of his property to furnish means for the protection of the rest; and this he is induced to do by the same prudence which in every other case advises him out of two evils to choose the least. *Wherefore*, security being the true design and end of government, it unanswerably follows that whatever *form* thereof appears most likely to ensure it to us, with the least expence and greatest benefit, is preferable to all others.

In order to gain a clear and just idea of the design and end of government, let us suppose a small number of persons settled in some sequestered part of the earth, unconnected with the rest, they will then represent the first peopling of any country, or of the world. In this state of natural liberty, society will be their first thought. A thousand motives will excite them thereto, the strength of one man is so unequal to his wants, and his mind so unfitted for perpetual solitude, that he is soon obliged to seek assistance and relief of another, who in his turn requires the same. Four or five united would be able to raise a tolerable dwelling in the midst of a wilderness, but *one* man might labour out the common period of life without accomplishing any thing; when he had felled his timber he could not remove it, nor erect it after it was removed; hunger in the mean time would urge him from his work, and every different want call him a different way. Disease, nay even misfortune would be death, for though neither might be mortal, yet either would disable him from living, and reduce him to a state in which he might rather be said to perish than to die.

Thus necessity, like a gravitating power, would soon form our newly arrived emigrants into society, the reciprocal blessings of which, would supersede, and render the obligations of law and government unnecessary while they remained perfectly just to each other; but as nothing but heaven is impregnable to vice, it will unavoidably happen, that in proportion as they surmount the first difficulties of emigration, which bound them together in a common cause, they will begin to relax in their duty and attachment to each other; and this remissness, will point out the necessity, of establishing some form of government to supply the defect of moral virtue.

Some convenient tree will afford them a State-House, under the branches of which, the whole colony may assemble to deliberate on public matters. It is more than probable that their first laws will have the title only of REGULATIONS, and be enforced by no other penalty than public disesteem. In this first parliament every man, by natural right, will have a seat.

But as the colony increases, the public concerns will increase likewise, and the distance at which the members may be separated, will render it too inconvenient for all of them to meet on every occasion as at first, when their number was small, their habitations near, and the public concerns few and trifling. This will point out the convenience of their consenting to leave the legislative part to be managed by a select number chosen from the whole body, who are supposed to have the same concerns at stake which those have who appointed them, and who will act in the same manner as the whole body would act were they present. If the colony continue increasing, it will become necessary to augment the number of the representatives, and that the interest of every part of the colony may be attended to, it will be found best to divide the whole into convenient parts, each part sending its proper number; and that the *elected* might never form to themselves an interest separate from the *electors*, prudence will point out the propriety of having elections often; because as the *elected* might by that means return and mix again with the general body of the *electors* in a few months, their fidelity to the public will be secured by the prudent reflexion of not making a rod for themselves. And as this frequent interchange will establish a common interest with every part of the community, they will mutually and naturally support each other, and on this (not on the unmeaning name of king) depends the *strength of government, and the happiness of the governed.*

Here then is the origin and rise of government; namely, a mode rendered necessary by the inability of moral virtue to govern the world; here too is the design and end of government, viz. freedom and security. And however our eyes may be dazzled with show, or our ears deceived by sound; however prejudice may warp our wills, or interest darken our understanding, the simple voice of nature and of reason will say, it is right.

I draw my idea of the form of government from a principle in nature, which no art can overturn, viz. that the more simple any thing is, the less liable it is to be disordered, and the easier repaired when disordered; and with this maxim in view, I offer a few remarks on the so much boasted constitution of England. That it was noble for the dark and slavish times in which it was erected, is granted. When the world was over run with tyranny the least remove therefrom was a glorious rescue. But that it is imperfect, subject to convulsions, and incapable of producing what it seems to promise, is easily demonstrated.

Absolute governments (tho' the disgrace of human nature) have this advantage with them, that they are simple; if the people suffer, they know the head from which their suffering springs, know likewise the remedy, and are not bewildered by a variety of causes and cures. But the constitution of England is so exceedingly complex, that the nation may suffer for years together without being able to discover in which part the fault lies, some will say in one and some in another, and every political physician will advise a different medicine.

I know it is difficult to get over local or long standing prejudices, yet if we will suffer ourselves to examine the component parts of the English constitution, we shall find them to be the base remains of two ancient tyrannies, compounded with some new republican materials.

First.—The remains of monarchical tyranny in the person of the king.

Secondly.—The remains of aristocratical tyranny in the persons of the peers.

Thirdly.—The new republican materials, in the persons of the commons, on whose virtue depends the freedom of England.

The two first, by being hereditary, are independent of the people; wherefore in a *constitutional sense* they contribute nothing towards the freedom of the state.

To say that the constitution of England is a *union* of three powers reciprocally *checking* each other, is farcical, either the words have no meaning, or they are flat contradictions.

To say that the commons is a check upon the king, presupposes two things.

First.—That the king is not to be trusted without being looked after, or in other words, that a thirst for absolute power is the natural disease of monarchy.

Secondly.—That the commons, by being appointed for that purpose, are either wiser or more worthy of confidence than the crown.

But as the same constitution which gives the commons a power to check the king by withholding the supplies, gives afterwards the king a power to check the commons, by empowering him to reject their other bills; it again supposes that the king is wiser than those whom it has already supposed to be wiser than him. A mere absurdity!

There is something exceedingly ridiculous in the composition of monarchy; it first excludes a man from the means of information, yet empowers him to act in cases where the highest judgment is required. The state of a king shuts him from the world, yet the business of a king requires him to know it thoroughly; wherefore the different parts, by unnaturally opposing and destroying each other, prove the whole character to be absurd and useless.

Some writers have explained the English constitution thus; the king, say they, is one, the people another; the peers are an house in behalf of the king; the commons in behalf of the people; but this hath all the distinctions of an house divided against itself; and though the expressions be pleasantly arranged, yet when examined they appear idle and ambiguous; and it will always happen, that the nicest construction that words are capable of, when applied to the description of some thing which either cannot exist, or is too incomprehensible to be within the compass of description, will be words of sound only, and though they may amuse the ear, they cannot inform the mind, for this explanation includes a previous question, viz. *How came the king by a power which the people are afraid to trust, and always obliged to check?* Such a power could not be the gift of a wise people, neither can any power, *which needs checking*, be from God; yet the provision, which the constitution makes, supposes such a power to exist.

But the provision is unequal to the task; the means either cannot or will not accomplish the end, and the whole affair is a felo de se; for as the greater weight will always carry up the less, and as all the wheels of a machine are put in motion by one, it only remains to know which power in the constitution has the most weight, for that will govern; and though the others, or a part of them, may clog, or, as the phrase is, check the rapidity of its motion, yet so long as they cannot stop it, their endeavors will be ineffectual; the first moving power will at last have its way, and what it wants in speed is supplied by time.

That the crown is this overbearing part in the English constitution needs not be mentioned, and that it derives its whole consequence merely from being the giver of places and pensions is self-evident, wherefore, though we have been wise enough to shut and lock a door against absolute monarchy, we at the same time have been foolish enough to put the crown in possession of the key.

The prejudice of Englishmen, in favour of their own government by king, lords and commons, arises as much or more from national pride than reason. Individuals are undoubtedly safer in England than in some other countries, but the *will* of the king is as much the *law* of the land in Britain as in France, with this difference, that instead of proceeding directly from his mouth, it is handed to the people under the more formidable shape of an act of parliament. For the fate of Charles the First, hath only made kings more subtle—not more just.

Wherefore, laying aside all national pride and prejudice in favour of modes and forms, the plain truth is, that *it is wholly owing to the constitution of the people, and not to the constitution of the government* that the crown is not as oppressive in England as in Turkey.

An inquiry into the *constitutional errors* in the English form of government is at this time highly necessary, for as we are never in a proper condition of doing justice to others, while we continue under the influence of some leading partiality, so neither are we capable of doing it to ourselves while we remain fettered by any obstinate prejudice. And as a man, who is attached to a prostitute, is unfitted to choose or judge of a wife, so any prepossession in favour of a rotten constitution of government will disable us from discerning a good one.

OF MONARCHY AND HEREDITARY SUCCESSION.

MANKIND being originally equals in the order of creation, the equality could only be destroyed by some subsequent circumstance; the distinctions of rich, and poor, may in a great measure be accounted for, and that without having recourse to the harsh ill sounding names of oppression and avarice. Oppression is often the *consequence*, but seldom or never the *means* of riches; and though avarice will preserve a man from being necessitously poor, it generally makes him too timorous to be wealthy.

But there is another and greater distinction for which no truly natural or religious reason can be assigned, and that is, the distinction of men into KINGS and SUBJECTS. Male and female are the distinctions of nature, good and bad the distinctions of heaven; but how a race of men came into the world so exalted above the rest, and distinguished like some new species, is worth enquiring into, and whether they are the means of happiness or of misery to mankind.

In the early ages of the world, according to the scripture chronology, there were no kings; the consequence of which was there were no wars; it is the pride of kings which throw mankind into confusion. Holland without a king hath enjoyed more peace for this last century than any of the monarchical governments in Europe. Antiquity favors the same remark; for the quiet and rural lives of the first patriarchs hath a happy something in them, which vanishes away when we come to the history of Jewish royalty.

Government by kings was first introduced into the world by the Heathens, from whom the children of Israel copied the custom. It was the most prosperous invention the Devil ever set on foot for the promotion of idolatry. The Heathens paid divine honors to their deceased kings, and the christian world hath improved on the plan by doing the same to their living ones. How impious is the title of sacred majesty applied to a worm, who in the midst of his splendor is crumbling into dust!

As the exalting one man so greatly above the rest cannot be justified on the equal rights of nature, so neither can it be defended on the authority of scripture; for the will of the Almighty, as declared by Gideon and the prophet Samuel, expressly disapproves of government by kings. All anti-monarchical parts of scripture have been very smoothly glossed over in monarchical governments, but they undoubtedly merit the attention of countries which have their governments yet to form. *"Render unto Cæsar the things which are Cæsar's"* is the scripture doctrine of courts, yet it is no support of monarchical government, for the Jews at that time were without a king, and in a state of vassalage to the Romans.

Near three thousand years passed away from the Mosaic account of the creation, till the Jews under a national delusion requested a king. Till then their form of government (except in extraordinary cases, where the Almighty interposed) was a kind of republic administred by a judge and the elders of the tribes. Kings they had none, and it was held sinful to acknowledge any being under that title but the Lord of Hosts. And when a man seriously reflects on the idolatrous homage which is paid to the persons of Kings, he need not wonder, that the Almighty ever jealous of his honor, should disapprove of a form of government which so impiously invades the prerogative of heaven.

Monarchy is ranked in scripture as one of the sins of the Jews, for which a curse in reserve is denounced against them. The history of that transaction is worth attending to.

The children of Israel being oppressed by the Midianites, Gideon marched against them with a small army, and victory, thro' the divine interposition, decided in his favour. The Jews elate with success, and attributing it to the generalship of Gideon, proposed making him a king, saying, *Rule thou over us, thou and thy son and thy son's son.* Here was temptation in its fullest extent; not a kingdom only, but an hereditary one, but Gideon in the piety of his soul replied, *I will not rule over you, neither shall my son rule over you.* THE LORD SHALL RULE OVER YOU. Words need not be more explicit; Gideon doth not *decline* the honor, but denieth their right to give it; neither doth he compliment them with invented declarations of his thanks, but in the positive stile of a prophet charges them with disaffection to their proper Sovereign, the King of heaven.

About one hundred and thirty years after this, they fell again into the same error. The hankering which the Jews had for the idolatrous customs of the Heathens, is something exceedingly unaccountable; but so it was, that laying hold of the misconduct of Samuel's two sons, who were entrusted with some secular concerns, they came in an abrupt and clamorous manner to Samuel, saying, *Behold thou art old, and thy sons walk not in thy ways, now make us a king to judge us like all the other nations.* And here we cannot but observe that their motives were bad, viz. that they might be *like* unto other nations, i. e. the Heathens, whereas their true glory laid in being as much *unlike* them as possible. *But the thing displeased Samuel when they said, Give us a king to judge us; and Samuel prayed unto the Lord, and the Lord said unto Samuel, Hearken unto the voice of the people in all that they say unto thee, for they have not rejected thee, but they have rejected me,* THAT I SHOULD NOT REIGN OVER THEM. *According to all the works which they have done since the day that I brought them up out of Egypt, even unto this day; wherewith they have forsaken me and served other Gods; so do they also unto thee. Now therefore hearken unto their voice, howbeit, protest solemnly unto them and shew them the manner of the king that shall reign over them,* i. e. not of any particular king, but the general manner of the kings of the earth, whom Israel was so eagerly copying after. And notwithstanding the great distance of time and difference of manners, the character is still in fashion. *And Samuel told all the words of the Lord unto the people, that asked of him a king. And he said, This shall be the manner of the king that shall reign over you; he will take your sons and appoint them for himself, for his chariots, and to be his horsemen, and some shall run before his chariots* (this description agrees with the present mode of impressing men) *and he will appoint him captains over thousands and captains over fifties, and will set them to ear his ground and to reap his harvest, and to make his instruments of war, and instruments of his chariots; and he will take your daughters to be confectionaries, and to be cooks and to be bakers* (this describes the expence and luxury as well as the oppression of kings) *and he will take your fields and your olive yards, even the best of them, and give them to his servants; and he will take the tenth of your seed, and of your vineyards, and give them to his officers and to his servants* (by which we see that bribery, corruption and favoritism are the standing vices of kings) *and he will take the tenth of your men servants, and your maid servants, and your goodliest young men and your asses, and put them to his work; and he will take the tenth of your sheep, and ye shall be his servants, and ye shall cry out in that day because of your king which ye shall have chosen,* AND THE LORD WILL NOT HEAR YOU IN THAT DAY. This accounts for the continuation of monarchy; neither do the characters of the few good kings which have lived since, either sanctify the title, or blot out the sinfulness of the origin; the high enco-mium given of David takes no notice of him *officially as a king,* but only as a *man* after God's own heart. *Nevertheless the People refused to obey the voice of Samuel, and they said, Nay, but we will have a king over us, that we may be like all the nations, and that our king may judge us, and go out before us, and fight our battles.* Samuel continued to reason with them, but to no purpose; he set before them their ingratitude, but all would not avail; and seeing them fully bent on their folly, he cried out, *I will call unto the Lord, and he shall send thun-der and rain* (which then was a punishment, being in the time of wheat harvest) *that ye may perceive and see that your wickedness is great which ye have done in the sight of the Lord,* IN ASKING YOU A KING. *So Samuel called unto the Lord, and the Lord sent thunder and rain that day, and all the people greatly feared the Lord and Samuel. And all the people said unto Samuel, Pray for thy servants unto the Lord thy God that we die not, for* WE HAVE ADDED UNTO OUR SINS THIS EVIL, TO ASK A KING. These portions of scripture are direct and positive. They admit of no equivocal construction. That the Almighty hath here entered his protest against monarchical government is true, or the scripture is false. And a man hath good reason to believe that there is as much of king-craft, as priest-craft, in withholding the scripture from the public in Popish countries. For monarchy in every instance is the Popery of government.

To the evil of monarchy we have added that of hereditary succession; and as the first is a degradation and lessening of ourselves, so the second, claimed as a matter of right, is an insult and an imposition on posterity. For all men being originally equals, no *one* by *birth* could have a right to set up his own family in perpetual preference to all others for ever, and though himself might deserve *some* decent degree of honors of his cotemporaries, yet his descendants might be far too unworthy to inherit them. One of the strongest *natural* proofs of the folly of hereditary right in kings, is, that nature disapproves it, otherwise she would not so frequently turn it into ridicule by giving mankind an *ass for a lion*.

Secondly, as no man at first could possess any other public honors than were bestowed upon him, so the givers of those honors could have no power to give away the right of posterity, and though they might say "We choose you for *our* head," they could not, without manifest injustice to their children, say "that your children and your childrens children shall reign over *ours* for ever." Because such an unwise, unjust, unnatural compact might (perhaps) in the next succession put them under the government of a rogue or a fool. Most wise men, in their private sentiments, have ever treated hereditary right with contempt; yet it is one of those evils, which when once established is not easily removed; many submit from fear, others from superstition, and the more powerful part shares with the king the plunder of the rest.

This is supposing the present race of kings in the world to have had an honorable origin; whereas it is more than probable, that could we take off the dark covering of antiquity, and trace them to their first rise, that we should find the first of them nothing better than the principal ruffian of some restless gang, whose savage manners or pre-eminence in subtility obtained him the title of chief among plunderers; and who by increasing in power, and extending his depredations, overawed the quiet and defenceless to purchase their safety by frequent contributions. Yet his electors could have no idea of giving hereditary right to his descendants, because such a perpetual exclusion of themselves was incompatible with the free and unrestrained principles they professed to live by. Wherefore, hereditary succession in the early ages of monarchy could not take place as a matter of claim, but as something

casual or complimental; but as few or no records were extant
in those days, and traditionary history stuffed with fables, it
was very easy, after the lapse of a few generations, to trump
up some superstitious tale, conveniently timed, Mahomet like,
to cram hereditary right down the throats of the vulgar. Perhaps the disorders which threatened, or seemed to threaten,
on the decease of a leader and the choice of a new one (for
elections among ruffians could not be very orderly) induced
many at first to favor hereditary pretensions; by which means
it happened, as it hath happened since, that what at first was
submitted to as a convenience, was afterwards claimed as a
right.

England, since the conquest, hath known some few good
monarchs, but groaned beneath a much larger number of bad
ones; yet no man in his senses can say that their claim under
William the Conqueror is a very honorable one. A French
bastard landing with an armed banditti, and establishing himself king of England against the consent of the natives, is in
plain terms a very paltry rascally original.—It certainly hath
no divinity in it. However, it is needless to spend much time
in exposing the folly of hereditary right, if there are any so
weak as to believe it, let them promiscuously worship the ass
and lion, and welcome. I shall neither copy their humility, nor
disturb their devotion.

Yet I should be glad to ask how they suppose kings came at
first? The question admits but of three answers, viz. either by
lot, by election, or by usurpation. If the first king was taken
by lot, it establishes a precedent for the next, which excludes
hereditary succession. Saul was by lot, yet the succession was
not hereditary, neither does it appear from that transaction
there was any intention it ever should. If the first king of any
country was by election, that likewise establishes a precedent
for the next; for to say, that the *right* of all future generations
is taken away, by the act of the first electors, in their choice
not only of a king, but of a family of kings for ever, hath no
parrallel in or out of scripture but the doctrine of original sin,
which supposes the free will of all men lost in Adam; and
from such comparison, and it will admit of no other, hereditary succession can derive no glory. For as in Adam all sinned,

and as in the first electors all men obeyed; as in the one all
mankind were subjected to Satan, and in the other to Sovereignty; as our innocence was lost in the first, and our authority in the last; and as both disable us from reassuming some
former state and privilege, it unanswerably follows that original sin and hereditary succession are parellels. Dishonorable
rank! Inglorious connexion! Yet the most subtile sophist cannot produce a juster simile.

As to usurpation, no man will be so hardy as to defend it;
and that William the Conqueror was an usurper is a fact not
to be contradicted. The plain truth is, that the antiquity of
English monarchy will not bear looking into.

But it is not so much the absurdity as the evil of hereditary
succession which concerns mankind. Did it ensure a race of
good and wise men it would have the seal of divine authority,
but as it opens a door to the *foolish*, the *wicked*, and the *improper*, it hath in it the nature of oppression. Men who look
upon themselves born to reign, and others to obey, soon
grow insolent; selected from the rest of mankind their minds
are early poisoned by importance; and the world they act in
differs so materially from the world at large, that they have
but little opportunity of knowing its true interests, and when
they succeed to the government are frequently the most ignorant and unfit of any throughout the dominions.

Another evil which attends hereditary succession is, that the
throne is subject to be possessed by a minor at any age; all
which time the regency, acting under the cover of a king,
have every opportunity and inducement to betray their trust.
The same national misfortune happens, when a king worn out
with age and infirmity, enters the last stage of human weakness. In both these cases the public becomes a prey to every
miscreant, who can tamper successfully with the follies either
of age or infancy.

The most plausible plea, which hath ever been offered in
favour of hereditary succession, is, that it preserves a nation
from civil wars; and were this true, it would be weighty;
whereas, it is the most barefaced falsity ever imposed upon
mankind. The whole history of England disowns the fact.
Thirty kings and two minors have reigned in that distracted
kingdom since the conquest, in which time there have been

(including the Revolution) no less than eight civil wars and nineteen rebellions. Wherefore instead of making for peace, it makes against it, and destroys the very foundation it seems to stand on.

The contest for monarchy and succession, between the houses of York and Lancaster, laid England in a scene of blood for many years. Twelve pitched battles, besides skirmishes and sieges, were fought between Henry and Edward. Twice was Henry prisoner to Edward, who in his turn was prisoner to Henry. And so uncertain is the fate of war and the temper of a nation, when nothing but personal matters are the ground of a quarrel, that Henry was taken in triumph from a prison to a palace, and Edward obliged to fly from a palace to a foreign land; yet, as sudden transitions of temper are seldom lasting, Henry in his turn was driven from the throne, and Edward recalled to succeed him. The parliament always following the strongest side.

This contest began in the reign of Henry the Sixth, and was not entirely extinguished till Henry the Seventh, in whom the families were united. Including a period of 67 years, viz. from 1422 to 1489.

In short, monarchy and succession have laid (not this or that kingdom only) but the world in blood and ashes. 'Tis a form of government which the word of God bears testimony against, and blood will attend it.

If we inquire into the business of a king, we shall find that in some countries they have none; and after sauntering away their lives without pleasure to themselves or advantage to the nation, withdraw from the scene, and leave their successors to tread the same idle round. In absolute monarchies the whole weight of business, civil and military, lies on the king; the children of Israel in their request for a king, urged this plea "that he may judge us, and go out before us and fight our battles." But in countries where he is neither a judge nor a general, as in England, a man would be puzzled to know what *is* his business.

The nearer any government approaches to a republic the less business there is for a king. It is somewhat difficult to find a proper name for the government of England. Sir William Meredith calls it a republic; but in its present state it is unworthy of the name, because the corrupt influence of the crown, by having all the places in its disposal, hath so effectually swallowed up the power, and eaten out the virtue of the house of commons (the republican part in the constitution) that the government of England is nearly as monarchical as that of France or Spain. Men fall out with names without understanding them. For it is the republican and not the monarchical part of the constitution of England which Englishmen glory in, viz. the liberty of choosing an house of commons from out of their own body—and it is easy to see that when republican virtue fails, slavery ensues. Why is the constitution of England sickly, but because monarchy hath poisoned the republic, the crown hath engrossed the commons?

In England a king hath little more to do than to make war and give away places; which in plain terms, is to impoverish the nation and set it together by the ears. A pretty business indeed for a man to be allowed eight hundred thousand sterling a year for, and worshipped into the bargain! Of more worth is one honest man to society and in the sight of God, than all the crowned ruffians that ever lived.

THOUGHTS ON THE PRESENT STATE OF AMERICAN AFFAIRS.

IN the following pages I offer nothing more than simple facts, plain arguments, and common sense; and have no other preliminaries to settle with the reader, than that he will divest himself of prejudice and prepossession, and suffer his reason and his feelings to determine for themselves; that he will put *on*, or rather that he will not put *off*, the true character of a man, and generously enlarge his views beyond the present day.

Volumes have been written on the subject of the struggle between England and America. Men of all ranks have embarked in the controversy, from different motives, and with various designs; but all have been ineffectual, and the period of debate is closed. Arms, as the last resource, decide the contest; the appeal was the choice of the king, and the continent hath accepted the challenge.

It hath been reported of the late Mr. Pelham (who tho' an

able minister was not without his faults) that on his being attacked in the house of commons, on the score, that his measures were only of a temporary kind, replied *"they will last my time."* Should a thought so fatal and unmanly possess the colonies in the present contest, the name of ancestors will be remembered by future generations with detestation.

The sun never shined on a cause of greater worth. 'Tis not the affair of a city, a country, a province, or a kingdom, but of a continent—of at least one eighth part of the habitable globe. 'Tis not the concern of a day, a year, or an age; posterity are virtually involved in the contest, and will be more or less affected, even to the end of time, by the proceedings now. Now is the seed time of continental union, faith and honor. The least fracture now will be like a name engraved with the point of a pin on the tender rind of a young oak; the wound will enlarge with the tree, and posterity read it in full grown characters.

By referring the matter from argument to arms, a new æra for politics is struck; a new method of thinking hath arisen. All plans, proposals, &c. prior to the nineteenth of April, *i. e.* to the commencement of hostilities, are like the almanacks of the last year; which, though proper then, are superceded and useless now. Whatever was advanced by the advocates on either side of the question then, terminated in one and the same point, viz. a union with Great-Britain; the only difference between the parties was the method of effecting it; the one proposing force, the other friendship; but it hath so far happened that the first hath failed, and the second hath withdrawn her influence.

As much hath been said of the advantages of reconciliation, which, like an agreeable dream, hath passed away and left us as we were, it is but right, that we should examine the contrary side of the argument, and inquire into some of the many material injuries which these colonies sustain, and always will sustain, by being connected with, and dependant on Great-Britain. To examine that connexion and dependance, on the principles of nature and common sense, to see what we have to trust to, if separated, and what we are to expect, if dependant.

I have heard it asserted by some, that as America hath

flourished under her former connexion with Great-Britain, that the same connexion is necessary towards her future happiness, and will always have the same effect. Nothing can be more fallacious than this kind of argument. We may as well assert that because a child has thrived upon milk, that it is never to have meat, or that the first twenty years of our lives is to become a precedent for the next twenty. But even this is admitting more than is true, for I answer roundly, that America would have flourished as much, and probably much more, had no European power had any thing to do with her. The commerce, by which she hath enriched herself are the necessaries of life, and will always have a market while eating is the custom of Europe.

But she has protected us, say some. That she hath engrossed us is true, and defended the continent at our expence as well as her own is admitted, and she would have defended Turkey from the same motive, viz. the sake of trade and dominion.

Alas, we have been long led away by ancient prejudices, and made large sacrifices to superstition. We have boasted the protection of Great-Britain, without considering, that her motive was *interest* not *attachment*; that she did not protect us from *our enemies* on *our account*, but from *her enemies* on *her own account*, from those who had no quarrel with us on any *other account*, and who will always be our enemies on the *same account*. Let Britain wave her pretensions to the continent, or the continent throw off the dependance, and we should be at peace with France and Spain were they at war with Britain. The miseries of Hanover last war ought to warn us against connexions.

It hath lately been asserted in parliament, that the colonies have no relation to each other but through the parent country, *i. e.* that Pennsylvania and the Jerseys, and so on for the rest, are sister colonies by the way of England; this is certainly a very round-about way of proving relationship, but it is the nearest and only true way of proving enemyship, if I may so call it. France and Spain never were, nor perhaps ever will be our enemies as *Americans*, but as our being the *subjects of Great-Britain*.

But Britain is the parent country, say some. Then the more

shame upon her conduct. Even brutes do not devour their young, nor savages make war upon their families; wherefore the assertion, if true, turns to her reproach; but it happens not to be true, or only partly so, and the phrase *parent* or *mother country* hath been jesuitically adopted by the king and his parasites, with a low papistical design of gaining an unfair bias on the credulous weakness of our minds. Europe, and not England, is the parent country of America. This new world hath been the asylum for the persecuted lovers of civil and religious liberty from *every part* of Europe. Hither have they fled, not from the tender embraces of the mother, but from the cruelty of the monster; and it is so far true of England, that the same tyranny which drove the first emigrants from home, pursues their descendants still.

In this extensive quarter of the globe, we forget the narrow limits of three hundred and sixty miles (the extent of England) and carry our friendship on a larger scale; we claim brotherhood with every European christian, and triumph in the generosity of the sentiment.

It is pleasant to observe by what regular gradations we surmount the force of local prejudice, as we enlarge our acquaintance with the world. A man born in any town in England divided into parishes, will naturally associate most with his fellow parishioners (because their interests in many cases will be common) and distinguish him by the name of *neighbour*; if he meet him but a few miles from home, he drops the narrow idea of a street, and salutes him by the name of *townsman*; if he travel out of the county, and meet him in any other, he forgets the minor divisions of street and town, and calls him *countryman*, i. e. *county-man*; but if in their foreign excursions they should associate in France or any other part of *Europe*, their local remembrance would be enlarged into that of *Englishmen*. And by a just parity of reasoning, all Europeans meeting in America, or any other quarter of the globe, are *countrymen*; for England, Holland, Germany, or Sweden, when compared with the whole, stand in the same places on the larger scale, which the divisions of street, town, and county do on the smaller ones; distinctions too limited for continental minds. Not one third of the inhabitants, even of this province, are of English descent. Wherefore I reprobate the phrase of parent or mother country applied to England only, as being false, selfish, narrow and ungenerous.

But admitting, that we were all of English descent, what does it amount to? Nothing. Britain, being now an open enemy, extinguishes every other name and title: And to say that reconciliation is our duty, is truly farcical. The first king of England, of the present line (William the Conqueror) was a Frenchman, and half the Peers of England are descendants from the same country; wherefore, by the same method of reasoning, England ought to be governed by France.

Much hath been said of the united strength of Britain and the colonies, that in conjunction they might bid defiance to the world. But this is mere presumption; the fate of war is uncertain, neither do the expressions mean any thing; for this continent would never suffer itself to be drained of inhabitants, to support the British arms in either Asia, Africa, or Europe.

Besides, what have we to do with setting the world at defiance? Our plan is commerce, and that, well attended to, will secure us the peace and friendship of all Europe; because, it is the interest of all Europe to have America a *free port*. Her trade will always be a protection, and her barrenness of gold and silver secure her from invaders.

I challenge the warmest advocate for reconciliation, to shew, a single advantage that this continent can reap, by being connected with Great Britain. I repeat the challenge, not a single advantage is derived. Our corn will fetch its price in any market in Europe, and our imported goods must be paid for buy them where we will.

But the injuries and disadvantages we sustain by that connection, are without number; and our duty to mankind at large, as well as to ourselves, instruct us to renounce the alliance: Because, any submission to, or dependance on Great-Britain, tends directly to involve this continent in European wars and quarrels; and sets us at variance with nations, who would otherwise seek our friendship, and against whom, we have neither anger nor complaint. As Europe is our market for trade, we ought to form no partial connection with any part of it. It is the true interest of America to steer clear of European contentions, which she never can do, while by her dependance on Britain, she is made the make-weight in the scale of British politics.

Europe is too thickly planted with kingdoms to be long at peace, and whenever a war breaks out between England and any foreign power, the trade of America goes to ruin, *because of her connection with Britain.* The next war may not turn out like the last, and should it not, the advocates for reconciliation now will be wishing for separation then, because, neutrality in that case, would be a safer convoy than a man of war. Every thing that is right or natural pleads for separation. The blood of the slain, the weeping voice of nature cries, 'TIS TIME TO PART. Even the distance at which the Almighty hath placed England and America, is a strong and natural proof, that the authority of the one, over the other, was never the design of Heaven. The time likewise at which the continent was discovered, adds weight to the argument, and the manner in which it was peopled encreases the force of it. The reformation was preceded by the discovery of America, as if the Almighty graciously meant to open a sanctuary to the persecuted in future years, when home should afford neither friendship nor safety.

The authority of Great-Britain over this continent, is a form of government, which sooner or later must have an end: And a serious mind can draw no true pleasure by looking forward, under the painful and positive conviction, that what he calls "the present constitution" is merely temporary. As parents, we can have no joy, knowing that *this government* is not sufficiently lasting to ensure any thing which we may bequeath to posterity: And by a plain method of argument, as we are running the next generation into debt, we ought to do the work of it, otherwise we use them meanly and pitifully. In order to discover the line of our duty rightly, we should take our children in our hand, and fix our station a few years farther into life; that eminence will present a prospect, which a few present fears and prejudices conceal from our sight.

Though I would carefully avoid giving unnecessary offence, yet I am inclined to believe, that all those who espouse the doctrine of reconciliation, may be included within the following descriptions. Interested men, who are not to be trusted;

weak men, who *cannot* see; prejudiced men, who *will not* see; and a certain set of moderate men, who think better of the European world than it deserves; and this last class, by an ill-judged deliberation, will be the cause of more calamities to this continent, than all the other three.

It is the good fortune of many to live distant from the scene of sorrow; the evil is not sufficiently brought to *their* doors to make *them* feel the precariousness with which all American property is possessed. But let our imaginations transport us for a few moments to Boston, that seat of wretchedness will teach us wisdom, and instruct us for ever to renounce a power in whom we can have no trust. The inhabitants of that unfortunate city, who but a few months ago were in ease and affluence, have now, no other alternative than to stay and starve, or turn out to beg. Endangered by the fire of their friends if they continue within the city, and plundered by the soldiery if they leave it. In their present condition they are prisoners without the hope of redemption, and in a general attack for their relief, they would be exposed to the fury of both armies.

Men of passive tempers look somewhat lightly over the offences of Britain, and, still hoping for the best, are apt to call out, *"Come, come, we shall be friends again, for all this."* But examine the passions and feelings of mankind, Bring the doctrine of reconciliation to the touchstone of nature, and then tell me, whether you can hereafter love, honour, and faithfully serve the power that hath carried fire and sword into your land? If you cannot do all these, then are you only deceiving yourselves, and by your delay bringing ruin upon posterity. Your future connection with Britain, whom you can neither love nor honour, will be forced and unnatural, and being formed only on the plan of present convenience, will in a little time fall into a relapse more wretched than the first. But if you say, you can still pass the violations over, then I ask, Hath your house been burnt? Hath your property been destroyed before your face? Are your wife and children destitute of a bed to lie on, or bread to live on? Have you lost a parent or a child by their hands, and yourself the ruined and wretched survivor? If you have not, then are you not a judge of those who have. But if you have, and still can shake hands with the murderers, then are you unworthy the name of husband, father, friend, or lover, and whatever may be your rank or title in life, you have the heart of a coward, and the spirit of a sycophant.

This is not inflaming or exaggerating matters, but trying them by those feelings and affections which nature justifies, and without which, we should be incapable of discharging the social duties of life, or enjoying the felicities of it. I mean not to exhibit horror for the purpose of provoking revenge, but to awaken us from fatal and unmanly slumbers, that we may pursue determinately some fixed object. It is not in the power of Britain or of Europe to conquer America, if she do not conquer herself by *delay* and *timidity*. The present winter is worth an age if rightly employed, but if lost or neglected, the whole continent will partake of the misfortune; and there is no punishment which that man will not deserve, be he who, or what, or where he will, that may be the means of sacrificing a season so precious and useful.

It is repugnant to reason, to the universal order of things, to all examples from former ages, to suppose, that this continent can longer remain subject to any external power. The most sanguine in Britain does not think so. The utmost stretch of human wisdom cannot, at this time, compass a plan short of separation, which can promise the continent even a year's security. Reconciliation is *now* a falacious dream. Nature hath deserted the connexion, and Art cannot supply her place. For, as Milton wisely expresses, "never can true reconcilement grow where wounds of deadly hate have pierced so deep."

Every quiet method for peace hath been ineffectual. Our prayers have been rejected with disdain; and only tended to convince us, that nothing flatters vanity, or confirms obstinacy in Kings more than repeated petitioning—and nothing hath contributed more than that very measure to make the Kings of Europe absolute: Witness Denmark and Sweden. Wherefore, since nothing but blows will do, for God's sake, let us come to a final separation, and not leave the next generation to be cutting throats, under the violated unmeaning names of parent and child.

To say, they will never attempt it again is idle and visionary, we thought so at the repeal of the stamp-act, yet a year or two undeceived us; as well may we suppose that nations, which have been once defeated, will never renew the quarrel.

As to government matters, it is not in the power of Britain to do this continent justice: The business of it will soon be too weighty, and intricate, to be managed with any tolerable degree of convenience, by a power, so distant from us, and so very ignorant of us; for if they cannot conquer us, they cannot govern us. To be always running three or four thousand miles with a tale or a petition, waiting four or five months for an answer, which when obtained requires five or six more to explain it in, will in a few years be looked upon as folly and childishness — There was a time when it was proper, and there is a proper time for it to cease.

Small islands not capable of protecting themselves, are the proper objects for kingdoms to take under their care; but there is something very absurd, in supposing a continent to be perpetually governed by an island. In no instance hath nature made the satellite larger than its primary planet, and as England and America, with respect to each other, reverses the common order of nature, it is evident they belong to different systems: England to Europe, America to itself.

I am not induced by motives of pride, party, or resentment to espouse the doctrine of separation and independance; I am clearly, positively, and conscientiously persuaded that it is the true interest of this continent to be so; that every thing short of *that* is mere patchwork, that it can afford no lasting felicity, — that it is leaving the sword to our children, and shrinking back at a time, when, a little more, a little farther, would have rendered this continent the glory of the earth.

As Britain hath not manifested the least inclination towards a compromise, we may be assured that no terms can be obtained worthy the acceptance of the continent, or any ways equal to the expence of blood and treasure we have been already put to.

The object, contended for, ought always to bear some just proportion to the expence. The removal of North, or the whole detestable junto, is a matter unworthy the millions we have expended. A temporary stoppage of trade, was an inconvenience, which would have sufficiently ballanced the repeal of all the acts complained of, had such repeals been obtained; but if the whole continent must take up arms, if every man must be a soldier, it is scarcely worth our while to fight against a contemptible ministry only. Dearly, dearly, do we pay for the repeal of the acts, if that is all we fight for; for in a just estimation, it is as great a folly to pay a Bunker-hill price for law, as for land. As I have always considered the independancy of this continent, as an event, which sooner or later must arrive, so from the late rapid progress of the continent to maturity, the event could not be far off. Wherefore, on the breaking out of hostilities, it was not worth the while to have disputed a matter, which time would have finally redressed, unless we meant to be in earnest; otherwise, it is like wasting an estate on a suit at law, to regulate the trespasses of a tenant, whose lease is just expiring. No man was a warmer wisher for reconciliation than myself, before the fatal nineteenth of April 1775*, but the moment the event of that day was made known, I rejected the hardened, sullen tempered Pharoah of England for ever; and disdain the wretch, that with the pretended title of FATHER OF HIS PEOPLE can unfeelingly hear of their slaughter, and composedly sleep with their blood upon his soul.

But admitting that matters were now made up, what would be the event? I answer, the ruin of the continent. And that for several reasons.

First. The powers of governing still remaining in the hands of the king, he will have a negative over the whole legislation of this continent. And as he hath shewn himself such an inveterate enemy to liberty, and discovered such a thirst for arbitrary power; is he, or is he not, a proper man to say to these colonies, *"You shall make no laws but what I please."* And is there any inhabitant in America so ignorant, as not to know, that according to what is called the *present constitution*, that this continent can make no laws but what the king gives leave to; and is there any man so unwise, as not to see, that (considering what has happened) he will suffer no law to be made

*Massacre at Lexington.

here, but such as suit *his* purpose. We may be as effectually enslaved by the want of laws in America, as by submitting to laws made for us in England. After matters are made up (as it is called) can there be any doubt, but the whole power of the crown will be exerted, to keep this continent as low and humble as possible? Instead of going forward we shall go backward, or be perpetually quarrelling or ridiculously petitioning.—We are already greater than the king wishes us to be, and will he not hereafter endeavour to make us less? To bring the matter to one point. Is the power who is jealous of our prosperity, a proper power to govern us? Whoever says *No* to this question is an *independant*, for independancy means no more, than, whether we shall make our own laws, or, whether the king, the greatest enemy this continent hath, or can have, shall tell us *"there shall be no laws but such as I like."*

But the king you will say has a negative in England; the people there can make no laws without his consent. In point of right and good order, there is something very ridiculous, that a youth of twenty-one (which hath often happened) shall say to several millions of people, older and wiser than himself, I forbid this or that act of yours to be law. But in this place I decline this sort of reply, though I will never cease to expose the absurdity of it, and only answer, that England being the King's residence, and America not so, makes quite another case. The king's negative *here* is ten times more dangerous and fatal than it can be in England, for *there* he will scarcely refuse his consent to a bill for putting England into as strong a state of defence as possible, and in America he would never suffer such a bill to be passed.

America is only a secondary object in the system of British politics, England consults the good of *this* country, no farther than it answers her *own* purpose. Wherefore, her own interest leads her to suppress the growth of *ours* in every case which doth not promote her advantage, or in the least interferes with it. A pretty state we should soon be in under such a second-hand government, considering what has happened! Men do not change from enemies to friends by the alteration of a name: And in order to shew that reconciliation *now* is a dangerous doctrine, I affirm, *that it would be policy in the king*

*at this time, to repeal the acts for the sake of reinstating himself
in the government of the provinces;* in order, that HE MAY AC-
COMPLISH BY CRAFT AND SUBTILTY, IN THE LONG RUN,
WHAT HE CANNOT DO BY FORCE AND VIOLENCE IN THE
SHORT ONE. Reconciliation and ruin are nearly related.

Secondly. That as even the best terms, which we can expect
to obtain, can amount to no more than a temporary expedient, or a kind of government by guardianship, which can last
no longer than till the colonies come of age, so the general
face and state of things, in the interim, will be unsettled and
unpromising. Emigrants of property will not choose to come
to a country whose form of government hangs but by a
thread, and who is every day tottering on the brink of com-
motion and disturbance; and numbers of the present inhabitants would lay hold of the interval, to dispose of their effects,
and quit the continent.

But the most powerful of all arguments, is, that nothing
but independance, i. e. a continental form of government, can
keep the peace of the continent and preserve it inviolate from
civil wars. I dread the event of a reconciliation with Britain
now, as it is more than probable, that it will be followed by a
revolt somewhere or other, the consequences of which may
be far more fatal than all the malice of Britain.

Thousands are already ruined by British barbarity; (thousands more will probably suffer the same fate) Those men
have other feelings than us who have nothing suffered. All
they *now* possess is liberty, what they before enjoyed is sacrificed to its service, and having nothing more to lose, they
disdain submission. Besides, the general temper of the colonies, towards a British government, will be like that of a
youth, who is nearly out of his time; they will care very little
about her. And a government which cannot preserve the
peace, is no government at all, and in that case we pay our
money for nothing; and pray what is it that Britain can do,
whose power will be wholly on paper, should a civil tumult
break out the very day after reconciliation? I have heard some
men say, many of whom I believe spoke without thinking,
that they dreaded an independance, fearing that it would produce civil wars. It is but seldom that our first thoughts are
truly correct, and that is the case here; for there are ten times

more to dread from a patched up connexion than from independance. I make the sufferers case my own, and I protest,
that were I driven from house and home, my property destroyed, and my circumstances ruined, that as a man, sensible
of injuries, I could never relish the doctrine of reconciliation,
or consider myself bound thereby.

The colonies have manifested such a spirit of good order
and obedience to continental government, as is sufficient to
make every reasonable person easy and happy on that head.
No man can assign the least pretence for his fears, on any
other grounds, than such as are truly childish and ridiculous,
viz. that one colony will be striving for superiority over another.

Where there are no distinctions there can be no superiority,
perfect equality affords no temptation. The republics of Europe are all (and we may say always) in peace. Holland and
Swisserland are without wars, foreign or domestic: Monarchical governments, it is true, are never long at rest; the crown
itself is a temptation to enterprizing ruffians at *home*; and that
degree of pride and insolence ever attendant on regal authority, swells into a rupture with foreign powers, in instances,
where a republican government, by being formed on more
natural principles, would negociate the mistake.

If there is any true cause of fear respecting independance, it
is because no plan is yet laid down. Men do not see their way
out—Wherefore, as an opening into that business, I offer the
following hints; at the same time modestly affirming, that I
have no other opinion of them myself, than that they may be
the means of giving rise to something better. Could the strag-
gling thoughts of individuals be collected, they would frequently form materials for wise and able men to improve into
useful matter.

Let the assemblies be annual, with a President only. The
representation more equal. Their business wholly domestic,
and subject to the authority of a Continental Congress.

Let each colony be divided into six, eight, or ten, convenient districts, each district to send a proper number of delegates to Congress, so that each colony send at least thirty.
The whole number in Congress will be at least 390. Each Con-

gress to sit   and to choose a president by the following
method. When the delegates are met, let a colony be taken
from the whole thirteen colonies by lot, after which, let the
whole Congress choose (by ballot) a president from out of
the delegates of *that* province. In the next Congress, let a
colony be taken by lot from twelve only, omitting that colony
from which the president was taken in the former Congress,
and so proceeding on till the whole thirteen shall have had
their proper rotation. And in order that nothing may pass into
a law but what is satisfactorily just, not less than three fifths of
the Congress to be called a majority. — He that will promote
discord, under a government so equally formed as this, would
have joined Lucifer in his revolt.

But as there is a peculiar delicacy, from whom, or in what
manner, this business must first arise, and as it seems most
agreeable and consistent that it should come from some inter-
mediate body between the governed and the governors, that
is, between the Congress and the people, let a CONTINENTAL
CONFERENCE be held, in the following manner, and for the
following purpose.

A committee of twenty-six members of Congress, viz. two
for each colony. Two members from each House of Assembly, or Provincial Convention; and five representatives of the
people at large, to be chosen in the capital city or town of
each province, for, and in behalf of the whole province, by
as many qualified voters as shall think proper to attend from
all parts of the province for that purpose; or, if more convenient, the representatives may be chosen in two or three of
the most populous parts thereof. In this conference, thus assembled, will be united, the two grand principles of business, *knowledge* and *power*. The members of Congress,
Assemblies, or Conventions, by having had experience in national concerns, will be able and useful counsellors, and the
whole, being impowered by the people, will have a truly legal authority.

The conferring members being met, let their business be to
frame a CONTINENTAL CHARTER, or Charter of the United
Colonies; (answering to what is called the Magna Charta of
England) fixing the number and manner of choosing members of Congress, members of Assembly, with their date of

sitting, and drawing the line of business and jurisdiction between them: (Always remembering, that our strength is continental, not provincial:) Securing freedom and property to all men, and above all things, the free exercise of religion, according to the dictates of conscience; with such other matter as is necessary for a charter to contain. Immediately after which, the said Conference to dissolve, and the bodies which shall be chosen comfortable to the said charter, to be the legislators and governors of this continent for the time being: Whose peace and happiness, may God preserve, Amen.

Should any body of men be hereafter delegated for this or some similar purpose, I offer them the following extracts from that wise observer on governments *Dragonetti*. "The science" says he "of the politician consists in fixing the true point of happiness and freedom. Those men would deserve the gratitude of ages, who should discover a mode of government that contained the greatest sum of individual happiness, with the least national expense.

Dragonetti on virtue and rewards."

But where says some is the King of America? I'll tell you Friend, he reigns above, and doth not make havoc of mankind like the Royal Brute of Britain. Yet that we may not appear to be defective even in earthly honors, let a day be solemnly set apart for proclaiming the charter; let it be brought forth placed on the divine law, the word of God; let a crown be placed thereon, by which the world may know, that so far as we approve of monarchy, that in America THE LAW IS KING. For as in absolute governments the King is law, so in free countries the law *ought* to be King; and there ought to be no other. But lest any ill use should afterwards arise, let the crown at the conclusion of the ceremony be demolished, and scattered among the people whose right it is.

A government of our own is our natural right: And when a man seriously reflects on the precariousness of human affairs, he will become convinced, that it is infinitely wiser and safer, to form a constitution of our own in a cool deliberate manner, while we have it in our power, than to trust such an interesting event to time and chance. If we omit it now,

some * Massanello may hereafter arise, who laying hold of
popular disquietudes, may collect together the desperate and
the discontented, and by assuming to themselves the powers
of government, may sweep away the liberties of the continent
like a deluge. Should the government of America return again
into the hands of Britain, the tottering situation of things, will
be a temptation for some desperate adventurer to try his fortune; and in such a case, what relief can Britain give? Ere she
could hear the news, the fatal business might be done; and
ourselves suffering like the wretched Britons under the oppression of the Conqueror. Ye that oppose independance
now, ye know not what ye do; ye are opening a door to eternal tyranny, by keeping vacant the seat of government. There
are thousands, and tens of thousands, who would think it
glorious to expel from the continent, that barbarous and
hellish power, which hath stirred up the Indians and Negroes
to destroy us, the cruelty hath a double guilt, it is dealing
brutally by us, and treacherously by them.

To talk of friendship with those in whom our reason forbids
us to have faith, and our affections wounded through a thousand pores instruct us to detest, is madness and folly. Every
day wears out the little remains of kindred between us and
them, and can there be any reason to hope, that as the relationship expires, the affection will increase, or that we shall
agree better, when we have ten times more and greater concerns to quarrel over than ever?

Ye that tell us of harmony and reconciliation, can ye restore
to us the time that is past? Can ye give to prostitution its
former innocence? Neither can ye reconcile Britain and
America. The last cord now is broken, the people of England
are presenting addresses against us. There are injuries which
nature cannot forgive; she would cease to be nature if she did.
As well can the lover forgive the ravisher of his mistress, as the
continent forgive the murders of Britain. The Almighty hath
implanted in us these unextinguishable feelings for good and

*Thomas Anello, otherwise Massanello, a fisherman of Naples, who after
spiriting up his countrymen in the public market place, against the oppression
of the Spaniards, to whom the place was then subject, prompted them to
revolt, and in the space of a day became King.

wise purposes. They are the guardians of his image in our hearts. They distinguish us from the herd of common animals. The social compact would dissolve, and justice be extirpated from the earth, or have only a casual existence were we callous to the touches of affection. The robber, and the murderer, would often escape unpunished, did not the injuries which our tempers sustain, provoke us into justice.

O ye that love mankind! Ye that dare oppose, not only the tyranny, but the tyrant, stand forth! Every spot of the old world is overrun with oppression. Freedom hath been hunted round the globe. Asia, and Africa, have long expelled her.— Europe regards her like a stranger, and England hath given her warning to depart. O! receive the fugitive, and prepare in time an asylum for mankind.

OF THE PRESENT ABILITY OF AMERICA, WITH SOME MISCELLANEOUS REFLEXIONS.

I HAVE never met with a man, either in England or America, who hath not confessed his opinion, that a separation between the countries, would take place one time or other: And there is no instance, in which we have shewn less judgment, than in endeavouring to describe, what we call, the ripeness or fitness of the Continent for independance.

As all men allow the measure, and vary only in their opinion of the time, let us, in order to remove mistakes, take a general survey of things, and endeavour, if possible, to find out the *very* time. But we need not go far, the inquiry ceases at once, for, the *time hath found us.* The general concurrence, the glorious union of all things prove the fact.

It is not in numbers, but in unity, that our great strength lies; yet our present numbers are sufficient to repel the force of all the world. The Continent hath, at this time, the largest body of armed and disciplined men of any power under Heaven; and is just arrived at that pitch of strength, in which, no single colony is able to support itself, and the whole, when united, can accomplish the matter, and either more, or, less than this, might be fatal in its effects. Our land force is already sufficient, and as to naval affairs, we cannot be insensible, that Britain would never suffer an American man of war to be built, while the continent remained in her hands. Wherefore, we should be no forwarder an hundred years hence in that branch, than we are now; but the truth is, we should be less so, because the timber of the country is every day diminishing, and that, which will remain at last, will be far off and difficult to procure.

Were the continent crowded with inhabitants, her sufferings under the present circumstances would be intolerable. The more sea port towns we had, the more should we have both to defend and to loose. Our present numbers are so happily proportioned to our wants, that no man need be idle. The diminution of trade affords an army, and the necessities of an army create a new trade.

Debts we have none; and whatever we may contract on this account will serve as a glorious memento of our virtue. Can we but leave posterity with a settled form of government, an independant constitution of it's own, the purchase at any price will be cheap. But to expend millions for the sake of getting a few vile acts repealed, and routing the present ministry only, is unworthy the charge, and is using posterity with the utmost cruelty; because it is leaving them the great work to do, and a debt upon their backs, from which, they derive no advantage. Such a thought is unworthy a man of honor, and is the true characteristic of a narrow heart and a pedling politician.

The debt we may contract doth not deserve our regard if the work be but accomplished. No nation ought to be without a debt. A national debt is a national bond; and when it bears no interest, is in no case a grievance. Britain is oppressed with a debt of upwards of one hundred and forty millions sterling, for which she pays upwards of four millions interest. And as a compensation for her debt, she has a large navy; America is without a debt, and without a navy; yet for the twentieth part of the English national debt, could have a navy as large again. The navy of England is not worth, at this time, more than three millions and an half sterling.

The first and second editions of this pamphlet were published without the following calculations, which are now given as a proof that the above estimation of the navy is a just one. *See Entic's naval history, intro.* page 56.

The charge of building a ship of each rate, and furnishing

her with masts, yards, sails and rigging, together with a proportion of eight months boatswain's and carpenter's sea-stores, as calculated by Mr. Burchett, Secretary to the navy.

		£.
For a ship of a 100 guns	. . . .	35,553
90	. . . .	29,886
80	. . . .	23,638
70	. . . .	17,785
60	. . . .	14,197
50	. . . .	10,606
40	. . . .	7,558
30	. . . .	5,846
20	. . . .	3,710

And from hence it is easy to sum up the value, or cost rather, of the whole British navy, which in the year 1757, when it was at its greatest glory consisted of the following ships and guns.

Ships.	Guns.	Cost of one.	Cost of all.
6	. . . . 100	35,553 *l.*	. . . . 213,318 *l.*
12	. . . . 90	29,886	 358,632
12	. . . . 80	23,638	 283,656
43	. . . . 70	17,785	 764,755
35	. . . . 60	14,197	 496,895
40	. . . . 50	10,606	. . . 424,240
45	. . . . 40	7,558	 340,110
58	. . . . 20	3,710	 215,180
85	Sloops, bombs, and fireships, one with another, at	2,000	 170,000

Cost 3,266,786

Remains for guns 233,214

3,500,000

No country on the globe is so happily situated, or so internally capable of raising a fleet as America. Tar, timber, iron, and cordage are her natural produce. We need go abroad for nothing. Whereas the Dutch, who make large profits by hiring out their ships of war to the Spaniards and Portuguese, are obliged to import most of the materials they use. We ought to view the building a fleet as an article of commerce, it being the natural manufactory of this country. It is the best money we can lay out. A navy when finished is worth more than it cost. And is that nice point in national policy, in which commerce and protection are united. Let us build; if we want them not, we can sell; and by that means replace our paper currency with ready gold and silver.

In point of manning a fleet, people in general run into great errors; it is not necessary that one fourth part should be sailors. The Terrible privateer, Captain Death, stood the hottest engagement of any ship last war, yet had not twenty sailors on board, though her complement of men was upwards of two hundred. A few able and social sailors will soon instruct a sufficient number of active landmen in the common work of a ship. Wherefore, we never can be more capable to begin on maritime matters than now, while our timber is standing, our fisheries blocked up, and our sailors and shipwrights out of employ. Men of war, of seventy and eighty guns were built forty years ago in New-England, and why not the same now? Ship-building is America's greatest pride, and in which, she will in time excel the whole world. The great empires of the east are mostly inland, and consequently excluded from the possibility of rivalling her. Africa is in a state of barbarism; and no power in Europe, hath either such an extent of coast, or such an internal supply of materials. Where nature hath given the one, she has withheld the other; to America only hath she been liberal of both. The vast empire of Russia is almost shut out from the sea; wherefore, her boundless forests, her tar, iron, and cordage are only articles of commerce.

In point of safety, ought we to be without a fleet? We are not the little people now, which we were sixty years ago; at that time we might have trusted our property in the streets, or fields rather; and slept securely without locks or bolts to our doors or windows. The case now is altered, and our methods of defence, ought to improve with our increase of property. A common pirate, twelve months ago, might have come up the Delaware, and laid the city of Philadelphia under instant contribution, for what sum he pleased; and the same might have happened to other places. Nay, any daring fellow, in a brig of fourteen or sixteen guns, might have robbed the whole Continent, and carried off half a million of money. These are circumstances which demand our attention, and point out the necessity of naval protection.

Some, perhaps, will say, that after we have made it up with Britain, she will protect us. Can we be so unwise as to mean, that she shall keep a navy in our harbours for that purpose? Common sense will tell us, that the power which hath endeavoured to subdue us, is of all others, the most improper to defend us. Conquest may be effected under the pretence of friendship; and ourselves, after a long and brave resistance, be at last cheated into slavery. And if her ships are not to be admitted into our harbours, I would ask, how is she to protect us? A navy three or four thousand miles off can be of little use, and on sudden emergencies, none at all. Wherefore, if we must hereafter protect ourselves, why not do it for ourselves? Why do it for another?

The English list of ships of war, is long and formidable, but not a tenth part of them are at any one time fit for service, numbers of them not in being; yet their names are pompously continued in the list, if only a plank be left of the ship: and not a fifth part, of such as are fit for service, can be spared on any one station at one time. The East, and West Indies, Mediterranean, Africa, and other parts over which Britain extends her claim, make large demands upon her navy. From a mixture of prejudice and inattention, we have contracted a false notion respecting the navy of England, and have talked as if we should have the whole of it to encounter at once, and for that reason, supposed, that we must have one as large; which not being instantly practicable, have been made use of by a set of disguised Tories to discourage our beginning thereon. Nothing can be farther from truth than this; for if America had only a twentieth part of the naval force of Britain, she would be by far an over match for her; because, as we neither have, nor claim any foreign dominion, our whole force would be employed on our own coast, where we should, in the long run, have two to one the advantage of those who had three or four thousand miles to sail over, before they could attack us, and the same distance to return in order to refit and recruit.

And although Britain by her fleet, hath a check over our trade to Europe, we have as large a one over her trade to the West-Indies, which, by laying in the neighbourhood of the Continent, is entirely at its mercy.

Some method might be fallen on to keep up a naval force in time of peace, if we should not judge it necessary to support a constant navy. If premiums were to be given to merchants, to build and employ in their service, ships mounted with twenty, thirty, forty, or fifty guns, (the premiums to be in proportion to the loss of bulk to the merchants) fifty or sixty of those ships, with a few guard ships on constant duty, would keep up a sufficient navy, and that without burdening ourselves with the evil so loudly complained of in England, of suffering their fleet, in time of peace to lie rotting in the docks. To unite the sinews of commerce and defence is sound policy; for when our strength and our riches, play into each other's hand, we need fear no external enemy.

In almost every article of defence we abound. Hemp flourishes even to rankness, so that we need not want cordage. Our iron is superior to that of other countries. Our small arms equal to any in the world. Cannon we can cast at pleasure. Saltpetre and gunpowder we are every day producing. Our knowledge is hourly improving. Resolution is our inherent character, and courage hath never yet forsaken us. Wherefore, what is it that we want? Why is it that we hesitate? From Britain we can expect nothing but ruin. If she is once admitted to the government of America again, this Continent will not be worth living in. Jealousies will be always arising; insurrections will be constantly happening; and who will go forth to quell them? Who will venture his life to reduce his own countrymen to a foreign obedience? The difference between Pennsylvania and Connecticut, respecting some unlocated lands, shews the insignificance of a British government, and fully proves, that nothing but Continental authority can regulate Continental matters.

Another reason why the present time is preferable to all others, is, that the fewer our numbers are, the more land there is yet unoccupied, which instead of being lavished by the king on his worthless dependants, may be hereafter applied, not only to the discharge of the present debt, but to the constant support of government. No nation under heaven hath such an advantage as this.

The infant state of the Colonies, as it is called, so far from being against, is an argument in favor of independance. We are sufficiently numerous, and were we more so, we might be less united. It is a matter worthy of observation, that the more a country is peopled, the smaller their armies are. In military numbers, the ancients far exceeded the moderns: and the reason is evident, for trade being the consequence of population, men become too much absorbed thereby to attend to any thing else. Commerce diminishes the spirit, both of patriotism and military defence. And history sufficiently informs us, that the bravest atchievements were always accomplished in the non-age of a nation. With the increase of commerce, England hath lost its spirit. The city of London, notwithstanding its numbers, submits to continued insults with the patience of a coward. The more men have to lose, the less willing are they to venture. The rich are in general slaves to fear, and submit to courtly power with the trembling duplicity of a Spaniel.

Youth is the seed time of good habits, as well in nations as in individuals. It might be difficult, if not impossible, to form the Continent into one government half a century hence. The vast variety of interests, occasioned by an increase of trade and population, would create confusion. Colony would be against colony. Each being able might scorn each other's assistance: and while the proud and foolish gloried in their little distinctions, the wise would lament, that the union had not been formed before. Wherefore, the *present time* is the *true time* for establishing it. The intimacy which is contracted in infancy, and the friendship which is formed in misfortune, are, of all others, the most lasting and unalterable. Our present union is marked with both these characters: we are young, and we have been distressed; but our concord hath withstood our troubles, and fixes a memorable æra for posterity to glory in.

The present time, likewise, is that peculiar time, which never happens to a nation but once, *viz.* the time of forming itself into a government. Most nations have let slip the opportunity, and by that means have been compelled to receive laws from their conquerors, instead of making laws for themselves.

First, they had a king, and then a form of government; whereas, the articles or charter of government, should be formed first, and men delegated to execute them afterward: but from the errors of other nations, let us learn wisdom, and lay hold of the present opportunity—*To begin government at the right end.*

When William the Conqueror subdued England, he gave them law at the point of the sword; and until we consent, that the seat of government, in America, be legally and authoritatively occupied, we shall be in danger of having it filled by some fortunate ruffian, who may treat us in the same manner, and then, where will be our freedom? where our property?

As to religion, I hold it to be the indispensible duty of all government, to protect all conscientious professors thereof, and I know of no other business which government hath to do therewith. Let a man throw aside that narrowness of soul, that selfishness of principle, which the niggards of all professions are so unwilling to part with, and he will be at once delivered of his fears on that head. Suspicion is the companion of mean souls, and the bane of all good society. For myself, I fully and conscientiously believe, that it is the will of the Almighty, that there should be diversity of religious opinions among us: It affords a larger field for our Christian kindness. Were we all of one way of thinking, our religious dispositions would want matter for probation; and on this liberal principle, I look on the various denominations among us, to be like children of the same family, differing only, in what is called, their Christian names.

In page thirty-three, I threw out a few thoughts on the propriety of a Continental Charter, (for I only presume to offer hints, not plans) and in this place, I take the liberty of re-mentioning the subject, by observing, that a charter is to be understood as a bond of solemn obligation, which the whole enters into, to support the right of every separate part, whether of religion, personal freedom, or property. A firm bargain and a right reckoning make long friends.

In a former page I likewise mentioned the necessity of a large and equal representation; and there is no political matter which more deserves our attention. A small number of electors, or a small number of representatives, are equally dangerous. But if the number of the representatives be not only small, but unequal, the danger is increased. As an instance of this, I mention the following; when the Associators petition was before the House of Assembly of Pennsylvania; twenty-eight members only were present, all the Bucks county members, being eight, voted against it, and had seven of the Chester members done the same, this whole province had been governed by two counties only, and this danger it is always exposed to. The unwarrantable stretch likewise, which that house made in their last sitting, to gain an undue authority over the Delegates of that province, ought to warn the people at large, how they trust power out of their own hands. A set of instructions for the Delegates were put together, which in point of sense and business would have dishonored a schoolboy, and after being approved by a *few*, a *very few* without doors, were carried into the House, and there passed *in behalf of the whole colony*, whereas, did the whole colony know, with what ill-will that House hath entered on some necessary public measures, they would not hesitate a moment to think them unworthy of such a trust.

Immediate necessity makes many things convenient, which if continued would grow into oppressions. Expedience and right are different things. When the calamities of America required a consultation, there was no method so ready, or at that time so proper, as to appoint persons from the several Houses of Assembly for that purpose; and the wisdom with which they have proceeded hath preserved this continent from ruin. But as it is more than probable that we shall never be without a CONGRESS, every well wisher to good order, must own, that the mode for choosing members of that body, deserves consideration. And I put it as a question to those, who make a study of mankind, whether *representation and election* is not too great a power for one and the same body of men to possess? When we are planning for posterity, we ought to remember, that virtue is not hereditary.

It is from our enemies that we often gain excellent maxims, and are frequently surprised into reason by their mistakes. Mr. Cornwall (one of the Lords of the Treasury) treated the petition of the New-York Assembly with contempt, because *that*

House, he said, consisted but of twenty-six members, which trifling number, he argued, could not with decency be put for the whole. We thank him for his involuntary honesty.*

To CONCLUDE, however strange it may appear to some, or however unwilling they may be to think so, matters not, but many strong and striking reasons may be given, to shew, that nothing can settle our affairs so expeditiously as an open and determined declaration for independance. Some of which are,

First.—It is the custom of nations, when any two are at war, for some other powers, not engaged in the quarrel, to step in as mediators, and bring about the preliminaries of a peace: but while America calls herself the Subject of Great-Britain, no power, however well disposed she may be, can offer her mediation. Wherefore, in our present state we may quarrel on for ever.

Secondly.—It is unreasonable to suppose, that France or Spain will give us any kind of assistance, if we mean only, to make use of that assistance for the purpose of repairing the breach, and strengthening the connection between Britain and America; because, those powers would be sufferers by the consequences.

Thirdly.—While we profess ourselves the subjects of Britain, we must, in the eye of foreign nations, be considered as rebels. The precedent is somewhat dangerous to *their peace*, for men to be in arms under the name of subjects; we, on the spot, can solve the paradox: but to unite resistance and subjection, requires an idea much too refined for common understanding.

Fourthly.—Were a manifesto to be published, and despatched to foreign courts, setting forth the miseries we have endured, and the peaceable methods we have ineffectually used for redress; declaring, at the same time, that not being able, any longer, to live happily or safely under the cruel disposition of the British court, we had been driven to the necessity of breaking off all connections with her; at the same time, assuring all such courts of our peaceable disposition towards

---

*Those who would fully understand of what great consequence a large and equal representation is to a state, should read Burgh's political Disquisitions.

them, and of our desire of entering into trade with them: Such a memorial would produce more good effects to this Continent, than if a ship were freighted with petitions to Britain.

Under our present denomination of British subjects, we can neither be received nor heard abroad: The custom of all courts is against us, and will be so, until, by an independance, we take rank with other nations.

These proceedings may at first appear strange and difficult; but, like all other steps which we have already passed over, will in a little time become familiar and agreeable; and, until an independance is declared, the Continent will feel itself like a man who continues putting off some unpleasant business from day to day, yet knows it must be done, hates to set about it, wishes it over, and is continually haunted with the thoughts of its necessity.

APPENDIX.

SINCE the publication of the first edition of this pamphlet, or rather, on the same day on which it came out, the King's Speech made its appearance in this city. Had the spirit of prophecy directed the birth of this production, it could not have brought it forth, at a more seasonable juncture, or a more necessary time. The bloody mindedness of the one, shew the necessity of pursuing the doctrine of the other. Men read by way of revenge. And the Speech, instead of terrifying, prepared a way for the manly principles of Independance.

Ceremony, and even, silence, from whatever motive they may arise, have a hurtful tendency, when they give the least degree of countenance to base and wicked performances; wherefore, if this maxim be admitted, it naturally follows, that the King's Speech, as being a piece of finished villany, de-served, and still deserves, a general execration both by the Congress and the people. Yet, as the domestic tranquillity of a nation, depends greatly, on the *chastity* of what may properly be called NATIONAL MANNERS, it is often better, to pass some things over in silent disdain, than to make use of such new methods of dislike, as might introduce the least innovation, on that guardian of our peace and safety. And, perhaps, it is chiefly owing to this prudent delicacy, that the King's Speech, hath not, before now, suffered a public execution. The Speech if it may be called one, is nothing better than a wilful audacious libel against the truth, the common good, and the existence of mankind; and is a formal and pompous method of offering up human sacrifices to the pride of tyrants. But this general massacre of mankind, is one of the privileges, and the certain consequence of Kings; for as nature knows them *not*, they know *not her*, and although they are beings of our *own* creating, they know not *us*, and are become the gods of their creators. The Speech hath one good quality, which is, that it is not calculated to deceive, neither can we, even if we would, be deceived by it. Brutality and tyranny appear on the face of it. It leaves us at no loss: And every line convinces, even in the moment of reading, that He, who hunts the woods for prey, the naked and untutored Indian, is less a Savage than the King of Britain.

Sir John Dalrymple, the putative father of a whining jesuitical piece, fallaciously called, *"The Address of the people of* ENGLAND *to the inhabitants of* AMERICA,*"* hath, perhaps, from a vain supposition, that the people *here* were to be frightened at the pomp and description of a king, given, (though very unwisely on his part) the real character of the present one: "But," says this writer, "if you are inclined to pay compliments to an administration, which we do not complain of," (meaning the Marquis of Rockingham's at the repeal of the Stamp Act) "it is very unfair in you to withhold them from that prince, *by whose* NOD ALONE *they were permitted to do any thing.*" This is toryism with a witness! Here is idolatry even without a mask: And he who can calmly hear, and digest such doctrine, hath forfeited his claim to rationality—an apostate from the order of manhood; and ought to be considered—as one, who hath not only given up the proper dignity of man, but sunk himself beneath the rank of animals, and contemptibly crawls through the world like a worm.

However, it matters very little now, what the king of England either says or does; he hath wickedly broken through every moral and human obligation, trampled nature and conscience beneath his feet; and by a steady and constitutional spirit of insolence and cruelty, procured for himself an universal hatred. It is *now* the interest of America to provide for herself. She hath already a large and young family, whom it is more her duty to take care of, than to be granting away her property, to support a power who is become a reproach to the names of men and christians—YE, whose office it is to watch over the morals of a nation, of whatsoever sect or denomination ye are of, as well as ye, who, are more immediately the guardians of the public liberty, if ye wish to preserve your native country uncontaminated by European corruption, ye must in secret wish a separation—But leaving the moral part to private reflection, I shall chiefly confine my farther remarks to the following heads.

First. That it is the interest of America to be separated from Britain.

Secondly. Which is the easiest and most practicable plan, RECONCILIATION or INDEPENDANCE? with some occasional remarks.

In support of the first, I could, if I judged it proper, produce the opinion of some of the ablest and most experienced men on this continent; and whose sentiments, on that head, are not yet publicly known. It is in reality a self-evident position: For no nation in a state of foreign dependance, limited in its commerce, and cramped and fettered in its legislative powers, can ever arrive at any material eminence. America doth not yet know what opulence is; and although the progress which she hath made stands unparalleled in the history of other nations, it is but childhood, compared with what she would be capable of arriving at, had she, as she ought to have, the legislative powers in her own hands. England is, at this time, proudly coveting what would do her no good, were she to accomplish it; and the Continent hesitating on a matter, which will be her final ruin if neglected. It is the commerce and not the conquest of America, by which England is to be benefited, and that would in a great measure continue, were the countries as independant of each other as France and Spain; because in many articles, neither can go to a better market. But it is the independance of this country on Britain or any other, which is now the main and only object worthy of contention, and which, like all other truths discovered by necessity, will appear clearer and stronger every day.

First. Because it will come to that one time or other.

Secondly. Because, the longer it is delayed the harder it will be to accomplish.

I have frequently amused myself both in public and private companies, with silently remarking, the specious errors of those who speak without reflecting. And among the many which I have heard, the following seems the most general, viz. that had this rupture happened forty or fifty years hence, instead of *now*, the Continent would have been more able to have shaken off the dependance. To which I reply, that our military ability, *at this time*, arises from the experience gained in the last war, and which in forty or fifty years time, would have been totally extinct. The Continent, would not, by that time, have had a General, or even a military officer left; and we, or those who may succeed us, would have been as ignorant of martial matters as the ancient Indians: And this single position, closely attended to, will unanswerably prove, that the present time is preferable to all others. The argument turns thus—at the conclusion of the last war, we had experience, but wanted numbers; and forty or fifty years hence, we should have numbers, without experience; wherefore, the proper point of time, must be some particular point between the two extremes, in which a sufficiency of the former remains, and a proper increase of the latter is obtained: And that point of time is the present time.

The reader will pardon this digression, as it does not properly come under the head I first set out with, and to which I again return by the following position, viz.

Should affairs be patched up with Britain, and she to remain the governing and sovereign power of America, (which, as matters are now circumstanced, is giving up the point intirely) we shall deprive ourselves of the very means of sinking the debt we have, or may contract. The value of the back lands which some of the provinces are clandestinely deprived of, by the unjust extention of the limits of Canada, valued only at five pounds sterling per hundred acres, amount to upwards of twenty-five millions, Pennsylvania currency; and the quit-rents at one penny sterling per acre, to two millions yearly.

It is by the sale of those lands that the debt may be sunk, without burthen to any, and the quit-rent reserved thereon, will always lessen, and in time, will wholly support the yearly expence of government. It matters not how long the debt is in paying, so that the lands when sold be applied to the discharge of it, and for the execution of which, the Congress for the time being, will be the continental trustees.

I proceed now to the second head, viz. Which is the easiest and most practicable plan, RECONCILIATION or INDEPENDANCE; with some occasional remarks.

He who takes nature for his guide is not easily beaten out of his argument, and on that ground, I answer *generally* —*That* INDEPENDANCE *being a* SINGLE SIMPLE LINE, *contained within ourselves; and reconciliation, a matter exceedingly perplexed and complicated, and in which, a treacherous capricious court is to interfere, gives the answer without a doubt.*

The present state of America is truly alarming to every man who is capable of reflexion. Without law, without government, without any other mode of power than what is founded on, and granted by courtesy. Held together by an unexampled concurrence of sentiment, which, is nevertheless subject to change, and which, every secret enemy is endeavouring to dissolve. Our present condition, is, Legislation without law; wisdom without a plan; a constitution without a name; and, what is strangely astonishing, perfect Independance contending for dependance. The instance is without a precedent; the case never existed before; and who can tell what may be the event? The property of no man is secure in the present unbraced system of things. The mind of the multitude is left at random, and seeing no fixed object before them, they pursue such as fancy or opinion starts. Nothing is criminal; there is no such thing as treason; wherefore, every one thinks himself at liberty to act as he pleases. The Tories dared not have assembled offensively, had they known that their lives, by that act, were forfeited to the laws of the state. A line of distinction should be drawn, between, English soldiers taken in battle, and inhabitants of America taken in arms. The first are prisoners, but the latter traitors. The one forfeits his liberty, the other his head.

Notwithstanding our wisdom, there is a visible feebleness in some of our proceedings which gives encouragement to dissentions. The Continental Belt is too losely buckled. And if something is not done in time, it will be too late to do any thing, and we shall fall into a state, in which, neither *Reconciliation* nor *Independance* will be practicable. The king and his worthless adherents are got at their old game of dividing the Continent, and there are not wanting among us, Printers, who will be busy in spreading specious falsehoods. The artful and hypocritical letter which appeared a few months ago in two of the New-York papers, and likewise in two others, is an evidence that there are men who want either judgment or honesty.

It is easy getting into holes and corners and talking of reconciliation: But do such men seriously consider, how difficult the task is, and how dangerous it may prove, should the Continent divide thereon. Do they take within their view, all the various orders of men whose situation and circumstances, as well as their own, are to be considered therein. Do they put themselves in the place of the sufferer whose *all* is *already* gone, and of the soldier, who hath quitted *all* for the defence of his country. If their ill judged moderation be suited to their own private situations *only*, regardless of others, the event will convince them, that "they are reckoning without their Host."

Put us, say some, on the footing we were on in sixty-three: To which I answer, the request is not *now* in the power of Britain to comply with, neither will she propose it; but if it were, and even should be granted, I ask, as a reasonable question, By what means is such a corrupt and faithless court to be kept to its engagements? Another parliament, nay, even the present, may hereafter repeal the obligation, on the pretence, of its being violently obtained, or unwisely granted; and in that case, Where is our redress?—No going to law with nations; cannon are the barristers of Crowns; and the sword, not of justice, but of war, decides the suit. To be on the footing of sixty-three, it is not sufficient, that the laws only be put on the same state, but, that our circumstances, likewise, be put on the same state; Our burnt and destroyed towns repaired or built up, our private losses made good, our public debts (contracted for defence) discharged; otherwise, we shall be millions worse than we were at that enviable period. Such a request, had it been complied with a year ago, would have won the heart and soul of the Continent—but now it is too late, "The Rubicon is passed."

Besides, the taking up arms, merely to enforce the repeal of a pecuniary law, seems as unwarrantable by the divine law, and as repugnant to human feelings, as the taking up arms to enforce obedience thereto. The object, on either side, doth not justify the means; for the lives of men are too valuable to be cast away on such trifles. It is the violence which is done and threatened to our persons; the destruction of our property by an armed force; the invasion of our country by fire and sword, which conscientiously qualifies the use of arms: And the instant, in which such a mode of defence became necessary, all subjection to Britain ought to have ceased; and the independancy of America, should have been considered, as dating its æra from, and published by, *the first musket that was fired against her*. This line is a line of consistency; neither drawn by caprice, nor extended by ambition; but produced by a chain of events, of which the colonies were not the authors.

I shall conclude these remarks, with the following timely and well intended hints. We ought to reflect, that there are three different ways, by which an independancy may hereafter be effected; and that *one* of those *three*, will one day or other, be the fate of America, viz. By the legal voice of the people in Congress; by a military power; or by a mob: It may not always happen that our soldiers are citizens, and the multitude a body of reasonable men; virtue, as I have already remarked, is not hereditary, neither is it perpetual. Should an independancy be brought about by the first of those means, we have every opportunity and every encouragement before us, to form the noblest purest constitution on the face of the earth. We have it in our power to begin the world over again. A situation, similar to the present, hath not happened since the days of Noah until now. The birthday of a new world is at hand, and a race of men, perhaps as numerous as all Europe contains, are to receive their portion of freedom from the event of a few months. The Reflexion is awful—and in this point of view, How trifling, how ridiculous, do the little, paltry cavellings, of a few weak or interested men appear, when weighed against the business of a world.

Should we neglect the present favorable and inviting period, and an Independance be hereafter effected by any other means, we must charge the consequence to ourselves, or to those rather, whose narrow and prejudiced souls, are habitually opposing the measure, without either inquiring or reflecting. There are reasons to be given in support of Independance, which men should rather privately think of, than be publicly told of. We ought not now to be debating whether we shall be independant or not, but, anxious to accomplish it on a firm, secure, and honorable basis, and uneasy rather that it is not yet began upon. Every day convinces us of its necessity. Even the Tories (if such beings yet remain among us) should, of all men, be the most solicitous to promote it; for, as the appointment of committees at first, protected them from popular rage, so, a wise and well established form of government, will be the only certain means of continuing it securely to them. *Wherefore*, if they have not virtue enough to be WHIGS, they ought to have prudence enough to wish for Independance.

In short, Independance is the only BOND that can tye and keep us together. We shall then see our object, and our ears will be legally shut against the schemes of an intriguing, as well, as a cruel enemy. We shall then too, be on a proper footing, to treat with Britain; for there is reason to conclude, that the pride of that court, will be less hurt by treating with the American states for terms of peace, than with those, whom she denominates, "rebellious subjects," for terms of accommodation. It is our delaying it that encourages her to hope for conquest, and our backwardness tends only to prolong the war. As we have, without any good effect therefrom, withheld our trade to obtain a redress of our grievances, let us *now* try the alternative, by *independantly* redressing them ourselves, and then offering to open the trade. The mercantile and reasonable part in England, will be still with us; because, peace *with* trade, is preferable to war *without* it. And if this offer be not accepted, other courts may be applied to.

On these grounds I rest the matter. And as no offer hath yet been made to refute the doctrine contained in the former editions of this pamphlet, it is a negative proof, that either the doctrine cannot be refuted, or, that the party in favour of it are too numerous to be opposed. WHEREFORE, instead of gazing at each other with suspicious or doubtful curiosity, let each of us, hold out to his neighbour the hearty hand of friendship, and unite in drawing a line, which, like an act of oblivion shall bury in forgetfulness every former dissention. Let the names of Whig and Tory be extinct; and let none other be heard among us, than those of *a good citizen, an open and resolute friend, and a virtuous supporter of the* RIGHTS *of* MANKIND *and of the* FREE AND INDEPEN-DANT STATES OF AMERICA.

To the Representatives of the Religious Society of the People called Quakers, or to so many of them as were concerned in publishing a late piece, entitled "The ANCIENT TESTIMONY and PRINCIPLES of the People called QUAKERS renewed, with Respect to the KING and GOVERNMENT, and touching the COMMOTIONS now prevailing in these and other parts of AMERICA addressed to the PEOPLE IN GENERAL."

THE Writer of this, is one of those few, who never dishonors religion either by ridiculing, or cavilling at any denomination whatsoever. To God, and not to man, are all men accountable on the score of religion. Wherefore, this epistle is not so properly addressed to you as a religious, but as a political body, dabbling in matters, which the professed Quietude of your Principles instruct you not to meddle with.

As you have, without a proper authority for so doing, put yourselves in the place of the whole body of the Quakers, so, the writer of this, in order to be on an equal rank with yourselves, is under the necessity, of putting himself in the place of all those, who, approve the very writings and principles, against which, your testimony is directed: And he hath chosen this singular situation, in order, that you might discover in him that presumption of character which you cannot see in yourselves. For neither he nor you can have any claim or title to *Political Representation.*

When men have departed from the right way, it is no wonder that they stumble and fall. And it is evident from the manner in which ye have managed your testimony, that politics, (as a religious body of men) is not your proper Walk; for however well adapted it might appear to you, it is, nevertheless, a jumble of good and bad put unwisely together, and the conclusion drawn therefrom, both unnatural and unjust.

The two first pages, (and the whole doth not make four) we give you credit for, and expect the same civility from you, because the love and desire of peace is not confined to Quakerism, it is the *natural,* as well the religious wish of all denominations of men. And on this ground, as men laboring to establish an Independant Constitution of our own, do we exceed all others in our hope, end, and aim. *Our plan is peace for ever.* We are tired of contention with Britain, and can see no real end to it but in a final separation. We act consistently, because for the sake of introducing an endless and uninterrupted peace, do we bear the evils and burthens of the present day. We are endeavoring, and will steadily continue to endeavor, to separate and dissolve a connexion which hath already filled our land with blood; and which, while the name of it remains, will be the fatal cause of future mischiefs to both countries.

We fight neither for revenge nor conquest; neither from pride nor passion; we are not insulting the world with our fleets and armies, not ravaging the globe for plunder. Beneath the shade of our own vines are we attacked; in our own houses, and on our own lands, is the violence committed against us. We view our enemies in the character of Highwaymen and Housebreakers, and having no defence for ourselves in the civil law, are obliged to punish them by the military one, and apply the sword, in the very case, where you have before now, applied the halter—Perhaps we feel for the ruined and insulted sufferers in all and every part of the continent, with a degree of tenderness which hath not yet made it's way into some of your bosoms. But be ye sure that ye mistake not the cause and ground of your Testimony. Call not coldness of soul, religion; nor put the *Bigot* in the place of the *Christian.*

O ye partial ministers of your own acknowledged principles. If the bearing arms be sinful, the first going to war must be more so, by all the difference between wilful attack and unavoidable defence. Wherefore, if ye really preach from conscience, and mean not to make a political hobby-horse of your religion, convince the world thereof, by proclaiming your doctrine to our enemies, *for they likwise bear* ARMS. Give us proof of your sincerity by publishing it at St. James's, to the commanders in chief at Boston, to the Admirals and Captains who are piratically ravaging our coasts, and to all the murdering miscreants who are acting in authority under HIM whom ye profess to serve. Had ye the honest soul of * *Barclay* ye would preach repentance to *your* king; Ye would tell the Royal Wretch his sins, and warn him of eternal ruin. Ye would not spend your partial invectives against the injured and the insulted only, but, like faithful ministers, would cry aloud and *spare none.* Say not that ye are persecuted, neither endeavour to make us the authors of that reproach, which, ye are bringing upon yourselves; for we testify unto all men, that we do not complain against you because ye are *Quakers,* but because ye pretend to *be* and are NOT Quakers.

Alas! it seems by the particular tendency of some part of your testimony, and other parts of your conduct, as if, all sin was reduced to, and comprehended in, *the act of bearing arms,* and that by the *people only.* Ye appear to us, to have mistaken party for conscience; because, the general tenor of

---

*"Thou hast tasted of prosperity and adversity: thou knowest what it is to be banished thy native country, to be over-ruled as well as to rule, and set upon the throne; and being *oppressed* thou hast reason to know how *hateful* the *oppressor* is both to God and man: If after all these warnings and advertisements, thou dost not turn unto the Lord with all thy heart, but forget him who remembered thee in thy distress, and give up thyself to follow lust and vanity, surely great will be thy condemnation.—Against which snare, as well as the temptation of those who may or do feed thee, and prompt thee to evil, the most excellent and prevalent remedy will be, to apply thyself to that light of Christ which shineth in thy conscience, and which neither can, nor will flatter thee, nor suffer thee to be at ease in thy sins."

Barclay's Address to Charles II.

your actions wants uniformity: And it is exceedingly difficult to us to give credit to many of your pretended scruples; because, we see them made by the same men, who, in the very instant that they are exclaiming against the mammon of this world, are nevertheless, hunting after it with a step as steady as Time, and an appetite as keen as Death.

The quotation which ye have made from Proverbs, in the third page of your testimony, that, "when a man's ways please the Lord, he maketh even his enemies to be at peace with him"; is very unwisely chosen on your part; because, it amounts to a proof, that the king's ways (whom ye are so desirous of supporting) do *not* please the Lord, otherwise, his reign would be in peace.

I now proceed to the latter part of your testimony, and that, for which all the foregoing seems only an introduction, viz.

"It hath ever been our judgment and principle, since we were called to profess the light of Christ Jesus, manifested in our consciences unto this day, that the setting up and putting down kings and governments, is God's peculiar prerogative; for causes best known to himself: And that it is not our business to have any hand or contrivance therein; nor to be busy bodies above our station, much less to plot and contrive the ruin, or overturn of any of them, but to pray for the king, and safety of our nation, and good of all men: That we may live a peaceable and quiet life, in all godliness and honesty; *under the government which God is pleased to set over us.*" — If these are *really* your principles why do ye not abide by them? Why do ye not leave that, which ye call God's Work, to be managed by himself? These very principles instruct you to wait with patience and humility, for the event of all public measures, and to receive *that event* as the divine will towards you. *Wherefore,* what occasion is there for your *political testimony* if you fully believe what it contains? And the very publishing it proves, that either, ye do not believe what ye profess, or have not virtue enough to practise what ye believe.

The principles of Quakerism have a direct tendency to make a man the quiet and inoffensive subject of any, and every government *which is set over him.* And if the setting up and putting down of kings and governments is God's peculiar prerogative, he most certainly will not be robbed thereof by us; wherefore, the principle itself leads you to approve of every thing, which ever happened, or may happen to kings as being his work. OLIVER CROMWELL thanks you. CHARLES, then, died not by the hands of man; and should the present Proud Imitator of him, come to the same untimely end, the writers and publishers of the Testimony, are bound, by the doctrine it contains, to applaud the fact. Kings are not taken away by miracles, neither are changes in governments brought about by any other means than such as are common and human; and such as we are now using. Even the dispersion of the Jews, though foretold by our Saviour, was effected by arms. Wherefore, as ye refuse to be the means on one side, ye ought not to be meddlers on the other; but to wait the issue in silence; and unless ye can produce divine authority, to prove, that the Almighty who hath created and placed this *new* world, at the greatest distance it could possibly stand, east and west, from every part of the old, doth, nevertheless, disapprove of its being independent of the corrupt and abandoned court of Britain, unless I say, ye can shew this, how can ye on the ground of your principles, justify the exciting and stirring up the people "firmly to unite in the *abhorrence* of all such *writings*, and *measures*, as evidence of desire and design to break off the *happy* connexion we have hitherto enjoyed, with the kingdom of Great-Britain, and our just and necessary subordination to the king, and those who are lawfully placed in authority under him." What a slap of the face is here! the men, who in the very paragraph before, have quietly and passively resigned up the ordering, altering, and disposal of kings and governments, into the hands of God, are now, recalling their principles, and putting in for a share of the business. Is it possible, that the conclusion, which is here justly quoted, can any ways follow from the doctrine laid down? The inconsistency is too glaring not to be seen; the absurdity too great not to be laughed at; and such as could only have been made by those, whose understandings were darkened by the narrow and crabby spirit of a dispairing political party; for ye are not to be considered as the whole body of the Quakers but only as a factional and fractional part thereof.

Here ends the examination of your testimony; (which I call

upon no man to abhor, as ye have done, but only to read and judge of fairly;) to which I subjoin the following remark; "That the setting up and putting down of kings," most certainly mean, the making him a king, who is yet not so, and the making him no king who is already one. And pray what hath this to do in the present case? We neither mean to *set up* nor to *put down*, neither to *make* nor to *unmake*, but to have nothing to *do* with them. Wherefore, your testimony in whatever light it is viewed serves only to dishonor your judgement, and for many other reasons had better have been let alone than published.

First, Because it tends to the decrease and reproach of all religion whatever, and is of the utmost danger to society, to make it a party in political disputes.

Secondly, Because it exhibits a body of men, numbers of whom disavow the publishing political testimonies, as being concerned therein and approvers thereof.

Thirdly, Because it hath a tendency to undo that continental harmony and friendship which yourselves by your late liberal and charitable donations hath lent a hand to establish; and the preservation of which, is of the utmost consequence to us all.

And here without anger or resentment I bid you farewell. Sincerely wishing, that as men and christians, ye may always fully and uninterruptedly enjoy every civil and religious right; and be, in your turn, the means of securing it to others; but that the example which ye have unwisely set, of mingling religion with politics, *may be disavowed and reprobated by every inhabitant of* AMERICA.

The Forester's Letters

LETTER I

April 1, 1776

TO CATO

To be *nobly wrong* is more manly than to be *meanly right*. Only let the error be disinterested—let it wear, *not the mask*, but the *mark* of principle and 'tis pardonable. It is on this large and liberal ground, that we distinguish between men and their tenets, and generously preserve our friendship for the one, while we combat with every prejudice of the other. But let not Cato take this compliment to himself; he stands excluded from the benefit of the distinction; he deserves it not—And if the sincerity of disdain can add a cubit to the stature of my sentiments, it shall not be wanting.

It is indifferent to me who the writers of Cato's letters are, and sufficient for me to know, that they are gorged with absurdity, confusion, contradiction, and the most notorious and willful falshoods. Let Cato and his faction be against Independance and welcome; their consequence will not *now* turn the scale: But let them have regard to justice, and pay some attention to the plain doctrine of reason. Where these are wanting, the sacred cause of truth applauds our anger, and dignifies it with the name of Virtue.

Four letters have already appeared under the specious name of Cato. What pretensions the writer of them can have to the signature, the Public will best determine; while, on my own part, I prophetically content myself with contemplating the similarity of their exits. The first of those letters promised a second, the second a third, the third a fourth; the fourth hath since made its appearance and still the writer keeps wide of the question. Why doth he thus loiter in the suburbs of the dispute? Why hath he not shewn us what the numerous blessings of reconciliation are, and *proved them practicable?* But he cunningly avoids the point. He cannot but discover the rock he is driving on. The fate of the Roman Cato is before his eyes: And that the Public may be prepared for his funeral, and

60

for his funeral oration, I will venture to predict the time and the manner of his exit. The moment he explains his terms of reconciliation the typographical Cato dies. If they be calculated to please the Cabinet they will not go down with the Colonies; and if they be suited to the Colonies they will be rejected by the Cabinet: The line of no-variation is yet unfound; and, like the philosophers stone, doth not exist. "I am bold," says Cato, "to declare and yet hope to make it evident to every honest man, that the true interest of America lies in *reconciliation* with Great-Britain on *constitutional principles.*"

This is a curious way of lumping the business indeed! And Cato may as well attempt to catch lions in a mouse-trap as to hope to allure the Public with such general and unexplained expressions. It is now a meer bug-bear to talk of *reconciliation* on *constitutional principles,* unless the terms of the first be produced and the sense of the other be defined; and unless he does this he does nothing.

To follow Cato through every absurdity and falshood in the compass of a * letter is impossible; neither is it *now* necessary. *Cassandra* (and I thank him) hath saved me much trouble; there is a spirit in his remarks which honesty only can inspire, and a uniformity in the conduct of his letter which the want of principle can never arrive at. Mark that, Cato.

One observation which I cannot help making on Cato's letters, is, that they are addressed *"To the People of Pennsylvania"* only. In almost any other writer this might have passed unnoticed, but we know it hath mischief in its meaning. The particular circumstance of a Convention is undoubtedly Provincial, but the great business of the day is Continental. And he who dares to endeavour to withdraw this province from the glorious union by which all are supported, deserves the reprobation of all men. It is the true interest of the whole to go hand in hand; and dismal in every instance would be the fate of that Colony which should retreat from the protection of the rest.

The first of Cato's letters is insipid in its stile, language and substance; crouded with personal and private innuendues, and directly levelled against *"the Majesty of the People of Penn-*

---

*The writer intended at first to have contained his remarks in one letter.

sylvania." The Committee could only call, propose, or recommend a Convention; but, like all other public measures, it still rested with the people at large, whether they would approve it or not; and Cato's reasoning on the right or wrong of that choice is contemptible; because, if the body of the people had thought, or should still think, that the Assembly (or any of their Delegates in Congress) by setting under the embarrassment of *oaths*, and entangled with *Government* and *Governors*, are not so perfectly free as they ought to be, they undoubtedly had, and still have, both the *right* and the *power* to place even the whole authority of the Assembly in any body of men they please; and whoever is hardy enough to say to the contrary is an enemy to mankind. The constitution of Pennsylvania hath been twice changed through the cunning of former Proprietors; surely, the people, whose right, power and property is greater than that of any single man, may make such alterations in their mode of government as the change of times and things require. Cato is exceedingly fond of impressing us with the importance of our *"chartered constitution."* Alas! We are not now, Sir, to be led away by the jingle of a phrase. Had we framed our conduct by the contents of the present charters, we had, ere now, been in a state of helpless misery. That *very assembly* you mention hath broken it, and been obliged to break it, in almost every instance of their proceedings. Hold it up to the Public and it is transparent with holes; pierced with as many deadly wounds as the body of McLeod. Disturb not its remains, Cato, nor dishonour it with another funeral oration.

There is nothing in Cato's first letter worthy of notice but the following insinuating falshood: "Grievous as the least restraint of the press must always be, to a *people* entitled to freedom, it must be the more so, when it is not only unwarranted by *those* to whom *they* have committed the care of *their* liberties, but cannot be warranted by *them*, consistent with liberty itself."—The rude and unscholastical confusion of persons in the above paragraph, though it throws an obscurity on the meaning, still leaves it discoverable. Who, Sir, hath laid any restraint on the liberty of the press? I know of no instance, in which the press hath been even the object of notice, in this province, except on account of the Tory letter from

Kent County which was published last spring in the *Pennsylvania Ledger*, and which it was the duty of every good man to detect, because the *honesty* of the press is as great an object to society as the *freedom* of it. If this is the restraint you complain of we know your true character at once; and that it is so, appears evident from the expression which immediately follows the above quotation; your words are, "Nevertheless, *we* readily submitted to it, while the least colourable pretence could be offered for requiring such a submission." Who submitted, Cato? *we* Whigs or *we* Tories? Until you clear up this, Sir, you must content yourself with being ranked among the rankest of the *writing* Tories; because, no other body of men can have any pretence to complain of want of freedom of the press. It is not your throwing out, now and then, a little popular phrase, which can protect you from suspicion; they are only the gildings under which the poison is conveyed, and without which you dared not to renew your attempts on the virtue of the people.

Cato's second letter, or the greatest part thereof, is taken up with the reverence due from us to the persons and authority of the Commissioners, whom Cato vainly and ridiculously stiles AMBASSADORS *coming to negociate a peace.* How came Cato not to be let a little better into the secret? The act of Parliament which describes the powers of these men, hath been in this city upwards of a month, and in the hands too of Cato's friends. No, Sir, they are not the *Ambassadors of peace*, but the distributors of pardons, mischief and insult. Cato discovers a gross ignorance of the British constitution, in supposing that these men *can* be empowered to act as Ambassadors. To prevent his future errors I will set him right. The present war differs from every other, in this instance, viz. that it is not carried on under the prerogative of the Crown as other wars have always been, but under the authority of the whole legislative power united, and as the barriers which stand in the way of a negociation, are not proclamations but acts of Parliament, it evidently follows, that were even the King of England here in person, he could not ratify the terms or conditions of a reconciliation; because, in the single character of King he could not stipulate for the repeal of any *acts* of Parliament, neither can the Parliament stipulate for him.

There is no body of men more jealous of their privileges than the Commons: because they sell them. Mark that, Cato.

I have not the least doubt upon me but that their business (exclusive of granting us pardons) is downright bribery and corruption. It is the machine by which they effect all their plans. We ought to view them as enemies of a most dangerous species, and he who means not to be corrupted by them will enter his protest in time. Are they not the very men who are paid for voting in every measure against us, and ought we not to suspect their designs? Can we view the barbarians as friends? Would it be prudent to trust the viper in our very bosoms? Or to suffer them to ramble at large among us while such doubtful characters as Cato have a being upon the Continent? Yet let their persons be safe from injury and outrage — but trust them not. Our business with them is short and explicit, viz. We are desirous of peace, Gentlemen; we are ready to ratify the terms, and will virtuously fulfil the conditions thereof; but we should deserve all and every misery which tyranny can inflict, were we, after suffering such a repetition of savage barbarities, to come under your government again.

Cato, by way of stealing into credit, says, that "the contest we are engaged in is founded on the most noble and virtuous principles which can animate the mind of man. We are contending, (says he) against an arbitrary Ministry for the rights of Englishmen." No, Cato, we are *now* contending against an arbitrary King to get clear of his tyranny. While the dispute rested in words only, it might be called "contending with the Ministry," but since it is broken out into open war, it is high time to have done with such silly and water-gruel definitions. But it suits not Cato to speak the truth. It is his interest to dress up the sceptered savage in the mildest colours. Cato's patent for a large tract of land is yet unsigned. Alas poor Cato!

Cato proceeds very importantly to tell us, *"that the eyes of all Europe are upon us."* This stale and hackneyed phrase, hath had a regular descent, from many of the King's speeches down to several of the speeches in Parliament; from thence, it took a turn among the little wits and bucks of St. James's; till after suffering all the torture of senseless repetition, and being reduced to a state of vagrancy, was charitably picked up to embellish the second letter of Cato. It is truly of the bug-bear kind, contains no meaning, and the very using it discovers a barrenness of invention. It signifies nothing to tell us "that the eyes of all Europe are upon us," unless he had likewise told us what they are looking at us *for*; which, as he hath not done, I will: They are looking at us, Cato, in hopes of seeing a final separation between Britain and the Colonies, that they, the *lookers on*, may partake of a free and uninterrupted trade with the whole Continent of America. Cato! thou reasonest *wrong*.

For the present, Sir, farewell. I have seen thy soliloquy and despise it. Remember, thou hast thrown me the glove, Cato, and either thee or I must tire. I fear not the field of fair debate, but thou hast stepped aside and made it personal— Thou hast tauntingly called on me by name; and if I cease to hunt thee from every lane and lurking-hole of mischief, and bring thee not a trembling culprit before the public bar, then brand me with reproach, by naming me in the list of your confederates.

Philadelphia, March 28, 1776.   THE FORESTER.

LETTER II

April 10, 1776

TO CATO

BEFORE I enter on the more immediate purpose of this letter; I think it necessary, once for all, to endeavour to settle as clearly as I can the following point, viz. How far personality is concerned in any political debate. The general maxim is, that measures, and not men, is the thing in question; and the maxim is undeniably just, when rightly understood. Cato, as a refuge for himself, hath quoted the author of *Common Sense*, who, in his preface, says, "That the object for attention is the *doctrine itself*, not the *man*;" that is, not the *rank* or *condition* of the man; for whether he is with those whose fortune is *already* made, or with those whose fortune is *yet* to make, or among those who seldom think or care whether they make *any*, is a matter wholly out of the question, and entirely confined to himself. But the political characters, political dependencies, and political Connections of men, being of a public nature, differ exceedingly from the circumstances of private life: And they are in many instances so nearly related to the measures they propose, that, to prevent our being deceived by the last, we *must* be acquainted with the first. A total ignorance of men lays us under the danger of mistaking plausibility for principle. Could the wolf bleat like the lamb, the flock would soon be inticed into ruin; wherefore, to prevent the mischief, he ought to be *seen*, as well as *heard*. There never was, nor ever will be, nor ever ought to be, any important political debate carried on, in which a total separation in all cases between men and measures could be admitted with sufficient safety. When hypocrisy shall be banished from the earth, the knowledge of men will be unnecessary, because, their measures cannot then be fraudulent; but until that time come (which never will come) they ought, under proper limitations, to go together. We have already too much secrecy in some things; and too little in others;—were men more known, and measures more concealed, we should have fewer hypocrites, and more security.

As the chief design of these letters is to detect and expose the falshoods and fallacious reasonings of Cato, he must not expect (when detected) to be treated like one who had debated fairly; for I will be bold to say, and to prove, that a grosser violation of truth and reason scarcely ever came from the pen of a writer; And the explanations which he hath endeavoured to impose on the passages which he hath quoted from *Common Sense*, are such as never existed in the mind of the author, nor can they be drawn from the words themselves. Neither must Cato expect to be spared, where his carelessness of expression, and visible want of compassion and sentiment, shall give occasion to raise any moral or philosophical reflection thereon. These things being premised, I now proceed to review the latter part of Cato's second letter.

In this place, Cato begins his first attack on *Common Sense*; but as he only discovers his ill-will, and neither offers any arguments against it, nor makes any quotation from it, I should in this place pass him by, were it not for the following strange assertion. "If little notice, says Cato (*little opposition he means*) has yet been taken of the publications concerning Independence, it is neither owing to the popularity of the doctrine, the unanswerable nature of the arguments, nor the fear of opposing them as the vanity of the author would suggest." As Cato hath given us the *negative* reasons, he ought to have given us the *real* ones; for as he *positively* tells what it was *not* owing to, he undoubtedly knows what it *was* owing to, that *he* delayed *his* answers so long; but instead of telling us that (which perhaps is not proper to be told) he flies from the argument with the following plump declaration—"nine tenths of the people of Pennsylvania (says he) yet abhor the doctrine." But stop, Cato! not quite so fast friend. If this be true, how came they, so late as the 2d of March last, to elect for a Burgess of this City a Gentleman of known *independent principles*, and one of the very few to whom the author of Common Sense shewed some part thereof while in manuscript.

Cato is just as unfortunate in the following paragraph. "Those, says he, who made the appeal (that is, published the pamphlet) have but little cause to triumph in its success. Of this they seem sensible, and, like true quacks, are constantly pestering us with additional doses, till the stomachs of their patients *begin wholly* to revolt." It is Cato's hard fate to be always detected: For perhaps there never was a pamphlet, since the use of letters were known, about which so little pains were taken, and of which so great a number went off in so short a time; I am certain that I am within compass when I say one hundred and twenty thousand. The book was turned upon the world like an orphan, to shift for itself; no plan was formed to support it, neither hath the author ever published a syllable on the subject from that time, till after the appearance of Cato's fourth letter; wherefore, what Cato says of additional doses administered by the author is an absolute falsity. Besides which, it comes with an ill-grace from one, who frequently publishes two letters in a week, and often puts them both into one paper. Cato here, Cato there, look where you will.

At the distance of a few lines from the above quotations, Cato presents us with a retrospective view of our former state, in which, says he, "we considered our connection with Great-Britain as our chief happiness. We flourished, grew rich and populous, to a degree not to be paralleled in history." This assertion is truly of the legerdemain kind, appearing at once both right and wrong. All writers on Cato's side have used the same argument, and conceived themselves invincible; nevertheless, a single expression, properly placed, dissolves the charm, for the cheat lies in putting the *consequence* for the *cause*; for had we not *flourished* the *connexion* had never *existed*, or never been *regarded*, and this is fully proved by the neglect shewn to the first settlers, who had every difficulty to struggle with, unnoticed and unassisted by the British Court.

Cato proceeds very industriously to sum up the former declarations of Congress and other public bodies, some of which were made upwards of a year ago, to prove that the doctrine of Independence hath no sanction from them. To this I shall give Cato one general answer, which is, that had he produced a thousand more such authorities they would *now* amount to nothing. They are out of date. Times and things are altered. The true character of the King was but little known among the body of the people a year ago,—willing to believe him good, they fondly called him so, but have since found, that Cato's Royal Sovereign is a Royal Savage.

Cato hath introduced the above-mentioned long quotation of authorities against independency with the following curious preface. "Nor have many weeks, says he, yet elapsed, since the first open proposition for independence was published to the world. By what men of consequence this scheme is supported, or whether by any, may possibly be the subject of future enquiry. Certainly it hath no countenance from the Congress, to whose sentiments we look up with reverence. On the contrary, it is *directly repugnant to every* declaration of that respectable body." Now Cato thou hast nailed thyself with a witness! directly repugnant to every declaration of that respectable body! mind that Cato, and mark what follows. It appears by an extract from the Resolves of the Congress, printed in the front of the Oration delivered by Dr. Smith, in honour of that brave man General Montgomery, that he (the

Doctor) was appointed by that honourable body to compose and deliver the same, in the *execution* of which, the orator exclaimed loudly against the doctrine of independence, but when a motion was afterwards made in Congress (according to former usage) to return the *Orator* thanks, and request a copy for the press, the motion was rejected from every part of the house, and thrown out without a division.

I now proceed to Cato's third letter, in the opening of which he deserts the subject of independence, and renews his attack on the Committee. Cato's manner of writing has as much order in it as the motion of a squirrel; he frequently writes as if he knew not what to write next, just as the other and jumps about only because he cannot stand still; though I am sometimes angry with him for his unprincipled method of writing and reasoning, I cannot help laughing at him at other times for his want of ingenuity: an instance of which he gives us, in kindly warning us against *"the foul pages of interested writers and strangers intermeddling in our affairs."* Were I to reply seriously, my answer would be this, thou seemest then ignorant, Cato, of that ancient and numerous order which are related to each other in all and every part of the globe, with whom the kindred is not formed by place or accident, but in principle and sentiment. A freeman, Cato, is a stranger no where, a slave, every where. But were I disposed to answer merrily, I should tell him, that as his notions of friendship were so very narrow and local, he obliges me to understand, that when he addresses the people with the tender title of *"my dear countrymen"* which frequently occurs in his letters, that he particularly means the long list of Mac's published in Donald MacDonald's commission.

In this letter Cato recommends the pamphlet called *Plain Truth*, a performance, which hath withered away like a sickly unnoticed weed, and which, even its advocates are displeased at, and the author ashamed to own. About the middle of this third letter Cato gives notice of his being ready to take the field. "I now proceed says he to give my reasons." How Cato hath managed the attack we are now to examine; and the first remark I shall offer on his conduct, is, that he hath most unluckily entered the list on the wrong side, and discharged his first fire among the Tories.

In order to prove this I shall give the paragraph entire—
"AGRICULTURE and COMMERCE, says Cato, have hitherto
been the happy employments by which these middle colonies
have risen into wealth and importance. By *them* the face of the
country have been changed from a barren wilderness into the
hospitable abodes of peace and plenty. Without *them*, we had
either never existed as Americans, or existed only as savages.
—The oaks would still have possessed their *native spots of
earth*, and never have *appeared in the form of ships and
houses*. What are now well cultivated fields, or flourishing
cities, would have remained only the solitary haunts of wild
beasts, or of men equally wild." The reader cannot help perceiving that through this whole paragraph, *our connection*
with Britain is left entirely out of the question, and our
present greatness attributed to internal causes *agriculture* and
commerce. This is a strange way, Cato, of overturning *Common Sense,* which says, "I challenge the warmest advocate for
reconciliation, to shew a single advantage which this continent can reap by being connected with Great-Britain; I repeat, says he, the challenge, not a single advantage is derived.
*Our corn will fetch its price in any market in Europe, and our
imported goods must be paid for, buy them where we will.*" Cato
introduces his next paragraph with saying "that much of our
former felicity was owing to the protection of England *is not
to be denied;*" yes Cato, I deny it wholly, and for the following
clear and simple reasons, viz. that our being connected with,
and submitting to be protected by her, made and will still make
all "*her* enemies *our* enemies, or as *Common Sense* says,
sets us at variance with nations who would otherwise seek
our friendship, and against whom we have neither anger nor
complaint."

The following passage is so glaringly absurd, that I shall
make but a short comment upon it. "And if hereafter, says
Cato, in the fulness of time, it shall be necessary to separate
from the land that gave birth to (*some of*) our ancestors, it will
be in a state of perfect manhood, when we can fully wield our
own arms, and *protect our commerce and coasts by our own
fleets.*" But how are we to come by *fleets* Cato, while Britain
hath the government of the continent? unless, we are to suppose, as you have hinted in the former paragraph, that our

oaks are to *grow* into ships, and be launched self-built from their "native spots of earth." It is Cato's misfortune, as a writer, not to distinguish justly between magic and imagination; while on the other hand there are many passages in his letters so seriously and deliberately false, that nothing but the most hardened effrontery, and a cast of mind bordering upon impiety would have uttered. He frequently forces me out of the common tract of civil language, in order, to do him justice; moderation and temper being really unequal to the task of exposing him.

Cato, unless he meant to destroy the ground he stood upon, ought not to have let the following paragraph been seen. "If our present *differences*, says he, can be accommodated, there is *scarce a probability* that Britain will ever *renew* her late fatal system of policy, or attempt again to employ force against us." How came Cato to admit the *probability* of our being brought *again* into the same bloody and expensive situation? but it is worth remarking, that those who write without principle, cannot help sometimes blundering upon truth. Then there is no *real security*, Cato, in this *reconciliation* of yours on *constitutional principles*? It still amounts to nothing, and after all this expence of life and wealth, we are to rest at last upon hope, hazard and uncertainty. Why then, by all that is sacred, *"it is time to part."*

But Cato, after admitting the *probability* of our being brought *again* into the same situation, proceeds to tell us, how we are to conduct ourselves in the second quarrel; and that is, by the very same methods we have done the present one, viz. to expend millions of treasure, and thousands of lives, in order to patch up a second *re-union*, that the way may be open for a *third quarrel*; and in this endless and chequered round of blood and treacherous peace hath Cato disposed of the continent of America.—That I may not be thought to do Cato injustice, I have quoted the whole passage; "But should Britain be so infatuated, says he, at any future period, as to think of subjugating us, either by the arts of corruption, or oppressive exertions of power, can we entertain a doubt but we shall AGAIN, with a virtue equal to the present, and with the *weapons of defence in our hands* (when necessary) convince her that we are willing, by a *constitutional connection* with her, to afford and receive reciprocal benefits; but although subjects of the same King we will not consent to be her slaves."—Come hither ye *little ones,* whom the poisonous hand of Cato is rearing for destruction, and remember the page that warns ye of your ruin!

Cato, in many of his expressions, discovers all that calm command over the passions and feelings, which always distinguishes the man who hath expelled them from his heart. Of this careless kind is the before mentioned phrase "our present differences," and the same unpardonable negligence is conveyed in the following one—"*Although* I consider her, says he, as having in her late conduct towards us, acted the part of a cruel step-dame." Wonderful sensibility indeed! All the havoc and desolation of unnatural war; the destruction of thousands; the burning and depopulating of towns and cities; the ruin and separation of friends and families, are just sufficient to extort from Cato, *this one* callous confession. But the cold and creeping soul of Cato is a stranger to the manly powers of sympathetic sorrow. He *moves* not, nor *can* he move in so pure an element. Accustomed to lick the hand that hath made him visible, and to breathe the gross atmosphere of servile and sordid dependance, his soul would *now* starve on virtue, and suffocate in the clear region of disinterested friendship.

Surely when Cato sat down to write, he either did not expect to be called to an account, or was totally regardless of reputation; otherwise, he would not have endeavoured to persuade the public, that the doctrine of independence was broached in a kind of seditious manner, at a time *"when says he, some gleams of reconciliation began first to break in upon us."* Come forth Cato, and prove the assertion! where do these gleams of reconciliation spring from? Are they to be found in the King's speech—in the address of either House of Parliament;—or in the act which lets loose a whole kennel of pirates upon our property, and commissions another sett to insult with pardons, the very men, whom their own measures had sought to ruin? Either prove the assertion, Cato, or take the reward of it, for it is the part of an incendiary to endeavour with specious falshoods, to mislead the credulity of unwary readers.—Cato likewise says, that while we continue united, and renounce all thoughts of independence, "that we have the *utmost assurance* of obtaining a *full redress* of our *grievances*, and an *ample security* against any *future violation* of our *just rights.*" If Cato means to insinuate that we have *received* such an assurance, let him read the conclusion of the preceding paragraph again, the same answer will serve for both.

Perhaps, when we recollect the long and unabated cruelty of the British Court toward us, and remember the many prayers which we have put up both *to* them and *for* them, that the following piece of declamation of Cato can hardly be equalled, either for absurdity or insanity: "If we now effect independence, says he, we must be considered as a *faithless people in the sight of all mankind, and could scarcely expect the confidence of any nation upon earth, or look up to heaven for its approving sentence.*" Art thou mad, Cato, or art thou foolish —or art thou *both*—or art thou *worse* than both? In *this passage* thou hast fairly gone beyond me. I have not language to bring thee back. Thou art safely entrenched indeed!—Rest therefore in thy strong-hold till HE who fortified thee in it shall come and fetch thee out.

Cato seems to be possessed of that jesuitical cunning, which always endeavours to disgrace what it cannot disprove; and this he sometimes effects, by unfairly introducing *our* terms into *his* arguments, and thereby begets a monster which he sends round the country for a show, and tells the good people that the name of it is *independance*. Of this character are several passages in his fourth and fifth letters, particularly where he quotes the term *"foreign assistance,"* which he ungenerously explains into a surrender of the continent to France and Spain. Such an unfair and sophistical reasoner doth not deserve the civility of good manners. He creates, likewise, the same confusion, by frequently using the word *peace* for *union*, and thereby charges us falsly by representing us as being determined to "reject all propositions of *peace*:" Whereas our wish is *peace*, but *not re-union*; and though we would gladly listen to the former, we are determined to resist every proposal for the latter, *come from where it will;* being fully persuaded, that in the present state of affairs *separation of governments is the only and best thing that can be done for both countries.*

The following case is unjustly put. "There never was a war, says Cato, so implacable, even among states naturally rivals and enemies, or among savages themselves, as not to have *peace* for its object as well as end." But was there ever a war, Cato, which had *union* for its object? No. What Cato means by states naturally rivals and enemies, I shall not enquire into, but this I know (for myself at least) that it was not in the power of France or Spain, or all the other powers in Europe, to have given such a wound or raised up such a mortal hatred Britain hath done. We feel the same kind of undescribed anger at her conduct, as we would at the sight of an animal devouring its young: And this particular species of anger is not generated in the transitory temper of the man, but in the chaste undefiled womb of nature.

Cato, towards the conclusion of his third letter (at which place I shall leave him for the present) compares the state of Britain and America to the quarrels of lovers, and from thence infers a probability that our affections will be renewed thereby. This I cannot help looking on as one of the most unnatural and distorted similies that can be drawn. Come hither ye that are lovers, or ye that *have been* lovers and decide the controversy between us! What comparison is there between the soft murmurs of an heart mourning in secret, and the loud horrors of war—between the silent fears of pensive sorrow, and rivers of wasted blood—between the *sweet* strife of affection, and the *bitter* strife of death—between the curable calamities of pettish lovers, and the sad sight of a thousand slain. "Get thee behind me," Cato, for thou hast not the feelings of a man.

THE FORESTER.

LETTER III

April 22, 1776

TO CATO

CATO's partizans may call me furious; I regard it not. There are men too, who have not virtue enough to be angry, and that crime perhaps is Cato's—He who dares not offend cannot be honest. Having thus balanced the charge, I proceed to Cato's fourth, fifth, sixth and seventh letters, all of which as they contain but little matter, I shall dismiss with as little trouble and less formality.

His fourth letter is introduced with a punning soliloquy— Cato's title to soliloquies is indisputable; because no man cares for his company*. However, he disowns the writing it, and assures his readers that it "was *really* put into his hands." I always consider this confirming mode of expression, as betraying a suspicion of one's self; and in this place, it amounts to just as much as if Cato had said, "you know my *failing*, Sirs, but what I tell you now is really true." Well! be it so, Cato; you shall have all the credit you ask for, and as to when, or where, or how you got it, who was the author, or who the giver, I shall not enquire after; being fully convinced, by the poetical merit of the performance, that tho' the writer of it may be an *Allen*, he'll never be a *Ramsay*†. Thus much for the soliloquy; and if this gentle chastisement should be the means of preventing Cato or his colleagues from mingling their punning nonsense with subjects of such a serious nature as the present one truly is, it will answer *one* of the ends it was intended for.

Cato's fourth, and the greatest part of his fifth letter, are constructed on a false meaning uncivilly imposed on a passage quoted from *Common Sense*; and for which, the author of that pamphlet hath a right to expect from Cato the usual concessions. I shall quote the passage entire, with Cato's additional meaning, and the inferences which he draws therefrom.

He introduces it with saying, "In my remarks on the pamphlet before me, I shall first consider those arguments on which he (the author) appears to lay his chief stress; and these are collected under four heads in his conclusion:" one of which is, "*It is the custom of nations when any two are at war, for some other powers, not engaged in the quarrel, to step in by way of mediators, and bring about the preliminaries of a peace; but while America calls herself the subject of Great-Britain, no*

---

*As this piece may possibly fall into the hands of some who are not acquainted with the word Soliloquy, for *their* information the sense of it is given, viz. "*talking to one's self.*"

†*Allan Ramsay*, a famous Scotch poet of *genuine* wit and humour.

power, however well-disposed she may be, can offer her mediation." The meaning contained in this passage is so exceedingly plain, and expressed in such easy and familiar terms, that it scarcely admits of being made plainer. No one, I think, could have understood it any other wise, than that, while we continue to call ourselves British subjects, the quarrel between us can only be called a *family quarrel*, in which it would be just as indelicate for any other nation to advise, or any ways to meddle or make, even with their offers of mediation, as it would be for a third person to interfere in a quarrel between a man and his wife. Whereas, were we to make use of that natural right which all other nations have done before us, and erect a government of our own, *independent of all the world*, the quarrel could then be no longer called a *family quarrel*, but a *regular war* between the two powers of Britain and America, in the same manner as one carried on between England and France; and in this state of political separation, the neutral powers might kindly tender their mediation, (as hath always been the practice) and bring about the preliminaries of a *peace*. Not a *union*, Cato, that is quite another thing. But instead of Cato's taking it in this easy and natural sense, he flies away on a wrong scent, *charges the author with proposing to call in foreign assistance*; and, under this wilful falshood, raises up a mighty cry after nothing at all. He begins his wild and unintelligible comment in the following manner: "Is this" says he, (meaning the passage already quoted) "*common sense*, or *common nonsense?* Surely peace * with Great Britain cannot be the object of this writer, after the horrible character he has given of the people of that country, and telling us, that reconciliation with them would be our ruin. The latter part of the paragraph seems to cast some light upon the former, altho' it contradicts it; for these mediators are not to interfere for making up the quarrel, but to widen it, by supporting us in a declaration, that we are not the subjects of Great-Britain: a new sort of business truly for mediators! But this," continues Cato, "leads us directly to the *main enquiry, what foreign*

---

*It is a strange thing that Cato cannot be taught to distinguish between *peace* and *union*.

power is able to give us this support?" What support, Cato? the passage you have quoted neither says a syllable, nor insinuates a hint about support: It speaks *only* of neutral powers in the neighbourly character of mediators between those which are at war; and says it is the custom of European Courts to do so. Cato hath already raised Commissioners into Ambassadors, but how he could transform mediators into men in arms, and mediation into military alliance, is surpassingly strange. Read the part over again, Cato; if you find I have charged you wrongfully and will point it out, I will engage that the author of *Common Sense* shall ask your pardon in the public papers with his name to it, but if the error be yours, the concession on your part follows as a duty.

Though I am fully persuaded that Cato does not believe one half of what himself has written, he, nevertheless, takes amazing pains to *frighten* his readers into a belief of the whole: Tells them of foreign troops (which he supposes we are going to send for) ravaging up and down the country; of their "bloody massacres, unrelenting persecutions which would *harrow up* (says he) the *very souls of protestants and freemen.*" Were they coming, Cato, which no one ever dreamed of but yourself (for thank God we want them not) it would be impossible for them to exceed, or even to equal the cruelties practised by the British army in the East-Indies: The tying men to the mouths of cannon and *"blowing them away,"* was never acted by any but an English General, or approved by any but a British Court*—read the proceeding of the Select Committee on India affairs.

From temporal fears Cato proceeds to spiritual ones, and in a hypocritical panic, asks, "To whose share will Pennsylvania fall—that of his most Catholic, or his most Christian King? I confess, continues he, that these questions stagger me." I dont wonder at it, Cato—I am glad to hear that some kind of remorse hath overtaken you—that you begin to *feel* that you are "heavy laden"—you have had a long run; and the stoutest heart must fail at last.

---

*Lord Clive, the chief of Eastern plunderers, received the thanks of Parliament for *"his honourable conduct in the East-Indies."*

Cato perceiving that the falsehoods in his fourth letter passed unreproved, ventured boldly on a fifth, in which he continues enlarging on the same convenient bug-bear. "In my last," says he "some notice was taken of the dangerous proposition held up by the author of *Common Sense*, for having recourse to foreign assistance." When will Cato learn to speak the truth! The assistance which we hope for from France, is not armies, (we want them not) but arms and ammunition. We have already received into this province only, near two hundred tons of salt-petre and gun-powder, besides muskets. Surely! we may continue to cultivate a useful acquaintance, without such malevolent beings as Cato raising his barbarous slander thereon. At *this time*, it is not only illiberal, but impolitic, and perhaps dangerous, to be pouring forth such torrents of abuse as his fourth and fifth letters contain, against the only power, that, in articles of defence, hath supplied our hasty wants.

Cato after expending near two letters in beating down an idol which himself *only* had set up, proudly congratulates himself on the defeat, and marches off to new exploits, leaving behind him the following proclamation. "Having thus," says Cato, "*dispatched* his" (the author of *Common Sense's*) "*main argument* for *independence*, which he founds on the necessity of calling in *foreign assistance*, I proceed to examine some other parts of his work." Not a syllable, Cato, doth any part of the pamphlet in question, say of calling in foreign assistance, or even forming military alliances. The dream is wholly your own; and is directly repugnant both to the letter and spirit of every page in the piece. The idea which *Common Sense*, constantly holds up, is, to have nothing to do with the political affairs of Europe. "As Europe, says the pamphlet, is our market for trade, we ought to form no political connections with *any part of it*. It is the true interest of America to steer clear of all European contentions." And where it proposes sending a manifesto to foreign courts (which it is high time to do) it recommends it, only, for the purpose of announcing to them the *impossibility of our living any longer under the British government, and of "assuring such Courts, of our peaceable disposition towards them, and of our desire of entering into trade with them."* Learn to be an honest man,

Cato, and then thou wilt not be thus exposed.—I have been the more particular in detecting Cato here, because it is on this *bubble* that his air-built battery against independance is raised—a poor foundation indeed! which even the point of a pin, or a pen if you please, can demolish with a touch, and bury the formidable Cato beneath the ruins of a vapour.

From this part of his fifth letter to the end of his seventh, he entirely deserts the subject of independance, and sets up the proud standard of Kings, in preference to a Republican form of government. My remarks on this part of the subject will be general and concise.

In this part of the debate, Cato shelters himself chiefly in quotations from other authors, without reasoning much on the matter himself;* in answer to which, I present him with a string of maxims and reflexions, drawn from the nature of things, without borrowing from any one. Cato may observe, that I scarcely ever quote; the reason is, I always think. But to return.

Government should always be considered as a matter of convenience, not of right. The scripture institutes no particular form of government, but it enters a protest against the monarchical form; and a negation on *one* thing, where *two only* are offered, and *one* must be chosen, amounts to an affirmative on the *other*. Monarchical government was first set up by the Heathens, and the Almighty permitted it to the Jews as a punishment. *"I gave them a King in mine anger."* Hosea xiii. 11. A Republican form of government is pointed out by nature—Kingly governments by an unequality of power. In Republican governments, the leaders of the people, if improper, are removeable by vote; Kings only by arms: an unsuccessful vote in the first case, leaves the voter safe; but an unsuccessful attempt in the latter, is death. Strange! that, that

---

*The following is an instance of Cato's method of conducting an argument, "If hereditary succession, says *Common Sense*, (meaning succession of monarchical governments) did ensure a race of good and wise men, it would have the seal of divine authority," *"thus we find him,"* says Cato, *"with his own hand affixing the seal of heaven to what he before told us the Devil invented and the Almighty entered his protest against."* Cato's 7th letter.—This is a strange argument indeed, Cato! or rather it is no argument at all, for hereditary succession does *not* ensure a race of good and wise men, consequently has *not* the *seal of divine authority*.

which is our *right* in the *one*, should be our *ruin* in the *other*—from which reflexion follows this maxim, That that mode of government in which our *right* becomes our *ruin*, cannot be the *right one*. If all human nature be corrupt, it is needless to strengthen the corruption by establishing a succession of Kings, who, be they ever so base are still to be obeyed; for the manners of a Court will always have an influence over the morals of a people. A Republican government hath more *true grandeur* in it than a Kingly one: On the part of the public it is more consistent with freemen to appoint their rulers than to have them born; and on the part of those who preside, it is far nobler to be a ruler by the choice of the people, than a King by the chance of birth. Every honest Delegate is more than a Monarch. Disorders will unavoidably happen in all States, but monarchical governments are the most subject thereto, because the balance hangs uneven. *"Nineteen rebellions and eight civil wars in England since the conquest."* Whatever commotions are produced in Republican States, are not produced by a Republican spirit, but by those who seek to extinguish it. A Republican State cannot produce its own destruction, it can only suffer it. No nation of people, in their true senses, when seriously reflecting on the rank which God hath given them, and the reasoning faculties he hath blessed them with, would ever, of their own consent, give any *one man* a negative power over the whole: No man since the fall hath ever been equal to the trust; wherefore, 'tis insanity in us to entrust them with it; and in this sense, all those who have had it have done us right by abusing us into reason. Nature seems sometimes to laugh at mankind, by giving them so many fools for Kings; at other times, she punishes their folly by giving them tyrants; but England must have offended highly to be curst with both in one. *Rosseau* proposed a plan for establishing a perpetual European peace; which was, for every State in Europe to send Ambassadors to form a General Council, and when any difference happened between any two nations, to refer the matter to arbitration instead of going to arms. This would be forming a kind of European Republic: But the proud and plundering spirit of Kings hath not peace for its object.—They look not at the good of mankind—They set not out upon that plan: And if the history of the Creation, and the history of Kings be compared together, the result will be this—that God hath made a world, and Kings have robbed him of it.

But that which sufficiently establishes the Republican mode of government, in preference to a Kingly one, even when all other arguments are left out, is this simple truth, that all men are Republicans by nature and Royalists only by fashion. And this is fully proved by that passionate adoration, which all men shew to that great and almost only remaining bulwark of natural rights, *trial by juries*, which is founded on a pure Republican basis. Here the power of Kings is shut out. No Royal negative can enter this Court. The Jury, which is here, supreme, is a *Republic*, a body of *Judges chosen from among the people*.

The charter which secures this freedom in England, was formed, not in the senate, but in the field; and insisted on by the people, not granted by the crown; the crown in that instance *granted nothing*, but only renounced its former tyrannies, and bound itself over to its future good behaviour.—It was the compromise, by which the wearer of it made his peace with the people, and the condition on which he was suffered to reign.

Here ends my reply to all the letters which have at present appeared under the signature of Cato, being at this time seven in number. I have made no particular remarks on his two last, which treats only of the mode of government, but answered to them generally. In one place I observe, he accuses the writer of *Common Sense* with inconsistency, in having declared, "That no man was a warmer wisher for reconciliation than himself, before the fatal 19th of April, 1775;" "that is, (says Cato) reconciliation to monarchical government:" to which I reply, that *war* ought to be no man's *wish*, neither ought any man to perplex a state, already formed, with his private opinions; "the mode of government being a proper consideration for those countries" only "which have their governments yet to form." *Common Sense*.

On a review of the ground which I have gone over in Cato's letters, (exclusive of what I have omitted) I find the following material charges against him:

First. He hath accused the Committee with crimes generally; stated none, nor proved, nor attempted to prove any. *N. B.* The pretence of charging the acts of a body of men on individuals, is too slender to be admitted*.

Secondly. He hath falsly complained to the public of the restraint of the press.

Thirdly. He hath wickedly asserted that "gleams of reconciliation had lately broken in upon us," thereby grossly deceiving the people.

Fourthly. He hath insinuated as if he wished the public to believe, that we had *received* "the utmost assurance of having all our grievances redressed, and an ample security against any future violation of our just rights.

Fifthly. He hath spread false alarms of calling in foreign troops.

Sixthly. He hath turned the scripture into a jest. Ez. 35.

These falshoods, if uncontradicted, might have passed for truths, and the minds of persons remote from better intelligence might have been greatly embarrassed thereby. Let our opinions be what they will, truth as to facts should be strictly adhered to. It was this affecting consideration that drew out the *Forester* (a perfect volunteer) to the painful task of writing three long letters, and occasioned to the public the trouble of reading them.

Having for the present closed my correspondence with Cato, I shall conclude this letter with a well-meant, affectionate address—

TO THE PEOPLE.

It is not a time to triffle. Men, who know they deserve nothing from their country, and whose hope is on the arm that hath sought to enslave ye, may hold out to you, as Cato hath done, the false light of reconciliation—There is no such thing. 'Tis gone! 'Tis past!—The grave hath parted us—and

---

*Cato and I differ materially in our opinion of Committees; I consider them as the *only constitutional* bodies at present in this province, and that for the following reason; they were duly elected by the people, and chearfully and faithfully do the service for which they were elected. The House of Assembly were likewise elected by the people, but do the business for which they *were not* elected. Their authority is truly unconstitutional, being self created. My charge is as a body, and *not* as individuals.

death, in the persons of the slain, hath cut the thread of life between Britain and America.

Conquest, and not reconciliation is the plan of Britain. But admitting even the last hope of the Tories to happen, which is, that our enemies after a long succession of losses, wearied and disabled, should despairingly throw down their arms and propose a re-union; in that case, what is to be done? Are defeated and disappointed tyrants, to be considered like mistaken and converted friends? Or would it be right, to receive those for Governors, who, had they been conquerors, would have hung us up for traitors? Certainly not. Reject the offer then, and propose another; which is, *we will make peace with you as with enemies, but we will never re-unite with you as friends.* This effected, and ye secure to yourselves the pleasing prospect of an eternal peace. America, remote from all the wrangling world, may live at ease. Bounded by the ocean and backed by the wilderness, what hath she to fear, but her GOD?

Be not deceived.—It is not a little that is at stake. Reconciliation will not now go down, even if it were offered. 'Tis a dangerous question; for the eyes of all men begin to open. There is now no secret in the matter; there ought to be none. It is a case that concerns every man, and every man ought to lay it to heart. He that *is* here and he that was *born* here are alike concerned. It is needless too, to split the business into a thousand parts, and perplex it with endless and fruitless investigations, in the manner that a writer signed a *Common Man* hath done. This unparalleled contention of nations is not to be settled like a school-boy's task of pounds, shillings, pence, and fractions. *That writer*, though he may mean well, is strangely below the mark: For the first and great question, and that which involves every other in it, and from which every other will flow, is *happiness.* Can this continent be happy under the government of Great-Britain or not? Secondly, can she be happy under a government of our own? To live beneath the authority of those whom we cannot love, is misery, slavery, or what name you please. In that case, there will never be peace. Security will be a thing unknown, because, a treacherous friend in power, is the most dangerous of enemies. The answer to the second question, can America be happy under a government of her own is short and simple, viz. as happy as she please; she hath a blank sheet to write upon. Put it not off too long.*

Painful as the task of speaking truth must sometimes be, yet I cannot avoid giving the following hint, because much, nay almost every thing depends upon it; and that is, *a thorough knowledge of the persons whom we trust*. It is the duty of the public, at this time, to scrutinize closely into the conduct of their Committee Members, Members of Assembly, and Delegates in Congress; to know *what* they do, and their motives for so doing. Without knowing this, we shall never know who to confide in; but shall constantly mistake friends for enemies, and enemies for friends, till in the confusion of persons we sacrifice the cause.—I am led to this reflexion by the following circumstance, That the Gentleman to whom the unwise and arbitrary instructions to the Delegates of this province owe their being, and who hath bestowed all his power to support them, is said to be the same person who, when the ships now on the stocks were wanting timber, *refused to sell it*, and thus by preventing our strength to cry out of our insufficiency.—But his hour of fame is past—he is hastening to his political exit.

THE FORESTER.

REPLY TO CATO'S EIGHTH LETTER

April 30, 1776

TO CATO.

WHEREAS Cato, in his eighth letter, and some of his partizans since, have made free with the Forester as having neither *"character nor connexion."* To which I answer, first, "better to have none than bad ones." Secondly, that the person supposed by some, and known by others, to be the author of Common Sense, and the Forester's letters, came a cabin passenger in Jeremiah Warder's ship, the London Packet, last Christmas twelvemonth, bringing with him two unsealed letters of introduction from Dr. Franklin to his friends here, in

*Forget not the hapless African.

which he says, *"I recommend the bearer hereof, Mr. ——, as a worthy ingenious, &c."*

I have published this at the request, and for the sake of those gentlemen whose acquaintance I am honored with—and in my turn call on Cato and his confederates to set forth, as I have done, what rank and recommendation they or their originals made their first appearance in ——

THE FORESTER.

LETTER IV

May 8, 1776

WHOEVER will take the trouble of attending to the progress and changeability of times and things, and the conduct of mankind thereon, will find that *extraordinary circumstances* do sometimes arise before us, of a species, either so purely natural or so perfectly original, that none but the man of nature can understand them. When precedents fail to assist us, we must return to the first principles of things for information; and *think*, as if we were the *first men* that *thought*. And this is the true reason, that in the present state of affairs, the wise are become foolish, and the foolish wise. I am led to this reflection by not being able to account for the conduct of the Quakers on any other; for although they do not seem to perceive it themselves, yet, it is amazing to hear with what unanswerable ignorance many of that body, wise in other matters, will discourse on the present one. Did they hold places or commissions under the King, were they Governors of provinces, or had they any interest apparently distinct from us, the mystery would cease; but as they have not, their folly is best attributed, to that superabundance of *worldly knowledge,* which in original matters is too cunning to be wise. Back to the first plain path of nature friends, and begin anew, for in this business your first footsteps were wrong. You have now travelled to the summit of inconsistency, and that, with such accelerated rapidity as to acquire autumnal ripeness by the first of May. Now your *resting time comes on.* You have done your utmost and must abide the consequences. Yet who can reflect on such conduct without feeling concern; Who can look unaffected, on a body of *thoughtfull* men, undoing in *one rash hour* the labour of seventy years: Or what can be said in their excuse, more, than that they have arrived at their second childhood, the infancy of threescore and ten.*

But my chief design, in this letter, is to set forth the inconsistency, partiality, and injustice of the *dependant faction*, and like an honest man, who courts no favor, to shew to them the dangerous ground they stand upon; in order to do which, I must refer to the *business, event,* and *probable consequences* of the late election.

The business of that day was to do what? Why, to elect four burgesses to assist those already elected, in conducting the military proceedings of this province, against the power of *that crown* by whose authority they pretend to sit: And those gentlemen when elected, are according to the rules of that house (as the rest have done) to take an oath of allegiance to serve the same King against whom this province, with themselves at the head thereof, are at war: And a necessary qualification required of many voters, was, that they likewise should swear allegiance to the same King against whose power the same house of assembly had just before obliged them, either, to fine or take up arms. Did ever national hypocrisy arise to such a pitch as this! Under the pretence of moderation we are running into the most damnable sins. It is now the duty of every man from the pulpit and from the press, in his family and in the street to cry out against it. Good God! Have we no remembrance of duty left to the King of Heaven! No conscientious awe to restrain this sacrifice of sacred things? Is this our chartered priviledge? This our boasted constitution, that

---

*The Quakers in 1704 who then made up the whole house of assembly, zealously guarded their own and the peoples rights against the encroaching power of the proprietor, who nevertheless, outwitted them by finding means to abolish the original charter and introduce another, of which they complained in the following words. "And then by a subtle contrivance and artifice, 'of thine,' laid deeper than the capacities of some could fathom, or the circumstances of many could admit time then to consider of, a way was found out, to lay the first charter aside and introduce another."—*Query,* Would these men have elected the proprietary persons which you have done?

we can sin and feel it not? The clergy of the English church, of which I profess myself a member, complain of *their* situation, and wish relief; in short, every *thinking man* must feel distress. — Yet, to the credit of the people be it spoken, the sin lies not at their door. We can trace the iniquity in this province to the fountain head, and see by what delusions it has imposed on others. The guilt centers in a few, and flows from the same source, that a few years ago avariciously suffered the frontiers of this province to be deluged in blood; and though the vengeance of Heaven hath slept since, it may awake too soon for their repose.

A motion was sometime ago made to elect a convention to take into consideration the state of the province, a more judicious proposal could not be thought of. Our present condition is alarming. We are worse off then other provinces — and such an enquiry is highly necessary. The House of Assembly in its present form is disqualified for such business, because it is a branch from that power against whom we are contending. Besides, they are in intercourse with the King's representative, and the members which compose the house have, as *members thereof*, taken an oath to discover to the King of England the very business, which, in that inquiry would unavoidably come before them. Their minds too are warped and prejudiced by the provincial instructions they have arbitrarily and without right issued forth. They are again improper, because, the enquiry would necessarily *extend to them as a body*, to see how far it is proper to trust men with such unlimited power as they have lately assumed. In times like these, we must trace to the root and origin of things; It being the only way to become right, when we are got systematically wrong. The motion for a Convention, alarmed the crown and proprietary dependants; but to every man of reflection, it had a cordial and restorative quality. The case is, first, we are got wrong — Secondly, how shall we get right? — Not by an House of Assembly; because they cannot sit as *Judges in a case*, where their *own existence* under their *present form and authority is to be judged of.* However, the objectors found out a way, as they thought, to supercede the necessity of a Convention, by promoting a bill for augmenting the number of representatives; not perceiving at the same time, that such an augmentation would *encrease* the *necessity* of a convention; because, the more any power is augmented, which derives it's authority from our enemies, the more unsafe and dangerous it becomes to us. Far be it from the writer of this to censure the individuals which compose that house; his aim being only against the chartered authority under which it acts. However the bill passed into a law (which shews, that in Pennsylvania, as well as in England, there is *no constitution*, but only *a temporary form of government**) While in order to shew the inconsistency of the house in its present state, the motion for a convention was postponed, and four conscientious independant gentlemen were proposed as candidates, on the augmentation, who, had they been elected would not have taken the oaths necessary to admit a person as member of that assembly. And in that case, the house would have had neither one kind of authority nor another. While the old part remained sworn to divulge to the King, what the new part thought it their duty to declare against him. Thus matters stood on the morning of the election.

On our side we had to sustain the loss of those gallant citizens who are now before the walls of Quebec, and other parts of the continent; while the tories by never stirring out, remain at home to take the advantage of elections; and this evil prevails more or less from the Congress down to the Committees. A numerous body of Germans, of property, zealots in the cause of freedom, were likewise excluded for non-allegiance: Notwithstanding which, the tory non-conformists, that is, those who are advertised as enemies to their country, were admitted to vote on the other side. A strange contradiction indeed! To which were added the testimonizing Quakers, who, after suffering themselves to be duped by the meanest of all passion, religious spleen, endeavoured in a vague uncharitable manner to possess the Roman Catholics of the same disease. These parties, with such others as they could influence, were headed by the proprietary dependants, to support the British and Proprietary power against the public. They had pompously given out that nine tenths of the people were on their side. A vast majority truly! But it so happened,

*This distinction will be more fully explained in some future letter.

that notwithstanding the disadvantages we laid under, of having many of our voters rejected, others disqualified for non allegiance, with the great loss sustained by absentees, the manœuvre of shutting up the doors between seven and eight o'clock, and circulating the report of adjourning and finishing the next morning, by which, several were deceived, it so happened, I say, that on casting up the tickets, that the first, in numbers, on the dependant side, and the first on the independant side, viz. Clymer and Allen, were a tye 923 each.*

To the description which I have already given of those who are against us, I may add, that they have neither associated nor assisted, or but very few of them; that they are a collection of different bodies blended by accident, having no natural relation to each other; that they have agreed rather out of spite than right; and that, as they met by chance, they will dissolve away again for the want of a cement.

On our side, our object was *single*, our cause was *one*; wherefore, we *cannot* separate, neither *will* we separate. We have stood the experiment of the election, for the sake of knowing the men who were against us. Alass what are they! One half of them ought to be now asking public pardon for their former offences; and the other half may think themselves well off that they are let alone. When the enemy enters the country, *can* they defend themselves? Or *will* they defend themselves? And if not, are they so foolish as to think, that in times like these, when it is our duty to search the corrupted wound to the bottom, that we, with ten times their strength and number (if the question were put to the people at large) will submit to be governed by cowards and tories.

He that is wise will reflect, that the safest asylum, especially in times of general convulsion when no settled form of government prevails, is, *the love of the people*. All property is safe under their protection. Even in countries where the lowest and most licentious of them have risen into outrage, they have never departed from the path of *natural* honour. Volunteers unto death in defence of the person or fortune of those who had served or defended them. Division of property never

*Mr. Samuel Howell, though in their ticket, was never considered by us a proprietary dependant.

entered the mind of the populace.—It is incompatible with that spirit which impels them into action. An avaricious mob was never heard of; nay, even a miser put in the midst of them, and catching their spirit, would, for that instant, cease to be covetous.

I shall conclude this letter with remarking, that the English fleet and army have of late gone upon a different plan of operation to what they first set out with; for instead of going against those Colonies where independance prevails *most*, they go against *those only* where they suppose it prevails *least*. They have quitted Massachusetts-Bay and gone to North-Carolina; supposing they had many friends there. Why are they expected at New-York? But because they imagine the inhabitants are *not* generally independants, (yet that province hath a large share of virtue, notwithstanding the odium which its House of Assembly brought upon it.) From which I argue, that the electing the King's Attorney for a Burgess of this city, is a fair invitation for them to come here; and in that case, will those who have invited them turn out to repulse them; I suppose not, for in their 923 votes there will not be found more than sixty armed men, perhaps not so many. Wherefore, should such an event happen, which probably will, I here give my *first vote* to levy the expence attending the expedition against them, *on the estates of those who have invited them.*

THE FORESTER.

The American Crisis

NUMBER I

December 19, 1776

THESE are the times that try men's souls: The summer soldier and the sunshine patriot will, in this crisis, shrink from the service of his country; but he that stands it NOW, deserves the love and thanks of man and woman. Tyranny, like hell, is not easily conquered; yet we have this consolation with us, that the harder the conflict, the more glorious the triumph. What we obtain too cheap, we esteem too lightly: — 'Tis dearness only that gives every thing its value. Heaven knows how to set a proper price upon its goods; and it would be strange indeed, if so celestial an article as FREEDOM should not be highly rated. Britain, with an army to enforce her tyranny, has declared, that she has a right (*not only to* TAX) but "*to* BIND *us in* ALL CASES WHATSOEVER," and if being *bound in that manner* is not slavery, then is there not such a thing as slavery upon earth. Even the expression is impious, for so unlimited a power can belong only to GOD.

Whether the Independence of the Continent was declared too soon, or delayed too long, I will not now enter into as an argument; my own simple opinion is, that had it been eight months earlier, it would have been much better. We did not make a proper use of last winter, neither could we, while we were in a dependent state. However, the fault, if it were one, was all our own; we have none to blame but ourselves*. But no great deal is lost yet; all that Howe has been doing for this month past is rather a ravage than a conquest, which the spirit of the Jersies a year ago would have quickly repulsed, and which time and a little resolution will soon recover.

---

*"The present winter" (meaning the last) "is worth an age, if rightly employed, but if lost, or neglected, the whole Continent will partake of the evil; and there is no punishment that man does not deserve, be he who, or what, or where he will, that may be the means of sacrificing a season so precious and useful."   COMMON SENSE.

I have as little superstition in me as any man living, but my secret opinion has ever been, and still is, that GOD almighty will not give up a people to military destruction, or leave them unsupportedly to perish, who had so earnestly and so repeatedly sought to avoid the calamities of war, by every decent method which wisdom could invent. Neither have I so much of the infidel in me, as to suppose, that HE has relinquished the government of the world, and given us up to the care of devils; and as I do not, I cannot see on what grounds the king of Britain can look up to heaven for help against us: A common murderer, a highwayman, or a housebreaker, has as good a pretence as he.

'Tis surprising to see how rapidly a panic will sometimes run through a country. All nations and ages have been subject to them: Britain has trembled like an ague at the report of a French fleet of flat bottomed boats; and in the fourteenth century the whole English army, after ravaging the kingdom of France, was driven back like men petrified with fear; and this brave exploit was performed by a few broken forces collected and headed by a woman, Joan of Arc. Would, that Heaven might inspire some Jersey maid to spirit up her countrymen, and save her fair fellow-sufferers from ravage and ravishment! Yet panics, in some cases, have their uses; they produce as much good as hurt. Their duration is always short; the mind soon grows thro' them, and acquires a firmer habit than before. But their peculiar advantage is, that they are the touchstones of sincerity and hypocrisy, and bring things and men to light, which might otherwise have lain for ever undiscovered. In fact, they have the same effect on secret traitors, which an imaginary apparition would upon a private murderer. They sift out the hidden thoughts of man, and hold them up in public to the world. Many a disguised Tory has lately shewn his head, that shall penitentially solemnize with curses the day on which Howe arrived upon the Delaware.

As I was with the troops at fort Lee, and marched with them to the edge of Pennsylvania, I am well acquainted with many circumstances, which those, who lived at a distance, know but little or nothing of. Our situation there was exceedingly cramped, the place being on a narrow neck of land between the North river and the Hackensack. Our force was inconsiderable, being not one fourth so great as Howe could bring against us. We had no army at hand to have relieved the garrison, had we shut ourselves up and stood on the defence. Our ammunition, light artillery, and the best part of our stores, had been removed upon the apprehension that Howe would endeavour to penetrate the Jersies, in which case fort Lee could be of no use to us; for it must occur to every thinking man, whether in the army or not, that these kind of field forts are only for temporary purposes, and last in use no longer than the enemy directs his force against the particular object, which such forts are raised to defend. Such was our situation and condition at fort Lee on the morning of the 20th of November, when an officer arrived with information, that the enemy with 200 boats had landed about seven or eight miles above: Major General Green, who commanded the garrison, immediately ordered them under arms, and sent express to his Excellency General Washington at the town of Hackensack, distant by the way of the ferry six miles. Our first object was to secure the bridge over the Hackensack, which laid up the river between the enemy and us, about six miles from us and three from them. General Washington arrived in about three quarters of an hour, and marched at the head of the troops towards the bridge, which place I expected we should have a brush for; however they did not chuse to dispute it with us, and the greatest part of our troops went over the bridge, the rest over the ferry, except some which passed at a mill on a small creek, between the bridge and the ferry, and made their way through some marshy grounds up to the town of Hackensack, and there passed the river. We brought off as much baggage as the waggons could contain, the rest was lost. The simple object was to bring off the garrison, and to march them on till they could be strengthened by the Jersey or Pennsylvania militia, so as to be enabled to make a stand. We staid four days at Newark, collected in our outposts with some of the Jersey militia, and marched out twice to meet the enemy on information of their being advancing, though our numbers were greatly inferiour to theirs. Howe, in my little opinion, committed a great error in generalship, in not throwing a body of forces off from Staaten Island through Amboy, by which means he might have seized all our stores at Brunswick, and intercepted our march into Pennsylvania: But, if we believe the power of hell to be limited, we must likewise believe that their agents are under some providential controul.

I shall not now attempt to give all the particulars of our retreat to the Delaware; suffice it for the present to say, that both officers and men, though greatly harassed and fatigued, frequently without rest, covering, or provision, the inevitable consequences of a long retreat, bore it with a manly and a martial spirit. All their wishes were one, which was, that the country would turn out and help them to drive the enemy back. Voltaire has remarked, that king William never appeared to full advantage but in difficulties and in action; the same remark may be made on General Washington, for the character fits him. There is a natural firmness in some minds which cannot be unlocked by triffles, but which, when unlocked, discovers a cabinet of fortitude; and I reckon it among those kind of public blessings, which we do not immediately see, that GOD hath blest him with uninterrupted health, and given him a mind that can even flourish upon care.

I shall conclude this paper with some miscellaneous remarks on the state of our affairs; and shall begin with asking the following question, Why is it that the enemy hath left the New-England provinces, and made these middle ones the seat of war? The answer is easy: New-England is not infested with Tories, and we are. I have been tender in raising the cry against these men, and used numberless arguments to shew them their danger, but it will not do to sacrifice a world to either their folly or their baseness. The period is now arrived, in which either they or we must change our sentiments, or one or both must fall. And what is a Tory? Good GOD! what is he? I should not be afraid to go with a hundred Whigs against a thousand Tories, were they to attempt to get into arms. Every Tory is a coward, for a servile, slavish, self-interested fear is the foundation of Toryism; and a man under such influence, though he may be cruel, never can be brave.

But before the line of irrecoverable separation be drawn between us, let us reason the matter together: Your conduct is an invitation to the enemy, yet not one in a thousand of you has heart enough to join him. Howe is as much deceived by you as the American cause is injured by you. He expects you will all take up arms, and flock to his standard with muskets on your shoulders. Your opinions are of no use to him, unless you support him personally; for 'tis soldiers, and not Tories, that he wants.

I once felt all that kind of anger, which a man ought to feel, against the mean principles that are held by the Tories: A noted one, who kept a tavern at Amboy, was standing at his door, with as pretty a child in his hand, about eight or nine years old, as most I ever saw, and after speaking his mind as freely as he thought was prudent, finished with this unfatherly expression, *"Well! give me peace in my day."* Not a man lives on the Continent but fully believes that a seperation must some time or other finally take place, and a generous parent would have said, *"If there must be trouble, let it be in my day, that my child may have peace;"* and this single reflection, well applied, is sufficient to awaken every man to duty. Not a place upon earth might be so happy as America. Her situation is remote from all the wrangling world, and she has nothing to do but to trade with them. A man may easily distinguish in himself between temper and principle, and I am as confident, as I am that GOD governs the world, that America will never be happy till she gets clear of foreign dominion. Wars, without ceasing, will break out till that period arrives, and the Continent must in the end be conqueror; for, though the flame of liberty may sometimes cease to shine, the coal never can expire.

America did not, nor does not, want force; but she wanted a proper application of that force. Wisdom is not the purchase of a day, and it is no wonder that we should err at first sitting off. From an excess of tenderness, we were unwilling to raise an army, and trusted our cause to the temporary defence of a well meaning militia. A summer's experience has now taught us better; yet with those troops, while they were collected, we were able to set bounds to the progress of the enemy, and, thank GOD! they are again assembling. I always considered a militia as the best troops in the world for a sudden exertion, but they will not do for a long campaign. Howe, it is probable, will make an attempt on this city; should he fail on this side the Delaware, he is ruined; if he succeeds, our cause is not ruined. He stakes all on his side against a part of ours; admitting he succeeds, the consequence will be, that armies from both ends of the Continent will march to assist their suffering friends in the middle States; for he cannot go every where, it is impossible. I consider Howe as the greatest enemy the Tories have; he is bringing a war into their country, which, had it not been for him and partly for themselves, they had been clear of. Should he now be expelled, I wish, with all the devotion of a Christian, that the names of Whig and Tory may never more be mentioned; but should the Tories give him encouragement to come, or assistance if he come, I as sincerely wish that our next year's arms may expell them from the Continent, and the Congress appropriate their possessions to the relief of those who have suffered in well doing. A single successful battle next year will settle the whole. America could carry on a two years war by the confiscation of the property of disaffected persons, and be made happy by their expulsion. Say not that this is revenge, call it rather the soft resentment of a suffering people, who, having no object in view but the GOOD of ALL, have staked their OWN ALL upon a seemingly doubtful event. Yet it is folly to argue against determined hardness; eloquence may strike the ear, and the language of sorrow draw forth the tear of compassion, but nothing can reach the heart that is steeled with prejudice.

Quitting this class of men, I turn with the warm ardour of a friend to those who have nobly stood, and are yet determined to stand the matter out: I call not upon a few, but upon all; not on THIS State or THAT State, but on EVERY State; up and help us; lay your shoulders to the wheel; better have too much force than too little, when so great an object is at stake. Let it be told to the future world, that in the depth of winter, when nothing but hope and virtue could survive, that the city and the country, alarmed at one common danger, came forth to meet and to repulse it. Say not, that thousands are gone, turn out your tens of thousands; throw not the burthen of the day upon Providence, but *"shew your faith by your works,"* that GOD may bless you. It matters not where you live, or what rank of life you hold, the evil or the blessing will reach you all. The far and the near, the home counties and the back, the rich and the poor, shall suffer or rejoice alike. The heart that feels not now, is dead: The blood of his children shall curse his cowardice, who shrinks back at a time when a little might have saved the whole, and made *them* happy. I love the man that can smile in trouble, that can gather strength from distress, and grow brave by reflection. 'Tis the business of little minds to shrink; but he whose heart is firm, and whose conscience approves his conduct, will pursue his principles unto death. My own line of reasoning is to myself as strait and clear as a ray of light. Not all the treasures of the world, so far as I believe, could have induced me to support an offensive war, for I think it murder; but if a thief break into my house, burn and destroy my property, and kill or threaten to kill me, or those that are in it, and to *"bind me in all cases whatsoever,"* to his absolute will, am I to suffer it? What signifies it to me, whether he who does it, is a king or a common man; my countryman or not my countryman? whether it is done by an individual villain, or an army of them? If we reason to the root of things we shall find no difference; neither can any just cause be assigned why we should punish in the one case, and pardon in the other. Let them call me rebel, and welcome, I feel no concern from it; but I should suffer the misery of devils, were I to make a whore of my soul by swearing allegiance to one, whose character is that of a sottish, stupid, stubborn, worthless, brutish man. I conceive likewise a horrid idea in receiving mercy from a being, who at the last day shall be shrieking to the rocks and mountains to cover him, and fleeing with terror from the orphan, the widow and the slain of America.

There are cases which cannot be overdone by language, and this is one. There are persons too who see not the full extent of the evil that threatens them; they solace themselves with hopes that the enemy, if they succeed, will be merciful. It is the madness of folly to expect mercy from those who have refused to do justice; and even mercy, where conquest is the object, is only a trick of war: The cunning of the fox is as murderous as the violence of the wolfe; and we ought to guard equally against both. Howe's first object is partly by threats and partly by promises, to terrify or seduce the people to deliver up their arms, and receive mercy. The ministry recommended the same plan to Gage, and this is what the Tories call making their peace; *"a peace which passeth all understanding"* indeed! A peace which would be the immediate forerunner of a worse ruin than any we have yet thought of. Ye men of Pennsylvania, do reason upon those things! Were the back counties to give up their arms, they would fall an easy prey to the Indians, who are all armed: This perhaps is what some Tories would not be sorry for. Were the home counties to deliver up their arms, they would be exposed to the resentment of the back counties, who would then have it in their power to chastise their defection at pleasure. And were any one State to give up its arms, THAT State must be garrisoned by all Howe's army of Britons and Hessians to preserve it from the anger of the rest. Mutual fear is a principal link in the chain of mutual love, and woe be to that State that breaks the compact. Howe is mercifully inviting you to barbarous destruction, and men must be either rogues or fools that will not see it. I dwell not upon the vapours of imagination; I bring reason to your ears; and in language, as plain as A, B, C, hold up truth to your eyes.

I thank GOD that I fear not. I see no real cause for fear. I know our situation well, and can see the way out of it. While our army was collected, Howe dared not risk a battle, and it is no credit to him that he decamped from the White Plains, and waited a mean opportunity to ravage the defenceless Jersies; but it is great credit to us, that, with an handful of men, we sustained an orderly retreat for near an hundred miles, brought off our ammunition, all our field-pieces, the greatest part of our stores, and had four rivers to pass. None can say that our retreat was precipitate, for we were near three weeks in performing it, that the country might have time to come in. Twice we marched back to meet the enemy and remained out till dark. The sign of fear was not seen in our camp, and had not some of the cowardly and disaffected inhabitants spread false alarms thro' the country, the Jersies had never been ravaged. Once more we are again collected and collecting; our new army at both ends of the Continent is recruiting fast, and we shall be able to open the next campaign with sixty thousand men, well armed and cloathed. This is our situation, and who will may know it. By perseverance and fortitude we have the prospect of a glorious issue; by cowardice and submission, the sad choice of a variety of evils—a ravaged country—a depopulated city—habitations without safety, and slavery without hope—our homes turned into barracks and baudy-houses for Hessians, and a future race to provide for whose fathers we shall doubt of. Look on this picture, and weep over it!—and if there yet remains one thoughtless wretch who believes it not, let him suffer it unlamented.

The American Crisis

NUMBER II

January 13, 1777

TO LORD HOWE.

"What's in the name of LORD that I should fear,
To bring my grievance to the public ear."   CHURCHILL.

UNIVERSAL empire is the prerogative of a writer. His concerns are with all mankind, and though he cannot command their obedience, he can assign them their duty. The Republic of Letters is more ancient than monarchy, and of far higher character in the world than the vassal court of Britain; he that rebels against reason is a real rebel, but he that in defence of reason, rebels against tyranny, has a better title to "DEFENDER OF THE FAITH" than George the Third.

As a military man your Lordship may hold out the sword of war, and call it the "ULTIMA RATIO REGUM:" *The last Reason of Kings;* we in return can show you the sword of justice, and call it, "The best Scourge of Tyrants." The first of these two may threaten, or even frighten, for a while, and cast a sickly languor over an insulted people, but reason will soon recover the debauch, and restore them again to tranquil fortitude. Your Lordship, I find, has now commenced author and published a proclamation; I too have published a crisis; as they stand, they are the antipodes of each other; both cannot rise at once, and one of them must descend: And so quick is the revolution of things, that your Lordship's performance, I see, has already fallen many degrees from its first place, and is now just visible on the edge of the political horizon.

It is surprising to what pitch of infatuation blind folly and obstinacy will carry mankind, and your Lordship's drowsy proclamation is a proof that it does not even quit them in their sleep. Perhaps you thought America too was taking a nap, and therefore, chose, like satan to Eve, to whisper the delusion softly, lest you should awaken her. This Continent, Sir, is too extensive to sleep all at once, and too watchful, even in its slumbers, not to startle at the unhallowed foot of an invader. You may issue your proclamations, and welcome, for we have learned to *"reverence ourselves"* and scorn the insulting ruffian that employs you. America for your deceased brother's sake would gladly have shown you respect, and it is a new aggravation to her feelings that *Howe* should be forgetful, and raise his sword against those, who at their own charge raised a monument to his brother. But your master has commanded, and you have not enough of nature left to refuse. Surely! there must be something strangely degenerating in the love of monarchy, that can so completely wear a man down to an ingrate, and make him proud to lick the dust that kings have trod upon. A few more years, should you survive them, will bestow on you the title of an old man, and in some hour of future reflection you may probably find the fitness of Woolsey's despairing penitence, *"Had I served my God as faithfully as I have served my king, he would not thus have forsaken me in my old age."*

The character you appear to us in is truly ridiculous. Your friends, the Tories, announced your coming with high descriptions of your unlimited powers; but your proclamation has given them the lie, by shewing you to be a Commissioner without authority. Had your powers been ever so great, they were nothing to us, farther than we pleased; because we had the same right which other nations had, to do what we thought was best. "THE UNITED STATES OF AMERICA," will sound as pompously in the world or in history as *"The Kingdom of Great-Britain;"* The character of *General Washington* will fill a page with as much luster as that of *Lord Howe*; and the *Congress* have as much right to command the *King and Parliament* of London, to desist from legislation, as *they* or *you* have to command the Congress. Only suppose how laughable such an edict would appear from us, and then, in that merry mood, do but turn the tables upon yourself, and you will see how your proclamation is received here. Having thus placed you in a proper position in which you may have a full view of folly and learn to despise it, I hold up to you, for that purpose, the following quotation from your own lunarian proclamation. "And We (Lord Howe and General Howe) do command, (and in his Majesty's name forsooth) all such

persons as are assembled together under the name of general
or provincial Congresses, Committees, Conventions, or other
Associations, by whatever name or names known or distinguished, to desist and cease from all such treasonable actings
and doings."

You introduce your proclamation by referring to your declarations of the 14th of July and 19th of September. In the last
of these, you sunk yourself below the character of a private
gentleman. That I may not seem to accuse you unjustly I shall
state the circumstance: By a verbal invitation of yours com-
municated to Congress by General Sullivan, then a prisoner
on his parole, you signified your desire of conferring with
some members of that body as private gentlemen. It was beneath the dignity of the American Congress to pay any regard
to a message that at best was but a genteel affront, and had
too much of the ministerial complexion of tampering with
private persons; and which might probably have been the
case, had the gentlemen who were deputed on that business,
possessed that easy kind of virtue which an English courtier is
so truly distinguished by. Your request however was complied
with, for honest men are naturally more tender of their civil
than their political fame. The interview ended as every sensible man thought it would; for your Lordship knows, as well
as the writer of the Crisis, that it is impossible for the king of
England to promise the repeal, or even the revisal, of any acts
of parliament; wherefore, on your part, you had nothing to
say, more than to request, in the room of demanding, the
entire surrender of the Continent; and then, if that was complied with, to promise that the inhabitants should escape with
their lives. This was the upshot of the conference. You informed the conferees that you were two months in soliciting
these powers. We ask, what powers? for as Commissioner you
have none. If you mean the power of pardoning, it is an
oblique proof that your master was determined to sacrifice all
before him; and that you were two months in dissuading him
from his purpose. Another evidence of his savage obstinacy!
From your own account of the matter we may justly draw
these two conclusions; first, that you serve a monster; and
secondly, that never was a commissioner sent on a more foolish errand than yourself. This plain language may perhaps

sound uncoothly to an ear viciated by courtly refinements; but words were made for use, and the fault lies in deserving them, or the abuse in applying them unfairly.

Soon after your return to New-York you published a very illiberal and unmanly hand bill against the Congress; for it was certainly stepping out of the line of common civility, first to screen your national pride by soliciting an interview with them as private gentlemen, and in the conclusion to endeavour to deceive the multitude by making an hand bill attack on the whole body of the Congress; you got them together under one name, and abused them under another. But the king you serve and the cause you support afford you so few instances of acting the gentleman, that out of pity to your situation the Congress pardoned the insult by taking no notice of it.

You say in that hand bill, "that they, the Congress, disavowed every purpose for reconciliation not consonant with their extravagant and inadmissible claim of Independence." Why, God bless me! what have you to do with our Independence? we ask no leave of yours to set it up; we ask no money of yours to support it; we can do better without your fleets and armies than with them; you may soon have enough to do to protect yourselves without being burthened with us. We are very willing to be at peace with you, to buy of you and sell to you, and, like young beginners in the world, to work for our own living; therefore, why do you put yourselves out of cash, when we know you cannot spare it, and we do not desire you to run into debt? I am willing, Sir, you should see your folly in every view I can place it, and for that reason descend sometimes to tell you in jest what I wish you to see in earnest. But to be more serious with you, why do you say "their" Independence? To set you right, Sir, we tell you, that the Independency is *ours* not *theirs*. The Congress were authorised by every State on the Continent to publish it to all the world, and in so doing are not to be considered as the inventors, but only as the heralds that proclaimed it, or the office from which the sense of the people receive a legal form; and it was as much as any or all their heads were worth, to have treated with you on the subject of submission under any name whatever. But we know the men in whom we have trusted; can England say the same of her parliament?

I come now more particularly to your proclamation of the 30th of November last. Had you gained an entire conquest over all the armies of America, and then put forth a proclamation, offering (what you call) mercy, your conduct would have had some specious show of humanity; but to creep by surprise into a province, and there endeavour to terrify and seduce the inhabitants from their just allegiance to the rest by promises, which you neither meant nor were able to fulfil, is both cruel and unmanly: Cruel in its effects; because, unless you can keep all the ground you have marched over, how are you, in the words of your proclamation, to secure to your proselytes "the enjoyment of their property?" What are to become either of your new adopted subjects, or your old friends the Tories, in Burlington, Bordentown, Trenton, Mountholly, and many other places, where you proudly lorded it for a few days, and then fled with the precipitation of a pursued thief? What, I say, are to become of those wretches? What are to become of those who went over to you from this city and State? What more can you say to them than *"Shift for yourselves?"* Or what more can they hope for than to wander like vagabonds over the face of the earth? You may now tell them to take their leave of America and all that once was theirs. Recommend them, for consolation, to your master's court; there perhaps they may make a shift to live on the scraps of some dangling parasite, and choose companions among thousands like themselves. A traitor is the foulest fiend on earth!

In a political sense we ought to thank you for thus bequeathing estates to the Continent; we shall soon, at this rate, be able to carry on a war without expence, and grow rich by the ill policy of Lord Howe and the generous defection of the Tories. Had you set your foot into this city you would have bestowed estates upon us which we never thought of, by bringing forth traitors we were unwilling to suspect. But these men, you'll say, *"are his majesty's most faithful subjects;"* let that honour then be all their fortune, and let his majesty take them to himself.

I am now thoroughly disgusted with them; they live in ungrateful ease and bend their whole minds to mischief. It seems as if GOD had given them over to a spirit of infidelity, and that they are open to conviction in no other line but that of punishment. It is time to have done with tarring, feathering, carting, and taking securities for their future good behaviour; every sensible man must feel a conscious shame at seeing a poor fellow hawked for a show about the streets, when it is known that he is only the tool of some principal villain, biased into his offence by the force of false reasoning, or bribed thereto through sad necessity. We dishonour ourselves by attacking such trifling characters, while greater ones are suffered to escape; 'tis our duty to find *them* out, and their proper punishment would be to exile them from the Continent for ever. The circle of them is not so great as some imagine; the influence of a few have tainted many who are not naturally corrupt. A continual circulation of lies among those who are not much in the way of hearing them contradicted, will in time pass for truth; and the crime lies not in the believer but the inventor. I am not for declaring war against every man that appears not so warm as myself: Difference of constitution, temper, habit of speaking and many other things will go a great way in fixing the outward character of a man, yet simple honesty may remain at bottom. Some men have naturally a military turn, and can brave hardships and the risk of life with a chearful face; others have not, no slavery appears to them so great as the fatigue of arms, and no terror so powerful as that of personal danger: What can we say? We cannot alter nature, neither ought we to punish the son because the father begot him in a cowardly mood. However, I believe most men have more courage than they know of, and that a little at first is enough to begin with. I knew the time when I thought that the whistling of a cannon ball would have frightened me almost to death; but I have since tried it, and find I can stand it with as little discomposure, and (I believe) with a much easier conscience than your Lordship. The same dread would return to me again were I in your situation, for my solemn belief of your cause is, that it is hellish and damnable, and under that conviction every thinking man's heart *must* fail him.

From a concern that a good cause should be dishonoured by the least disunion among us, I said in my former paper, No. 1. "That should the enemy now be expelled, I wish, with all the sincerity of a Christian, that the names of Whig and

Tory might never more be mentioned;" but there is a knot of men among us of such a venomous cast that they will not admit even one's good wishes to act in their favour. Instead of rejoicing that Heaven had, as it were, providentially preserved this city from plunder and destruction, by delivering so great a part of the enemy into our hands with so little effusion of blood, they stubbornly affected to disbelieve it till within an hour, nay half an hour, of the prisoners arriving: And the Quakers put forth a testimony, dated the 20th of December, signed *"John Pemberton,"* declaring their attachment to the British government.* These men are continually harping on the great sin of *our* bearing arms, but the king of Britain may lay waste the world in blood and famine, and they, poor fallen souls, have nothing to say.

In some future paper I intend to distinguish between the different kind of persons who have been denominated *Tories*, for this I am clear in, that all are not so who have been called so, nor all men Whigs who were once thought so; and as I mean not to conceal the name of any true friend when there shall be occasion to mention him, neither will I that of an enemy who ought to be known, let his rank, station or religion be what it may. Much pains have been taken by some to set your Lordship's private character in an amiable light, but as it has chiefly been done by men who know nothing about you, and who are no ways remarkable for their attachment to us, we have no just authority for believing it. George the Third was imposed upon us by the same arts, but TIME, at length, has done him justice, and the same fate may probably attend your Lordship. Your avowed purpose here, is to kill, conquer, plunder, pardon and enslave; and the ravages of your army through the Jersies have been marked with as much barbarism as if you had openly professed yourself the

*I have ever been careful of charging offences upon whole societies of men, but as the paper referred to is put forth by an unknown set of men, who claim to themselves the right of representing the whole; and while the whole society of Quakers admit its validity by a silent acknowledgment, it is impossible that any distinction can be made by the public; and the more so because the New-York paper, of the 30th of December, printed by permission of our enemies, says that *"the Quakers begin to speak openly of their attachment to the British constitution."* We are certain that we have many friends among them, and wish to know them.

prince of ruffians; not even the appearance of humanity has been preserved either on the march or the retreat of your troops; no general order, that I could ever learn, has ever been issued to prevent or even forbid your troops from robbery wherever they came, and the only instance of justice, if it can be called such, which has distinguished you for impartiality, is, that you treated and plundered all alike; what could not be carried away have been destroyed, and mohogony furniture have been deliberately laid on the fire for fuel, rather than the men should be fatigued with cutting wood.* There was a time when the Whigs confided much in your supposed candour, and the Tories rested themselves on your favour; the experiments have now been made, and failed; and every town, nay every cottage, in the Jersies, where your arms have been, is a testimony against you. How you may rest under this sacrifice of character I know not, but this I know, that you sleep and rise with the daily curses of thousands upon you; perhaps the misery which the Tories have suffered by your proffered mercy may give them some claim to their country's pity, and be in the end the best favour you could show them.

In a folio general order book belonging to Colonel Rohl's battalion, taken at Trenton, and now in the possession of the Council of Safety for this State, the following barbarous order is frequently repeated, *"His Excellency the* COMMANDER IN CHIEF *orders, that all inhabitants which shall be found with arms, not having an officer with them, shall be immediately taken and hung up."* How many you may thus have privately sacrificed we know not, and the account can only be settled in another world. Your treatment of prisoners, in order to distress them to enlist into your infernal service, is not to be equalled by any instance in Europe. Yet this is the humane Lord Howe and his brother, whom the Tories and their three quarter kindred the Quakers, or some of them at least, have been holding up for patterns of justice and mercy!

A bad cause will ever be supported by bad means and bad

---

*As some people may doubt the truth of such wanton destruction, I think it necessary to inform, that one of the people called Quakers, who lives at Trenton, gave me this information at the house of Mr. Michael Hutchinson (one of the same profession) who lives near to Trenton ferry, on the Pennsylvania side; Mr. Hutchinson being present.

men, and whoever will be at the pains of examining strictly into things, will find that one and the same spirit of oppression and impiety, more or less, governs through your whole party in both countries: Not many days ago I accidently fell in company with a person of this city, noted for espousing your cause, and on my remarking to him, "that it appeared clear to me, by the late providential turn of affairs, that GOD Almighty was visibly on our side," he replied, "We care nothing for that, you may have HIM, and welcome; if we have but enough of the devil on our side we shall do." However carelessly this might be spoken matters not, 'tis still the insensible principle that directs all your conduct, and will at last most assuredly deceive and ruin you.

If ever a nation was mad and foolish, blind to its own interest and bent on its own destruction, it is Britain. There are such things as national sins, and though the punishment of individuals may be reserved to *another* world, national punishment can only be inflicted in *this* world. Britain, as a nation, is in my inmost belief the greatest and most ungrateful offender against GOD on the face of the whole earth: Bless'd with all the commerce she could wish for, and furnished by a vast extension of dominion with the means of civilizing both the eastern and western world, she has made no other use of both than proudly to idolize her own "Thunder," and rip up the bowels of whole countries for what she could get;—like Alexander she has made war her sport, and inflicted misery for prodagality sake. The blood of India is not yet repaid, nor the wretchedness of Africa yet requitted. Of late she has enlarged her list of national cruelties by her butcherly destruction of the Caribbs of St. Vincents, and in returning an answer by the sword to the meek prayer for *"Peace, Liberty and Safety."* These are serious things; and whatever a foolish tyrant, a debauched court, a trafficking legislature or a blinded people may think, the national account with Heaven must some day or other be settled: All countries have sooner or later been called to their reckoning; the proudest empires have sunk when the balance was struck; and Britain, like an individual penitent, must undergo her day of sorrow, and the sooner it happens to her the better. As I wish it over, I wish it to come, but withal wish that it may be as light as possible.

Perhaps your Lordship has no taste for serious things; by your connexions in England I should suppose not: Therefore I shall drop this part of the subject, and take it up in a line in which you will better understand me.

By what means, may I ask, do you expect to conquer America? If you could not effect it in the summer when our army was less than yours, nor in the winter when we had none, how are you to do it? In point of generalship you have been outwitted, and in point of fortitude outdone; your advantages turn out to your loss, and show us that it is in our power to ruin you by gifts: Like a game of drafts we can move out of *one* square to let you come in, in order that we may afterwards take two or three for one; and as we can always keep a double corner for ourselves, we can always prevent a total defeat. You cannot be so insensible as not to see that we have two to one the advantage of you, because we conquer by a drawn game, and you lose by it. Burgoyne might have taught your Lordship this knowledge; he has been long a student in the doctrine of chances.

I have no other idea of conquering countries than by subduing the armies which defend them: Have you done this, or can you do this? If you have not, it would be civil in you to let your proclamations alone for the present; otherwise, you will ruin more Tories by your grace and favour than you will Whigs by your arms.

Were you to obtain possession of this city, you would not know what to do with it more than to plunder it. To hold it, in the manner you hold New-York, would be an additional dead weight upon your hands; and if a general conquest is your object, you had better be without the city than with it. When you have defeated all our armies, the cities will fall into your hands of themselves; but to creep into them in the manner you got into Princetown, Trenton, &c. is like robbing an orchard in the night before the fruit be ripe, and running away in the morning. Your experiment in the Jersies is sufficient to teach you that you have something more to do than barely to get into other people's houses; and your new converts, to whom you promised all manner of protection, and seduced into new guilt by pardoning them from their former virtues, must begin to have a very contemptible opinion both of your power and your policy. Your authority in the Jersies is now reduced to the small circle which your army occupies, and your proclamation is no where else seen unless it be to be laughed at. The mighty subduers of the Continent are retreated into a nutshell, and the proud forgivers of our sins are fled from those they came to pardon; and all this at a time when they were dispatching vessel after vessel to England with the great news of every day. In short, you have managed your Jersey expedition so very dexterously that the dead only are conquerors, because none will dispute the ground with them.

In all the wars you have formerly been concerned in, you had only armies to contend with; in this case you have both an army and a country to combat with. In former wars, the countries followed the fate of their capitals; Canada fell with Quebec, and Minorca with Port Mahon or St. Philips; by subduing those, the conquerors opened a way into, and became masters of the country: here it is otherwise; if you get possession of a city here, you are obliged to shut yourselves up in it, and can make no other use of it, than to spend your country's money in. This is all the advantage you have drawn from New-York; and you would draw less from Philadelphia, because it requires more force to keep it, and is much farther from the sea. A pretty figure you and the Tories would cut in this city, with a river full of ice, and a town full of fire; for the immediate consequence of your getting here would be, that you would be cannonaded out again and the Tories be obliged to make good the damage; and this, sooner or later, will be the fate of New-York.

I wish to see the city saved, not so much from military as from natural motives. 'Tis the hiding-place of women and children, and Lord Howe's proper business is with our armies. When I put all the circumstances together which ought to be taken, I laugh at your notion of conquering America. Because you lived in a little country where an army might run over the whole in a few days, and where a single company of soldiers might put a multitude to the route, you expected to find it the same here. It is plain that you brought over with you all the narrow notions you were bred up with, and imagined that a proclamation in the king's name was to do great things; but Englishmen always travel for knowledge, and your Lordship, I hope, will return, if you return at all, much wiser than you came.

We may be surprised by events we did not expect, and in that interval of recollection you may gain some temporary advantage: Such was the case a few weeks ago, but we soon ripen again into reason, collect our strength, and while you are preparing for a triumph we came upon you with a defeat. Such it has been, and such it would be were you to try it an hundred times over. Were you to garrison the places you might march over, in order to secure their subjection, (for remember you can do it by no other means) your army would be like a stream of water running to nothing. By the time you reached from New-York to Virginia you would be reduced to a string of drops not capable of hanging together; while we, by retreating from State to State, like a river turning back upon itself, would acquire strength in the same proportion as you lost it, and in the end be capable of overwhelming you. The country in the mean time would suffer, but 'tis a day of suffering, and we ought to expect it. What we contend for is worthy the affliction we may go through. If we get but bread to eat, and any kind of rayment to put on, we ought, not only to be contented, but thankful. More than *that* we ought not to look for, and less than *that* Heaven has not yet suffered us to want. He that would sell his Birthright for a little *salt*, is as worthless as he who sold it for *porridge* without salt. And he that would part with it for a gay coat, or a *plain* coat, ought for ever to be a slave in buff. What are salt, sugar and finery to the inestimable blessings of "Liberty and Safety?" Or what are the inconveniencies of a few months to the tributary bondage of ages? The meanest peasant in America, bless'd with these sentiments, is a happy man compared with a New-York Tory; he can eat his morsel without repining, and when he has done, can sweeten it with a repast of wholesome air; he can take his child by the hand and bless it, without feeling the conscious shame of neglecting a parent's duty.

In publishing these remarks I have several objects in view: On your part they are, to expose the folly of your pretended authority as a Commissioner; the wickedness of your cause in general; and the impossibility of your conquering us at any rate. On the part of the public my meaning is, to show them their true and solid interest; to encourage them to their own good, to remove the fears and falsities which bad men had spread and weak men had encouraged; and to excite in all men a love for union, and a chearfulness for duty.

I shall submit one more case to you respecting your conquest of this country, and then proceed to new observations:

Suppose our armies in every part of the Continent were immediately to disperse, every man to his home, or where else he might be safe, and engage to re-assemble again on a certain future day; it is clear that you would then have no army to contend with, yet you would be as much at a loss in that case as you are now; you would be afraid to send your troops in parties over the Continent, either to disarm, or prevent us from assembling, lest they should not return; and while you kept them together, having no army of ours to dispute with, you could not call it a conquest; you might furnish out a pompous page in the London Gazette or the New-York paper, but when we returned at the appointed time, you would have the same work to do you had at first.

It has been the folly of Britain to suppose herself more powerful than she really is, and by that means have arrogated to herself a rank in the world she is not entitled to; for more than this century past she has not been able to carry on a war without foreign assistance. In Marlborough's campaigns, and from that day to this, the number of German troops and officers assisting her have been about equal with her own; ten thousand Hessians were sent to England last war to protect her from a French invasion; and she would have cut but a poor figure in her Canadian and West-Indian expeditions, had not America been lavish both of her money and men to help her along. The only instance in which she was engaged singly, that I can recollect, was against the rebellion in Scotland in forty-five and forty-six, and in that, out of three battles, she was twice beaten, till by thus reducing their numbers (as we shall yours) and taking a supply-ship that was coming to Scotland with cloaths, arms and money (as we have often done) she was at last enabled to defeat them. England was never famous by land; her officers have generally been suspected of cowardice, have more of the air of a dancing-master than a soldier, and by the sample we have taken prisoners we begin to give the preference to ourselves. Her strength of late has laid in her extravagance; but as her finances and her credit are now low, her sinews in that line begin to fail fast. As a nation she is the poorest in Europe; for were the whole kingdom, and all that is in it, to be put up to sale like the estate of a bankrupt, it would not fetch as much as she owes: Yet this thoughtless wretch must go to war, and with the avowed design too of making us beasts of burthen, to support her in riot and debauchery, and to assist her afterwards in distressing those nations who are now our best friends. This ingratitude may suit a Tory, or the unchristian peevishness of a fallen Quaker, but none else.

'Tis the unhappy temper of the English to be pleased with any war, right or wrong, be it but successful; but they soon grow discontented with ill fortune, and it is an even chance that they are as clamorous for peace next summer, as the king and his ministers were for war last winter. In this natural view of things, your Lordship stands in a very ugly critical situation: Your whole character is staked upon your laurels; if they wither, you wither with them; if they flourish, you cannot live long to look at them; and at any rate, the black account hereafter is not far off. What lately appeared to us misfortunes, were only blessings in disguise; and the seeming advantages on your side have turned out to our profit. Even our loss of this city, as far as we can see, might be a principal gain to us: The more surface you spread over, the thinner you will be, and the easier wiped away; and our consolation under that apparent disaster would be, that the estates of the Tories would become securities for the repairs. In short, there is no old ground we can fail upon, but some new foundation rises again to support us. *"We have put, Sir, our hands to the plough, and cursed be he that looketh back."*

Your king, in his speech to parliament last spring, declared to them, *"That he had no doubt but the great force they had enabled him to send to America, would effectually reduce the rebellious Colonies."* It has not, neither can it; but it has done just enough to lay the foundation of its own next year's ruin. You are sensible that you left England in a divided distracted state of politics, and, by the command you had here, you became a principal prop in the court party; their fortunes rest on yours; by a single express you can fix their value with the public, and the degree to which their spirits shall rise or fall; they are in your hands as stock, and you have the secret of the ally with you. Thus situated and connected, you become the unintentional mechanical instrument of your own and their overthrow. The king and his ministers put conquest out of doubt, and the credit of both depended on the proof. To support them in the interim, it was necessary you should make the most of every thing; and we can tell by Hugh Gaine's New-York paper what the complexion of the London Gazette is. With such a list of victories the nation cannot expect you will ask new supplies; and to confess your want of them, would give the lie to your triumphs, and impeach the king and his ministers of treasonable deception. If you make the necessary demand at home, your party sinks; if you make it not, you sink yourself; to ask it now is too late, and to ask it before was too soon, and unless it arrive quickly will be of no use. In short, the part you have to act, cannot be acted; and I am fully persuaded that all you have to trust to, is to do the best you can with what force you have got, or little more. Though we have greatly excelled you in point of generalship and bravery of men, yet, as a people, we have not entered into the full soul of enterprize; for I, who know England and the disposition of the people well; am confident that it is easier for us to effect a revolution there, than you a conquest here: A few thousand men landed in England with the declared design of deposing the present king, bringing his ministers to trial, and setting up the duke of Gloucester in his stead, would assuredly carry their point, while you were groveling here ignorant of the matter. As I send all my papers to England, this, like COMMON SENSE, will find its way there; and though it may put one party on their guard, it will inform the other and the nation in general of our design to help them.

Thus far, Sir, I have endeavoured to give you a picture of present affairs: You may draw from it what conclusions you please. I wish as well to the true prosperity of England as you can, but I consider *Independence as America's natural Right and Interest*, and never could see any real disservice it would be to Britain. If an English merchant receives an order and is paid for it, it signifies nothing to him who governs the country—This is my creed of politics. If I have any where expressed myself overwarmly, 'tis from a fixt immovable hatred I have, and ever had, to cruel men and cruel measures. I have likewise an aversion to monarchy, as being too debasing to the dignity of man; but I never troubled others with my notions till very lately, nor ever published a syllable in England in my life. What I write is pure nature, and my pen and my soul have ever gone together. My writings I have always given away, reserving only the expence of printing and paper, and sometimes not even that. I never courted either fame or interest, and my manner of life, to those who know it, will justify what I say. My study is to be useful, and if your Lordship love mankind as well I do, you would, seeing you cannot conquer us, cast about and lend your hand towards accomplishing a peace. Our Independence, with GOD's blessing, we will maintain against all the world; but as we wish to avoid evil ourselves, we wish not to inflict it on others. I am never over-inquisitive into the secrets of the Cabinet, but I have some notion, that if you neglect the present opportunity, that it will not be in our power to make a separate peace with you afterwards; for whatever treaties or alliances we form, we shall most faithfully abide by; wherefore you may be deceived if you think you can make it with us at any time. A lasting independent peace is my wish, end and aim; and to accomplish that *"I pray God the"* Americans *"may never be defeated, and I trust while they have good officers, and are well commanded,"* and willing to be commanded, *"that they* NEVER WILL.*"*

COMMON SENSE.

Philadelphia, January 13, 1777.

The American Crisis

NUMBER III

April 19, 1777

IN the progress of politics, as in the common occurrences of life, we are not only apt to forget the ground we have travelled over, but frequently neglect to gather up experience as we go. We expend, if I may so say, the knowledge of every day on the circumstances that produce it, and journey on in search of new matter and new refinements: But as it is pleasant, and sometimes useful, to look back, even to the first periods of infancy, and trace the turns and windings through which we have passed, so we may likewise derive many advantages by halting a while in our political career, and taking a review of the wondrous complicated labyrinth of little more than yesterday.

Truly, may we say, that never did man grow old in so short a time! We have crouded the business of an age into the compass of a few months, and have been driven through such a rapid succession of things, that, for the want of leisure to think, we unavoidably wasted knowledge as we came, and have left nearly as much behind us as we brought with us: But the road is yet rich with the fragments, and, before we fully lose sight of them, will repay us for the trouble of stopping to pick them up.

Were a man to be totally deprived of memory, he would be incapable of forming any just opinion; every thing about him would seem a chaos; he would have even his own history to ask from every one; and by not knowing how the world went on in his absence, he would be at a loss to know how it *ought* to go on when he recovered, or rather, returned to it again. In like manner, tho' in a less degree, a too great inattention to past occurrences retards and bewilders our judgment in every thing; while, on the contrary, by comparing what is past with what is present, we frequently hit on the true character of both, and become wise with very little trouble. It is a kind of countermarch, by which we get into the rear of Time, and mark the movements and meaning of things as we make our return. There are certain circumstances, which, at the time of their happening, are kind of riddles, and as every riddle is to be followed by its answer, so those kind of circumstances will be followed by their events, and those events are always the true solution. A considerable space of time may lapse between, and unless we continue our observations from the one to the other, the harmony of them will pass away unnoticed: But the misfortune is, that partly from the pressing necessity of some instant things, and partly from the impatience of our own tempers, we are frequently in such a hurry to make out the meaning of every thing as fast as it happens, that we thereby never truly understand it; and not only start new difficulties to ourselves by so doing, but, as it were, embarrass Providence in her good designs.

I have been civil in stating this fault on a large scale, for, as it now stands, it does not appear to be levelled against any particular set of men; but were it to be refined a little farther, it might afterwards be applied to the Tories with a degree of striking propriety: Those men have been remarkable for drawing sudden conclusions from single facts. The least apparent mishap on our side, or the least seeming advantage on the part of the enemy, have determined with them the fate of a whole campaign. By this hasty judgment they have converted a retreat into a defeat; mistook generalship for error; while every little advantage purposely given the enemy, either to weaken their strength by dividing it, embarrass their councils by multiplying their objects, or to secure a greater post by the surrender of a less, has been instantly magnified into a conquest. Thus, by quartering ill policy upon ill principles, they have frequently promoted the cause they designed to injure, and injured that which they intended to promote.

It is probable the campaign may open before this Number comes from the press. The enemy have long lain idle and amused themselves with carrying on the war by proclamations only. While they continue their delay our strength encreases, and were they to move to action now, it is a circumstantial proof they have no reinforcement coming; wherefore, in either case, the comparative advantage will be ours. Like a wounded disabled whale they want only time and room to die in; and though in the agony of their exit, it may be unsafe to live within the flapping of their tail, yet every hour shortens their date and lessens their power of mischief. If any thing happens while this Number is in the press, it will afford me a subject for the last pages of it. At present I am tired of waiting; and as neither the enemy, nor the state of politics, have *yet* produced any thing new, I am thereby left in the field of general matter undirected by any striking or particular object. This Crisis, therefore, will be made up rather of variety than novelty, and consist more of things useful than things wonderful.

The success of the cause, the union of the people, and the means of supporting and securing both, are points which cannot be too much attended to. He who doubts of the former is a desponding coward, and he who wilfully disturbs the latter is a traitor. Their characters are easily fixt, and under these short descriptions I leave them for the present.

One of the greatest degrees of sentimental union which America ever knew, was in denying the right of the British parliament *"to bind the Colonies in all cases whatever."* The declaration is in its form an almighty one, and is the loftiest stretch of arbitrary power that ever one set of men, or one country claimed over another. Taxation was nothing more than the putting the declared right into practice; and this failing, recourse was had to arms, as a means to establish both the right *and* the practice, or to answer a worse purpose, which will be mentioned in the course of this Number. And in order to repay themselves the expence of an army, and to profit by their own injustice, the Colonies were, by another law, declared to be in a state of actual rebellion, and of consequence all property therein would fall to the conquerors.

The Colonies, on their part, FIRST, denied the right; SECONDLY, they suspended the use of taxable articles, and petitioned against the practice of taxation: and these failing, they, THIRDLY, defended their property by force, as soon as it was forcibly invaded, and in answer to the declaration of rebellion and non-protection, published their declaration of Independence and right to self-protection.

These, in a few words, are the different stages of the quarrel; and the parts are so intimately and necessarily connected with each other as to admit of no separation. A person, to use a trite phrase, must be a Whig or a Tory in the lump. His feelings, as a man, may be wounded; his charity, as a Christian, may be moved; but his political principles must go through all the cases on one side or the other. He cannot be a Whig in *this* stage, and a Tory in *that*. If he says he is against the United Independence of the Continent, he is to all intents and purposes against her in all the rest; because THIS LAST comprehends the whole. And he may just as well say, that Britain was right in declaring us rebels; right in taxing us; and right in declaring her *"right to bind the Colonies in all cases whatsoever."* It signifies nothing what neutral ground, of his own creating, he may skulk upon for shelter, for the quarrel in no stage of it hath afforded any such ground; and either we or Britain are absolutely right or absolutely wrong through the whole.

Britain, like a gamester nearly ruined, hath now put all her losses into one bet, and is playing a desperate game for the total. If she win it, she wins from *me* my life; she wins the Continent as the forfeited property of rebels; the right of taxing those that are left as reduced subjects; and the power of binding them as slaves: And the single die which determines this unparalleled event is, Whether we support our Independence or she overturn it. This is coming to the point at once. Here is the touch-stone to try men by. *He that is not a supporter of the Independent States of America, in the same degree that his religious and political principles would suffer him to support the government of any other country, of which he called himself a subject, is, in the American sense of the word,* A TORY; *and the instant that he endeavours to bring his Toryism into practice, he becomes* A TRAITOR. The first can only be detected by a general test, and the law hath already provided for the latter.

It is unnatural and impolitic to admit men who would root up our Independence to have any share in our legislation, either as electors or representatives; because the support of our Independence rests in a great measure on the vigour and purity of our public bodies. Would Britain, even in time of peace, much less in war, suffer an elector to be carried by men who professed themselves not to be her subjects, or allow such to sit in parliament? Certainly not.

But there are a certain species of Tories with whom conscience or principle hath nothing to do, and who are so from avarice only. Some of the first fortunes in the Continent, on the part of the Whigs, are staked on the issue of our present measures. And shall disaffection only be rewarded with security? Can any thing be a greater inducement to a miserly man, than the hope of making his mammon safe? And though the scheme be fraught with every character of folly, yet, so long as he supposes, that by doing nothing materially criminal against America on one part, and by expressing his private disapprobation against Independence, as a palliative with the enemy on the other part, he stands thereby in a safe line between both, while, I say, this ground be suffered to remain, craft and the spirit of avarice will point it out, and men will not be wanting to fill up this most contemptible of all characters.

These men, ashamed to own the sordid cause from whence their disaffection springs, add thereby meanness to meanness, by endeavouring to shelter themselves under the mask of hypocrisy; that is, they had rather be thought to be Tories from *some kind of principle*, than Tories by having *no principle at all*. But till such time as they can show some real reason, natural, political or conscientious, on which their objections to Independence are founded, we are not obliged to give them credit for being Tories of the first stamp, but must set them down as Tories of the last.

In the Second Number of the Crisis I endeavoured to show the impossibility of the enemy making any conquest of America; that nothing was wanting on our part but patience and perseverance, and that, with these virtues, our success, as far as human speculation could discern, seemed as certain as fate. But as there are many among us, who, influenced by others, have regularly gone back from the principles they once held, in proportion as we have gone forward; and as it is the unfortunate lot of many a good man to live within the neighbourhood of disaffected ones; I shall therefore, for the sake of confirming the one and recovering the other, endeavour, in the space of a page or two, to go over some of the leading principles in support of Independence. It is a much pleasanter task to prevent vice than to punish it; and however our tempers may be gratified by resentment, or our national expences eased by forfeited estates, harmony and friendship is nevertheless the happiest condition a country can be blest with.

The principal arguments in support of Independence may be comprehended under the four following heads,

FIRST,—The natural right of the Continent to Independence.

SECONDLY,—Her interest in being independent.

THIRDLY,—The necessity.—And

FOURTHLY,—The moral advantages arising therefrom.

I. The NATURAL RIGHT of the Continent to Independence, is a point which never yet was called in question. It will not even admit of a debate. To deny such a right, would be a kind of atheism against nature: And the best answer to such an objection would be, *"The fool hath said in his heart, There is no God."*

II. The INTEREST of the Continent in being independent is a point as clearly right as the former. America, by her own internal industry, and unknown to all the powers of Europe, was at the beginning of the dispute, arrived at a pitch of greatness, trade and population, beyond which it was the interest of Britain not to suffer her to pass, lest she should grow too powerful to be kept subordinate. She began to view this country with the same uneasy malicious eye, with which a covetous guardian would view his ward whose estate he had been enriching himself by for twenty years, and saw him just arriving at manhood. And America owes no more to Britain for her present maturity, than the ward would to his guardian for being twenty-one years of age. That America hath flourished *at the time* she was under the government of Britain, is true; but there is every natural reason to believe, that had she been an independent country from the first settlement thereof, uncontrouled by any foreign power, free to make her own laws, regulate and encourage her own commerce, she had by this time been of much greater worth than now. The case is simply this, The first settlers in the different Colonies were left to shift for themselves, unnoticed and unsupported by any European government; but as the tyranny and persecution of the old world daily drove numbers to the new, and, as by the favour of Heaven on their industry and perseverance, they grew into importance, so, in a like degree, they became an object of profit to the greedy eyes of Europe. It was impossible in this state of infancy, however thriving and promising, that they could resist the power of any armed invader that should seek to bring them under his authority. In this situation Britain thought it worth her while to claim them, and the Continent received and acknowledged the claimer. It was, in reality, of no very great importance who was her master, seeing, that from the force and ambition of the different powers of Europe she must, till she acquired strength enough to assert her own right, acknowledge some one. As well, perhaps, Britain as another; and it might have been as well to have been under the States of Holland as any. The same hopes of engrossing and profiting by her trade, by not oppressing it too much, would have operated alike with any master, and produced to the Colonies the same effects. The clamor of protection, likewise, was all a farce; because, in order to make *that* protection necessary, she must first, by her own quarrels create us enemies. Hard terms, indeed!

To know whether it be the interest of the Continent to be independent, we need only ask this easy, simple question: Is it the interest of a man to be a boy all his life? The answer to one will be the answer to both. America hath been one continued scene of legislative contention from the first king's representative to the last; and this was unavoidably founded in the natural opposition of interest between the old country and the new. A governor sent from England, or receiving his authority therefrom, ought never to have been considered in any other light than that of a genteel commissioned spy, whose private business was information, and his public business a kind of civilized oppression. In the first of these characters he was to watch the tempers, sentiments and disposition of the people, the growth of trade, and the encrease of private fortunes; and in the latter, to suppress all such acts of the Assemblies, however beneficial to the people, which did not directly or indirectly throw some encrease of power or profit into the hands of those who sent him.

America, till now, could never be called a *free country*, because her legislation depended on the will of a man three thousand miles distant, whose interest was in opposition to ours, and who, by a single "NO," could forbid what law he pleased.

The freedom of trade, likewise, is, to a trading country, an article of such vast importance, that the principal source of wealth depends upon it; and it is impossible that any country can flourish, as it otherwise might do, whose commerce is engrossed, cramped and fettered by the laws and mandates of another—yet these evils, and more than I can here enumerate, the Continent has suffered by being under the government of Great-Britain. By an Independence we clear the whole at once—put an end to the business of unanswered petitions and fruitless remonstrances—exchange Britain for Europe—shake hands with the world—live at peace with mankind—and trade to any market where we best can buy and sell.

III. The NECESSITY, likewise, of being independent, even before it was declared, became so evident and important, that the Continent ran the risk of being ruined every day she delayed it. There were reasons to believe that Britain would endeavour to make a European matter of it, and rather than lose the whole, would dismember it like Poland, and dispose of her several claims to the highest bidder. Genoa, failing in her attempts to reduce Corsica, made a sale of it to the French, and such traffics have been common in the old world. We had at that time no Ambassador in any part of Europe, to counteract her negociations, and by that means she had the range of every foreign Court uncontradicted on our part. We even knew nothing of the treaty for the Hessians till it was concluded, and the troops ready to embark. Had we been independent before, we had probably prevented her obtaining them. We had no credit abroad, because of our rebellious dependency. Our ships could claim no protection in foreign ports, because we afforded them no justifiable reason for granting it to us. The calling ourselves subjects, and at the same time fighting against the power we acknowledged, was a dangerous precedent to all Europe. If the grievances justified our taking up arms, they justified our separation; if they did not justify our separation, neither could they justify our taking up arms. All Europe was interested in reducing us as rebels, and all Europe (or the greatest part at least) is interested in supporting us as Independent States. At home our condition was still worse: Our currency had no foundation, and the fall of it would have ruined Whig and Tory alike. We had no other law than a kind of moderated passion; no other civil power than an honest mob; and no other protection than the temporary attachment of one man to another. Had Independence been delayed a few months longer, this Continent would have been plunged into irrecoverable confusion: Some violent for it, some against it, till in the general cabal the rich would have been ruined, and the poor destroyed. It is to Independence that every Tory owes the present safety he lives in; for by *that*, and *that only*, we emerged from a state of dangerous suspense, and became a regular people.

The necessity likewise of being independent, had there been no rupture between Britain and America, would in a little time have brought one on. The encreasing importance of commerce, the weight and perplexity of legislation, and the entangled state of European politics, would daily have shewn to the Continent the impossibility of continuing subordinate; for, after the coolest reflections on the matter, *this must* be allowed, that Britain was too jealous of America, to govern it justly; too ignorant of it, to govern it well; and too distant from it, to govern it at all.

IV. But, what weigh most with all men of serious reflection are the MORAL ADVANTAGES arising from Independence: War and desolation are become the trades of the old world; and America neither could, nor can be under the government of Britain without becoming a sharer of her guilt, and a partner in all the dismal commerce of death. The spirit of duelling, extended on a national scale, is a proper character for European wars. They have seldom any other motive than pride, or any other object than fame. The conquerors and the conquered are generally ruined alike, and the chief difference at last is, that the one marches home with his honours, and the other without them. 'Tis the natural temper of the English to fight for a feather, if they suppose *that feather* to be an affront; and America, without the right of asking why, must have abetted in every quarrel and abided by its fate. It is a shocking situation to live in, that one country must be brought into all the wars of another, whether the measure be right or wrong, or whether she will or not; yet this, in the fullest extent, was, and ever would be, the unavoidable consequence of the connection. Surely! the Quakers forgot their own principles, when in their late testimony they called *this connection* with these military and miserable appendages hanging to it, *"The happy constitution."*

Britain, for centuries past, have been nearly fifty years out of every hundred at war with some power or other. It certainly ought to be a conscientious as well as political consideration with America, not to dip her hands in the bloody work of Europe. Our situation affords us a retreat from their cabals, and the present happy union of the States bids fair for extirpating the future use of arms from one quarter of the world; yet such have been the irreligious politics of the present leaders of the Quakers, that, for the sake of they scarce know what, they would cut off every hope of such a blessing by tying this Continent to Britain, like Hector to the chariot-wheel of Achilles, to be dragged through all the miseries of endless European wars.

The connection, viewed from this ground, is distressing to every man who has the feelings of humanity. By having Britain for our master, we became enemies to the greatest part of Europe, and they to us; and the consequence was war inevitable. By being our own masters, independent of any foreign one, we have Europe for our friends, and the prospect of an endless peace among ourselves. Those who were advocates for the British government over these Colonies, were obliged to limit both their arguments and their ideas to the period of a European peace only: The moment Britain became plunged in war, every supposed convenience to us vanished away, and all we could hope for was *not to be ruined.* Could this be a desirable condition for a young country to be in?

Had the French pursued their fortune immediately after the defeat of Braddock last war, this city and province had then experienced the woful calamities of being a British subject. A scene of the same kind might happen again; for America, considered as a subject to the crown of Britain, would ever have been the seat of war and the bone of contention between the two powers.

On the whole, If the future expulsion of arms from one quarter of the world be a desirable object to a peaceable man;—if the freedom of trade to every part of it can engage the attention of a man of business,—if the support or fall of millions of currency can affect our interest;—if the entire possession of estates, by cutting off the lordly claims of Britain over the soil, deserves the regard of landed property;—and if the right of making our own laws, uncontrouled by royal or ministerial spies or mandates, be worthy our care as freemen;—then are all men interested in the support of Independence, and may he that supports it not, be driven from the blessing, and live unpitied beneath the servile sufferings of scandalous subjection!

We have been amused with the tales of ancient wonders; we have read, and wept over, the histories of other nations; applauded, censured, or pitied, as their cases affected us.—The fortitude and patience of the sufferers—the justness of their cause—the weight of their oppressions and oppressors—the object to be saved or lost—with all the consequences of a defeat or a conquest—have, in the hour of sympathy, bewitched our hearts and chained it to their fate: But where is the power that ever made war upon petitioners? Or where is the war on which a world was staked till now?

We may not, perhaps, be wise enough to make all the advantages we ought of our Independence; but they are, nevertheless, marked and presented to us with every character of GREAT and GOOD, and worthy the hand of Him who sent them. I look through the present trouble to a time of tranquillity, when we shall have it in our power to set an example of peace to all the world. Were the Quakers really impressed and influenced by the quiet principles they profess to hold, they would, however they might disapprove the means, be the first of all men to approve of INDEPENDENCE, because, by separating from the cities of Sodom and Gomorrah, it affords an opportunity, never given to man before, of carrying their favourite principle of peace into general practice, by establishing governments that shall hereafter exist without wars. Oh ye fallen, cringing priest- and Pemberton-ridden people! what more can we say of ye than that a religious Quaker is a valuable character, and a political Quaker a real Jesuit.

Having thus gone over some of the principal points in support of Independence, I must now request the reader to return back with me to the period when it first began to be a public doctrine, and examine the progress it has made among the various classes of men. The era I mean to begin at, is the breaking out of hostilities, April 19th, 1775. Until this event happened, the Continent seemed to view the dispute as a kind of lawsuit for a matter of right, litigating between the old country and the new; and she felt the same kind and degree of horror, as if she had seen an oppressive plaintiff, at the head of a band of ruffians, enter the court, while the cause was before it, and put the judge, the jury, the defendant and his council to the sword. Perhaps a more heart-felt convulsion never reached a country with the same degree of power and rapidity before, and never may again. Pity for the sufferers, mixt with indignation at the violence and heightened with apprehensions of undergoing the same fate, made the affair of Lexington the affair of the Continent. Every part of it felt the shock, and all vibrated together. A general promotion of sentiment took place: Those who had drank deeply into Whiggish principles, that is, the right and necessity not only of opposing, but wholly setting aside the power of the Crown as soon as it became practically dangerous (for in theory it was always so) stept into the first stage of Independence; while another class of Whigs, equally sound in principle, but not so sanguine in enterprize, attached themselves the stronger to the cause and fell close in with the rear of the former; their partition was a mere point. Numbers of the moderate men, whose chief fault, *at that time*, arose from their entertaining a better opinion of Britain than she deserved, convinced now of their mistake, gave her up and publicly declared themselves good Whigs. While the Tories, seeing it was no longer a laughing matter, either slunk into silent obscurity, or contented themselves with coming forth and abusing General Gage: Not a single advocate appeared to justify the action of that day; it seemed to appear to every one with the same magnitude, struck every one with the same force, and created in every one the same abhorrence. From this period we may date the growth of Independence.

If the many circumstances, which happened at this memorable time, be taken in one view, and compared with each other, they will justify a conclusion which seems not to be attended to, I mean a fixt design in the king and ministry of driving America into arms, in order that they might be furnished with a pretence for seizing the whole Continent as the immediate property of the Crown. A noble plunder for hungry courtiers!

It ought to be remembered, that the first petition from the Congress was at this time unanswered on the part of the British king. That the motion, called Lord North's motion, of the 20th of February, 1775, arrived in America the latter end of March. This motion was to be laid by the several governors, then in being, before the Assembly of each province; and the first Assembly before which it was laid, was the Assembly of Pennsylvania in *May* following. This being a just state of the case, I then ask, why were hostilities commenced between the time of passing the resolve in the House of Commons, of the 20th of February, and the time of the Assemblies meeting to deliberate upon it? Degrading and infamous as that motion was, there is, nevertheless, reason to believe, that the king and his adherents were afraid the Colonies would agree to it, and lest they should, took effectual care they should not, by provoking them with hostilities in the interim. They had not the least doubt at that time of conquering America at one blow; and what they expected to get by a conquest being infinitely greater than any thing they could hope to get either by taxation or accommodation, they seemed determined to prevent even the possibility of hearing each other, lest America should disappoint their greedy hopes of the whole, by listening even to their own terms. On the one hand they refused to hear the petition of the Continent, and on the other hand took effectual care the Continent should not hear them.

That the motion of the 20th of February and the orders for commencing hostilities were both concerted by the same PERSON or persons, and not the latter by General Gage, as was falsely imagined at first, is evident from an extract of a letter of his to administration, read among other papers in the House of Commons; in which he informs his masters, *That though their idea of his disarming certain counties was a right one, yet it required him to be master of the country, in order to enable him to execute it.* This was prior to the commencement of hostilities, and consequently before the motion of the 20th of February could be deliberated on by the several Assemblies.

Perhaps it may be asked, why was the motion past, if there was at the same time a plan to aggravate the Americans not to listen to it? Lord North assigned one reason himself, which was, *a hope of dividing them.* This was publicly tempting them to reject it; that if, in case, the injury of arms should fail of provoking them sufficiently, the insult of such a declaration might fill it up. But by passing the motion and getting it afterwards rejected in America, it enabled them, in their wretched idea of politics, among other things, to hold up the Colonies to foreign powers with every possible mark of disobedience and rebellion. They had applied to those powers not to supply the Continent with arms, ammunition, &c. and it was necessary they should incense them against us, by assigning on their own part some seeming reputable reason why. By dividing, it had a tendency to weaken the States, and likewise to perplex the adherents of America in England. But the principal scheme, and that which has marked their character in every part of their conduct, was a design of precipitating the Colonies into a state which they might afterwards deem rebellion, and under that pretence put an end to all future complaints, petitions or remonstrances, by seizing the whole at once. They had ravaged one part of the globe, till it could glut them no longer; their prodigality required new plunder, and through the East-India article TEA they hoped to transfer their rapine from that quarter of the world to this. — Every designed quarrel has its pretence; and the same barbarian avarice accompanied the *Plant* to America, which ruined the country that produced it.

That men never turn rogues without turning fools, is a maxim, sooner or later, universally true. The commencement of hostilities, being in the beginning of April, was, of all times, the worst chosen: The Congress were to meet the tenth of May following, and the distress the Continent felt at this unparalleled outrage gave a stability to *That Body*, which no other circumstance could have done. It suppressed too all inferior debates, and bound them together by a necessitous affection, without giving them time to differ upon trifles. The suffering likewise, softened the whole body of the people into a degree of pliability, which laid the principal foundation stone of union, order and government; and which, at any other time, might only have fretted and then faded away unnoticed and unimproved: But Providence, who best knows how to time her misfortunes as well as her immediate favours, chose this to be the time: And who dares dispute it?

It did not seem the disposition of the people at this crisis to heap petition upon petition, while the former remained unanswered: The measure, however, was carried in Congress, and a second petition was sent; of which I shall only remark, that it was submissive even to a dangerous fault, because the prayer of it appealed solely to, what is called, the prerogative of the Crown, while the matter in dispute was confessed to be constitutional. But even this Petition, flattering as it was, was still not so harmonious as the chink of cash, and consequently not sufficiently grateful to the tyrant and his ministry. From every circumstance it is evident, that it was the determination of the British court to have nothing to do with America but to conquer it fully and absolutely. They were certain of success, and the field of battle was to be the only place of treaty. I am confident there are thousands and tens of thousands in America who wonder *now* they should ever think otherwise; but the sin of that day was the sin of Civility, yet it operated against our present good in the same manner that a civil opinion of the devil would against our future peace.

Independence was a doctrine scarce and rare even towards the conclusion of the year Seventy-five: All our politics had been founded on the hope or expectation of making the matter up—a hope, which, though general on the side of America, had never entered the head or heart of the British court. Their hope was conquest and confiscation. Good Heavens! what volumes of thanks does America owe to Britain! What infinite obligations to the fool, that fills, with paradoxical vacancy, the throne! Nothing but the sharpest essence of villany, compounded with the strongest distillation of folly, could have produced a menstruum that would have effected a separation. The Congress in Seventy-four administered an abortive medicine to Independence, by prohibiting the importation of goods, and the succeeding Congress rendered the dose still more dangerous by continuing it. Had Independence been a settled system with America (as Britain has advanced) she ought to have *doubled* her importation, and prohibited in some degree her exportation. And this single circumstance is sufficient to acquit America before any jury of nations of having a Continental plan of Independence in view: A charge, which had it been true, would have been honourable, but is so grossly false, that either the amazing ignorance, or the wilful dishonesty, of the British court is effectually proved by it.

The second petition like the first produced no answer; it was scarcely acknowledged to be received; the British court were too determined in their villany even to act it artfully, and in their rage for conquest neglected the necessary subtleties for obtaining it. They might have divided, distracted and played a thousand tricks with us had they been as cunning as they were cruel.

This last indignity gave a new spring to Independence. Those who knew the savage obstinacy of the king and the jobbing gambling spirit of the court predicted the fate of the petition as soon as it was sent from America; for the men being known, their measures were easily foreseen. As politicians we ought not so much to ground our hope on the reasonableness of the thing we ask, as on the reasonableness of the person of whom we ask it: Who would expect discretion from a fool, candour from a tyrant, or justice from a villain?

As every prospect of an accommodation seemed now to fail fast, men began to think seriously on the matter; and their reason being thus stript of the false hope which had long encompassed it, became approachable by fair debate; yet still the bulk of the people hesitated; they startled at the novelty of Independence, without once considering that our getting into arms at first was a more extraordinary novelty, and that all other nations had gone through the work of Independence before us. They doubted, likewise, the ability of the Continent to support it, without reflecting, that it required the same force to obtain an accommodation by arms as an Independence. If the one was acquireable, the other was the same; because, to accomplish either, it was necessary that our strength should be too great for Britain to subdue; and it was too unreasonable to suppose, that with the power of being masters, we should submit to be servants.* Their caution, at this time, was exceedingly misplaced; for if they were able to defend their property and maintain their rights by arms, they consequently were able to defend and support their Independence; and in proportion as these men saw the necessity and rightness of the measure, they honestly and openly declared and adopted it, and the part they have acted since, have done them honour, and fully established their characters. Error in opinion has this peculiar advantage with it, that the foremost point of the contrary ground may at any time be reached by the sudden exertion of a thought; and it frequently happens in sentimental differences that some striking circumstance, or some forcible reason, quickly conceived, will effect in an instant what neither argument nor example could produce in an age.

I find it impossible in the small compass I am limited to, to trace out the progress which Independence has made on the minds of the different classes of men, and the several reasons by which they were moved. With some, it was a passionate abhorrence against the king of England and his ministry as a set of savages and brutes; and these men, governed by the agony of a wounded mind, were for trusting every thing to

*In this state of political suspense the pamphlet *Common Sense* made its appearance, and the success it met with does not become me to mention. Dr. Franklin, Mr. Samuel and John Adams were severally spoken of as the supposed Author. I had not, at that time, the pleasure either of personally knowing or being known to the two last Gentlemen. The favour of Dr. Franklin's friendship I possessed in England, and my introduction to this part of the world was through his patronage. I happened, when a school boy, to pick up a pleasing natural history of Virginia, and my inclination from that day of seeing the western side of the atlantic never left me. In October, Seventy-five, Dr. Franklin proposed giving me such materials as were in his hands, towards compleating a history of the present transaction, and seemed desirous of having the first volume out by the next spring. I had then formed the outlines of Common Sense, and finished nearly the first part; and as I supposed the Doctor's design in getting out a history, was to open the new year with a new system, I expected to surprize him with a production on that subject much earlier than he thought of; and without informing him of what I was doing, got it ready for the press as fast as I conveniently could, and sent him the first pamphlet that was printed off.

hope and Heaven and bidding defiance at once. With others, it was a growing conviction that the scheme of the British court was to create, ferment and drive on a quarrel for the sake of confiscated plunder: Men of this cast ripened into Independence in proportion as the evidence encreased. While a third class, conceiving it was the true interest of America, internally and externally, to be her own master, gave their support to Independence, step by step, as they saw her abilities to maintain it enlarge. With many it was a compound of all these reasons; while those, who were too callous to be reached by neither, remained, and still remain Tories.

The *legal necessity* of being independent, with several collateral reasons, is pointed out in an elegant, masterly manner, in a charge to the grand jury for the district of Charlestown, by the Hon. WILLIAM HENRY DRAYTON, Esq; Chief Justice of South-Carolina. This performance, and the ADDRESS of the CONVENTION of New-York, are pieces, in my humble opinion, of the first rank in America.

The principal causes why Independence has not been so universally supported as it ought, are, *fear* and *indolence*, and the causes why it has been opposed, are, *avarice, downright villany,* and *lust of personal power.* There is not such a Being in America as a Tory from conscience: Some secret defect or other is interwoven in the character of all those, be they men or women, who can look with patience on the brutality, luxury and debauchery of the British court, and the violations of their army here. A woman's virtue must sit very lightly on her who can even hint a favourable sentiment in their behalf. It is remarkable that the whole race of prostitutes in New-York were Tories; and the schemes for supporting the Tory cause, in this city, for which several are now in jail, and one hanged, were concerted and carried on in common baudy-houses, assisted by those who kept them.

The connection between vice and meanness is a fit object for satire, but when the satire is a fact, it cuts with the irresistible power of a diamond. If a Quaker, in defence of his just rights, his property and the chastity of his house, takes up a musket, he is expelled the meeting; but the present king of England, who reduced and took into keeping a sister of their society, is reverenced and supported with repeated testimonies, while the friendly noodle from whom she was taken, (and who is now in this city) continues a drudge in the service of his rival, as if proud of being cuckolded by a creature called a king.

Our support and success depend on such a variety of men and circumstances, that every one, who does but wish well, is of some use: There are men who have a strange awkwardness to arms, yet have hearts to risk every shilling in the cause, or in support of those who have better talents for defending it. Nature, in the arrangement of mankind, has fitted some for every service in life: Were all soldiers, all would starve and go naked, and were none soldiers, all would be slaves. As *disaffection* to Independence is the badge of a Tory, so *affection* to it is the mark of a Whig; and the different services of the Whigs down from those who nobly contribute every thing, to those who have nothing to render but their wishes, tend all to the same centre, though with different degrees of merit and ability. The larger we make the circle, the more we shall harmonize, and the stronger we shall be. All we want to shut out, is disaffection, and *that excluded*, we must accept from each other such duties as we are best fitted to bestow. A narrow system of politics, like a narrow system of religion, is calculated only to sour the temper, and live at variance with mankind.

All we want to know in America is simply this, Who is for Independence, and who is not? Those who are for it, will support it, and the remainder will undoubtedly see the reasonableness of their paying the charges; while those who oppose, or seek to betray it, must expect the more rigid fate of the jail and the gibbet. There is a kind of bastard generosity, which, by being extended to all men, is as fatal to society, on one hand, as the want of true generosity is on the other. A lax manner of administring justice, falsely termed moderation, has a tendency both to dispirit public virtue and promote the growth of public evils. Had the late Committee of Safety taken cognizance of the last testimony of the Quakers, and proceeded against such delinquents as were concerned therein, they had, probably, prevented the treasonable plans which have been concerted since. When one villain is suffered to escape, it encourages another to proceed, either from a hope of escaping likewise, or an apprehension that we dare not punish. It has been a matter of general surprise, that no notice was taken of the incendiary publication of the Quakers, of the 20th of November last: A publication evidently intended to promote sedition and treason, and encourage the enemy, who were then within a day's march of this city, to proceed on and possess it. I here present the reader with a memorial, which was laid before the Board of Safety a few days after the testimony appeared. Not a member of that Board, that I conversed with but expressed the highest detestation of the perverted principles and conduct of the Quaker junto, and that the Board would take the matter up; notwithstanding which, it was suffered to pass away unnoticed, to the encouragement of new acts of treason, the general danger of the cause, and the disgrace of the State.

To the HONOURABLE the COUNCIL OF SAFETY of the State of Pennsylvania.

At a meeting of a reputable number of the inhabitants of the city of Philadelphia, impressed with a proper sense of the justice of the cause which this Continent is engaged in, and animated with a generous fervor for supporting the same, it was resolved, that the following be laid before the Board of Safety:

"WE profess liberality of sentiment to all men; with this distinction *only*, that those who do *not* deserve it, would become wise and *seek* to deserve it. We hold the pure doctrine of universal liberty of conscience, and conceive it our duty to endeavour to secure that sacred right to others, as well as to defend it for ourselves; for we undertake not to judge of the religious rectitude of tenets, but leave the whole matter to Him who made us.

"We persecute no man, neither will we abet in the persecution of any man for religion sake; our common relation to others being that of fellow-citizens and fellow-subjects of one civil community; and in this line of connection we hold out the right hand of fellowship to all men. But we should conceive ourselves to be unworthy members of the FREE AND INDEPENDENT STATES OF AMERICA, were we unconcernedly to see or suffer any treasonable wound, public or private, directly or indirectly, to be given against the peace and safety of the same. We enquire not into the rank of the offenders, nor their religious persuasion; we have no business with either, our part being only to find them out, and exhibit them to justice.

"A printed paper, dated the 20th of November, and signed *'John Pemberton,'* whom we suppose to be an inhabitant of this city, has lately been dispersed abroad, a copy of which accompanies this. Had the framers and publishers of that paper conceived it their duty to exhort the youth, and others, of their society, to a patient submission under the present trying visitations, and humbly to wait the event of Heaven towards them, they had therein shewn a Christian temper, and we had been silent; but the anger and political virulence with which their instructions are given, and the abuse with which they stigmatize all ranks of men, not thinking like themselves, leave no doubt on our minds from what spirit their publication proceeded: And it is disgraceful to the pure cause of truth, that men can dally with words of the most sacred import, and play them as mechanically off as if religion consisted only in contrivance. We know of no instance, in which the Quakers have been compelled to bear arms, or do any thing which might strain their conscience; wherefore their advice *'to withstand and refuse to submit to the arbitrary instructions and ordinances of men,'* appear to us a false alarm, and could only be treasonably calculated to gain favour with our enemies, when they were seemingly on the brink of invading this State, or, what is still worse, to weaken the hands of our defence, that their entrance into this city might be made practicable and easy.

"We disclaim all tumult and disorder in the punishment of offenders; and wish to be governed, not by temper but by reason, in the manner of treating them. We are sensible that our cause has suffered by the two following errors; first, by an ill-judged lenity to traiterous persons in some cases; and secondly, by only a passionate treatment of them in others. For the future we disown both, and wish to be steady in our proceedings, and serious in our punishments.

"Every State in America has by the repeated voice of its

inhabitants, directed and authorised the Continental Congress to publish a formal Declaration of Independence of, and
Separation from, the oppressive king and parliament of Great-
Britain; and we look on every man an enemy who does not in
some line or other give his assistance towards supporting the
same; at the same time we consider the offence to be heightened to a degree of unpardonable guilt, when such persons,
under the shew of religion, endeavour, either by writing,
speaking, or otherwise, to subvert, overturn, or bring reproach upon the Independence of this Continent as declared
by Congress.

"The publishers of the paper, signed *'John Pemberton,'* have
called in a loud and passionate manner on their friends and
connections, to *'withstand and refuse'* obedience to whatever
'instructions or ordinances' may be published, not warranted
by (what they call) 'THAT HAPPY CONSTITUTION UNDER
WHICH THEY AND OTHERS LONG ENJOYED TRANQUILLITY
AND PEACE.' If this be not treason, we know not what may
properly be called by that name.

"To us it is a matter of surprise and astonishment, that men
with the word *'peace, peace'* continually on their lips, should
be so fond of living under, and supporting a government and
at the same time calling it *'happy,'* which is never better
pleased than when at war—that hath filled India with carnage
and famine—Africa with slavery—and tampered with Indians
and Negroes to cut the throats of the freemen of America. We
conceive it a disgrace to this State to harbour or wink at such
palpable hypocrisy. But as we seek not to hurt the hair of any
man's head, when we can make ourselves safe without, we
with such persons to restore peace to themselves and us, by
removing themselves to some part of the king of Britain's dominions, as by that means they may live unmolested by us or
we by them; for our fixt opinion is, that those who do not
deserve a place among us, ought not to have one.

"We conclude, with requesting the Council of Safety to take
into their consideration the paper signed *'John Pemberton;'*
and if it shall appear to them to be of a dangerous tendency,
or of a treasonable nature, that they would commit the signer,
together with such other persons as they can discover were
concerned therein, into custody, until such time as some

mode of trial shall ascertain the full degree of their guilt and punishment; in the doing of which, we wish their judges, whoever they may be, to disregard the man, his connections, interest, riches, poverty or principles of religion, and to attend to the nature of his offence only."

The most cavilling sectarian cannot accuse the foregoing with containing the least ingredient of persecution. The free spirit on which the American cause is founded, disdains to mix with such an impurity, and leave it a rubbish fit only for narrow and suspicious minds to grovel in: Suspicion and persecution are weeds of the same dunghill, and flourish best together. Had the Quakers minded their religion and their business, they might have lived through this dispute in enviable ease, and none would have molested them. The common phrase with these people is, *"Our principles are peace."* To which may be replied, *and your practices are the reverse*; for never did the conduct of men oppose their own doctrine more notoriously than the present race of the Quakers. They have artfully changed themselves into a different sort of people to what they used to be, and yet have the address to persuade each other they are not altered; like antiquated virgins they see not the havoc deformity hath made upon them, but pleasantly mistaking wrinkles for dimples, conceit themselves yet lovely, and wonder at the stupid world for not admiring them.

Did no injury arise to the public by this apostacy of the Quakers from themselves, the public would have nothing to do with it; but as both the design and consequences are pointed against a cause in which the whole community are interested, it is therefore no longer a subject confined to the cognizance of the meeting only, but comes as a matter of criminality before either the authority of the particular State *in which* it is acted, or of the Continent *against which* it operates. Every attempt now to support the authority of the king or parliament of Great-Britain over America, is treason against *every* State; therefore it is impossible that any *one* can pardon or screen from punishment an offender against *all*.

But to proceed: While the infatuated Tories of this and other States were last spring talking of Commissioners, accommodation, making the matter up and the Lord knows what stuff and nonsense, their *good* king and ministry were glutting themselves with the revenge of reducing America to an *unconditional submission*, and solacing each other with the certainty of conquering it in *one campaign*. The following quotations are from the Parliamentary Register of the debates of the House of Lords, March 5th, 1776.

"The Americans," says Lord *Talbot**, "have been obstinate, undutiful and ungovernable from the very beginning, from their first early and infant settlements; and I am every day more and more convinced that this people will never be brought back to their duty, and the subordinate relation they stand in to this country, till *reduced to an unconditional effectual submission; no concession on our part, no lenity, no endurance,* will have any other effect but that of encreasing their insolence."

"'The struggle," says Lord *Townsend*†, "is now a struggle for power; the die is cast, and the ONLY POINT which now remains to be determined, is, in what manner the war can be most effectually prosecuted and speedily finished, in order to procure that *unconditional submission*, which has been so ably stated by the noble Earl with the white staff" (meaning Lord Talbot); "and I have no reason to doubt that the measures now pursuing will put an end to the war in the course of a SINGLE CAMPAIGN. Should it linger longer, we shall then have reason to expect that some foreign power will interfere, and take advantage of our domestic troubles and civil distractions."

Lord *Littleton*, "My sentiments are pretty well known. I shall only observe now, that lenient measures have had no other effect than to produce insult after insult; that the more we conceded, the higher America rose in her demands, and the more insolent she has grown. It is for this reason that I am now for the most effective and decisive measures; and am of opinion, that no alternative is left us, but to relinquish America for ever, or finally determine to compel her to acknowledge the legislative authority of this country; and it is

---

*Steward of the king's houshold.

†Formerly General Townsend at Quebec, and late Lord Lieutenant of Ireland.

the principle of an *unconditional submission* I would be for maintaining."

Can words be more expressive than these? Surely the Tories will believe the Tory Lords! The truth is, they *do believe them*, and know as fully as any Whig on the Continent knows, that the king and ministry never had the least design of an accommodation with America, but an absolute unconditional conquest. And the part which the Tories were to act, was, by downright lying, to endeavour to put the Continent off its guard, and to divide and sow discontent in the minds of such Whigs as they might gain an influence over. In short, to keep up a distraction here, that the force sent from England might be able to conquer in *"one campaign."* They and the ministry were, by a different game, playing into each other's hands. The cry of the Tories in England was, *"No reconciliation, no accommodation,"* in order to obtain the greater military force; while those in America were crying nothing but *"reconciliation and accommodation,"* that the force sent might conquer with the less resistance.

But *this "single campaign"* is over, and America not conquered. The whole work is yet to do, and the force much less to do it with. Their condition is both despicable and deplorable: Out of cash — out of heart — and out of hope. A country furnished with arms and ammunition, as America now is, with three millions of inhabitants, and three thousand miles distant from the nearest enemy that can approach her, is able to look and laugh them in the face.

Howe appears to have two objects in view, either to go up the North river, or come to Philadelphia.

By going up the North river, he secures a retreat for his army thro' Canada, but the ships must return, if they return at all, the same way they went; and as our army would be in the rear, the safety of their passage down is a doubtful matter. By such a motion he shuts himself from all supplies from Europe but thro' Canada, and exposes his army and navy to the danger of perishing. The idea of his cutting off the communication between the eastern and southern States, by means of the North river, is merely visionary. He cannot do it by his shipping; because no ship can lay long at anchor in any river within reach of the shore; a single gun would drive a first rate from such a station: This was fully proved last October at fort Washington and Lee, where one gun only, on each side the river, obliged two frigates to cut and be towed off in an hour's time. Neither can he cut it off by his army; because the several posts they must occupy, would divide them almost to nothing, and expose them to be picked up by ours like pebbles on a river's bank; but admitting he could, where is the injury? Because while his whole force is cantoned out, as centries over the water, they will be very innocently employed, and the moment they march into the country, the communication opens.

The most probable object is Philadelphia, and the reasons are many. Howe's business in America is to conquer it, and in proportion as he finds himself unable to the task, he will employ his strength to distress women and weak minds, in order to accomplish through *their* fears what he cannot effect by his *own* force. His coming or attempting to come to Philadelphia is a circumstance that proves his weakness: For no general, that felt himself able to take the field and attack his antagonist, would think of bringing his army into a city in the summer time; and this mere shifting the scene from place to place, without effecting any thing, has feebleness and cowardice on the face of it, and holds him up in a contemptible light to any one who can reason justly and firmly. By several informations from New-York, it appears that their army in general, both officers and men, have given up the expectation of conquering America; their eye, now, is fixt upon the spoil. They suppose Philadelphia to be rich with stores, and as they think to get more by robbing a town than by attacking an army, their movement towards this city is probable. We are not now contending against an army of soldiers, but against a band of thieves, who had rather plunder than fight, and have no other hope of conquest than by cruelty.

They expect to get a mighty booty and strike another general panic by making a sudden movement and getting possession of this city, but unless they can march *out* as well as *in*, or get the entire command of the river, to remove off their plunder, they may probably be stopt with the stolen goods upon them. They have never yet succeeded wherever they have been opposed but at fort Washington. At Charlestown their defeat was effectual. At Ticonderoga they ran away. In every skirmish at Kingsbridge and the White Plains they were obliged to retreat, and the instant our arms were turned upon them in the Jersies, they turned likewise, and those that turned not were taken.

The necessity of always fitting our internal police to the circumstances of the times we live in, is something so strikingly obvious that no sufficient objection can be made against it. The safety of all societies depend upon it; and where this point is not attended to, the consequence will either be a general languor or a tumult. The encouragement and protection of the good subjects of any State, and the suppression and punishment of bad ones, are the principal objects for which all authority is instituted, and the line in which it ought to operate. We have in this city a strange variety of men and characters, and the circumstances of the times require they should be publicly known; it is not the number of Tories that hurt us, so much, as the not finding out who they are; men must now take one side or the other, and abide by the consequences: The Quakers, trusting to their short sighted sagacity, have, most unluckily for them, made their declaration in their last testimony, and we ought *now* to take them at their word. They have voluntarily read themselves out of the Continental meeting, and cannot hope to be restored to it again, but by payment and penitence. Men whose political principles are founded on avarice, are beyond the reach of reason, and the only cure for Toryism of this cast, is to tax it. A substantial good drawn from a real evil, is of the same benefit to society, as if drawn from a virtue; and where men have not public spirit to render themselves serviceable, it ought to be the study of government to draw the best use possible from their vices. When the governing passion of any man or set of men is once known, the method of managing them is easy; for even misers, whom no public virtue can impress, would become generous, could a heavy tax be laid upon covetousness.

The Tories have endeavoured to insure their property with the enemy, by forfeiting their reputation with us; from which may be justly inferred, that their governing passion is avarice. Make them as much afraid of losing on one side as the other, and you stagger their Toryism; make them more so, and you reclaim them; for their principle is to worship any power they are most afraid of.

This method of considering men and things together, opens into a large field for speculation, and affords me opportunity of offering some observations on the state of our currency, so as to make the support of it go hand in hand, with the suppression of disaffection and the encouragement of public spirit.

The thing which first presents itself in inspecting the state of the currency, is, that we have too much of it, and that there is a necessity of reducing the quantity, in order to encrease the value. Men are daily growing poor by the very means they take to get rich, for in the same proportion that the prices of all goods on hand are raised, the value of all money laid by is reduced. A simple case will make this clear: Let a man have one hundred pounds cash, and as many goods on hand as will to-day sell for £ 20, but not content with the present market-price, he raises them to 40, and by so doing, obliges others in their own defence to raise cent per cent likewise; in this case, it is evident that his hundred pounds laid by is reduced fifty pounds in value; whereas, had the markets dropt cent per cent, his goods would have sold but for ten, but his hundred pounds would have risen in value to two hundred; because it would then purchase as many goods again, or support his family as long again as before. And strange as it may seem, he is one hundred and fifty pounds the poorer for raising his goods, to what he would have been had he lowered them; because the forty pounds his goods sold for, is by the general rise of the markets, cent per cent, rendered of no more value than the ten pounds would be had the market fallen in the same proportion; and consequently the whole difference of gain or loss is on the different values of the hundred pounds laid by, viz. from fifty to two hundred. This rage for raising goods is for several reasons much more the fault of the Tories than the Whigs; and yet the Tories (to their shame and confusion ought they to be told of it) are by far the most noisy and discontented. The greatest part of the Whigs, by being now either in the army or employed in some public service, are *buyers* only and not *sellers*, and as this evil has its origin in trade, it cannot be charged on those who are out of it.

But the grievance is now become too general to be remedied by partial methods, and the only effectual cure is to reduce the quantity of money; with half the quantity we should be richer than we are now, because the value of it would be doubled, and consequently our attachment to it increased; for it is not the number of dollars a man has, but how far they will go, that makes him either rich or poor.

These two points being admitted, viz. that the quantity of money is too great, and that the prices of goods can be only effectually reduced by reducing the quantity of the money, the next point to be considered is, The method how to reduce it?

The circumstances of the times, as before observed, require that the public characters of all men should *now* be fully understood, and the only general method of ascertaining it is by an oath or affirmation, renouncing all allegiance to the king of Great-Britain, and to support the Independency of the United States as declared by Congress. Let, at the same time, a tax of ten, fifteen or twenty per cent per annum, to be collected quarterly, be levied on all property. These alternatives, by being perfectly voluntary, will take in all sorts of people. Here is the test; here is the tax. He who takes the former, conscientiously proves his affection to the cause, and binds himself to pay his quota by the best *services* in his power, and is thereby justly exempt from the latter; and those who chuse the latter, pay their quota in money, to be excused from taking the former, or rather 'tis the price paid to us for their supposed, though mistaken, insurance with the enemy.

But this is only a part of the advantage which would arise by knowing the different characters of men. The Whigs stake every thing on the issue of their arms, while the Tories, by their disaffection, are sapping and undermining their strength, and, of consequence, the property of the Whigs is the more exposed thereby; and whatever injury their estates may sustain by the movements of the enemy, must either be borne by themselves, who have done every thing which have *yet* been done, or by the Tories, who have not only done nothing, but have by their disaffection, invited the enemy on.

In the present crisis we ought to know square by square, and house by house, who are in real allegiance with the United Independent States, and who are not. Let but the line be made clear and distinct, and all men will then know what they are to trust to. It would not only be good policy, but strict justice, to raise fifty or an hundred thousand pounds, or more, if it is necessary, out of the estates and property of the king of England's votaries, resident in Philadelphia, to be distributed, as a reward to those inhabitants of the city and State, who should turn out and repulse the enemy, should they attempt their march this way; and likewise, to bind the property of all such persons to make good the damages which that of the Whigs might sustain. In the undistinguishable mode of conducting a war, we frequently make reprisals at sea, on the vessels of persons in England who are friends to our cause compared with the residentiary Tories among us.

In every former publication of mine, from Common Sense down to the last Crisis, I have generally gone on the charitable supposition, that the Tories were rather a mistaken than a criminal people, and have applied argument after argument with all the candour and temper I was capable of, in order to set every part of the case clearly and fairly before them, and if possible to reclaim them from ruin to reason. I have done my duty by them and have now done with that doctrine, taking it for granted, that those who yet hold their disaffection, are, either a set of avaricious miscreants, who would sacrifice the Continent to save themselves, or a banditti of hungry traitors, who are hoping for a division of the spoil. To which may be added, a list of Crown or Proprietary dependents, who, rather than go without a portion of power, would be content to share it with the devil. Of such men there is no hope; and their obedience will only be according to the danger that is set before them, and the power that is exercised over them.

A time will shortly arrive, in which, by ascertaining the characters of persons now, we shall be guarded against their mischiefs then; for in proportion as the enemy despair of conquest, they will be trying the arts of seduction and the force of fear by all the mischiefs they can inflict. But in war we may be certain of these two things, viz. that cruelty in an enemy, and motions made with more than usual parade, are always signs of weakness. He that can conquer, finds his mind too free and pleasant to be brutish; and he that intends to conquer, never makes too much show of his strength.

We now know the enemy we have to do with. While drunk with the certainty of victory they disdained to be civil; and in proportion as disappointment makes them sober, and their apprehensions of an European war alarm them, they will become cringing and artful; honest they cannot be. But our answer to them, in either condition they may be in, is short and full, "As Free and Independent States we are willing to make peace with you to-morrow, but we can neither hear nor reply in any other character."

If Britain cannot conquer us, it proves, that she is neither able to govern or protect us, and our particular situation now is such, that any connection with her would be unwisely exchanging a half defeated enemy for two powerful ones. Europe, by every appearance and information, is now on the eve, nay, on the morning twilight of a war, and any alliance with *George the Third* brings *France* and *Spain* upon our backs; a separation from him attach them to our side; therefore, the only road to *Peace, Honour* and *Commerce* is INDEPENDENCE.

COMMON SENSE.

Philadelphia, April 19, 1777.

And in the Fourth year of the UNION, *which GOD preserve!*

The American Crisis

NUMBER IV

September 12, 1777

THOSE who expect to reap the blessings of Freedom, must, like men, undergo the fatigue of supporting it. The event of yesterday is one of those kind of alarms, which is just sufficient to rouse us to duty, without being of consequence enough to depress our fortitude. It is not a field of a few acres of ground, but a cause that we are defending, and whether we defeat the enemy in one battle, or by degrees, the consequence will be the same.

Look back at the events of last winter and the present year, there you will find that the enemy's successes have always contributed to reduce them. What they have gained in ground, they paid so dearly for in numbers, that their victories have in the end amounted to defeats. We have always been masters at the last push, and always shall while we do our duty. Howe has been once on the banks of the Delaware, and from thence driven back with loss and disgrace; and why not be again driven from the Schuylkill? His condition and ours are very different. He has every body to fight, we have only his *one* army to cope with and which wastes away at every engagement; we can not only reinforce, but can redouble our numbers; he is cut off from all supplies, and must sooner or later inevitably fall into our hands.

Shall a band of ten or twelve thousand robbers, who are this day fifteen hundred or two thousand men less in strength than they were yesterday, conquer America, or subdue even a single state? The thing cannot be, unless we sit down and suffer them to do it. Another such a brush, notwithstanding we lost the ground, would, by still reducing the enemy, put them in a condition to be afterwards totally defeated.

Could our whole army have come up to the attack at one time, the consequences had probably been otherwise; but our having different parts of the Brandywine creek to guard, and the uncertainty which road to Philadelphia the enemy would attempt to take, naturally afforded them an opportunity of passing with their main body at a place where only a part of ours could be posted; for, it must strike every thinking man with conviction, that it requires a much greater force to oppose an enemy in several places, than is sufficient to defeat them in any one place.

Men who are sincere in defending their freedom, will always feel concern at every circumstance, which seems to make against them; it is the natural and honest consequence of all affectionate attachments, and the want of it is a vice. But the dejection lasts only for a moment; they soon rise out of it with additional vigor; the glow of hope, courage and fortitude, will, in a little time, supply the place of every inferior passion, and kindle the whole heart into heroism.

There is a mystery in the countenance of some causes, which we have not always present judgment enough to explain. It is distressing to see an enemy advancing into a country, but it is the only place in which we can beat them, and in which we have always beaten them, whenever they made the attempt. The nearer any disease approaches to a crisis, the nearer it is to a cure: Danger and deliverance make their advances together, and it is only at the last push, that one or the other takes the lead.

There are many men who will do their duty when it is not wanted; but a genuine Public spirit always appears most when there is most occasion for it. Thank GOD! our army, though fatigued, is yet entire. The attack made by us yesterday was under many disadvantages, naturally arising from the uncertainty of knowing which route the enemy would take; and from that circumstance, the whole of our force could not be brought up together time enough to engage all at once. Our strength is yet reserved; and it is evident that Howe does not think himself a gainer by the affair, otherwise, he would this morning have moved down and attacked General Washington.

Gentlemen of the city and country, It is in your power, by a spirited improvement of the present circumstance, to turn it to a real advantage: Howe is now weaker than before, and every shot will contribute to reduce him. You are more immediately interested than any other part of the Continent; your

All is at stake; it is not so with the general cause; you are devoted by the enemy to plunder and destruction: It is the encouragement which Howe, the chief of plunderers, has promised his army. Thus circumstanced, you may save yourselves by a manly resistance, but you can have no hope in any other conduct. I never yet knew our brave General, or any part of the army, officers or men, out of heart, and I have seen them in circumstances a thousand times more trying than the present. It is only those that are not in action, that feel languor and heaviness, and the best way to rub it off is to turn out, and make sure work of it.

Our army must undoubtedly feel fatigue, and want a reinforcement of rest, though not of valour. Our own interest and happiness call upon us to give them every support in our power, and make the burden of the day, on which the safety of this city depends, as light as possible. Remember, Gentlemen, that we have forces both to the Northward and Southward of Philadelphia, and if the enemy be but stopt till those can arrive, this city will be saved, and the enemy finally routed. You have too much at stake to hesitate. You ought not to think an hour upon the matter, but to spring to action at once. Other States have been invaded, and have likewise driven off the invaders. Now OUR time and turn is come, and perhaps the finishing stroke is reserved for us. When we look back on the dangers we have been saved from, and reflect on the successes we have been blest with, it would be sinful either to be idle or despair.

I close this paper with a short address to General Howe. You, sir, are only lingering out the period that shall bring with it your defeat. You have yet scarce began upon the war; and the farther you enter, the faster will your troubles thicken. What you now enjoy is only a respite from ruin; an invitation to destruction; a something, that will lead on to our deliverance at your expence. We know the cause we are engaged in, and though a passionate fondness for it may make us grieve at every injury which threatens it, yet, when the moment of concern is over, the determination to duty returns. We are not the hireling slaves of a beggarly tyrant, nor the cringing flatterers of an infamous court. We are not moved by the gloomy smile of a worthless king, but by the ardent glow of generous patriotism. We fight, not to enslave, but to set a country free, and to make room upon the earth for honest men to live in. In such a cause we are sure we are right; and we leave to you the despairing reflection of being the tool of a miserable tyrant.

COMMON SENSE

Philadelphia, Sept. 12, at Noon.

The American Crisis

NUMBER V

March 21, 1778

TO GENERAL SIR WILLIAM HOWE.

To argue with a man who has renounced the use and authority of reason, and whose philosophy consists in holding humanity in contempt, is like administring medicine to the dead, or endeavouring to convert an Atheist by scripture. Enjoy, Sir, your insensibility of feeling and reflecting. It is the prerogative of animals. And no man will envy you those honours, in which a savage only can be your rival and a bear your master.

As the generosity of this country rewarded your brother's services last war with an elegant monument in Westminster Abbey, it is consistent that she should bestow some mark of distinction upon you. You certainly deserve her notice, and a conspicuous place in the catalogue of extraordinary persons. Yet it would be a pity to pass you from the world in state, and consign you to magnificent oblivion among the tombs, without telling the future beholder why. Judas is as much known as John, yet history ascribes their fame to very different actions.

Sir William hath undoubtedly merited a monument: But of what kind, or with what inscription, where placed or how embellished, is a question that would puzzle all the Heralds of St James's in the profoundest mood of historical deliberation. We are at no loss, Sir, to ascertain your real character, but somewhat perplexed how to perpetuate it's identity, and preserve it uninjured from the transformations of time or mistake. A statuary may give a false expression to your bust, or decorate it with some equivocal emblems, by which you may happen to steal into reputation and impose upon the hereafter traditionary world. Ill nature or ridicule may conspire, or a variety of accidents combine, to lessen, enlarge, or change Sir William's fame; and no doubt but he who has taken so much pains to be singular in his conduct, would choose to be just as singular in his exit, his monument and his epitaph.

The usual honours of the dead, to be sure, are not sufficiently sublime to escort a character like you to the republic
of dust and ashes; for however men may differ in their ideas of
grandeur or government here, the grave is nevertheless a perfect republic. Death is not the monarch of the dead, but of
the dying. The moment he obtains a conquest he loses a subject, and, like the foolish King you serve, will, in the end, war
himself out of all dominion.

As a proper preliminary towards the arrangement of your
funeral honors, we readily admit your new rank of *Knighthood*. The title is perfectly in character, and is your own, more
by merit than creation. There are Knights of various orders
from the Knight of the Windmill to the Knight of the Post.
The former is your patron for exploits, and the latter will assist you in settling your accounts. No honorary title could be
more happily applied! The ingenuity is sublime! And your
royal master hath discovered more genius in fitting you therewith, than in generating the most finished figure for a button,
or discanting on the properties of a button-mould.

But how, Sir, shall we dispose of you? The invention of a
Statuary is exhausted, and Sir William is yet unprovided with
a monument. America is anxious to bestow her funeral favors
upon you, and wishes to do it in a manner that shall distinguish you from all the deceased heroes of the last war. The
Egyptian method of embalming is not known to the present
age, and hieroglyphical pageantry hath out-lived the science
of decyphering it. Some other method, therefore, must be
thought of to immortalize the new Knight of the Windmill
and Post. Sir William, thanks to his stars, is not oppressed
with very delicate ideas. He has no ambition of being wrapt
up and handed about in myrrh, aloes and cassia. Less chargeable odors will suffice; and it fortunately happens, that the
simple genius of America hath discovered the art of preserving
bodies and embellishing them too, with much greater frugality than the ancients. In a balmage, Sir, of humble tar, you
will be as secure as Pharoah, and in a hieroglyphic of feathers
rival in finery all the mummies of Egypt.

As you have already made your exit from the moral world,
and by numberless acts both of passionate and deliberate injustice engraved an "HERE LYETH" on your deceased honor,

it must be meer affectation in you to pretend concern at the humours or opinions of mankind respecting you. What remains of you may expire at any time. The sooner the better. For he who survives his reputation, lives out of spite to himself, like a man listening to his own reproach.

Thus entombed and ornamented I leave you to the inspection of the curious, and return to the history of your yet surviving actions. — The character of Sir William hath undergone some extraordinary revolutions since his arrival in America. It is now fix'd and known; and we have nothing to hope from your candor or to fear from your capacity. Indolence and inability have too large a share in your composition ever to suffer you to be any thing more than the hero of little villainies and unfinished adventures. That, which to some persons appeared moderation in you at first, was not produced by any real virtue of your own, but by a contrast of passions dividing and holding you in perpetual irresolution. One vice will frequently expel another without the least merit in the man, as powers in contrary directions reduce each other to rest.

It became you, to have supported a dignified solemnity of character; to have shewn a superior liberality of soul; to have won respect by an obstinate perseverance in maintaining order, and to have exhibited, on all occasions, such an unchangeable graciousness of conduct, that while we beheld in you the resolution of an enemy we might admire in you the sincerity of a man. You came to America under the high-sounding titles of Commander and Commissioner; not only to suppress what you call rebellion by arms, but to shame it out of countenance by the excellence of your example. Instead of which, you have been the patron of low and vulgar frauds, the encourager of Indian cruelties; and have imported a cargo of vices blacker than those you pretended to suppress.

Mankind are not universally agreed in their determination of right and wrong; but there are certain actions which the consent of all nations and individuals hath branded with the unchangeable name of MEANNESS. In the list of human vices we find some of such a refined constitution, that they cannot be carried into practice without seducing some virtue to their assistance; but *meanness* hath neither alliance nor apology. It is generated in the dust and sweepings of other vices, and is of such a hateful figure that all the rest conspire to disown it. Sir William, the Commissioner of George the Third, hath at last vouchsafed to give it rank and pedigree. He has placed the fugitive at the Council Board, and dubbed it companion of the order of knighthood.

The particular act of meanness which I allude to in this description, is forgery. You, Sir, have abetted and patronised the forging and uttering counterfeit continental bills. In the same New-York news-papers in which your own proclamation under your master's authority was published, offering, or pretending to offer, pardon and protection to the inhabitants of these States, there were repeated advertisements of counterfeit money for sale, and persons who have come officially from you and under the sanction of your flag, have been taken up in attempting to put them off.

A conduct so basely mean in a public character is without precedent or pretence. Every nation on earth, whether friends or enemies, will unite in despising you. 'Tis an incendiary war upon society which nothing can excuse or palliate—An improvement upon beggarly villainy—and shews an inbred wretchedness of heart made up between the venomous malignity of a serpent and the spiteful imbecility of an inferior reptile.

The laws of any civilized country would condemn you to the gibbet without regard to your rank or titles, because it is an action foreign to the usage and custom of war; and should you fall into our hands, which pray God you may, it will be a doubtful matter whether we are to consider you as a military prisoner or a prisoner for felony.

Besides, it is exceedingly unwise and impolitic in you, or any persons in the English service, to promote, or even encourage, or wink at, the crime of forgery in any case whatever. Because, as the riches of England, as a nation, is chiefly in paper, and the far greater part of trade among individuals is carried on by the same medium, that is, by notes and drafts on one another, they, therefore, of all people in the world ought to endeavour to keep forgery out of sight, and, if possible, not to revive the idea of it. It is dangerous to make men familiar with a crime which they may afterwards practise to much greater advantage against those who first taught them. Several officers in the English army have made their exit at the gallows for forgery on their agents; for we all know, who know any thing of England, that there is not a more necessitous body of men, taking them generally, than what the English officers are. They contrive to make a shew at the expence of the taylor, and appear clean at the charge of the washerwoman.

England hath at this time nearly two hundred millions pounds sterling of public money in paper, for which she hath no real property, besides a large circulation of bank notes, bank post bills, and promissary notes and drafts of private bankers, merchants and tradesmen. She hath the greatest quantity of paper currency and the least quantity of gold and silver of any nation in Europe; the real specie, which is about sixteen millions sterling, serve only as change in large sums, which are always made in paper, or for payment in small ones. Thus circumstanced, the nation is put to its wit's ends, and obliged to be severe almost to criminality, to prevent the practice and growth of forgery. Scarcely a session passes at the Old Bailey, or an execution at Tyburn, but witnesseth this truth. Yet you, Sir, regardless of the policy which her necessity obliges her to adopt, have made your whole army intimate with the crime. And as all armies, at the conclusion of a war, are too apt to carry into practice the vices of the campaign, it will probably happen, that England will hereafter abound in forgeries, to which Art, the practitioners were first initiated under your authority in America. You, Sir, have the honor of adding a new vice to the military catalogue; and the reason, perhaps, why the invention was reserved for you, is, because no General before was mean enough even to think of it.

That a man whose soul is absorbed in the low traffic of vulgar vice, is incapable of moving in any superior region, is clearly shewn in you by the event of every campaign. Your military exploits have been without plan, object or decision. Can it be possible that you or your employers can suppose the possession of Philadelphia to be any ways equal to the expence or expectation of the nation which supports you? What advantages does England derive from any atchievements of yours? To *her* it is perfectly indifferent what place you are in, so long as the business of conquest is unperformed and the charge of maintaining you remains the same.

If the principal events of the three campaigns be attended to, the balance will appear strongly against you at the close of each; but the last, in point of importance to us, hath exceeded the former two. It is pleasant to look back on dangers past, and equally as pleasant to meditate on present ones when the way out begins to appear. *That* period is now arrived, and the long doubtful winter of war is changing to the sweeter prospects of victory and joy. At the close of the campaign in seventy-five, you were obliged to retreat from Boston. In the summer of seventy-six, you appeared with a numerous fleet and army in the harbour of New-York. By what miracle the Continent was preserved in that season of danger is a subject of admiration! If instead of wasting your time against Long-Island, you had run up the North River and landed any where above New-York, the consequence must have been, that either you would have compelled General Washington to fight you with very unequal numbers, or he must have suddenly evacuated the city with the loss of nearly all the stores of the army, or have surrendered for want of provisions, the situation of the place naturally producing one or other of these events.

The preparations made to defend New-York were, nevertheless, wise and military; because your forces were then at sea, their numbers uncertain; storms, sickness, or a variety of accidents might have disabled their coming, or so diminished them on their passage, that those which survived would have been incapable of opening the campaign with any prospect of success; in which case the defence would have been sufficient and the place preserved; for cities that have been raised from nothing with an infinitude of labor and expence, are not to be thrown away on the bare probability of their being taken. On these grounds, the preparations made to maintain New-York were as judicious as the retreat afterwards. While you, in the interim, let slip the *very* opportunity which seemed to put conquest in your power.

Through the whole of that campaign you had nearly double the forces which General Washington immediately commanded. The principal plan, at that time, on our part, was to wear away the season with as little loss as possible, and to raise the army for the next year. Long-Island, New-York, Forts Washington and Lee were not defended, after your superior force was known, under any expectation of their being finally maintained, but as a range of out works, in the attacking of which, your time might be wasted, your numbers reduced, and your vanity amused by possessing them on our retreat. It was intended to have withdrawn the garrison from Fort Washington after it had answered the former of those purposes, but the fate of that day put a prize into your hands without much honour to yourselves.

Your progress through the Jerseys was accidental; you had it not even in contemplation, or you would not have sent so principal a part of your force to Rhode-Island before-hand. The utmost hope of America in the year seventy-six reached no higher than that she might not *then* be conquered. She had no expectation of defeating you in that campaign. Even the most cowardly Tory allowed, that, could she withstand the shock of *that* summer her independence would be past a doubt. You had *then* greatly the advantage of her. You were formidable. Your military knowledge was supposed to be compleat. Your fleets and forces arrived without an accident. You had neither experience nor reinforcements to wait for. You had nothing to do but to begin, and your chance lay in the first vigorous onset.

America was young and unskilled. She was obliged to trust her defence to time and practice; and hath, by meer dint of perseverance, maintained her cause, and brought her enemy to a condition, in which, she is now capable of meeting him on any grounds.

It is remarkable that in the campaign of seventy-six, you gained no more, notwithstanding your great force, than what was given you by consent of evacuation, except Fort Washington: While every advantage obtained by us was by fair and hard fighting. The defeat of Sir Peter Parker was compleat. The conquest of the Hessians at Trenton by the remains of a retreating army, which, but a few days before, you affected to despise, is an instance of heroic perseverance very seldom to be met with. And the victory over the British troops at

Princeton, by a harrassed and wearied party, who had been engaged the day before and marched all night without refreshment, is attended with such a scene of circumstances and superiority of Generalship, as will ever give it a place on the first line in the history of great actions.

When I look back on the gloomy days of last winter and see America suspended by a thread, I feel a triumph of joy at the recollection of her delivery, and a reverence for the characters which snatched her from destruction. To doubt *now* would be a species of infidelity, and to forget the instruments which saved us *then* would be ingratitude.

The close of that campaign left us with the spirits of conquerors. The Northern districts were relieved by the retreat of General Carleton over the lakes. The army under your command were hunted back and had their bounds prescribed. The Continent began to feel its military importance, and the winter passed pleasantly away in preparations for the next campaign.

However confident you might be on your first arrival, the course of the year seventy-six gave you some idea of the difficulty, if not impossibility, of conquest. To this reason I ascribe your delay in opening the campaign in seventy-seven. The face of matters, on the close of the former year, gave you no encouragement to pursue a discretionary war as soon as the spring admitted the taking the field; for though conquest, in that case, would have given you a double portion of fame, yet the experiment was too hazardous. The Ministry, had you failed, would have shifted the whole blame upon you, charged you with having acted without orders, and condemned at once both your plan and execution.

To avoid those misfortunes, which might have involved you and your money accounts in perplexity and suspicion, you prudently waited the arrival of a plan of operations from England, which was, that you should proceed for Philadelphia by way of Chesapeak, and that Burgoyne, after reducing Ticonderoga, should take his route by Albany, and, if necessary, join you.

The splendid laurels of the last campaign have flourished in the North. In that quarter America hath surprized the world, and laid the foundation of her this year's glory. The conquest

of Ticonderoga (if it may be called a conquest) has, like all
your other victories, led on to ruin. Even the provisions taken
in that fortress, (which by General Burgoyne's return was sufficient in bread and flour for nearly 5000 men for ten weeks,
and in beef and pork for the same number of men for one
month) served only to hasten his overthrow, by enabling him
to proceed for Saratoga the place of his destruction. A short
review of the operations of the last campaign will shew the
condition of affairs on both sides.

You have taken Ticonderoga and marched into Philadelphia. These are all the events which the year hath produced
on your part. A trifling campaign indeed, compared with the
expences of England and the conquest of the Continent. On
the other side, a considerable part of your Northern force
has been routed by the New-York militia under General
Herkimer. Fort Stanwix hath bravely survived a compounded
attack of soldiers and savages, and the besiegers have fled. The
battle of Bennington has put a thousand prisoners into our
hands, with all their arms, stores, artillery and baggage. General Burgoyne in two engagements has been defeated; himself, his army, and all that were his and theirs are now ours.
Ticonderoga and Independence are retaken, and not the
shadow of an enemy remains in all the Northern districts. At
this instant we have upwards of eleven thousand prisoners,
between sixty and seventy pieces of brass ordnance, besides
small arms, tents, stores, &c. &c.

In order to know the real value of those advantages we
must reverse the scene, and suppose General Gates, and the
force he commanded, to be at your mercy as prisoners, and
General Burgoyne with his army of soldiers and savages to be
already joined to you in Pennsylvania. So dismal a picture can
scarcely be looked at. It hath all the traces and colourings of
horror and despair; and excites the most swelling emotions of
gratitude by exhibiting the miseries we are so graciously preserved from.

I admire this distribution of laurels around the Continent.
It is the earnest of future union. South-Carolina has had her
day of suffering and of fame; and the other Southern States
have exerted themselves in proportion to the force that invaded or insulted them. Towards the close of the campaign in

seventy-six, these middle States were called upon and did their duty nobly. They were witnesses to the almost expiring flame of human freedom. It was the close struggle of life and death. The line of invisible division; and on which, the unabated fortitude of a Washington prevailed, and saved the spark, that has since blazed in the North with unrivalled lustre.

Let me ask, Sir, what great exploits have you performed? Through all the variety of changes and opportunities which this war hath produced, I know no one action of yours that can be stiled masterly. You have moved in and out, backward and forward, round and round, as if valor consisted in a military jig. The history and figure of your movements would be truly ridiculous could they be justly delineated. They resemble the labors of a puppy pursuing his tail; the end is still at the same distance, and all the turnings round must be done over again.

The first appearance of affairs at Ticonderoga wore such an unpromising aspect, that it was necessary, in July, to detach a part of the forces to the support of that quarter, which were otherwise destined or intended to act against you, and this, perhaps, has been the means of postponing your downfal to another campaign. The destruction of one army at a time is work enough. We know, Sir, what we are about, what we have to do, and how to do it.

Your progress from Chesapeak was marked by no capital stroke of policy or heroism. Your principal aim was to get General Washington between the Delaware and Schuylkill and between Philadelphia and your army. In that situation, with a river on each of his flanks, which united about five miles below the city, and your army above him, you could have intercepted his reinforcements and supplies, cut off all his communication with the country, and, if necessary, have dispatched assistance to open a passage for General Burgoyne. This scheme was too visible to succeed, for had General Washington suffered you to command the open country above him, I think it a very reasonable conjecture that the conquest of Burgoyne would not have taken place, because you could, in that case, have relieved him. It was therefore necessary, while that important victory was in suspense, to trepan *you* into a situation, in which you could only be on the defensive without the power of affording him assistance. The manœuvre had its effect and Burgoyne was conquered.

There has been something unmilitarily passive in you from the time of your passing the Schuylkill and getting possession of Philadelphia to the close of the campaign. You mistook a trap for a conquest, the probability of which has been made known to Europe, and the edge of your triumph taken off by our own information long before.

Having got you into this situation, a scheme for a general attack upon you at Germantown was carried into execution on the fourth of October, and though the success was not equal to the excellence of the plan, yet the attempting it proved the genius of America to be on the rise and her power approaching to superiority. The obscurity of the morning was your best friend, for a fog is always favorable to a hunted enemy. Some weeks after this, you, likewise, planned an attack on General Washington while at Whitemarsh, marched out with infinite parade, but on finding him preparing to attack you the next morning, you prudently cut about and retreated to Philadelphia with all the precipitation of a man conquered in imagination.

Immediately after the battle of Germantown, the probability of Burgoyne's defeat gave a new policy to affairs in Pennsylvania, and it was judged most consistent with the general safety of America to wait the issue of the Northern campaign. Slow and sure is sound work. The news of that victory arrived in our camp on the 18th of October, and no sooner did the shout of joy, and the report of the thirteen cannon reach your ears, than you resolved upon a retreat, and the next day, that is, on the 19th, you withdrew your drooping army into Philadelphia. This movement was evidently dictated by fear; and carried with it a positive confession that you dreaded a second attack. It was hiding yourself among women and children, and sleeping away the choicest part of the campaign in expensive inactivity. An army in a city can never be a conquering army. The situation admits only a defence. It is meer shelter; and every military power in Europe will conclude you to be eventually defeated.

The time when you made this retreat was the very time you ought to have fought a battle, in order to put yourself in a condition of recovering in Pennsylvania what you had lost at Saratoga. And the reason why you did not, must be either prudence or cowardice; the former supposes your inability, and the latter needs no explanation. I draw no conclusions, Sir, but such as are naturally deduced from known and visible facts, and such as will always have a being while the facts which produced them remain unaltered.

After this retreat a new difficulty arose which exhibited the power of Britain in a very contemptible light, which was the attack and defence of Mud-Island. For several weeks did that little unfinished fortress stand out against all the attempts of Admiral and General Howe. It was the fable of Bender realized on the Delaware. Scheme after scheme and force upon force were tried and defeated. The garrison, with scarce any thing to cover them but their bravery, survived in the midst of mud, shot and shells, and were at last obliged to give it up more to the powers of time and gun-powder than to the military superiority of the besiegers.

It is my sincere opinion that matters are in much worse condition with you than what is generally known. Your master's speech at the opening of Parliament is like a soliloquy on ill luck. It shews him to be coming a little to his reason, for sense of pain is the first symptom of recovery in profound stupefactions. His condition is deplorable. He is obliged to submit to all the insults of France and Spain without daring to know or resent them, and thankful for the most trivial evasions to the most humble remonstrances. The time *was* when he could not *deign* an answer to a petition from America, and the time now *is* when he dare not *give* an answer to an affront from France. The capture of Burgoyne's army will sink his consequence as much in Europe as in America. In his speech he expresses his suspicions at the warlike preparations of France and Spain, and as he has only the one army which you command to support his character in the world with, it remains very uncertain when, or in what quarter, it will be most wanted or can be best employed, and this will partly account for the great care you take to keep it from action and attacks, for should Burgoyne's fate be yours, which it probably will, England may take her endless farewell not only of all America but of all the West-Indies.

Never did a nation invite destruction upon itself with the eagerness and the ignorance with which Britain has done. Bent upon the ruin of a young and unoffending country, she hath drawn the sword that hath wounded herself to the heart, and in the agony of her resentment hath applied a poison for a cure. Her conduct towards America is a compound of rage and lunacy; she aims at the government of it, yet preserves neither dignity nor character in her methods to obtain it. Were government a mere manufacture or article of commerce immaterial by whom it should be made or sold, we might as well employ her as another, but when we consider it as the fountain from whence the general manners and morality of a country take their rise, that the persons entrusted with the execution thereof are by their serious example an authority to support these principles, how abominably absurd is the idea of being hereafter governed by a set of men who have been guilty of forgery, perjury, treachery, theft, and every species of villainy which the lowest wretches on earth could practise or invent. What greater public curse can befal any country than to be under such authority, and what greater blessing than to be delivered therefrom. The soul of any man of sentiment would rise in brave rebellion against them and spurn them from the earth.

The malignant and venemous tempered Gen. Vaughan has amused his savage fancy in burning the whole town of Kingston, in York government, and the late Governor of that State, Mr. Tryon, in his letter to General Parsons, has endeavoured to justify it, and declared his wish to burn the houses of every Committee-man in the country. Such a confession from one who was once entrusted with the powers of civil government, is a reproach to the character. But it is the wish and the declaration of a man whom anguish and disappointment have driven to despair, and who is daily decaying into the grave with constitutional rottenness.

There is not in the compass of language a sufficiency of words to express the baseness of your King, his Ministry and his Army. They have refined upon villainy till it wants a name. To the fiercer vices of former ages they have added the dregs and scummings of the most finished rascality, and are so completely sunk in serpentine deceit, that there is not left among them *one* generous enemy.

From such men and such masters may the gracious hand of
Heaven preserve America! And though the sufferings she now
endures are heavy and severe, they are like straws in the wind
compared to the weight of evils she would feel under the government of your King, and his pensioned Parliament.

There is something in meanness which excites a species of
resentment that never subsides, and something in cruelty
which stirs up the heart to the highest agony of human
hatred; Britain hath filled up both these characters till no
addition can be made, and hath not reputation left with
us to obtain credit for the slightest promise. The will of God
hath parted us, and the deed is registered for eternity. When
she shall be a spot scarcely visible among the nations,
America shall flourish the favorite of Heaven and the friend
of mankind.

For the domestic happiness of Britain and the peace of the
world I wish she had not a foot of land but what is circumscribed within her own island. Extent of dominion hath been
her ruin, and instead of civilizing others hath brutalized herself. Her late reduction of India under Clive and his successors, was not so properly a conquest as an extermination of
mankind. She is the only power who could practise the prodigal barbarity of tying men to mouths of loaded cannon and
blowing them away. It happens that General Burgoyne, who
made the report of that horrid transaction in the House of
Commons, is now a prisoner with us, and though an enemy, I
can appeal to him for the truth of it, being confident that he
neither can nor will deny it. Yet Clive received the approba-
tion of the last Parliament.

When we take a survey of mankind we cannot help cursing
the wretch, who, to the unavoidable misfortunes of nature
shall wilfully add the calamities of war. One would think there
were evils enough in the world without studying to increase
them, and that life is sufficiently short without shaking the
sand that measures it. The histories of Alexander, and Charles
of Sweden, are the histories of human devils; a good man
cannot think of their actions without abhorrence nor of their
deaths without rejoicing. To see the bounties of Heaven destroyed, the beautiful face of nature laid waste, and the choicest works of creation and art tumbled into ruin, would fetch a

curse from the soul of piety itself. But in this country the aggravation is heightened by a new combination of affecting circumstances. America was young, and, compared with other countries, was virtuous. None but a Herod of uncommon malice would have made war upon infancy and innocence, and none but a people of the most finished fortitude dared, under those circumstances, have resisted the tyranny. The natives, or their ancestors, had fled from the former oppressions of England, and with the industry of bees had changed a wilderness into a habitable world. To Britain they were indebted for nothing. The country was the gift of Heaven, and God alone is their Lord and Sovereign.

The time, Sir, will come when you, in a melancholy hour, shall reckon up your miseries by your murders in America. Life, with you, begins to wear a clouded aspect. The vision of pleasurable delusion is wearing away, and changing to the barren wild of age and sorrow. The poor reflection of having served your King will yield you no consolation in your parting moments. He will crumble to the same undistinguished ashes with yourself, and have sins enough of his own to answer for. It is not the farcical benedictions of a Bishop, nor the cringing hypocrisy of a court of Chaplains, nor the formality of an act of Parliament, that can change guilt into innocence, or make the punishment *one* pang the less. You may, perhaps, be unwilling to be serious, but this destruction of the goods of Providence, this havoc of the human race, and this sowing the world with mischief, must be accounted for to him who made and governs it. To us they are only present sufferings, but to him they are deep rebellions.

If there is a sin superior to every other it is that of willful and offensive war. Most other sins are circumscribed within narrow limits, that is, the power of *one* man cannot give them a very general extension, and many kind of sins have only a mental existence from which no infection arises; but he who is the author of a war, lets loose the whole contagion of Hell, and opens a vein that bleeds a nation to death. We leave it to England and Indians to boast of these honors; we feel no thirst for such savage glory; a nobler flame, a purer spirit animates America. She hath taken up the sword of virtuous defence; she hath bravely put herself between Tyranny and

Freedom, between a curse and a blessing, determined to expel the one, and protect the other.

It is the object only of war that makes it honorable. And if there were ever *a just* war since the world began, it is this which America is now engaged in. She invaded no land of yours. She hired no mercenaries to burn your towns, nor Indians to massacre their inhabitants. She wanted nothing from you and was indebted for nothing to you; and thus circumstanced, her defence is honorable and her prosperity certain.

Yet it is not on the *justice* only, but likewise on the *importance* of this cause that I ground my seeming enthusiastical confidence of our success. The vast extension of America makes her of too much value in the scale of Providence, to be cast, like a pearl before swine, at the feet of a European island; and of much less consequence would it be that Britain were sunk in the sea than that America should miscarry. There has been such a chain of extraordinary events in the discovery of this country at first, in the peopling and planting it afterwards, in the rearing and nursing it to its present State, and in the protection of it through the present war, that no man can doubt, but Providence hath some nobler end to accomplish than the gratification of the petty Elector of Hanover or the ignorant and insignificant King of Britain.

As the blood of the martyrs hath been the seed of the Christian Church, so the political persecutions of England will, and hath already enriched America with industry, experience, union and importance. Before the present æra she was a meer chaos of uncemented Colonies, individually exposed to the ravages of the Indians and the invasion of any power that Britain should be at war with. She had nothing she could call her own. Her felicity depended upon accident. The convulsions of Europe might have thrown her from one conqueror to another, till she had been the slave of all and ruined by every one; for until she had spirit enough to become her own master, there was no knowing to which master she should belong. *That* period, thank God, is past, and she is no longer the dependent, disunited Colonies of Britain, but the independent and united States of America, knowing no master but Heaven and herself. You or your King may call this "Delusion," "Rebellion," or what name you please. To us it is perfectly indifferent. The issue will determine the character and Time will give it a name as lasting as his own.

You have now, Sir, tried the fate of three campaigns, and can fully declare to England, that nothing is to be got on your part but blows and broken bones, and nothing on hers but waste of trade and credit and an encrease of poverty and taxes. You are now only where you might have been two years ago without the loss of a single ship, and yet not a step the forwarder towards the conquest of the Continent; because, as I have already hinted, "An army in a city can never be a conquering army." The full amount of your losses since the beginning of the war exceeds twenty thousand men, besides millions of treasure for which you have nothing in exchange. Our expences, though great, are circulated within ourselves. Yours is a direct sinking of money, and that from both ends at once; first in hiring troops out of the nation, and in paying them afterwards, because the money in neither case can return to Britain. We are already in possession of the prize, you only in suit for it. To us it is a real treasure, to you it would be only an empty triumph. Our expences will repay themselves with ten fold interest, while yours entail upon you everlasting poverty.

Take a review, Sir, of the ground you have gone over, and let it teach you policy, if it cannot honesty. You stand but on a very tottering foundation. A change of the Ministry in England may probably bring your measures into question and your head to the block. Clive, with all his successes, had some difficulty in escaping, and yours being all a war of losses, will afford you less pretensions and your enemies more grounds for impeachment.

Go home, Sir, and endeavor to save the remains of your ruined country by a just representation of the madness of her measures. A few moments well applied may yet preserve her from political destruction. I am not one of those who wish to see Europe in a flame, because I am persuaded such an event will not shorten the war. The rupture, at present, is confined between the two powers of America and England. England finds she cannot conquer America, and America has no wish to conquer England. You are fighting for what you can never obtain, and we defending what we mean never to part with. A few words, therefore, settle the bargain. Let England mind her own business and we will mind ours. Govern yourselves and we will govern ourselves. You may then trade where you please unmolested by us, and we will trade where we please unmolested by you; and such articles as we can purchase of each other better than elsewhere may be mutually done. If it were possible that you could carry on the war for twenty years you must still come to this point at last, or worse, and the sooner you think of it the better it will be for you.

My official situation enables me to know the repeated insults which Britain is obliged to put up with from foreign powers, and the wretched shifts she is driven to, to gloss them over. Her reduced strength and exhausted coffers in a three years war with America have given a powerful superiority to France and Spain. She is not now a match for them—But if neither counsels can prevail on her to think, nor sufferings awaken her to reason, she must e'en go on, till the honor of England becomes a proverb of contempt, and Europe dub her the Land of Fools.

I am, Sir,
With every wish for an honorable peace,
Your friend, enemy, and countryman,
COMMON SENSE.

YORK-TOWN,
March 18, 1778.

TO THE INHABITANTS OF AMERICA.

WITH all the pleasure with which a man exchanges bad company for good, I take my leave of Sir William and return to you. It is now nearly three years since the tyranny of Britain received its first repulse by the arms of America. A period, which has given birth to a new world and erected a monument to the folly of the old.

I cannot help being sometimes surprised at the complimentary references which I have seen and heard made to antient histories and transactions. The wisdom, civil governments, and sense of honor of the States of Greece and Rome, are frequently held up as objects of excellence and imitation. Mankind have lived for very little purpose, if, at this period of the world, they must go two or three thousand years back for lessons and examples. We do dishonorary injustice to ourselves by placing them in such a superior line. We have no just authority for it, neither can we tell why it is that we should suppose ourselves inferior.

Could the mist of antiquity be taken away, and men and things viewed as they then really were, it is more than probable that they would admire us, rather than we them. America has surmounted a greater variety and combination of difficulties than, I believe, ever fell to the share of any one people, in the same space of time, and has replenished the world with more useful knowledge and sounder maxims of civil government than were ever produced in any age before. Had it not been for America there had been no such thing as freedom left throughout the whole universe. England hath lost hers in a long chain of right reasoning from wrong principles, and it is from this country now she must learn the resolution to redress herself, and the wisdom how.

The Grecians and Romans were strongly possessed of the *spirit* of liberty but *not* the *principle*, for at the time they were determined not to be slaves themselves, they employed their power to enslave the rest of mankind. But this distinguished era is blotted by no one misanthropical vice. In short, if the principle on which the cause is founded, the universal blessings that are to arise from it, the difficulties that accompanied it, the wisdom with which it has been debated, the fortitude by which it has been supported, the strength of the power we had to oppose, and the condition in which we undertook it, be all taken in one view, we may justly stile it the most virtuous and illustrious revolution that ever graced the history of mankind.

A good opinion of ourselves is exceedingly necessary in private life, but absolutely necessary in public life, and of the utmost importance in supporting national character. I have no notion of yielding the palm of the United States to any Grecians or Romans that were ever born. We have equalled the bravest in times of danger, and excelled the wisest in the construction of civil governments, *no one in America excepted.*

From this agreeable eminence let us take a review of present affairs. The spirit of corruption is so inseparably interwoven with British politics, that their Ministry suppose all mankind are governed by the same motive. They have no idea of a people submitting even to temporary inconvenience from an attachment to rights and privileges. Their plans of business are calculated *by* the hour and *for* the hour, and are uniform in nothing but the corruption which gives them birth. They never had, neither have they at this time, any regular plan for the conquest of America by arms. They know not how to go about it, neither have they power to effect it if they could know. The thing is not within the compass of human practicability, for America is too extensive either to be fully conquered or *passively* defended. But she may be *actively* defended by defeating or making prisoners of the army that invades her. And this is the only system of defence that can be effectual in a large country.

There is something in a war carried on by invasion which makes it differ in circumstances from any other mode of war, because he who conducts it cannot tell whether the ground he gains, be for him, or against him, when he first makes it. In the winter seventy six General Howe marched with an air of victory through the Jerseys, the consequence of which was his defeat, and General Burgoyne at Saratoga experienced the same fate from the same cause. The Spaniards about two years ago were defeated by the Algerines in the same manner, that is, their first triumphs became a trap in which they were totally routed. And whoever will attend to the circumstances and events of a war carried on by invasion, will find, that any invader, in order to be finally conquered must first begin to conquer.

I confess myself one of those who believe the loss of Philadelphia to be attended with more advantages than injuries. The case stood thus. The enemy imagined Philadelphia to be of more importance to us than it really was; for we all know that it had long ceased to be a port, not a cargo of goods had been brought into it for near a twelve-month, nor any fix'd manufactories, nor even ship building carried on in it; yet as the enemy believed the conquest of it to be practicable, and to that belief added the absurd idea that the soul of all

America was centered there and would be conquered there, it naturally follows, that their possession of it, by not answering the end proposed, must break up the plans they had so foolishly gone upon, and either oblige them to form a new one, for which their present strength is not sufficient, or to give over the attempt.

We never had so small an army to fight against, nor so fair an opportunity of final success as *now*. The death wound is already given. The day is ours if we follow it up. The enemy by his situation is within our reach, and by his reduced strength is within our power. The Ministers of Britain may rage as they please, but our part is to conquer their armies. Let them wrangle and welcome, but let it not draw our attention from the *one* thing needful. *Here*, in *this* spot is our business to be accomplished, our felicity secured. What we have now to do is as clear as light, and the way to do it is as strait as a line. It needs not to be commented upon, yet, in order to be perfectly understood, I will put a case that cannot admit of a mistake.

Had the armies under the Generals Howe and Burgoyne been united and taken post at Germantown, and had the Northern army under General Gates been joined to that under General Washington at Whitemarsh, the consequence would have been a general action; and if in that action we had killed and taken the same number of officers and men, that is, between nine and ten thousand, with the same quantity of artillery, arms, stores, &c. as have been taken to the Northward, and obliged General Howe with the remains of his army, that is, with the same number he now commands, to take shelter in Philadelphia, we should certainly have thought ourselves the greatest heroes in the world; and should, as soon as the season permitted, have collected together all the force of the Continent and laid siege to the city, for it requires a much greater force to besiege an enemy in a town than to defeat them in the field. The case *now* is just the same as if it had been produced by the means I have here supposed. Between nine and ten thousand have been killed and taken, all their stores are in our possession, and General Howe, in consequence of that victory, has thrown himself for shelter into Philadelphia. He, or his trifling friend Galloway, may form what pretences they please, yet no just reason can be given for their going into winter quarters so early as the 19th of October, but their apprehension of a defeat if they continued out, or their conscious inability of keeping the field with safety. I see no advantage which can arise to America by hunting the enemy from State to State. It is a triumph without a prize, and wholly unworthy the attention of a people determined to conquer. Neither can any State promise itself security while the enemy remain in a condition to transport themselves from one part of the Continent to another. Howe, likewise, cannot conquer where we have no army to oppose, therefore any such removals in him are mean and cowardly, and reduces Britain to a common pilferer. If he retreats from Philadelphia, he will be despised; if he stays, he may be shut up and starved out, and the country, if he advances into it, may become his Saratoga. He has his choice of evils and we of opportunities. If he moves early, it is not only a sign but a proof that he expects no reinforcement, and his delays will prove that he either waits for the arrival of a plan to go upon, or force to execute it, or both; in *which* case, our strength will encrease more than his, therefore in *any* case we cannot be wrong if we do but proceed.

The particular condition of Pennsylvania deserves the attention of all the other States. Her military strength must not be estimated by the number of inhabitants. Here are men of all nations, characters, professions and interests. Here are the firmest Whigs, surviving, like sparks in the ocean, unquenched and uncooled in the midst of discouragement and disaffection. Here are men losing their all with chearfulness, and collecting fire and fortitude from the flames of their own estates. Here are others skulking in secret, many making a market of the times, and numbers who are changing Whig and Tory with the circumstances of every day.

It is by meer dint of fortitude and perseverance that the Whigs of this State have been able to maintain so good a countenance, and do even what they have done. We want help, and the sooner it can arrive the more effectual it will be. The invaded State, be it which it may, will always feel an additional burthen upon its back, and be hard set to support its civil power with sufficient authority; and this difficulty will always rise or fall, in proportion as the other States throw in their assistance to the common cause.

The enemy will most probably make many manœuvres at the opening of this campaign, to amuse and draw off the attention of the several States from the *one thing needful*. We may expect to hear of alarms and pretended expeditions to *this* place and *that* place, to the Southward, the Eastward and the Northward, all intended to prevent our forming into one formidable body. The less the enemy's strength is, the more subtleties of this kind will they make use of. Their existence depends upon it, because the force of America, when collected, is sufficient to swallow their present army up. It is therefore our business to make short work of it, by bending our whole attention to *this one principal point*, for the instant that the main body under General Howe is defeated, all the inferior alarms throughout the Continent, like so many shadows, will follow his downfall.

The only way to finish a war with the least possible bloodshed, or perhaps without any, is to collect an army, against the power of which, the enemy shall have no chance. By not doing this, we prolong the war, and double both the calamities and expences of it. What a rich and happy country would America be, were she, by a vigorous exertion, to reduce Howe as she has reduced Burgoyne. Her currency would rise to millions beyond its present value. Every man would be rich, and every man would have it in his power to be happy. And why not do these things? What is there to hinder? America is her own mistress and can do what she pleases.

If we had not at this time a man in the field, we could, nevertheless, raise an army in a few weeks sufficient to overwhelm all the force which General Howe at present commands. Vigor and determination will do any thing and every thing. We began the war with this kind of spirit, why not end it with the same? Here, Gentlemen, is the enemy. Here is the army. The interest, the happiness, of all America is centered in this half ruined spot. Come on and help us. Here are laurels, come and share them. Here are Tories, come and help us to expel them. Here are Whigs that will make you welcome, and enemies that dread your coming.

The worst of all policy is that of doing things by halves.

Penny-wise and pound foolish has been the ruin of thousands. The present spring, if rightly improved, will free us from all our troubles, and save us the expence of millions. We have now only one army to cope with. No opportunity can be fairer; no prospect more promising. I shall conclude this paper with a few outlines of a plan either for filling up the battalions with expedition, or for raising an additional force for any limited time, on any sudden emergency.

That in which every man is interested is every man's duty to support. And any burthen which falls equally on all men, and, from which every man is to receive an equal benefit, is consistent with the most perfect ideas of liberty. I would wish to revive something of that virtuous animation which first called America into the field. Then every man was eager to do his part, and perhaps the principal reason why we have in any degree fallen therefrom, is, because we did not set a sufficient value by it at first, but left it to blaze out of itself, instead of regulating and preserving it by just proportions of rest and service.

Suppose any State whose number of effective inhabitants were 80,000, should be required to furnish 3200 men towards the defence of the Continent on any very sudden emergency.

First, Let the whole number of effective inhabitants be divided into hundreds; then if each of those hundreds turn out four men, the whole number of 3200 will be had.

2dly, Let the names of each hundred men be entered in a book, and let four dollars be collected from each man, with as much more as any of the gentlemen whose abilities can afford it shall please to throw in, which gifts shall likewise be entered against the donors names.

3dly, Let the sums so collected be offered as a present, over and above the bounty of twenty dollars, to any four who may be inclined to propose themselves as volunteers; if more than four offer, the majority of the subscribers present shall determine which; if none offers, then four out of the hundred shall be taken by lot, who shall be entitled to the said sums, and shall either go, or provide others that will, in the space of six days.

4thly, As it will always happen, that in the space of ground on which any hundred men shall live, there will always be a number of persons who, by age and infirmity, are incapable of doing personal service, and as such persons are generally possessed of the greatest part of property in any country, their portion of service, therefore, will be to furnish each man with a blanket, which will make a regimental coat jacket and breeches, or cloaths in lieu thereof, and another for a watch cloak, and two pair of shoes — for however choice people may be of these things matters not in cases of this kind — Those who live always in houses can find many ways to keep themselves warm, but it is a shame and a sin to suffer a soldier in the field to want a blanket while there is one in the country.

Should the cloathing not be wanted, the superannuated or infirm persons possessing property, may, in lieu thereof, throw in their money subscriptions towards encreasing the bounty, for though age will naturally exempt a person from personal service, it cannot exempt him from his share of the charge, because the men are raised for the defence of property and liberty jointly.

There never was a scheme against which objections might not be raised. But this alone is not a sufficient reason for rejection. The only line to judge truly upon, is, to draw out and admit all the objections which can fairly be made, and place against them all the contrary qualities, conveniences and advantages, then by striking a balance you come at the true character of any scheme, principle or position.

The most material advantages of the plan here proposed are ease, expedition, and cheapness; yet the men so raised get a much larger bounty than is any where at present given; because all the expences, extravagance, and consequent idleness of recruiting are saved or prevented. The country incurs no new debt, nor interest thereon; the whole matter being all settled at once and entirely done with. It is a subscription answering all the purposes of a tax, without either the charge or trouble of collecting. The men are ready for the field with the greatest possible expedition, because it becomes the duty of the inhabitants themselves, in every part of the country, to find up their proportion of men, instead of leaving it to a recruiting Serjeant, who, be he ever so industrious, cannot know always where to apply.

I do not propose this as a regular digested plan, neither will the limits of this paper admit of any further remarks upon it. I believe it to be a hint capable of much improvement, and as such submit it to the Public.

COMMON SENSE.

Lancaster, March 21, 1778.

Prospects for War Between Britain and France

June 10, 1778

TO THE PEOPLE OF AMERICA.

As the country appears greatly amused with expectations of the enemy quitting Philadelphia, and lest that amusement should lull us into some unlooked for misfortune, I take the liberty, thro' the channels of the several news-papers, to point out the grounds upon which the politics of the enemy may, I think, be understood, or at least ought to be considered.

Whether they will quit Philadelphia or not is a question, which neither we, nor the General who commands there, can determine. He acts by orders from England, and we can judge only by appearances. He may expect to receive such, and may, nevertheless, receive orders to the contrary.

The state of European affairs, after the treaty with France was signed, rendered a war between France and England probable; and under that expectation, the Commander of the British troops would consequently pack up, and hold himself in readiness to obey *any* orders he might receive, upon a supposition that such orders would be sudden and peremptory. He must know that Philadelphia is no station for him, in case of an European war. He cannot help seeing that he is subject to an attack from France and America unitedly, and that the army he commands will be wanted elsewhere. Should such an event take place, he will move instantly, and therefore will, in the interim, always hold himself in readiness to move. And this, I presume, accounts for his preparations, which rather indicates his apprehensions than his intentions.

As I would not be misunderstood by using an undefined nicety of expression, I choose therefore to say, that we have a sett of as vile and treacherous characters to deal with, as were ever permitted to work out their own destruction, or suffered to live as a scourge to mankind. I mean the present King of England and his Ministers. As there is no act of baseness they would not commit, so there is no meanness they will not submit to. They would, I believe, suffer themselves to be kicked by every power in Europe, if by that submission they could go on unmolested with their schemes against America. *Here* they have fixed their object, and their eyes and ears are shut against every other.

There is *one* and *only* one way, by which they may creditably avoid a rupture with France, and likewise put themselves in a condition of making peace with America; and which if they omit doing, we may be sure there is mischief lurking behind, viz. *To acknowledge, on their part, the Independence of America.* Because such an acknowledgment admits France to the undisturbed enjoyment of her treaty with us as a matter of *right*, and consequently no quarrel can take place on the part of Britain. In this case, the capture of French vessels will be confined to those laden with military stores and cloathing made up, which likewise, according to the custom of nations, is not a legal cause for a declaration of war on the part of France.

Should this be their conduct, they will keep clear of a war with France, and consequently their apprehensions of immediate danger from their situation in Philadelphia will subside; after which, they will think themselves at liberty to hold or evacuate it as *future* occasions may arise. They know that their strongest fortification is their being mixed among the inhabitants, who must be exposed to the same mischief with themselves by an attack.

So if they do not accede to the Independence of America, and yet avoid a rupture with France, we may justly attribute such conduct to a mixture of secret villainy and public meanness, and may likewise be sure they have no intentions of quitting Philadelphia, and will have none, unless forced to it; and every expectation of their voluntarily doing it, tends only to lull us into a state of drowsiness and danger. I have here stated three cases, which are all that can happen.

First. A war with France.

Secondly. An acknowledgment of our independence, on the part of Britain, by which such a war may be *creditably* avoided. And,

Thirdly. Her submission to every indignity which France

has or may show, by which submission a war may be *meanly* avoided.

The first leads to an immediate evacuation of Philadelphia, and perhaps New-York. The second and third do not. And tho' I may possibly be wrong in my conjecture, yet I think it more than probable that the *last* of the three will be the Ministry's line of conduct. The character of the men favours this supposition.

But taking either of the two last to happen, we shall be exposed to consequences that we ought immediately to prepare against. The apparent probability of a war with France has given the British King and Ministry *new and popular pretensions for raising more troops,* which they may yet employ against us, if they can *any ways* avoid employing them against France; while we, amused with delusive appearances, may be most unwarily taken in.

This is not a time to trifle, neither are these trifling matters. I do not undertake to say what *will* happen, I only state what *may* happen; and as one of these three *must* happen, it is our part to be guarded against all. Not a man now ought to be absent from his proper post; and I submit it to the judgment of every State, whether the present time is not as politically critical, and may, by remissness, be as distressing as any which has yet happened. A reinforcement of eight hundred men has very lately arrived at New-York, which does not look much like an evacuation. They are yet tampering with the Indians. The burning Col. Kirkbride's and Mr. Borden's is but a recent affair, since which they have burnt a considerable number of houses in the state of Rhode-Island, and all these at the time they are pretending to negociate. If any thing can determine what confirmed villainy is, it must be conduct like this.

On our part we cannot be wrong, but by mistake or delusion. A fairer prospect we need not wish for, if we do but improve it. We have at present steered with safety thro a rough sea, and are bringing the ship into port, let us take care she is not shipwreck'd in the harbour.

The danger arising to Britain by the mean policy which I suppose she will adopt is, that by sending her forces to America, and failing at the same time in making fair weather with France, she will expose herself to be conquered at home, while she aims at conquest abroad. But as there is no act of absurdity she is not capable of committing, we should, therefore, not depend on the *wise* things she *ought* to do, but prepare against the *mad* things she will *most probably* do.

COMMON SENSE.

York-Town, June 10, 1778.

N. B. *The* CRISIS, No. 6, *which is ready for the press, will be published as soon as possible. It has been delayed in order to take in a larger compass of affairs than was at first intended. The author cannot promise the exact time, as it is lengthy and the printers very busy. Such News-papers as choose to publish the above remarks, are desired to insert this note.*

C. S.

The Crisis

NUMBER VI

October 20, 1778

TO THE EARL OF CARLISLE, GENERAL CLINTON, AND WILLIAM EDEN, ESQ; BRITISH COMMISSIONERS, AT NEW-YORK.

THERE is a dignity in the warm passions of a whig, which is never to be found in the cold malice of a tory. In the one, nature is only heated—in the other she is poisoned. The instant the former has it in his power to punish, he feels a disposition to forgive; but the canine venom of the latter knows no relief but in revenge. This general distinction will, I believe, apply in all cases, and suit as well the meridian of England as America.

As I presume your last proclamation will undergo the strictures of other pens, I shall confine my remarks to only a few parts thereof. All that you have said might have been comprised in half the compass. It is tedious and unmeaning, and only a repetition of your former follies, with here and there an offensive aggravation. Your cargo of pardons will have no market—It is unfashionable to look at them—Even speculation is at an end. They are become a perfect drug, and no ways calculated for the climate.

In the course of your proclamation you say, "The policy as well as the *benevolence of Great-Britain*, have thus far checked the extremes of war, when they tended to distress a people still considered as our fellow subjects, and to desolate a country shortly to become again a source of mutual advantage." What you mean by "the *benevolence* of Great-Britain," is to me inconceivable. To put a plain question: Do you consider yourselves men or devils? For until this point is settled, no determinate sense can be put upon the expression. You have already equalled, and in many instances excelled, the savages of either Indies; and if you have yet a cruelty in store, you must have imported it, unmixed with every human material, from the original ware-house of Hell.

To the interposition of Providence, and her blessings on our endeavours, and not to *British benevolence*, are we indebted for the short chain that limits your ravages. Remember you do not, at this time, command a foot of land on the Continent of America. Staten-Island, York-Island, a small part of Long-Island, and Rhode-Island, circumscribe your power; and even those you hold at the expence of the West-Indies. To avoid a defeat and prevent a desertion of your troops, you have taken up your quarters in holes and corners of inaccessible security; and in order to conceal what every one can conceive, you now endeavour to impose your weakness upon us for an act of mercy. If you think to succeed by such shadowy devises, you are but infants in the political world; you have the A, B, C, of stratagem yet to learn; and are wholly ignorant of the people you have to contend with. Like men in a state of intoxication, you forget that the rest of the world have eyes, and that the same stupidity which conceals you from yourselves, exposes you to their satire and contempt.

The paragraph I have quoted, stands as an introduction to the following, "But when that country (America) professes the unnatural design, not only of estranging herself from us, but of mortgaging herself and her resources to our enemies, the whole contest is changed; and the question is, how far Great-Britain may, by every means in her power, destroy or render useless, a connection contrived for her ruin and the aggrandizement of France. Under such circumstances, the laws of self-preservation must direct the conduct of Britain, and if the British Colonies are to become an accession to France, will direct her to render that accession of as little avail as possible to her enemy."

I consider you in this declaration like madmen biting in the hour of death. It contains likewise a fraudulent meanness; for, in order to justify a barbarous conclusion, you have advanced a false position. The treaty we have formed with France is open, noble and generous. It is true policy founded on sound philosophy, and neither a surrender or mortgage, as you would scandalously insinuate. I have seen every article, and speak from positive knowledge. In France we have found an affectionate friend and a faithful ally; from Britain nothing but tyranny, cruelty and infidelity.

But the happiness is, that the mischief you threaten is not in your power to execute; and if it were, the punishment would return upon you in a tenfold degree. The humanity of America hath hitherto restrained her from acts of retaliation, and the affection she retains for many individuals in England, who have fed, cloathed, and comforted her prisoners, has, to the present day, warded off her resentment, and operated as a screen to the whole. But even these considerations must cease when national objects interfere and oppose them. Repeated aggravations will provoke a retort, and policy justify the measure. We mean now to take you seriously up upon your own ground and principle, and as you do so shall you be done by.

You ought to know, gentlemen, that England and Scotland are far more exposed to incendiary desolation than America in her present State can possibly be. We occupy a country with but few towns, and whose riches consists in land and annual produce. The two last can suffer but little, and that only within a very limited compass. In Britain it is otherwise. Her wealth lies chiefly in cities and large towns, the repositories of manufactures, and fleets of merchant men. There is not a Nobleman's country seat but may be laid in ashes by a single person. Your own may probably contribute to the proof: In short, there is no evil which cannot be returned when you come to incendiary mischief. The ships in the Thames may certainly be as easily set on fire as the temporary bridge was a few years ago; yet of that affair no discovery was ever made; and the loss you would sustain by such an event, executed at a proper season, is infinitely greater than any you can inflict. The East-India house and the Bank, neither are nor can be secure from this sort of destruction, and as Doctor Price justly observes, a fire at the latter would bankrupt the nation. It has never been the custom of France and England, when at war, to make those havocs on each other, because the ease with which they could retaliate, rendered it as impolitic as if each had destroyed his own.

But think not gentlemen that our distance secures you, or our invention fails us. We can much easier accomplish such a point than any nation in Europe. We talk the same language, dress in the same habit, and appear with the same manners as yourselves. We can pass from one part of England to another unsuspected, many of us are as well acquainted with the country as you are, and should you impoliticly provoke our will, you will most assuredly lament the effects of it. Mischiefs of this kind require no army to execute them. The means are obvious, and the opportunities unguardable. I hold up a warning piece to your senses, if you have any left, and *"to the unhappy people likewise whose affairs are committed to you."** I call not with the rancour of an enemy, but with the earnestness of a friend on the deluded people of England, lest between your blunders and theirs, they sink beneath the evils contrived for us.

"He who lives in a glass house, says the Spanish proverb, should never begin throwing stones." This, gentlemen, is exactly your case; and you must be the most ignorant of mankind, or suppose us so, not to see on which side the balance of accounts will fall. There are many other modes of retaliation, which for several reasons I choose not to mention. But be assured of this, that the instant you put a threat in execution, a counter blow will follow it. If you *openly* profess yourselves savages, it is high time we should treat you as such, and if nothing but distress can recover you to reason, to punish will become an office of charity.

While your fleet lay last Winter in the Delaware I offered my service to the Pennsylvania Navy Board then at Trenton, as one who would make a party with them, or any four or five gentlemen on an expedition down the river to set fire to it, and though it was not then accepted, nor the thing *personally* attempted, it is more than probable, that your own folly will provoke a much heavier stroke in some more vulnerable part. Say not when the mischief is done that you had not warning, and remember that we do not begin it, but mean to repay it. Thus much for your savage and impolitic threat.

In another part of your proclamation you say, "But if the honours of a military life are become the object of the Americans, let them seek those honours under the banners of their *rightful Sovereign*, and in fighting the battles of the united British empire, against our late *mutual and natural enemies*." Surely! The union of absurdity with madness was never

*General Clinton's letter to Congress.

marked in more distinguishable lines than those. Your *rightful Sovereign* as you call him may do well enough for you, who dare not enquire into the humble capacities of the man; but we who estimate persons and things by their real worth, cannot suffer our judgments to be so imposed upon; and unless it is your wish to see him exposed, it ought to be your endeavour to keep him out of sight. The less you have to say about him the better. We have *done with him*, and that ought to be answer enough. You have been often told so. Strange! that the answer must be so often repeated. You go a begging with your King as with a brat, or with some unsaleable commodity you were tired of; and though every body tells you no, no, still you keep hawking him about. But there is *one* that will have him in a little time, and as we have no inclination to disappoint you of a customer we shall bid nothing for him.

The impertinent folly of the paragraph I have just quoted, deserves no other notice than to be laughed at and thrown by, but the principle on which it is founded is detestable. *We are invited to submit to a man who has attempted by every cruelty to destroy us, and to join him in making war against France, who is already at war against him for our support.* Can Bedlam in concert with Lucifer form a more mad and devilish request? Were it possible that a people could sink into such apostacy, they would deserve to be swept from the earth like the inhabitants of Sodom and Gomorrah. The proposition is an universal affront to the rank which man holds in the creation. An indignity to him who placed him there. It supposes him made up without a spark of honour, and under no obligation to God or man.

What sort of men or christians must you suppose the Americans to be, who after seeing their most humble petitions insultingly rejected; the most grievous laws passed to distress them in every quarter; an undeclared war let loose upon them, and Indians and Negroes invited to the slaughter: Who after seeing their kindred murdered, their fellow citizens starved to death in prisons, and their houses and property destroyed and burned: Who after the most serious appeals to Heaven, the most solemn abjuration by oath of all government connection with you, and the most heart-felt pledges and protestations of faith to each other; and who after soliciting the friendship and entering into alliances with other nations, should at last break through all these obligations civil and divine, by complying with your horrid and infernal proposal. Ought we ever after to be considered as a part of the human race? Or ought we not rather to be blotted from the society of mankind and become a spectacle of misery to the world?—But there is something in corruption, which, like a jaundiced eye, transfers the colour of itself to the object it looks upon, and sees every thing stained and impure; for unless you were capable of such conduct yourselves, you would never have supposed such a character in us. The offer fixes your infamy. It exhibits you as a nation without faith; with whom oaths and treaties are considered as trifles, and the breaking them as the breaking of a bubble. Regard to decency or to rank might have taught you better, or pride inspired you though virtue could not. There is not left a step in the degradation of character to which you can now descend; you have put your foot on the ground floor and the key of the dungeon is turned upon you.

That the invitation may want nothing of being a complete monster, you have thought proper to finish it with an assertion which has no foundation either in fact or philosophy; and as Mr. Ferguson your Secretary, is a man of letters, and has made civil society his study and published a treatise on that subject, I address this part to him.

In the close of the paragraph which I last quoted, France is stiled the *"natural enemy"* of England, and by way of lugging us into some strange idea, she is likewise stiled the *late mutual and natural enemy* of both countries. I deny that she ever was the natural enemy of either, and that there does not exist in nature such a principle. The expression is an unmeaning barbarism, and wholly unphilosophical when applied to beings of the same species, let their rank in the creation be what it may. We have a perfect idea of a *natural* enemy when we think of the *Devil*, because the enmity is perpetual, unalterable and unabateable. It admits of neither peace, truce or treaty; consequently the warfare is eternal, and therefore it is natural. But man with man cannot arrange in the same opposition. Their quarrels are accidental and equivocally created.

They become friends or enemies as the change of temper or the cast of interest inclines them. The Creator of man did not constitute him the natural enemy of each other. He has not made any one order of beings so. Even wolves may quarrel, still they herd together. If any two nations are so, then must all nations be so, otherwise it is not nature but custom, and the offence frequently originates with the accuser. England is as truly the natural enemy of France as France is of England, and perhaps more so. Separated from the rest of Europe she has contracted an unsociable habit of manners, and imagines in others the jealousy she creates in herself. Never long satisfied with peace, she supposes the discontent universal, and buoyed up with her own importance, conceives herself the only object pointed at. The expression has been often used, and always with a fraudulent design, for when the idea of a *natural enemy* is conceived it prevents all other enquiries, and the real cause of the quarrel is hidden in the universality of the conceit. Men start at the notion of a natural enemy and ask no other questions. The cry obtains credit like the alarm of a mad dog, and is one of those kind of tricks, which, by operating on the common passions, secures their interest through their folly.

But we, Sir, are not to be thus imposed upon. We live in a large world, and have extended our ideas beyond the limits and prejudices of an island. We hold out the right hand of fellowship to all the universe, and we conceive there to be a sociality in the manners of France, which is much better disposed to peace and negociation than that of England, and until the latter become more civilized she cannot expect to live long at peace with any power. Her common language is vulgar and offensive, and children with their milk suck in the rudiments of insult *"The arm of Britain! The mighty arm of Britain! Britain that shakes the earth to its center and its poles! The scourge of France! The terror of the world! That governs with a nod and pours down vengeance like a God!"* This language neither makes a nation great or little, but it shews a savageness of manners, and has a tendency to keep national animosity alive. The entertainments of the stage are calculated to the same end, and almost every publick exhibition is tinctured with insult. Yet England is always in dread of France. Terrified at the apprehension of an invasion. Suspicious of being outwitted in a treaty, and privately cringing though she is publickly offending. Let her, therefore, reform her manners and do justice, and she will find the idea of a *natural enemy* to be only a phantom of her own imagination.

Little did I think, at this period of the war, to see a proclamation which could promise you no one useful purpose whatever, and tend only to expose you. One would think that you were just awakened from a four years dream, and knew nothing of what had passed in the interval. Is this a time to be offering pardons, or renewing the long forgotten subjects of charters and taxation? Is it worth your while, after every force has failed you, to retreat under the shelter of argument and persuasion? Or can you think that we, with nearly half your army prisoners, and in alliance with France, are to be begged or threatened into submission by a piece of paper? But as Commissioners, at a hundred pounds sterling a week each, you conceived yourselves bound to do something, and the genius of ill fortune told you you must write.

For my own part, I have not put pen to paper these several months. Convinced of our superiority by the issue of every campaign, I was inclined to hope, that that, which all the rest of the world can see, would become visible to you, and therefore felt unwilling to ruffle your temper by fretting you with repetitions or discoveries. There have been intervals of hesitation in your conduct, from which it seemed a pity to disturb you, and a charity to leave you to yourselves. You have often stopt, as if you intended to think, but your thoughts have ever been too early or too late.

There was a time when Britain disdained to answer, and even to hear a petition from America. *That* time is past, and she in her turn is petitioning our acceptance. We now stand on higher ground and offer her peace; and the time will come when she, perhaps in vain, will ask it from *us*. The latter case is as probable as the former ever was. She cannot refuse to acknowledge our Independence with greater obstinacy than she before refused to repeal her laws, and if America alone could bring her to the one, united with France she will reduce her to the other. There is something in obstinacy which

differs from every other passion, whenever it fails it never recovers, but either breaks like iron or crumbles sulkily away
like a fractured arch. Most other passions have their periods of
fatigue and rest; their suffering and their cure; but obstinacy
has no resource, and the first wound is mortal. You have already began to give it up, and you will, from the natural construction of the vice, find yourselves both obliged and
inclined to do so.

If you look back you see nothing but loss and disgrace. If
you look forward the same scene continues, and the close is
an impenetrable gloom. You may plan and execute little mischiefs, but are they worth the expence they cost you, or will
such partial evils have any effect on the general cause? Your
expedition to Egg-Harbour will be felt at a distance like an
attack upon a hen roost, and expose you in Europe with a
sort of childish phrensy. Is it worth while to keep an army to
protect you in writing proclamations, or to get once a year
into winter quarters? Possessing yourselves of towns is not
conquest, but convenience, and in which you will one day
or other be trepanned. Your retreat from Philadelphia was
only a timely escape, and your next expedition may be less
fortunate.

It would puzzle all the politicians in the universe to conceive what you stay for, or why you have staid so long. You
are prosecuting a war in which you confess you have neither
object nor hope, and that conquest, could it be effected,
would not repay the charge: In the mean while the rest of
your affairs are running to ruin, and a European war kindling
against you. In such a situation there is neither doubt or difficulty; the first rudiments of reason will determine the choice,
for if peace can be procured with more advantages than even
a conquest can be obtained, he must be an ideot indeed that
hesitates.

But you are probably buoyed up by a set of wretched mor-
tals, who, having deceived themselves, are cringing with the
duplicity of a spaniel for a little temporary bread. Those men
will tell you just what you please. It is their interest to amuse
in order to lengthen out their protection. They study to keep
you amongst them for that very purpose; and in proportion as

you disregard their advice and grow callous to their complaints, they will stretch into improbability, and pepper off their flattery the higher. Characters like these are to be found in every country, and every country will despise them.

COMMON SENSE.

Philadelphia, October 20th, 1778.

The Crisis

NUMBER VII

November 11, 1778

TO THE PEOPLE OF ENGLAND.

THERE are stages in the business of serious life in which to amuse is cruel, but to deceive is to destroy; and it is of little consequence, in the conclusion, whether men deceive themselves, or submit, by a kind of mutual consent, to the impositions of each other. That England has been long under the influence of delusion or mistake, needs no other proof than the unexpected and wretched situation she is now involved in: And so powerful has been the influence, that no provision was ever made or thought of against the misfortune, because the possibility of its happening was never conceived.

The general and successful resistance of America, the conquest of Burgoyne, and a war with France, were treated in Parliament as the dreams of a discontented opposition, or a distempered imagination. They were beheld as objects unworthy of a serious thought, and the bare intimation of them afforded the Ministry a triumph of laughter. Short triumph indeed! For every thing which has been predicted has happened, and all that was promised have failed. A long series of politics so remarkably distinguished by a succession of misfortunes, without one alleviating turn, must certainly have something in it systematically wrong. It is sufficient to awaken the most credulous into suspicion, and the most obstinate into thought. Either the means in your power are insufficient, or the measures ill planned; either the execution has been bad, or the thing attempted impracticable; or to speak more emphatically, either you are not able, or Heaven is not willing. For, why is it that you have not conquered us? Who, or what has prevented you? You have had every opportunity you could desire, and succeeded to your utmost wish in every preparatory means. Your fleets and armies have arrived in America without an accident. No uncommon misfortune hath intervened. No foreign nation hath interfered until the time you had allotted for victory was past. The opposition either in or out of Parliament, neither disconcerted your measures, retarded or diminished your force. They only foretold your fate. Every ministerial scheme was carried with as high a hand as if the whole nation had been unanimous. Every thing wanted was asked for, and every thing asked for was granted. A greater force was not within the compass of your abilities to send, and the time you sent it was of all others the most favourable. You were then at rest with the whole world beside. You had the range of every court in Europe uncontradicted by us. You amused us with a tale of Commissioners of Peace, and under that disguise collected a numerous army and came almost unexpectedly upon us. The force was much greater than we looked for; and that which we had to oppose it with, was unequal in numbers, badly armed, and poorly disciplined; beside which, it was embodied only for a short time, and expired within a few months after your arrival. We had governments to form; measures to concert; an army to raise and train, and every necessary article to import or to create. Our non-importation scheme had exhausted our stores, and your command by sea intercepted our supplies. We were a people unknown, and unconnected with the political world, and strangers to the disposition of foreign powers. Could you possibly wish for a more favourable conjunction of circumstances? Yet all these have happened and passed away, and as it were left you with a laugh. They are likewise events of such an original nativity as can never happen again, unless a new world should arise from the ocean.

If any thing can be a lesson to presumption, surely the circumstances of this war will have their effect. Had Britain been defeated by any European power, her pride would have drawn consolation from the importance of her conquerors; but in the present case, she is excelled by those she affected to despise, and her own opinions, retorting on herself, become an aggravation of her disgrace. Misfortune and experience are lost upon mankind when they produce neither reflection nor reformation. Evils, like poisons, have their uses, and there are diseases which no other remedy can reach. It has been the crime and folly of England to suppose herself invincible, and *that*, without acknowledging or perceiving that a full third of her strength was drawn from the country she is now at war with. The arm of Britain has been spoken of as the arm of the Almighty, and she has lived of late as if she thought the whole world created for her diversion. Her politics, instead of civilizing, has tended to brutalize mankind, and under the vain unmeaning title of *"Defender of the Faith,"* she has made war like an Indian against the religion of humanity. Her cruelties in the East-Indies will *never, never* be forgotten; and it is somewhat remarkable that the produce of that ruined country, transported to America, should there kindle up a war to punish the destroyer. The chain is continued, though with a kind of mysterious uniformity, both in the crime and the punishment. The latter runs parallel with the former; and time and fate will give it a perfect illustration.

Where information is with-held, ignorance becomes a reasonable excuse; and one would charitably hope that the people of England do not encourage cruelty from choice but from mistake. Their recluse situation, surrounded by the sea, preserves them from the calamities of war, and keeps them in the dark as to the conduct of their own armies. They see not, therefore they feel not. They tell the tale that is told them and believe it, and accustomed to no other news than their own, they receive it, stript of its horrors and prepared for the palate of the nation, through the channel of the London Gazette. They are made to believe that their Generals and armies differ from those of other nations, and have nothing of rudeness or barbarity in them. They suppose them what they wish them to be. They feel a disgrace in thinking otherwise, and naturally encourage the belief from a partiality to themselves. There was a time when I felt the same prejudices and reasoned from the same errors; but experience, sad and painful experience has taught me better. What the conduct of former armies was I know not, but what the conduct of the present is I well know. It is low, cruel, indolent, and profligate; and had the people of America no other cause for separation than what the army has occasioned, *that alone* is cause enough.

The field of politics in England is far more extensive than that of news. Men have a right to reason for themselves, and though they cannot contradict the intelligence in the London Gazette, they may frame upon it what sentiments they please.

But the misfortune is, that a general ignorance has prevailed over the whole nation respecting America. The Ministry and the Minority have both been wrong. The former was always so; the latter only lately so. Politics to be executively right, must have a unity of means and time, and a defect in either overthrows the whole. The Ministry rejected the plans of the Minority while they were practicable, and joined in them when they became impracticable. From wrong measures they got into wrong time, and have now compleated the circle of absurdity by closing it upon themselves.

It was my fate to come to America a few months before the breaking out of hostilities. I found the disposition of the people such, that they might have been led by a thread and governed by a reed. Their suspicion was quick and penetrating, but their attachment to Britain was obstinate, and it was, at that time, a kind of treason to speak against it. They disliked the Ministry, but they esteemed the nation. Their ideas of grievance operated without resentment, and their single object was reconciliation. Bad as I believed the Ministry to be, I never conceived them capable of a measure so rash and wicked as the commencing of hostilities; much less did I imagine the nation would encourage it. I viewed the dispute as a kind of law-suit, in which I supposed the parties would find a way either to decide or settle it. I had no thoughts of independence or of arms. The world could not then have persuaded me that I should be either a soldier or an author. If I had any talents for either they were buried in me, and might ever have continued so, had not the necessity of the times dragged and driven them into action. I had formed my plan of life, and conceiving myself happy, wished every body else so. But when the country, into which I had but just put my foot, was set on fire about my ears it was time to stir. It was time for every man to stir. Those who had been long settled had something to defend; those who were just come had something to pursue; and the call and the concern was equal and universal. For in a country where all men were once adventurers, the difference of a few years in their arrival could make none in their right.

The breaking out of hostilities opened a new suspicion in

the politics of America, which though at that time very rare, has been since proved to be very right. What I allude to is, *a secret and fixt determination in the British Cabinet to annex America to the Crown of England as a conquered country.* If this be taken as the object, then the whole line of conduct pursued by the Ministry, though rash in its origin, and ruinous in its consequences, is nevertheless uniform and consistent in its parts. It applies to every case and resolves every difficulty. But if taxation of any thing else be taken in its room, then is there no proportion between the object and the charge. Nothing but the whole soil and property of the country can be placed as a possible equivalent against the millions which the Ministry expended. No taxes raised in America could possibly repay it. A revenue of two millions sterling a year would not discharge the sum and interest accumulating thereon, in twenty years.

Reconciliation never appear to have been the wish or the object of administration, they looked on conquest as certain and infallible, and under that persuasion, sought to drive the Americans into what they might stile a general rebellion, and then crushing them with arms in their hands, reap the rich harvest of a general confiscation and silence them forever. The dependants at Court were too numerous to be provided for in England. The market for plunder in the East-Indies was over; and the profligacy of government required that a new mine should be opened, and that mine could be no other than America conquered and forfeited. They had no where else to go. Every other channel was drained, and extravagance, with the thirst of a drunkard, was gaping for supplies.

If the Ministry deny this to have been their plan, it becomes them to explain what was their plan. For either they have abused us in coveting property they never laboured for, or they have abused you in expending an amazing sum upon an incompetent object. Taxation, as I mentioned before could never be worth the charge of obtaining it by arms, and any kind of formal obedience which America could have made, would have weighed with the lightness of a laugh against such a load of expence. It is therefore most probable, that the Ministry will at last justify their policy by their dishonesty, and openly declare that their original design was conquest: And in this case it well becomes the people of England to consider how far the nation would have been benefited by the success.

In a general view there are very few conquests that repay the charge of making them, and mankind are pretty well convinced that it can never be worth their while to go to war for profit sake. If they are made war upon, their country invaded, or their existence at stake, it is their duty to defend and preserve themselves, but in every other light and from every other cause is war inglorious and detestable. But to return to the case in question —

When conquests are made of foreign countries, it is supposed that the *commerce* and *dominion* of the country which made them are extended. But this could neither be the object nor the consequence of the present war. You enjoyed the whole commerce before. It could receive no possible addition by a conquest, but on the contrary, must diminish as the inhabitants were reduced in numbers and wealth. You had the same *dominion* over the country which you used to have, and had no complaint to make against her for breach of any part of the compact between you and her, or contending against any established custom commercial, political, or territorial. The country and the commerce were both your own when you *began* to conquer, in the same manner and form as they had been your own a hundred years before. Nations have sometimes been induced to make conquests for the sake only of reducing the power of their enemies, or bringing it to a balance with their own. But this could be no part of your plan. No foreign authority was claimed here, neither was any such authority suspected by you, or acknowledged, or imagined by us. What then, in the name of Heaven, could you go to war for? or what chance could you possibly have in the event, but either to hold the same country which you held before, and that in a much worse condition, or to lose with an amazing expence what you might have retained without a farthing charge?

War never can be the interest of a trading nation, any more than quarreling can be profitable to a man in business. But to make war upon those who trade with us, is like setting a bulldog upon a customer at the shop door. The least degree of common sense shews the madness of the latter, and it will apply with the same force of conviction to the former. Piratical nations, having neither commerce or commodities of their own to lose, may make war upon all the world and lucratively find their account in it. But it is quite otherwise with Britain. For besides the stoppage of trade in time of war, she exposes more of her own property to be lost, than she has the chance of taking from others. Some ministerial gentlemen in Parliament have mentioned the greatness of her trade as an apology for the greatness of her loss. This is miserable politics indeed! because it ought to have been given as a reason for her not engaging in war at first. The coast of America commands the West India trade almost as effectually as the coast of Africa does that of the Streights, and England can no more carry on the former without the consent of America, than she can the latter without a Mediterranean pass.

In whatever light the war with America is considered upon commercial principles, it is evidently the interest of the people of England not to support it; and why it has been supported so long against the clearest demonstrations of truth and national advantage, is to me, and must be to all the reasonable world, a matter of astonishment. Perhaps it may be said that I live in America, and write this from interest. To this I reply, that my principles are universal. My attachment is to all the world and not to any particular part, and if what I advance is right, no matter where or who it comes from. We have given the proclamation of your Commissioners a currency in our news-papers, and I have no doubt but you will give this a place in yours. To oblige and be obliged is fair.

Before I dismiss this part of my address I shall mention one more circumstance in which I think the people of England have been equally mistaken; and then proceed to other matter.

There is such an idea existing in the world as that of *national honor*, and this, falsely understood, is oftentimes the cause of war. In a christian and philosophical sense mankind seem to have stood still at individual civilization, and to retain as nations all the original rudeness of nature. Peace, by treaty, is only a cessation of violence, not a reformation of sentiment. It is a substitute for a principle that is wanting, and ever will

be wanting till the idea of *national honor* be rightly understood. As individuals we profess ourselves christians, but as
nations we are heathens, Romans, and what not. I remember
the late Admiral Saunders declaring in the House of Commons, and that in the time of peace *"that the city of Madrid
laid in ashes was not a sufficient atonement for the Spaniards
taking off the rudder of an English sloop of war."* I do not ask
whether this is christianity or morality, I ask whether it is decency? whether it is proper language for a nation to use? In
private life we should call it by the plain name of bullying, and
the elevation of rank cannot alter its character. It is I think
exceedingly easy to define what ought to be understood by
national honour, for *that* which is the best character for an
individual is the best character for a nation; and wherever the
latter exceeds or falls beneath the former, there is a departure
from the line of true greatness.

I have thrown out this observation with a design of applying it to Great-Britain. Her idea of national honour seems
devoid of that benevolence of heart, that universal expansion
of philanthropy, and that triumph over the rage of vulgar
prejudice, without which man is inferior to himself, and a
companion of common animals. To know whom she shall regard or dislike, she asks what country they are of, what religion they profess, and what property they enjoy. Her idea of
national honour seems to consist in national insult, and that
to be a great people, is to be neither a christian, a philosopher, or a gentleman, but to threaten with the rudeness of a
bear, and to devour with the ferocity of a lion. This perhaps
may sound harsh and uncourtly, but it is too true, and the
more is the pity.

I mention this only as her general character. But towards
America she has observed no character at all, and destroyed
by her conduct what she assumed in her title. She set out with
the stile of *Parent* or *Mother Country*. The association of ideas
which naturally accompany this expression are filled with
every thing that is fond, tender, and forbearing. They have an
energy particular to themselves, and overlooking the accidental attachment of common affections, apply with peculiar soft-
ness to the first feelings of the heart. It is a political term
which every mother can feel the force of, and every child can

judge of. It needs no painting of mine to set it off, for nature only can do it justice.

But has any part of your conduct to America corresponded with the title you set up? If in your general national character you are unpolished and severe, in this you are inconsistent and unnatural; and you must have exceeding false notions of national honour, to suppose that the world can admire a want of humanity, or that national honour depends on the violence of resentment, the inflexibility of temper, or the vengeance of execution.

I would willingly convince you, and that with as much temper as the times will suffer me to do, that as you opposed your own interest by quarreling with us, so likewise your national honour, rightly conceived and understood, was no ways called upon to enter into a war with America. Had you studied true greatness of heart, the first and fairest ornament of mankind, you would have acted directly contrary to all that you have done, and the world would have ascribed it to a generous cause, besides which, you had (*though with the assistance of this country*) secured a powerful name by the last war. You were known and dreaded abroad; and it would have been wise in you to have suffered the world to have slept undisturbed under that idea. It was to you, a force existing without expence. It produced to you all the advantages of real power; and you were stronger through the universality of *that charm* than any future fleets and armies may probably make you. Your greatness was so secured and interwoven with your silence that you ought never to have awakened mankind, and had nothing to do but to be quiet. Had you been true politicians you would have seen all this, and continued to draw from the magic of a name, the force and authority of a nation.

Unwise as you were in breaking the charm, you were still more unwise in the manner of doing it. *Sampson* only *told the secret*, but *you* have *performed the operation*; you have shaven your own head, and wantonly thrown away the locks. America was the hair from which the charm was drawn that infatuated the world. You ought to have quarrelled with *no* power; but with *her* upon *no* account. You had nothing to fear from any condescension you might make. You might have humoured her, even if there had been no justice in her claims, without any risk to your reputation; for Europe fascinated by your fame, would have ascribed it to your beneficence, and America, intoxicated by the grant, would have slumbered in her fetters.

But this method of studying the progress of the passions, in order to ascertain the probable conduct of mankind, is a philosophy in politics, which those who preside at St. James's have no conceptions of. They know no other influence than corruption, and reckon all their probabilities from precedent. A new case is to them a new world, and while they are seeking for a parallel they get lost. The talents of Lord Mansfield can be estimated at best no higher than those of a Sophist. He understands the subtleties but not the elegance of nature; and by continually viewing mankind through the cold medium of the law, never thinks of penetrating into the warmer region of the mind. As for Lord North, it is his happiness to have in him more philosophy than sentiment, for he bears flogging like a top and sleeps the better for it. His punishment becomes his support, for while he suffers the lash for his sins, he keeps himself up by twirling about. In politics, he is a good arithmetician, and in every thing else nothing at all.

There is one circumstance which comes so much within Lord North's province as a financer, that I am surprised it should escape him, which is, the different abilities of the two countries in supporting the expence; for, strange as it may seem, England is not a match for America in this particular. By a curious kind of revolution in accounts, the people of England seem to mistake their poverty for their riches, that is, they reckon their national debt as a part of their national wealth. They make the same kind of error which a man would do, who after mortgaging his estate, should add the money borrowed, to the full value of the estate in order to count up his worth, and in this case he would conceit that he got rich by running into debt. Just thus it is with England. The Government owed at the beginning of this war One Hundred and Thirty-five millions sterling, and though the individuals to whom it was due, had a right to reckon their shares as so much private property yet to the nation collectively it was so much poverty. There is as effectual limits to public debts as to private ones, for when once the money borrowed is so great

as to require the whole yearly revenue to discharge the interest thereon, there is an end to all farther borrowing; in the
same manner as when the interest of a man's debts amounts
to the yearly income of his estate there is an end to his credit.
This is nearly the case with England, the interest of her
present debt being at least equal to one half of her yearly
revenue, so that out of Ten Million annually collected by
taxes, she has but Five she can call her own.

The very reverse of this was the case with America. She
began the war without any debt upon her, and in order to
carry it on, she neither raised money by taxes, nor borrowed it
upon interest, but *created* it, and her situation, at this time,
continues so much the reverse of yours, that taxing would
make her rich, whereas it would make you poor. When we
shall have sunk the sum which we have created, we shall then
be out of debt, be just as rich as when we began, and all the
while we are doing it, shall feel no difference, because the
value will rise as the quantity decreases.

There was not a country in the world so capable of bearing
the expence of a war as America; not only because she was not
in debt when she began, but because the country is young
and capable of infinite improvement, and has an almost
boundless tract of new lands in store; whereas England has
got to her extent of age and growth, and has no unoccupied
lands or property in reserve. The one is like a young heir coming to a large improveable estate; the other like an old man
whose chances are over, and his estate mortgaged for half its
worth.

In the second number of the Crisis, which I find has been
re-published in England, I endeavoured to set forth the im-
practicability of conquering America. I stated every case, that
I conceived could possibly happen, and ventured to predict its
consequences. As my conclusions were drawn not artfully but
naturally, they have all proved to be true. I was upon the
spot; knew the politics of America, her strength and resources, and by a train of services, the best in my power to
render, was honoured with the friendship a Congress, the
army and the people. I considered the cause a just one. I
know and feel it a just one, and under that confidence never
made my own profit or loss an object. My endeavour was to

have the matter well understood on both sides, and I conceived myself rendering a general service, by setting forth to the one the impossibility of being conquered, and to the other the impossibility of conquering. Most of the arguments made use of by the Ministry for supporting the war, are the very arguments that ought to have been used against supporting it; and the plans, by which they thought to conquer, are the very plans in which they were sure to be defeated. They have taken every thing up at the wrong end. Their ignorance is astonishing, and were you in my situation you would see it. They may perhaps have your confidence, but I am persuaded they would make very indifferent Members of Congress. I know what England is, and what America is, and from this compound of knowledge, am better enabled to judge of the issue, than what the King or any of his Ministers can be.

In this number I have endeavoured to shew the ill policy and disadvantages of the war. I believe many of my remarks are new. Those which are not so, I have studied to improve and place in a manner that may be clear and striking. Your failure is, I am persuaded, as certain as fate. America is above your reach. She is at least your equal in the world, and her Independence neither rests upon your consent, or can be prevented by your arms. In short, you spend your substance in vain, and impoverish yourselves without a hope.

But suppose you had conquered America, what advantage, collectively or individually, as merchants, manufacturers, or conquerors, could you have looked for. This is an object you never seem to have attended to. Listening for the sound of victory, and led away by the phrensy of arms, you neglected to reckon either the cost or the consequences. You must all pay towards the expence; the poorest among you must bear his share, and it is both your right and your duty to weigh seriously the matter. Had America been conquered, she might have been parcelled out in grants to the favourites at court, but no share of it would have fallen to you. Your taxes would not have been lessened, because she would have been in no condition to have paid any towards your relief. We are rich by a contrivance of our own, which would have ceased as soon as you became masters. Our paper money will be of no use in England, and gold and silver we have none. In the last war you made many conquests, but were any of your taxes lessened thereby? On the contrary, were you not taxed to pay for the charge of making them, and have not the same been the case in every war?

To the Parliament I beg to address myself in a particular manner. They appear to have supposed themselves partners in the chace, and to have hunted with the lion from an expectation of a right in the booty; but in this it is most probable they would, as legislators, have been disappointed. The case is quite a new one, and many unforeseen difficulties would have arisen thereon. The Parliament claimed a legislative right over America, and the war originated from that pretence. But the army is supposed to belong to the crown, and if America had been conquered through their means, the claim of the Legislature would have been suffocated in the conquest. Ceded or conquered countries are supposed to be out of the authority of Parliament. Taxation is exercised over them by prerogative and not by law. It was attempted to be done in the Granades a few years ago, and the only reason why it was not done was because the crown had made a prior relinquishment of its claim. Therefore, Parliament have been all this while supporting measures for the establishment of their authority, in the issue of which, they would have been triumphed over by the prerogative. This might have opened a new and interesting opposition between the Parliament and the Crown. The Crown would have said that it conquered for itself, and that to conquer for Parliament was an unknown case. The Parliament might have replied, that America not being a *foreign* country, but only a country in *rebellion*, could not be said to be *conquered*, but *reduced*; and thus continued their claim by disowning the term. The Crown might have rejoined, that however America might be considered at *first*, she became foreign at *last* by a declaration of Independence and a *treaty with France*; and that her case being, by *that treaty*, put within the law of nations, was out of the law of Parliament. The Parliament might have maintained, that as their claim over America had never been *surrendered*, so neither could it be *taken away*. The Crown might have insisted, that though the claim of Parliament could *not be taken away*, yet being an *inferior* it might be *superceded*; and that, whether the claim was withdrawn from the object, or the object taken from the claim, the same separation ensued; and that America being subdued after a treaty with France, was to all intents and purposes a regal conquest, and of course the sole property of the King. The Parliament, as the legal delegates of the people, might have contended against the term *"inferior"* and rested the case upon the antiquity of power, and this would have brought on a set of interesting and rational questions.

First, What is the original fountain of power and honour in any country?

Secondly, Whether the prerogative does not belong to the people?

Thirdly, Whether there is any such a thing as the English constitution?

Fourthly, Of what use is the Crown to the people?

Fifthly, Whether he who invented a crown was not an enemy to mankind?

Sixthly, Whether it is not a shame for a man to spend a million a year and do no good for it, and whether the money might not be better applied?

Seventhly, Whether such a man is not better dead than alive?

Eighthly, Whether a Congress, constituted like that of America, is not the most happy and consistent form of government in the world? —With a number of others of the same import.

In short, the contention about the dividend might have distracted the nation; for nothing is more common than to agree in the conquest and quarrel for the prize; therefore it is, perhaps, a happy circumstance that our successes have prevented the dispute.

If the Parliament had been thrown out in *their* claim, which it is most probable they would, the nation likewise would have been thrown out in *their* expectation; for as the taxes would have been laid on by the Crown without the Parliament, the revenue arising therefrom, if any could have arose, would not have gone into the Exchequer, but into the privy purse, and so far from lessening their taxes, would not even have been added to them, but served only as pocket money to the Crown. The more I reflect on this matter the more am I astonished at the blindness and ill policy of my countrymen, whose wisdom seem to operate without discernment, and their strength without an object.

To the great bulwark of the nation, I mean the mercantile and manufacturing part thereof, I likewise present my address. It is your interest to see America an independent country and *not* a conquered one. If conquered, she is ruined; and if ruined, poor; consequently the trade will be a trifle, and her credit doubtful. If independent she flourish, and from *her flourishing* must *your profits* arise. It matters nothing to you who governs America, if your manufactures find a consumption there. Some articles will consequently be obtained from other places, and right they should, but the demand of others will encrease by the great influx of inhabitants which a state of independence and peace will occasion, and on the final event you may be enriched. The commerce of America is perfectly free, and ever will be so. She will consign away no part of it to any nation. She has not to her friends, and certainly will not to her enemies, though it is probable that your narrow minded politicians, thinking to please you thereby, may some time or other make such an unnecessary proposal. Trade flourishes best when it is free, and it is weak policy to attempt to fetter it. Her treaty with France is on the most liberal and generous principles, and the French in their conduct towards her has proved themselves to be philosophers, politicians and gentlemen.

To the Ministry I likewise address myself. You, gentlemen, have studied the ruin of your country, from which it is not within your abilities to rescue her. Your attempts to recover are as ridiculous as your plans which involved her are detestable. The Commissioners being about to depart, will probably bring you this, and with it my sixth number to them; and in so doing they carry back more *Common Sense* than they brought, and you likewise will have more than when you sent them.

Having thus addressed you severally, I conclude by addressing you collectively. It is a long lane that has no turning. A period of sixteen years of misconduct and misfortune, is certainly long enough for any one nation to suffer under; and upon a supposition that war is not declared between France and you, I beg to place a line of conduct before you that will easily lead you out of all your troubles. It has been hinted before, and cannot be too much attended to.

Suppose America had remained unknown to Europe till the present year, and that Mr. Banks and Dr. Solander, in another voyage round the world, had made the first discovery of her, in the self same condition she is now in of arts, arms, numbers, and civilization. What I ask in that case, would have been your conduct towards her, for *that* will point out what it ought to be now? The problems and their solutions are equal, and the right line of the one is the parallel of the other. The question takes in every circumstance that can possibly arise. It reduces politics to a simple thought, and is moreover a mode of investigation, in which, while you are studying your interest, the simplicity of the case will cheat you into good temper. You have nothing to do but to suppose you have found America and she appears sound to your hand, and while in the joy of your heart you stand still to admire her, the path of politics rises strait before you.

Were I disposed to paint a contrast, I could easily set off what you *have done* in the *present case* against what you *would have done* in *that case,* and by justly opposing them, conclude a picture that would make you blush. But as when any of the prouder passions are hurt, it is much better philosophy to let a man slip into a good temper than to attack him in a bad one: for that reason therefore, I only state the case and leave yourselves to reflect upon it.

To go a little back into politics, it will be found, that the true interest of Britain lay in proposing and promoting the independence of America immediately after the last peace, for the expence which Britain had then incurred by defending America as HER OWN DOMINIONS, ought to have shewn her the policy and necessity of changing the *stile* of the country, as the *best* probable method of preventing future wars and expence, and the *only* method by which she could hold the commerce without the charge of sovereignty. Besides which, the title she assumed of *Parent country* naturally led to, and pointed out, the propriety, wisdom and advantage of a separation; for as in private life children grow into men, and by setting up for themselves extend and secure the interest of the whole family, so in the settlement of colonies large enough to admit of maturity, the same policy should be pursued and the same consequences would follow. Nothing hurts the affections both of parents and children so much, as living too closely connected, and keeping up the distinction too long. Domineering will not do over those, who by a progress in life are become equal in rank to their parents, that is, when they have families of their own; and though they may conceive themselves the subjects of their advice, will not suppose themselves the objects of their government. I do not, by drawing this parallel, mean to admit the title of *Parent country*, because, if due any where, it is due to Europe collectively and the first settlers from England were driven here by persecution. I mean only to introduce the term for the sake of the policy, and to show from your title, the line of your interest.

When you saw the state of strength and opulence, and that by her own industry, which America had arrived at, you ought to have advised her to have set up for herself, and proposed an alliance of interest with her, and in so doing, you would have drawn, and that at her *own* expence, more real advantage, and more military supplies and assistance both of ships and men, than from any weak and wrangling government you could exercise over her. In short, had you studied only the domestic politics of a family, you would have learned how to govern the state; but instead of this easy and natural line, you flew out into every thing which was wild and outrageous, till by following the passion and stupidity of the pilot you wrecked the vessel within sight of the shore.

Having shown what you *ought to have done*, I now proceed to shew the reason why it was *not done*. The caterpillar circle of the Court, had an interest to pursue distinct from, and opposed to yours, for though by the independence of America and an alliance therewith, the trade would have continued if not encreased, as in many articles neither country can go to a better market, and though by defending and protecting herself, she would have been no expence to you, and consequently your national charges would have decreased and your taxes might have been proportionably lessened thereby, yet the striking off so many places from the Court Calendar was put in opposition to the interests of the nation. The loss of thirteen governmentships with their appendages here and in England is a shocking sound to the ear of a hungry courtier. Your present King and Ministry will be the ruin of you; and you had better risk a revolution and call a Congress than be thus led on from madness to despair, and from despair to ruin. America has set you the example, and may you follow it and be free.

I now come to the last part, *a war with France.* This is what no man in his senses will advise you to, and all good men would wish to prevent. Whether France will declare war against you, is not for me in this place to mention or to hint even if I knew it, but it must be madness in you to do it first. The matter is now come to a *full crisis,* and peace is easy if willingly set about. Whatever you may think, France has behaved handsomely to you. She would have been unjust to herself to have acted otherwise than she did; and having accepted our offer of alliance, she gave you genteel notice of it. There was nothing in her conduct reserved or indelicate, and while she announced her determination to support her treaty she left you to give the first offence. America, on her part, has exhibited a character of firmness to the world. Unprepared and unarmed, without form or government she singly opposed a nation that domineered over half the globe. The greatness of the deed demands respect; and though you may feel resentment, you are compelled both to WONDER and ADMIRE.

HERE I rest my arguments and finish my address. Such as it is, it is a gift and you are welcome. It was always my design to dedicate a *Crisis* to you, when the time should come that would properly *make it a Crisis;* and when, likewise, I should catch myself in a temper to write it, and suppose you in a condition to read it. *That* time is now arrived, and with it, the opportunity of conveyance. For the Commissioners—*poor Commissioners!*—having proclaimed, that *"yet forty days and Ninevah shall be overthrown,"* have waited out the date, and discontented with their God, are returning to their goard. And all the harm I wish them is, that it may not *wither* about their ears, and that they may not make their exit in the belly of a Whale.

COMMON SENSE.

Philadelphia, November 11, 1778.

P. S. Though in the tranquility of my mind I have concluded with a laugh, yet I have something to mention to the *Commissioners*, which to them is serious and worthy their attention. Their authority is derived from an act of Parliament which likewise describes and *limits* their *official* powers. Their commission, therefore, is only a recital, and personal investiture, of those powers, or a nomination and description of the persons who are to execute them. Had it contained any thing contrary to, or gone beyond the line of, the written law from which it is derived and by which it is bound, it would, by the English constitution, have been treason in the Crown, and the King been subject to an impeachment. He dared not, therefore, have put in his commission what you have put into your proclamation, that is, he dared not have authorised you in that commission to burn and destroy, or to threaten to burn and destroy, any thing in America. You are both in the *Act* and in the *Commission* stiled *Commissioners for restoring peace,* and the methods for doing it are there pointed out. Your last proclamation is signed by you as Commissioners *under that Act.* You make Parliament the patron of its contents. Yet in the body of it, you insert matters contrary both to the spirit and letter of the Act, and what likewise your King dared not have put in his commission to you. The state of things in England, Gentlemen, is too ticklish for you to run hazards. You are *accountable to Parliament for the execution of that Act according to the letter of it.* Your heads may pay for breaking it, for you certainly have broke it by exceeding it. And as a friend, who would wish you to escape the paw of the Lion as well as the belly of the Whale, I civilly hint to you, *to keep within compass.*

Sir Harry Clinton, strictly speaking, is as accountable as the rest; for though a General, he is likewise a Commissioner, acting under a superior authority. His first obedience is to the Act; and his plea of being a General will not and cannot clear him as a Commissioner, for that would suppose the Crown, in its single capacity, to have a power of dispensing with an Act of Parliament. Your situations, Gentlemen, are nice and critical, and the more so because England is unsettled. Take heed! Remember the times of Charles the first! For Laud and Strafford fell by trusting to a hope like yours.

Having thus shewn you the danger of your proclamation, I now shew you the folly of it. The means contradict the design. You threatened to lay waste in order to render America a useless acquisition of alliance to France. I reply, that the more destruction you commit (if you could do it) the more valuable to France would you make that alliance. You can destroy only houses and goods; and by so doing you encrease our demand upon her for materials and merchandize, for the wants of one nation, provided it has FREEDOM and CREDIT, naturally produces riches to the other; and as you can neither ruin the land nor prevent the vegitation, you would encrease the exportation of our produce as payment, which to her would be a new fund of wealth. In short, had you cast about for a plan on purpose to enrich your enemies you could not have hit upon a better.

C. S.

Portion of a Letter to Henry Laurens

1778?

As we are forming Government on a new system, *that of representation*, I will give you my thoughts on the various classes and merits of men in society so far as relates to each other.

The first useful class of citizens are the farmers and cultivators. These may be called citizens of the first necessity, because every thing comes originally from the earth.

After these follow the various orders of manufacturers and mechanics of every kind. These differ from the first class in this particular, that they contribute to the accommodation rather than to the first necessities of life.

Next follow those called merchants and shopkeepers. These are occasionally convenient but not important. They produce nothing themselves as the two first classes do, but employ their time in exchanging one thing for another and living by the profits.

Perhaps you will say that in this classification of citizens I have marked no place for myself; that I am neither farmer, manufacturer, mechanic, merchant nor shopkeeper. I believe, however, I am of the first class. I am *a Farmer of thoughts*, and as all the crops I raise I give away, I please myself with making you a present of the thoughts in this letter.

Response to "Observations on the American Revolution"

March 20, 1779

FOR THE PENNSYLVANIA PACKET.

MR. DUNLAP,

THROUGH the channel of your paper, I take the liberty of remarking on a passage in a pamphlet just come into my hands, entitled, *"Observations on the American Revolution, published according to a Resolution of Congress. By their Committee."*

The gentlemen who, principally, if not wholly, conducted this work were Governeur Morriss, Esq; Delegate from the state of New-York, and W. H. Drayton, Esq; late Delegate from South-Carolina; and of those two Mr. Morriss had the chief share. Consequently, the honours or errors it contain, are claimable by, or chargeable on, the compilers and conductors only.

The work consists of a collection of the principal state papers, which are connected with the rise and progress of the present revolution, and are arranged in the following order:

A part of the proceedings of Congress in 1774. The motion, commonly called Lord North's conciliatory motion, in February, 1775, and the resolution of Congress thereon. A paper delivered to Congress by a British emissary. Resolutions of Congress respecting the defence of New York. Declaratory reasons of Congress for taking up arms, dated July 6th, 1775. Petition of Congress to the King of England July 8th, 1775. Address to the people of Great-Britain, July 8th, 1775. Resolutions of Congress, for granting commissions to privateers, of November 29th, 1775, and March 23d, 1776. Resolution of Congress recommending the taking up new governments, May 15th, 1776. Declaration of Independence, July 4th, 1776. Conference on Staten-Island with Lord Howe, reported September 17th, by the Committee of Congress appointed on that business. Draught of the bills of the British Parliament, received by Congress at York-Town April the 21st, 1778, and the resolutions of Congress thereon, April 22d, 1778. Address of Congress to the people of America, May 4th, 1778. Collection of letters, &c. &c. which passed between Congress and the British Commissioners. The work closes with the Proclamation and Manifesto of the said British Commissioners, dated New-York, October 3d, 1778, and the Manifesto of Congress in answer thereto, October 30th, 1778. The greatest part, if not the whole, of those publications, have, at different times, appeared in most of the Newspapers on the continent.

The above making up the substance of the work, the only thing that is new in it is the historical connection by which the several declarations, resolutions, &c. are formed into a continued chain, and in this part there is an evident defect amounting to injustice.

It cannot be supposed that the historical part should be compleat in so short a compass, but that is no reason that it should be unjust in the gross; and as Mr. Morriss and Mr. Drayton are the only persons accountable for the defect I shall here take notice of, to them, only, I address these remarks.

The reader, by casting his eye on the arrangement of papers in the order in which I have placed them, which is the order they stand in in the pamphlet, will see there is a skip (a flying over I may call it) from the conference on Staten Island, September 1776, to the receipt of the British bills at York-Town, April 21st, 1778. I shall give the paragraph entire, (for there is but one) which unites those two events so widely distant in time, and, on the part of the enemy, so different in complexion.

Page 6: "From this moment," that is, from the conference on Staten-Island, "the war raged with the utmost violence, and was prosecuted by the enemy with unabated vigour and barbarity. To recite the numerous instances in which their faith, solemnly pledged, hath been broken, would be tedious and perhaps useless: Victory declared herself for a long time in favour of their superior numbers and superior discipline, and their insolence was equal to their success. Unable to comprehend the whole of the object they had undertaken, and over-joyed at the acquisition of the minuter parts, already the needy, greedy parasites of a voluptuous court had, in imagination, carved out our possessions among them, and wantoned in the prospect of enjoying the fruits of our laborious industry. Every thing, therefore, which looked like conciliation was treated as a concession flowing from feebleness of soul. The spirit of despotism, flushed with hope and inured to guilt, turned a *hard, unfeeling eye* upon the miseries of human nature, and directed, well pleased, the storm of vengeance on the head of freedom. *But that full tide of success which had carried their expectations so high, began to ebb away: The gallant army, commanded by Burgoyne, checked by impediments which nature had thrown in his course,* at length submitted, notwithstanding the efforts of their accomplished General, to the determined bravery of their foes. The splendor of our success in that quarter called the attention of Europe to our fortitude and perseverance. The weight and importance of a country which could resist the astonishing efforts made by Great-Britain, were evident to the most careless observation. The acknowledgment of our Independence became therefore an object of serious deliberation. Awakened from their dream of glory to a view of their danger, the Ministry of England determined, if possible, to recover what they had wantonly thrown away.

"On the 21st day of April, 1778, the Congress, then sitting at York-Town, received a letter from the General inclosing a printed paper from Philadelphia to the following effect:

"Draught of a bill for declaring the intentions of the Parliament of Great-Britain," &c. &c. &c.

I have marked the exceptionable parts in italics. The first, which is immaterial to the history, though of some moment to the writer, is a false rhetorical figure, for "*hard* and *unfeeling*" are not, in any case, properties of the eye, but sentimentally, of the heart. A hard unfeeling—heart; a deaf—ear; and a scornful—eye; are epithets expressive of possible qualities in the parts they are applied to: But according to this gentleman's derangement of them, he might as well say a scornful ear or a deaf eye. A man must be but little acquainted with feelings, not to know which is their place of residence.

As the sense of the reader would have supplied the above defect in the writer, I should not have gone out of my way to have made the remark, had it been in any other paragraph than that which I have quoted, on account of a more important inattention.

The insolence of the enemy after the engagement on Long Island, and their barbarity after taking Fort Washington, were far greater than their vigor at any one time of that campaign. I speak this from better knowledge than either Mr. Morriss or Mr. Drayton can have, as I was out with the army from the first marching of the associators early in August, and after their return was with General Green at Fort Lee till the evacuation and continued with the army till after their passing the Delaware on the eighth of December. I had began the first number of the Crisis while on the retreat at Newark, with a design of publishing it in the Jersies, as it was Gen. Washington's intentions to have made a stand at Newark, could he have been timely reinforced instead of which, near half the army left him at that place, or soon after, their time being out.

To use a plain phrase, the enemy were then masters of the field, and had it in their power to carry every thing before them. "Flushed with hope and inured to guilt," and in full expectation of conquest, their confidence betrayed them into carelessness, and enabled General Washington to defeat them by a spirited and judicious improvement of their neglects: And I ask Mr. Morriss and Mr. Drayton, *when it was* that their, the enemy's, "*full tide of success began to ebb away?*" Truth will, and history ought to say, that it turned at Trenton and was additionally impelled by the subsequent, and more masterly, stroke at Princeton. These two actions disabled and laid the enemy dormant for more than six months afterwards; and by throwing a spirit of joy into the continent gave life and vigor to the recruiting service for the next campaign. They were hard bought victories, under every disadvantage of winter and misfortune. But the tide, once turned, went on, and the conquest of Burgoyne was, properly speaking, the high water mark of our successes.

Why Mr. Morriss and Mr. Drayton have, in utter silence, passed over the affairs of Trenton and Princeton, and taken a flight from Staten-Island to Saratoga, I cannot conceive. As historians they have reversed the line of facts, and as writers they have not made the most of their metaphor; for had they given honor where it was justly due, and shewn where the tide *began* to turn in *our* favor, it would have enabled them to have shewn its full encrease in the reduction of Burgoyne, where they have only placed its beginning.

The remains of the army which at that time continued with Gen. Washington, and the citizens of this state and of Jersey, who turned out to repel the torrent which threatened distruction to America, must feel themselves injured by such a partial representation, published under the authority of a Committee of Congress. Their services are done away, as if they had never been; and an omission, amounting to oblivion, stands as a contradiction to the fact. This could not unintentionally happen, as the natural order both of time and circumstances threw the whole in their way, and half a page, judiciously compiled, would have united the several links of the chain. I wonder that the metaphor of a tide should not revive in Mr. Drayton an idea of its progress; as he has, I am told, been an *Admiral*—of the *yellow*, I suppose.

But this is not the only injustice in the paragraph I have quoted. The compilers say, that "the gallant army commanded by Burgoyne, checked by impediments *which nature had thrown in his course*, at length submitted, notwithstanding the efforts of their accomplished General, to the determined bravery of their foes."

The conquest at Bennington by General Stark, which laid the foundation of Burgoyne's defeat, is here unjustly buried under a general description of *impediments which nature threw in his course.*

There is no part in the pamphlet, where half a dozen pages might have been employed to more honour and advantage, than in concisely setting forth the principal circumstances which passed between the conference on Staten-Island and the arrival of the draughts of the British bills at York-Town; for the want of which, the circumstantial connection is lost, and that which is omitted, as well as that which is told, have an appearance of injustice.

Mr. Morriss and Mr. Drayton have each of them been so exceedingly industrious in supporting Mr. Deane's impositions, that they seem not to have had time to attend any other kind of duty, and as, I believe, Mr. Deane is now looked on by half that House as a dishonest man, and the other half dare not support him, it will become these two gentlemen to show on what grounds they have abetted him. The suspicions against Mr. Deane are now too strong to be suffocated, and the evidence too full to be rejected or explained away, and he can but perceive that his character is every day sinking with the public—That he negociated a profered present into a purchase, and either stole, or was privy to the stealing the dispatches to cover the imposition, are circumstances which I have no reason to disbelieve.

COMMON SENSE.

P. S. As the pamphlet I have referred to is sent to all the states, the Printers in each will do an act of justice to those whose merits are in that performance so greatly neglected, by inserting this piece in their papers.

C— S—.

Response to the Riot Outside
James Wilson's House

October 16, 1779

SIR,

WHEN passion and mistake give way to candor and benevolence, we sensibly forget the injury in contemplating the effect, and pay a reverence to virtue tho' provoked into action by a fault. The late unfortunate affair of the fourth inst. will, to different minds, administer a different medicine. Surviving relations will feel as nature teaches, their part requires no invention, needs no apology, and whoever were to blame they are to be pitied. Those who unfortunately fell on either side, have paid a martyrdom to mistake, and distinguished themselves as the lamented victims of wasted bravery. In the softer sentiments of a thoughtful world, the whole affair will become a subject of concern; and the only consolation it affords is the hope of seeing the same degree of spirit exerted against the enemy, which, warped by error and aggravated by passion, produced a tumult in which no one enemy fell.

The countenance of the city during that affair, wore an unusual contemplative gloominess. It had nothing of that heated appearance which accompanies the disturbances of other countries, and was totally void of that eagerness of enterprise which takes place against a known enemy. Neither Whig nor Tory could rejoice; all were at a stand; concern produced in the one what dread created in the other; and for once the city was afflictedly united.

Neither can I see any hope the enemy can derive, when they learn the story with its causes and consequences. As a misfortune which we lament, it may to them become a matter of malignant joy; but it promises them nothing; it neither gives encouragement to their arms, nor invitation to their artifice; it neither indicates unwillingness to the field, nor wariness in resisting. On the contrary, it holds out to them a redundancy of zeal, a vehemence of spirit, which, however injudicious in its plans, or unfortunate in its effects, was intentionally aimed at their abettors.

It was the fourth of October. The anniversary of the action at Germantown. A day, distinguished by perplexities and consigned to misfortune. Whether the circumstance occurred at the time the matter was concerted, is what I have not authority even to guess upon, but be that as it may, we cannot but lament that the events of the evening should, in both instances, close with a tear the spirits of the morning.

As it is one of those occurrences which it is unpleasant to enquire into, I wish not to know more than I already know, nor indulge any other thoughts on the subjects than what may tend to abate the painfulness of remembrance, and extinguish the acrimony which error may have kindled. It is over, and thank God it was no worse. But were nothing said the matter might suffer abroad by aggravated misrepresentation. The deaths of three men might be multiplied into as many hundreds, and perpetuity be added to the contention of an hour.

That nothing more was meant by those who assembled on the Commons than to remove persons suspected of disaffection, is universally consented to, and in this light their design was naturally prompted by an attachment to the cause of an injured country. The difficulty of attempting such a measure, the hazard of executing it, and the consequences which might probably ensue, without first obtaining an authoritative sanction and consent, were matters which do not always accompany an excess of zeal. Those whose talent it is to act, are seldom much devoted to deliberate thinking; and feeling that they mean well they suppose it impossible to be wrong, and in the confidence of success overlook the trouble that lies concealed. Where is the man who has not, in his turn, exclaimed, that the Tories ought to be removed; and who had those men laid hold of, that could be deemed a Whig? The measure, while it existed in words, was a measure of popularity; and every one who has promoted it in conversation, has prompted them on.

On what occasion, or by what contrivance a number of Gentlemen were brought together in Mr. Wilson's house, makes up the most mysterious part of the business. As far as I can discover, I cannot find the least trace whereon to conclude that any one who went there had the least reason to be apprehensive of his own safety. They must, in general, have been induced by misrepresentation tho' some, I am well assured, were led by a generous intention of preventing mischief; and pity it is their advice was not taken. That Mr. Wilson is not a favourite in the State, is a matter which, I presume, he is fully sensible of, yet the difference is exceedingly great, between not being in favor and being considered as an enemy. But that he who never armed when the country was in danger, should arm his house to provoke danger, and draw to it a number of Gentlemen at the hazard of their lives, when a timely application to the Civil Power might have prevented every thing, was at once both unconstitutional and unfriendly, a disregard to the laws of the State and the peace of the city. By this imprudent conduct, parties became pitted who knew not each other; and that which had the appearance of a challenge, produced an action.

The affliction which followed, soon extended itself over the city. Every one asked what was the matter; how it began; who were the persons, with every other question of curiosity concern, and still the matter was inveloped in darkness; some supposed one thing, and some another, without being able to satisfy themselves or those who enquired. But when the parties in and out of the house were known, and became known to each other, the animosity began to subside; and the whole, exclusive of the imprudence, explained itself into a tragedy of errors.

It generally happens that distress is the forerunner of benevolence; at least it serves to quicken into action that which might otherwise take a longer time to awake. The sickness which has so generally prevailed through the city, added to the misfortune already mentioned, has been the means of setting on foot two well intended subscriptions; the one for the relief of the families of those who were killed or wounded on the fourth instant, the other for relief of the sick and distressed in the several wards. Both of them have been liberally supported; and most of the persons both in and out of the house, who could afford it, have been ample contributors.

How different this, to that spirit of rancor which generally accompanies, and most assuredly succeeds, premeditated domestic feuds. It calls back the mind to a state of serenity; and shews, by the most convincing proofs, that the affair, now too late to be remedied, was not the quarrel of enemies or of parties, but the unfortunate blunder of friends.

C—— S——.

The Crisis

NUMBER VIII

February 26, 1780

ADDRESSED TO THE PEOPLE OF ENGLAND,
BY THE AUTHOR OF COMMON SENSE.

"Trusting, (says the King of England in his speech of November last) in the Divine Providence, and in the justice of my cause, I am firmly resolved to prosecute the war with vigor, and to make every exertion in order to compel our enemies to equitable terms of peace and accommodation." To this declaration the United States of America and the Confederated Powers of Europe, will reply, *If Britain will have war, she shall have enough of it.*

Five years have nearly elapsed since the commencement of hostilities, and every campaign, by a gradual decay, has lessened your ability to conquer, without producing in you a serious thought on your condition or your fate. Like a prodigal lingering in an habitual consumption, you feel the relicks of life and mistake them for recovery. New schemes, like new medicines, have administered fresh hopes and prolonged the disease instead of curing it. A change of Generals, like a change of physicians, served only to keep the flattery alive, and furnish new pretences for new extravagance.

*"Can Britain fail?"** has been proudly asked at the commencement of every enterprize, and that *"whatever she wills is fate,"*† has been given with the solemnity of prophetic confidence, and tho' the question has been constantly replied to by disappointment, and the prediction falsified by misfortune, yet still the insult continued, and your catalogue of national evils encreased therewith. Eager to persuade the world of her power, she considered destruction as the minister of greatness, and conceived that the glory of a nation, like that of

---

*Whitehead's new-years ode for 1776.
†Ode at the installation of Lord North for Chancellor of the University of Oxford.

an Indian, lay in the number of its scalps and the miseries it inflicts.

Fire, sword and want, as far as the arms of Britain could extend them, have been spread with wanton cruelty along the coast of America; and while you, remote from the scene of suffering, had nothing to lose and as little to dread, the information reached you like a tale of antiquity, in which the distance of time defaces the conception, and changes the severest sorrows into conversable amusement.

This makes the second paper, addressed perhaps in vain, to the people of England. That advice should be taken where example has failed, or precept be regarded where warning is ridiculed, is like a picture of hope resting on dispair: But when time shall stamp with universal currency, the facts you have long encountered with a laugh, and the irresistible evidence of accumulated losses, like the hand writing on the wall, shall add terror to distress, you will then, in a conflict of sufferings, learn to sympathise with others by feeling for yourselves.

The triumphant appearance of the combined fleets in the channel and at your harbour's mouth, and the expedition of Captain Paul Jones on the western and eastern coast of England and Scotland, will, by placing you in the condition of an endangered country, read to you a stronger lecture on the calamities of invasion, and bring to your minds a truer picture of promiscuous distress, than the most finished rhetoric can describe or the keenest imagination conceive.

Hitherto you have experienced the expences, but nothing of the miseries of war. Your disappointments have been accompanied with no immediate suffering, and your losses came to you only by intelligence. Like fire at a distance, you heard not even the cry; you felt not the danger, you saw not the confusion. To you every thing has been foreign but the taxes to support it. You knew not what it was to be alarmed at midnight with an armed enemy in the streets. You were strangers to the distressing scene of a family in flight, and to the thousand restless cares and tender sorrows that incessantly arose. To see women and children wandering in the severity of winter with the broken remains of a well furnished house, and seeking shelter in every crib and hut, were matters you had no conception of. You knew not what it was to stand by and see your goods chopt up for fuel, and your beds ript to pieces to make packages for plunder. The misery of others, like a tempestuous night, added to the pleasures of your own security. You even enjoyed the storm, by contemplating the difference of conditions; and that which carried sorrow into the breasts of thousands, served but to heighten in you a species of tranquil pride. Yet these are but the fainter sufferings of war, when compared with carnage and slaughter, the miseries of a military hospital, or a town in flames.

The people of America by anticipating distress had fortified their minds against every species you could inflict. They had resolved to abandon their homes, to resign them to destruction, and to seek new settlements rather than submit. Thus familiarised to misfortune, before it arrived, they bore their portion with the less regret: The justness of their cause was a continual source of consolation, and the hope of final victory, which never left them, served to lighten the load and sweeten the cup alloted them to drink.

But when their sufferings shall become yours, and invasion be transferred upon the invaders, you will have neither their extended wilderness to fly to, their cause to comfort you, nor their hopes to rest on. Distress with them was sharpened by no self-reflection. They had not brought it on themselves. On the contrary, they had by every proceeding endeavoured to avoid it, and had descended even below the mark of congressional character to prevent a war. The national honor or the advantages of independence are matters, which at the commencement of the dispute, they had never studied, and it was only at the last moment that the measure was resolved on. Thus circumstanced, they naturally and conscientiously felt a dependence upon Providence. They had a clear pretension to it, and had they failed therein, infidelity had gained a triumph.

But your condition is the reverse of theirs. Every thing you suffer you have sought; nay, had you created mischiefs on purpose to inherit them, you could not have secured your title by a firmer deed. The world awakens with no pity at your complaints. You felt none for others; you deserve none for yourselves. Nature does not interest herself in cases like yours, but on the contrary turns from them with dislike and abandons them to punishment. You may now present memorials to what Court you please, but so far as America is the object, none will listen. The policy of Europe and the propensity there is in every mind to curb insulting ambition, and bring cruelty to judgment, are unitedly against you; and where nature and interest reinforces each other, the compact is too intimate to be dissolved.

Make but the case of others your own, and your own theirs, and you will then have a clear idea of the whole. Had France acted towards her Colonies as you have done, you would have branded her with every epithet of abhorrence; and had you, like her, stept in to succour a struggling people, all Europe must have echoed with your own applauses. But entangled in the passion of dispute, you see it not as you ought, and form opinions thereon which suit with no interest but your own. You wonder America does not rise in union with you to impose on herself a portion of your taxes and reduce herself to unconditional submission. You are amazed that the Southern Powers of Europe do not assist you in conquering a country which is afterwards to be turned against themselves; and that the northern ones do not contribute to reinstate you in America, who already enjoy the market for naval stores by the separation. You seem surprised that Holland does not pour in her succours to maintain you mistress of the seas, when her own commerce is suffering by your Act of navigation, or that any country should study her own interests while yours is on the carpet.

Such excesses of passionate folly, and unjust as well as unwise resentment, have driven you on, like Pharoah, to unpitied miseries, and while the importance of that quarrel shall perpetuate your disgrace, the flag of America will carry it round the world. The natural feelings of every rational being will take against you, and wherever the story shall be told, you will have neither excuse nor consolation left. With an unsparing hand and an unsatiable mind, you have havocked the world, both to gain dominion and to lose it, and while, in a frenzy of avarice and ambition, the east and west were doomed to tributary bondage, you rapidly earned destruction as the wages of a nation.

At the thoughts of a war at home every man amongst you

ought to tremble. The prospect is far more dreadful there than in America. Here the party that was against the measures of the continent were in general a kind of neutrals who added strength to neither army. There does not exist a being so devoid of sense and sentiment as to covet *"unconditional submission,"* and therefore no man in America could be with you in principle. Several might from a cowardice of mind, *prefer* it to the hardships and dangers of *opposing* it; but the same disposition that gave them such a choice, unfitted them to act either for or against. But England is rent into parties, with equal shares of resolution. The principle which produced the war, divides the nation. Their animosities are in the highest state of fermentation, and both sides by a call of the militia, are in arms. No human foresight can discern, no conclusion can be formed, what turn a war might take, if once set on foot by an invasion. She is not now in a fit disposition, to make a common cause of her own affairs, and having no conquests to hope for abroad, and nothing but expences arising at home, her every thing is staked upon a defensive combat, and the further she goes the worse she is off.

There are situations a nation may be in, in which peace or war, abstracted from every other consideration, may be politically right or wrong. When nothing can be lost by a war, but what must be lost without it, war is then the policy of that country; and such was the situation of America at the commencement of hostilities: But when no security can be gained by a war, but what may be accomplished by a peace, the case becomes reversed, and such now is the situation of England.

That America is beyond the reach of conquest, is a fact which experience has shewn and time confirmed, and this admitted, what, I ask, is now the object in contention? If there be any honor in pursuing self-destruction with inflexible passion; if national suicide be the perfection of national glory, you may, with all the pride of criminal happiness, expire unenvied and unrivalled.—But when the tumult of war shall cease, and the tempest of present passions be succeeded by calm reflection, or when those who surviving its fury, shall inherit from you a legacy of debts and misfortunes, when the yearly revenue shall scarcely be able to discharge the interest of the one, and no possible remedy be left for the other;

ideas, far different to the present, will arise, and embitter the remembrance of former follies. A mind disarmed of its rage, feels no pleasure in contemplating a frantic quarrel. Sickness of thought, the sure consequence of conduct like yours, leaves no ability for enjoyment, no relish for resentment; and tho' like a man in a fit, you feel not the injury of the struggle, nor distinguish between strength and disease, the weakness will nevertheless be proportioned to the violence, and the sense of pain encrease with the recovery.

To what persons or to whose system of politics you owe your present state of wretchedness is a matter of total indifference to America. They have contributed, however unwillingly, to set her above themselves, and she in the tranquility of conquest resigns the enquiry. The case now is not so properly who began the war, as who continues it. That there are men in all countries to whom a state of war is a mine of wealth, is a fact never to be doubted. Characters like these naturally breed in the putrefaction of distempered times, and after fattening on the disease they perish with it, or impregnated with the stench retreat into obscurity.

But there are several erroneous notions to which you likewise owe a share of your misfortunes, and which if continued will only increase your trouble and your losses. An opinion hangs about the gentlemen of the minority, that America would relish measures under *their* administration, which she would not from the present cabinet. On this rock Lord Chatham would have split had he gained the helm, and several of his survivors are steering the same course. Such distinctions in the infancy of the argument had some degree of foundation, but they now serve no other purpose than to lengthen out a war, in which the limits of the dispute, being fixt by the fate of arms, and guarantied by treaties, are not to be changed or altered by trivial circumstances.

The Ministry and many of the minority sacrifice their time in disputing on a question with which they have nothing to do, namely, whether America shall be independant or not? Whereas the only question that can come under their determination, is, whether they will accede to it or not? They confound a military question with a political one, and undertake to supply by a vote what they lost by a battle. Say, she shall not be independant, and it will signify as much as if they voted against a decree of fate, or say that she shall, and she will be no more independant than before. Questions, which when determined, cannot be executed, serve only to shew the folly of dispute and the weakness of disputants.

From a long habit of calling America your own, you suppose her governed by the same prejudices and conceits which govern yourselves. Because you have set up a particular denomination of religion to the exclusion of all others, you imagine she must do the same, and because you, with an unsociable narrowness of mind, have cherished animosity against France and Spain, you suppose her alliance must be defective in friendship. Copying her notions of the world from you, she formerly thought as you instructed, but now feeling herself free, and the prejudice removed, she thinks and acts upon a different system. It frequently happens that in proportion as we are taught to dislike persons and countries not knowing why, we feel an ardor of esteem upon a removal of the mistake; It seems as if something was to be made amends for, and we eagerly give into every office of friendship to attone for the injury of the error.

But perhaps there is something in the extent of countries, which among the generality of people, insensibly communicates extention to the mind. The soul of an Islander in its native State, seems bounded by the foggy confines of the water's edge, and all beyond, affords to him matter only for profit or curiosity, not for friendship. His island is to him his world, and fixt to that his every thing centers in it; while those, who are inhabitants of a continent, by casting their eye over a larger field, takes in likewise a larger intellectual circuit, and thus approaching nearer to an acquaintance with the universe, their atmosphere of thought is extended, and their liberality fills a wider space. In short, our minds seem to be measured by countries when we are men, as they are by places, when we are children, and until something happens to disentangle us from the prejudice, we serve under it without perceiving it.

In addition to this, it may be remarked, that men who study any universal science, the principles of which are universally known, or admitted, and applied without distinction to the common benefit of all countries, obtain thereby a larger share of philanthropy than those who only study national arts and improvements. Natural philosophy, mathematics and astronomy, carry the mind from the country to the creation, and give it a fitness suited to the extent. It was not Newton's honor, neither could it be his pride, that he was an Englishman, but that he was a philosopher: The Heavens had liberated him from the prejudices of an island, and science had expanded his soul as boundless as his studies.

(To be concluded in a subsequent paper.)

The Crisis

NUMBER IX

June 9, 1780

HAD America pursued her advantages with half the spirit she resisted her misfortunes, she would, before now, have been a conquering and a peaceful people; but lulled in the lap of soft tranquility she rested on her hopes, and adversity only has convulsed her into action. Whether subtilty or sincerity at the close of the last year, induced the enemy to an appearance for peace, is a point not material to know; it is sufficient that we see the effects it has had on our politics, and that we sternly rise to resent the delusion.

The war on the part of America, has been a war of natural feeling. Brave in distress; serene in conquest; drowsy when at rest; and in every situation generously disposed to peace. A dangerous calm, and the most heightened zeal, have, as circumstances varied, succeeded each other. Every passion, but that of dispair, has been called to a tour of duty; and so mistaken has been the enemy of our abilities and disposition, that when she supposed us conquered, we rose the conquerors. The extensiveness of the United States and the variety of their resources; the universality of their cause, the quick operation of their feelings, and the similarity of their sentiments, have, in every trying situation, produced a *something*, which favoured by Providence, and pursued with ardour, has accomplished in an instant the business of a campaign. We have never deliberately sought victory, but snatched it; and bravely undone in an hour, the plotted operations of a season.

The reported fate of Charlestown, like the misfortunes of seventy-six, has at last called forth a spirit, and kindled up a flame, which perhaps no other event could have produced. If the enemy has circulated a falsehood, they have unwisely aggravated us into life, and if they have told us a truth, they have unintentionally done us a service. We were returning with folded arms from the fatigues of war and thinking, and sitting leisurely down to enjoy repose. The dependence that has been put upon Charlestown, threw a drowsiness over America. We looked on the business done—the conflict over—the matter settled—or that all which remained unfinished would follow of itself. In this state of dangerous relax, exposed to the poisonous infusions of the enemy, and having no common danger to attract our attention, we were extinguishing by stages the ardour we began with, and surrendering by peacemeals the virtue that defended us.

Afflicting as the loss of Charlestown may be, yet if it universally rouse us from the slumber of a twelve months past, and renew in us the spirit of former days, it will produce an advantage more important than its loss. America ever *is* what she *thinks* herself to be. Governed by sentiment, and acting her own mind, she becomes as she pleases the victor or the victim.

It is not the conquest of towns, nor the accidental capture of garrisons, that can reduce a country so extensive as this. The sufferings of one part can ever be relieved by the exertions of another, and there is no situation the enemy can be in, that does not afford to us, the same advantages she seeks herself. By dividing her force, she leaves every post attackable. It is a mode of war, that carries with it a confession of weakness, and goes on the principle of distress, rather than conquest.

The decline of the enemy is visible not only in their operations but in their plans; Charlestown originally made but a secondary object in their system of attack, and it is now become their principal one, because they have not been able to succeed else where. It would have carried a cowardly appearance in Europe, had they formed their grand expedition in seventy-six, against a part of the Continent, where there was no army, or not a sufficient one to oppose them; but failing year after year, in their impression here, and to the eastward and northward, they deserted their first capital design, and prudently contenting themselves with what they can get, give a flourish of honor to conceal disgrace.

But this piece meal work is not conquering the Continent. It is discredit in them to attempt it, and in us to suffer it. It is now full time to put an end to a war of aggravations, which on one side, has no possible object, and on the other, has every inducement which honor, interest, safety and happiness, can inspire. If we suffer them much longer to remain among us, we shall become as bad as themselves. An association of vices will reduce us more than the sword. A nation hardened in the practice of iniquity, knows better how to profit by it, than a young country newly corrupted. We are not a match for them in the line of advantageous guilt, nor they to us, on the principles we bravely set out with. Our first days were our days of honor. They have marked the character of America wherever the story of her wars are told; and convinced of this, we have nothing to do, but wisely and unitedly to tread the well known track.

The progress of a war, is often as ruinous to individuals, as the issue of it is to a nation; and it is not only necessary that our force be such, that we be conquerors in the end, but that by timely exertions, we be secure in the interim. The present campaign will afford an opportunity which has never presented itself before, and the preparation for it, are equally necessary, whether Charlestown stand or fall. Suppose the first, it is in that case, only a failure of the enemy, not a defeat. All the conquest a besieged town can hope for, is not to be conquered; and compelling an enemy to raise the siege is to the besieged a victory. But there must be a probability amounting almost to certainty, that would justify a garrison marching out to attack a retreat. Therefore should Charlestown *not* be taken, and the enemy abandon the siege, every other part of the Continent should prepare to meet them; and on the contrary, *should it be taken*, the same preparations are necessary, to balance the loss, and put ourselves in a condition to co-operate with our allies, immediately on their arrival.

We are not now fighting our battles alone, as we were in seventy-six. England, from a malicious disposition to America, has *not* only not declared war against France and Spain, but the better to prosecute her passions here, has afforded those Powers no military object, and avoids them, to distress us. She will suffer her West-India Islands to be over run by France, and her southern settlements taken by Spain, rather than quit the object that gratifies revenge. This conduct, on the part of Britain, has pointed out the propriety of France sending a naval and land force to co-operate with America on the spot.

Their arrival cannot be very distant, nor the ravages of the enemy long. In the mean time the part necessary to us, needs no illustration. The recruiting the army, and procuring the supplies, are the two things needful, and a capture of either of the enemy's divisions, will restore to America peace and plenty.

At a Crisis, big, like the present, with expectation and events, the whole country is called to unanimity and exertion. Not an ability ought now to sleep that can produce but a mite to the general good, nor even a whisper suffered to pass that militates against it. The necessity of the case, and the importance of the consequences, admit no delay from a friend, no apology from an enemy. To spare now, would be the height of extravagance, and to consult present ease, would sacrifice it, perhaps, for ever.

America, rich in patriotism and produce, can want neither men nor supplies, when a serious necessity calls them forth. The slow operation of taxes, owing to the extensiveness of collection, and their depreciated value before they arrived in the Treasury, have, in many instances, thrown a burthen upon Government, which has been artfully interpreted by the enemy into a general decline throughout the country. Yet this, inconvenient as it may at first appear, is not only remediable, but may be turned to an immediate advantage; for it makes no real difference, whether a certain number of men, or company of militia, (and in this country every man is a militia man) are directed by law, to send a recruit at their own expence, or whether a tax is laid on them for that purpose and the man hired by government afterwards. The first, if there is any difference, is both cheapest and best, because it saves the expence which would attend collecting it as a tax, and brings the man sooner into the field, than the modes of recruiting formerly used: And on this principle, a law has been passed in this State, for recruiting two men from each company of militia, which will add upwards to a thousand to the force of the country.

But the flame, which has broke forth in this city, since the report from New-York, of the loss of Charlestown, not only does honor to the place, but like the blaze of seventy-six, will kindle into action, the scattered sparks throughout America. The valour of a country may be learned by the bravery of its soldiery, and the general cast of its inhabitants, but confidence of success is best discovered by the active measures pursued by men of property; and when the spirit of enterprize becomes so universal, as to act at once on all ranks of men, a war may then, and not till then, be stiled truly popular.

In seventy-six the ardour of the enterprising part was considerably checked by the real revolt of some, and the coolness of others. But in the present case there is a firmness in the substance and property of the country to the public cause. An association has been entered into by the merchants, tradesmen, and principal inhabitants of the city, to receive and support the new State money at the value of gold and silver; a measure, which, while it does them honour, will likewise contribute to their interest, by rendering the operations of the campaign convenient and effectual.

Neither has the spirit of exertion stopt here. A voluntary subscription is likewise began to raise a fund of hard money, to be given as bounties to fill up the full quota of the Pennsylvania line. It has been the remark of the enemy, that every thing in America has been done by the force of government; but when she sees the individuals throwing in their voluntary aids, and facilitating the public measures in concert with the established powers of the country, it will convince her that the cause of America stands not on the will of a few but on the broad foundation of property and popularity.

Thus aided and thus supported, disaffection will decline, and the withered head of tyranny expire in America. The ravages of the enemy will be short and limited, and like all their former ones will produce a victory over themselves.

COMMON SENSE.

Philadelphia, June 9, 1780.

At the time of writing this number of the Crisis, the loss of Charlestown, though believed by some, was more confidently disbelieved by others. But there ought to be no longer a doubt on the matter. Charlestown is gone, and I believe for the want of a sufficient supply of provisions. The man that does not now feel for the honor of the best and noblest cause that ever a country engaged in and exert himself accordingly, is no longer worthy a peacable residence among a people determined to be free.

C. S.

The Crisis Extraordinary

October 4, 1780

IT is impossible to sit down and think seriously on the affairs
of America, but the original principles on which she resisted,
and the glow and ardor they inspired, will occur like the un-
defaced remembrance of a lovely scene. To trace over in
imagination the purity of the cause, the voluntary sacrifices
made to support it, and all the various turnings of the war in
its defence, is at once both paying and receiving respect. The
principles deserve to be remembered, and to remember them
rightly is repossessing them. In this indulgence of generous
recollection we become gainers by what we seem to give, and
the more we bestow the richer we become.

So extensively right was the ground on which America proceeded, that it not only took in every just and liberal sentiment which could impress the heart, but made it the direct
interest of every class and order of men to defend the country.
The war, on the part of Britain, was originally a war of covetousness. The sordid and not the splendid passions gave it
being. The fertile fields and prosperous infancy of America
appeared to her as mines for tributary wealth. She viewed the
hive, and disregarding the industry that had enriched it,
thirsted for the honey. But in the present stage of her affairs,
the violence of temper is added to the rage of avarice; and
therefore, that which, at our first setting out, proceeded from
purity of principle and public interest, is now heightened by
all the obligations of necessity; for it requires but little knowledge of human nature to discern what would be the consequence, were America again reduced to the subjection of
Britain. Uncontrouled power, in the hands of an incensed,
imperious and rapacious conqueror, is an engine of dreadful
execution; and woe be to that country over which it can be
exercised. The names of Whig and Tory would then be sunk
in the general term of Rebel, and the oppression, whatever it
might be, would, with very few instances of exception, light
equally on all.

Britain did not go to war with America for the sake of dominion, because she was then in possession; neither was it for the extension of trade and commerce, because she had monopolized the whole and the country had yielded to it; neither was it to extinguish what *she* might call rebellion, because before she began no resistance existed. It could then be from no other motive than avarice, or a design of establishing, in the first instance, the same taxes in America as are paid in England (which, as I shall presently show, are above eleven times heavier than the taxes we now pay for the present year 1780) or, in the second instance, to confiscate the whole property of America, in case of resistance and conquest, of the latter of which she had then no doubt.

I shall now proceed to show what the taxes in England are, and what the yearly expence of the present war is to her— What the taxes of this country amount to, and what the annual expence of defending it effectually will be to us; and shall endeavor concisely to point out the cause of our difficulties, and the advantages on one side, or the consequences on the other, in case we do, or do not, put ourselves in an effectual state of defence. I mean to be open, candid and sincere. I see a universal wish to expel the enemy from the country, a murmuring because the war is not carried on with more vigour, and my intention is to show as shortly as possible both the reason and the remedy.

The number of souls in England (exclusive of Scotland and Ireland) is seven millions*, and the number of souls in America is three millions.

The amount of the taxes in England (exclusive of Scotland and Ireland) was, before the present war commenced, eleven millions six hundred and forty two thousand six hundred and fifty three pounds sterling, which on an average is no less a sum than one pound thirteen shillings and threepence sterling per head per annum men, women, and children; besides county taxes, taxes for the support of the poor, and a tenth of all the produce of the earth for the support of the bishops and clergy†. Nearly five millions of this sum went annually to pay

*This is taking the highest number that the people of England have been or can be rated at.

†The following is taken from Dr. Price's state of the taxes of England, pages 96, 97, 98.

the interest of the national debt contracted by former wars, and the remaining sum of six millions six hundred and forty two thousand six hundred pounds was applied to defray the yearly expence of government, the peace establishment of the army and navy, placemen pensioners, &c. consequently the whole of her enormous taxes being thus appropriated, she had nothing to spare out of them towards defraying the expences of the present war or any other. Yet had she not been in debt at the beginning of the war as we were not, and like us had only a land and not a naval war to carry on, her then revenue of eleven millions and a half pounds sterling would defray all her annual expences of war and government within each year.

But this not being the case with her, she is obliged to borrow about ten million pounds sterling yearly, to prosecute the war she is now engaged in (this year she borrowed twelve) and lay on new taxes to discharge the interest; and allowing that the present war has cost her only fifty millions sterling, the interest thereon at five per cent. will be two millions and

---

"An account of the money drawn from the public by taxes annually, being the medium of three years before the year 1776.

Amount of customs in England, ... £.	2,528,275
Amount of the excise in England, ...	4,649,892
Land tax at 3 s.	1,300,000
Land tax at 1 s. in the pound, ...	450,000
Salt duties, ...	218,739
Duties on stamps, cards, dice, advertisements, bonds, leases, indentures, newspapers, almanacks, &c.	280,788
Duties on houses and windows, ...	385,369
Post office, seizures, wine licences, hackney coaches, &c. . . .	250,000
Annual profit from lotteries, ...	150,000
Expence of collecting the excises in England, ...	297,887
Expence of collecting the customs in England, ...	468,703
Interest of loans on the land tax at 4 s. expences of collection, militia, &c.	250,000
Perquisites, &c. to custom house officers, &c. supposed	250,000
Expence of collecting the salt duties in England, 10 d. 1-2 per cent.	27,000
Bounties on fish exported.	18,000
Expence of collecting the duties on stamps, cards, advertisements, &c. 5 and 1-4 per cent.	18,000
Total,	£.11,642,653

an half, therefore the amount of her taxes now must be fourteen millions, which on an average is no less than forty
shillings sterling per head, men, women and children
throughout the nation. Now as this expence of fifty millions
was borrowed on the hopes of conquering America, and as it
was avarice which first induced her to commence the war,
how truly wretched and deplorable would the condition of
this country be, were she, by her own remissness, to suffer an
enemy of such a disposition, and so circumstanced, to reduce
her to subjection.

I now proceed to the revenues of America.

I have already stated the number of souls in America to be
three millions, and by a calculation I have made, which I have
every reason to believe is sufficiently right, the whole expence
of the war, and the support of the several governments, may
be defrayed for two million pounds sterling, annually; which,
on an average, is thirteen shillings and four pence per head,
men, women and children, and the peace establishment at the
end of the war will be but three quarters of a million, or five
shillings sterling per head. Now throwing out of the question
every thing of honor, principle, happiness, freedom, and reputation in the world, and taking it up on the simple ground of
interest, I put the following case.

Suppose Britain was to conquer America, and as conquerors was to lay her under no other conditions than to pay
the same proportions toward her annual revenue which the
people of England pay; our share, in that case, would be six
million pounds sterling yearly; can it then be a question,
whether it is best to raise two millions to defend the country,
and govern it ourselves, and only three quarters of a million
afterwards, or pay six millions to have it conquered, and let
the enemy govern it.

Can it be supposed that conquerors would chuse to put
themselves in a worse condition than what they granted to
the conquered. In England, the tax on rum is five shillings
and one penny sterling per gallon, which is one silver dollar
and fourteen coppers. Now would it not be laughable to
imagine, that after the expence they have been at, they would
let either Whig or Tory in America drink it cheaper than
themselves. Coffee which is so considerable an article of con-

sumption and support here is there loaded with a duty, which makes the price between five and six shillings sterling a pound, and a penalty of fifty pounds sterling on any person detected in roasting it in his own house. There is scarce an article of life you can eat, drink, wear, or enjoy that is not there loaded with a tax; even the light from heaven is only permitted to shine into their dwellings by paying eighteen pence sterling per window annually; and the humblest drink of life, small beer, cannot there be purchased without a tax of nearly two coppers a gallon, besides a heavy tax upon the malt, and another on the hops before it is brewed, exclusive of a land tax on the earth which produces them. In short, the condition of that country in point of taxation is so oppressive, the number of her poor so great, and the extravagance and rapaciousness of the court so enormous, that were they to effect a conquest of America, it is then only that the distresses of America would begin. Neither would it signify any thing to a man whether he be what we call a Whig or a Tory. The people of England and the ministry of that country know us by no such distinctions. What they want is clear solid revenue, and the modes they would take to procure it, would operate alike on all. Their manner of reasoning would be short, because they would naturally infer that if we were able to carry on a war of five or six years against them, we are able to pay the same taxes which they do.

I have already stated that the expence of conducting the present war, and the government of the several states, may be done for two millions sterling, and the establishment in time of peace, for three quarters of a million*.

As to navy matters, they flourish so well, and are so well attended to, in the hands of individuals, that I think it consistent on every principle of real use and œconomy, to turn the navy into hard money (keeping only three or four packets) and apply it to promote the service of the army. We shall not have a ship the less; the use of them, and the benefit from them, will be greatly increased, and their expences saved. We

---

*I have made the calculations in sterling, because it is a rate generally known in all the states, and because likewise it admits of an easy comparison between our expences to support the war and those of the enemy. Four silver dollars and an half is one pound sterling and threepence over.

are now allied with a formidable naval power, from whom we derive the assistance of a navy. And the line in which we can prosecute the war, so as to reduce the common enemy and benefit the alliance most effectually, will be by attending closely to the land service.

I estimate the charge of keeping up and maintaining an army, officering them, and all expences included, sufficient for the defence of the country, to be equal to the expence of forty thousand men at thirty pounds sterling per head, which is one million two hundred thousand pounds.

I likewise allow four hundred thousand pounds for Continental expences at home and abroad.

And four hundred thousand pounds for the support of the several state governments, the amount then will be,

For the army,	1,200,000
Continental expences at home and abroad,	400,000
Government of the several states,	400,000
Total	2,000,000

I take the proportion of this state, Pennsylvania, to be an eighth part of the Thirteen United States, the quota then for us to raise will be two hundred and fifty thousand pounds sterling; two hundred thousand of which will be our share for the support and pay of the army and Continental expences at home and abroad, and fifty thousand pounds for the support of state government.

In order to gain an idea of the proportion in which the raising such a sum will fall, I make the following calculation:

Pennsylvania contains three hundred and seventy five thousand inhabitants, men, women and children, which is likewise an eighth part of the whole inhabitants of the United States: therefore two hundred and fifty thousand pounds sterling to be raised among three hundred and seventy five thousand persons, is, on an average, thirteen shillings and fourpence sterling per head per annum, or something more than one shilling sterling per month. And our proportion of three quarters of a million for the government of the country, in time of peace, will be ninety three thousand seven hundred and fifty pounds sterling, fifty thousand of which will be for the government expences of the state, and forty three thou-

sand seven hundred and fifty pounds for Continental expences at home and abroad.

The peace establishment then will, on an average, be five
shillings sterling per head. Whereas was England now to stop,
and the war cease, her peace establishment would continue
the same as it is now, viz. forty shillings per head; therefore
was our taxes necessary for carrying on the war as much per
head as hers now is, and the difference to be only whether we
should, at the end of the war, pay at the rate of five shillings
per head, or forty shillings per head, the case needs no thinking of. But as we can securely defend and keep the country
for one third less than what our burthen would be if it was
conquered, and support the governments afterward for an
eighth of what Britain would levy on us, and could I find a
miser whose heart never felt the emotion of a spark of principle, even that man, uninfluenced by every love but the love
of money, and capable of no attachment but to his interest,
would, and must, from the frugality which govern him contribute to the defence of the country, or he ceases to be a
miser and becomes an ideot. But when we take in with it
every thing that can ornament mankind; when the line of our
interest becomes the line of our happiness; when all that can
chear and animate the heart; when sense of honor, fame, character, at home and abroad, are interwoven not only with the
security but the increase of property, there exists not a man in
America, unless he be a hired emissary, who does not see that
his good is connected with keeping up a sufficient defence.

I do not imagine that an instance can be produced in the
world, of a country putting herself to such an amazing charge
to conquer and enslave another as Britain has done. The sum
is too great for her to think of with any tolerable degree of
temper; and when we consider the burthen she sustains as
well as the disposition she has shewn, it would be the height
of folly in us to suppose that she would not reimburse herself
by the most rapid means, had she once more America within
her power. With such an oppression of expence, what would
an empty conquest be to her! what relief under such circumstances could she derive from a victory without a prize? It was
money, it was revenue, she first went to war for, and nothing
but *that* would satisfy her. It is not the nature of avarice to be

satisfied with any thing else. Every passion that acts upon mankind has a peculiar mode of operation. Many of them are temporary and fluctuating; they admit of cessation and variety: But avarice is a fixed uniform passion. It neither abates of its vigour nor changes its object; and the reason why it does not is founded in the nature of things, for wealth has not a rival where avarice is a ruling passion. One beauty may excel another, and extinguish from the mind of a man the pictured remembrance of a former one: But wealth is the phœnix of avarice, and therefore cannot seek a new object, because there is not another in the world.

I now pass on to shew the value of the present taxes, and compare them with the annual expence; but this I shall preface with a few explanatory remarks.

There are two distinct things which make the payment of taxes difficult; the one is the large and real value of the sum to be paid, and the other is the scarcity of the thing in which the payment is to be made; and although these appear to be one and the same, they are in several instances not only different, but the difficulty springs from different causes.

Suppose a tax was to be laid equal to one half of what every man's yearly income is, such a tax could not be paid because the property could not be spared; and on the other hand, suppose a very trifling tax was laid to be collected in *pearls,* such a tax likewise could not be paid, because it could not be had. Now any person may see that these are distinct cases, and the latter of them is a representation of ours.

That the difficulty cannot proceed from the former, that is, from the real value or weight of the tax, is evident at first view to any person who will consider it.

The amount of the quota of taxes for this state for the present year, 1780 (and so in proportion for every other state) is twenty millions of dollars, which at seventy for one is but sixty four thousand two hundred and eighty pounds three shillings sterling, and on an average is no more than three shillings and five pence sterling per head per annum men, women and children, or five pence per head per month. Now here is a clear positive fact, that cannot be contradicted, and which proves that the difficulty cannot be in the weight of the tax, for in itself it is a trifle and far from being adequate to our quota of the expence of the war. The quit rents of one penny sterling per acre on only one half the state, come to upwards of fifty thousand pounds, which is almost as much as all the taxes of the present year, and as those quit rents made no part of the taxes then paid, and are now discontinued, the quantity of money drawn for public service this year, exclusive of the militia fines, which I shall take notice of in the process of this work, is less than what was paid and payable in any year preceding the revolution, and since the last war; what I mean is that the quit rents and taxes taken together came to a larger sum then than the present taxes without the quit rents do now.

My intention by these arguments and calculations is to place the difficulty to the right cause, and shew that it does not proceed from the weight or worth of the tax, but from the scarcity of the medium in which it is paid; and to illustrate this point still farther, I shall now shew, that if the tax of twenty millions of dollars was of four times the real value it now is or nearly so, which would be about two hundred and fifty thousand pounds sterling, and would be our full quota, that this sum would have been raised with more ease, and less felt, than the present sum of only sixty four thousand two hundred and eighty pounds.

The convenience or inconvenience of paying a tax in money arises from the quantity of money that can be spared out of trade.

When the emissions stopt, the continent was left in possession of two hundred millions of dollars, perhaps as equally dispersed as it was possible for trade to do it. And as no more was to be issued, the rise or fall of prices could neither increase nor diminish the quantity. It therefore remained the same through all the fluctuations of trade and exchange.

Now had the exchange stood at twenty for one, which was the rate congress calculated upon when they quoted the states the latter end of last year, trade would have been carried on for nearly four times less money than it is now, and consequently the twenty millions would have been spared with much greater ease, and when collected would have been of almost four times the value they now are. And on the other hand, was the depreciation to be at ninety or one hundred for one, the quantity required for trade would be more than at sixty or seventy for one, and though the value of the tax would be less, the difficulty of sparing the money out of trade would be greater. And on these facts and arguments I rest the matter, to prove, that it is not the want of property, but the scarcity of the medium by which the proportion of property for taxation is to be measured out, that makes the embarrassment we lie under. There *is not* money enough, and what is equally as true, the people will not let there be money enough.

While I am on the subject of the currency, I shall offer one remark which will appear true to every body, and can be accounted for by nobody, which is, that the better the times were, the worse the money grew; and the worse the times were, the better the money stood. It never depreciated by any advantage obtained by the enemy. The troubles of seventy six, and the loss of Philadelphia in seventy seven, made no sensible impression on it, and every one knows that the surrender of Charlestown did not produce the least alteration in the rate of exchange, which for long before, and for more than three months after, stood at sixty for one. It seems as if the certainty of its being our own made us careless of its value, and that the most distant thoughts of losing it made us hug it the closer, like something we were loth to part with; or that we depreciate it for our pastime, which, when called to seriousness by the enemy, we leave off to renew again at our leisure. In short our good luck seem to break us, and our bad make us whole.

Passing on from this digression, I shall now endeavor to bring into one view the several parts I have already stated, and form thereon some propositions, and conclude.

I have placed before the reader, the average tax per head paid by the people in England; which is forty shillings sterling.

And I have shewn the rate on an average per head, which will defray all the expence of the war to us, and support the several governments without running the country into debt, which is thirteen shillings and fourpence.

I have shewn what the peace establishment may be conducted for, viz. an eighth part of what it would be, if under the government of Britain.

And I have likewise shewn what the average per head of the

present taxes are, namely, three shillings and five pence sterling or five pence per month; and that their whole yearly value in sterling is only sixty four thousand two hundred and eighty pounds. Whereas our quota to keep the payments equal with the expences, is two hundred and fifty thousand pounds. Consequently there is a deficiency of one hundred and eighty five thousand seven hundred and twenty pounds, and the same proportion of defect, according to the several quotas, happens in every other state. And this defect is the cause why the army has been so indifferently fed, cloathed and paid. It is the cause, likewise, of the nerveless state of the campaign, and the insecurity of the country. Now if a tax equal to thirteen and fourpence per head will remove all these difficulties, make people secure in their homes, leave them to follow the business of their stores and farms unmolested, and not only keep out, but drive out the enemy from the country; and if the neglect of raising this sum will let them in, and produce the evils which might be prevented, on which side, I ask, does the wisdom, interest and policy lie? Or rather would it not be an insult to reason to put the question. The sum when portioned out according to the several abilities of the people, can hurt no one, but an inroad from the enemy ruins hundreds of families.

Look at the destruction done in this city. The many houses totally destroyed, and others damaged; the waste of fences in the country round it, besides the plunder of furniture, forage and provision. I do not suppose that half a million sterling would reinstate the sufferers, and does this, I ask, bear any proportion to the expence that would make us secure. The damage on an average is at least ten pound sterling per head, which is as much as thirteen shillings and fourpence per head comes to for fifteen years. The same has happened on the frontiers, and in the Jersies, New York, and other places, where the enemy has been, Carolina and Georgia is likewise suffering the same fate.

That the people generally do not understand the insufficiency of the taxes to carry on the war, is evident, not only from common observation, but from the construction of several petitions, which were presented to the assembly of this state, against the recommendation of congress of the 18th of

March last, for taking up and funding the present currency at forty for one, and issuing new money in its stead. The prayer of the petitions was, *That the currency might be appreciated by taxes* (meaning the present taxes) *and that part of the taxes be applied to the support of the army, if the army could not be otherwise supported.* Now it could not have been possible for such a petition to have been presented, had the petitioners known, that so far from *part* of the taxes being sufficient for the support of the army, the *whole* of them falls three fourths short of the year's expences.

Before I proceed to propose methods by which a sufficiency of money may be raised, I shall take a short review of the general state of the country.

Notwithstanding the weight of the war, the ravages of the enemy, and the obstructions she has thrown in the way of trade and commerce, so soon does a young country outgrow misfortune, that America has already surmounted many that once heavily oppressed her. For the first year or two of the war, we were shut up within our ports, scarce venturing to look towards the ocean. Now our rivers are beautified with large and valuable vessels, our stores filled with merchandize, and the produce of the country has a ready market, and an advantageous price. Gold and silver, that for a while seemed to have retreated again within the bowels of the earth, is once more risen into circulation, and every day adds new strength to trade, commerce, and agriculture. In a pamphlet written by Sir John Dalrymple, and dispersed in America in the year 1775, he asserted, that, *two twenty gun ships, nay,* says he, *the tenders of those ships, stationed between Albermarle sound and Chesapeak bay, would shut up the trade of America for 600 miles.* How little did Sir John Dalrymple know of the abilities of America!

While under the government of Britain, the trade of this country was loaded with restrictions. It was only a few foreign ports she was allowed to sail to. Now it is otherwise; and allowing that the quantity of trade is but half what it was before the war, the case must shew the vast advantage of an open trade, because the present quantity under her restrictions could not support itself; from which I infer, that if half the quantity without the restrictions can bear itself up nearly, if not quite, as well as the whole when subject to them, how prosperous must the condition of America be when the whole shall return open with all the world. By trade I do not mean the employment of a merchant only, but the whole interest and business of the country taken collectively.

It is not so much my intention, by this publication, to propose particular plans for raising money, as it is to shew the necessity and the advantages to be derived from it. My principal design is to form the disposition of the people to such measures which I am fully persuaded is their interest and duty to adopt, and which needs no other force to accomplish them than the force of being felt. But as every hint may be useful, I shall throw out a sketch, and leave others to make such improvements upon it as to them may appear reasonable.

The annual sum wanted is two millions, and the average rate in which it falls is thirteen shillings and fourpence per head.

Suppose then that we raise half the sum and sixty thousand pounds over. The average rate thereof will be seven shillings per head.

In this case we shall have half the supply we want, and an annual fund of sixty thousand pounds whereon to borrow the other million; because sixty thousand pounds is the interest of a million at six per cent. and if at the end of another year we should be obliged, by the continuance of the war, to borrow another million, the taxes will be increased to seven shillings and sixpence; and thus for every million borrowed, an additional tax equal to sixpence per head must be levied.

The sum then to be raised next year will be one million and sixty thousand pounds: One half of which I would propose should be raised by duties on imported goods and prize goods, and the other half by a tax on landed property and houses, or such other means as each state may devise.

But as the duties on imports and prize goods must be the same in all the states, therefore the rate per cent. or in what other form the duty shall be laid, must be ascertained and regulated by congress, and ingrafted in that form into the law of each state; and the monies arising therefrom carried into the treasury of each state. The duties to be paid in gold or silver.

There are many reasons why a duty on imports is the most convenient duty or tax that can be collected, one of which is, because the whole is payable in a few places in a country, and it likewise operates with the greatest ease and equality, because as every one pays in proportion to what he consumes, so people in general consume in proportion to what they can afford, and therefore the tax is regulated by the abilities which every man supposes himself to have, or in other words every man becomes his own assessor, and pays by a little at a time when it suits him to buy. Besides, it is a tax which people may pay or let alone by not consuming the articles; and though the alternative may have no influence on their conduct, the power of choosing is an agreeable thing to the mind. For my own part, it would be a satisfaction to me, was there a duty on all sorts of liquors during the war, as in my idea of things, it would be an addition to the pleasure of society, to know, that when the health of the army goes round, a few drops from every glass become theirs. How often have I heard an emphatical wish almost accompanied with a tear, *"Oh, that our poor fellows in the field had some of this!"* Why then need we suffer under a fruitless sympathy, when there is a way to enjoy both the wish and the entertainment at once?

But the great national policy of putting a duty upon imports is, that it either keeps the foreign trade in our own hands or draws something for the defence of the country from every foreigner who participates it with us.

Thus much for the first half of the taxes, and as each state will best devise means to raise the other half, I shall confine my remarks to the resources of this state.

The quota then of this state of one million and sixty thousand pounds will be one hundred and thirty-three thousand two hundred and fifty pounds, the half of which is sixty-six thousand six hundred and twenty-five pounds; and supposing one fourth part of Pennsylvania inhabited, then a tax of one bushel of wheat on every twenty acres of land, one with another, would produce the sum, and all the present taxes to cease. Whereas the tythes of the bishops and clergy in England, exclusive of the taxes, are upwards of half a bushel of wheat on *every single* acre of land, good and bad, throughout the nation.

In a former part of this paper I mentioned the militia fines, but reserved speaking to the matter, which I shall now do: The ground I shall put it upon is, that two millions sterling a year will support a sufficient army, and all the expences of war, and government, without having recourse to the inconvenient method of continually calling men from their employments, which of all others is the most expensive and the least substantial. I consider the revenue created by taxes as the first and principal thing, and fines only as secondary and accidental things. It was not the intention of the militia law to apply the militia fines to any thing else but the support of the militia, neither do they produce any revenue to the state, yet these fines amount to more than all the taxes; for taking the muster roll to be sixty thousand men, the fine on forty thousand who may not attend, will be sixty thousand pounds sterling, and those who muster, will give up a portion of time equal to half that sum, and if the eight classes should be called within the year, and one third turn out, the fine on the remaining forty thousand would amount to seventy two millions of dollars, besides the fifteen shillings on every hundred pounds property, and the charge of seven and a half per cent for collecting in certain instances, which on the whole would be upwards of two hundred and fifty thousand pounds sterling.

Now if those very fines disable the country from raising a sufficient revenue without producing an equivalent advantage, would it not be to the ease and interest of all parties to encrease the revenue, in the manner I have proposed, or any better, if a better can be devised, and cease the operation of the fines. I would still keep the militia as an organized body of men, and should there be a real necessity to call them forth, pay them out of the proper revenues of the state, and encrease the taxes a third or fourth per cent. on those who did not attend. My limits will not allow me to go farther into this matter, which I shall therefore close with this remark; that fines are, of all modes of revenue, the most unsuited to the mind of a free country. When a man pays a tax, he knows the public necessity requires it, and therefore feels a pride in discharging his duty; but a fine seems an attonement for neglect of duty, and of consequence is paid with discredit, and frequently levied with severity.

I have now only one subject more to speak to, with which I shall conclude, which is, the resolve of congress of the 18th of March last, for taking up and funding the present currency at forty for one, and issuing new money in its stead.

Every one knows I am not the flatterer of congress, but in this instance *they are right*; and if that measure is supported, the currency will acquire a value, which without it, it will not. But this is not all: It will give relief to the finances until such time as they can be properly arranged, and save the country from being immediately double taxed under the present mode. In short, support that measure, and it will support you.

I have now waded through a tedious course of difficult business, and over an untrodden path. The subject on every point it could be viewed was entangled with perplexities, and inveloped in obscurity, yet such are the resources of America, that she wants nothing but system to insure success.

COMMON SENSE.

Philadelphia, October 4, 1780.

P. S. While this paper was preparing for the press, the treachery of General Arnold became known, and engrossed the attention and conversation of the public; and that, not so much on account of the traitor as the magnitude of the treason, and the providence evident in the discovery. The matter, as far as is at present known, is thus briefly related.

General Arnold about six weeks before had obtained the command of the important post of West Point, situated on the North river, about sixty miles above New York, and an hundred below Albany, there being no other defenceable pass between it and the last mentioned place. At what time, or in what manner, he first entered into a negociation with the enemy for betraying the fort and garrison into their hands, does not yet appear.

While Arnold commanded at West Point, General Washington and the minister of France went to Hartford in Connecticut, to consult on matters, in concert with Admiral Terney commander of the French fleet stationed at Rhode Island. In the mean time Arnold held a conference with major Andre, Adjutant General to General Clinton, whom he traiterously furnished with plans of the fort, state of the garrison, minutes of the last council of war, and the manner in which he would post the troops when the enemy should attempt a surprise; and then gave him a pass, by the name of Mr. John Anderson, to go to the lines at the White Plains or lower, if he Mr. Anderson thought proper, he being (the pass said) on public business.

Thus furnished, Andre parted from Arnold, set off for New York, and had nearly arrived at the extent of our lines, when he was stopped by a party of militia, to whom he produced his pass, but they, not being satisfied with his account, insisted on taking him before the commanding officer Lieut. Col. Jamieson. Finding himself in this situation, and hoping to escape by a bribe, he offered them his purse, watch and a promise of any quantity of goods they would accept, which these honest men nobly and virtuously scorned, and consistent with their duty took him to the proper officer. On examination there was found on him the above mentioned papers and several others, all in the hand writing of General Arnold, and finding himself thus detected, he confessed his proper name and character; he was accordingly made a close prisoner, and the papers sent off by express to West Point, at which place General Washington had arrived soon after the arrival of the packet. On this disclosure, he went in quest of Arnold, whom he had not seen that day, but all that could be learned was, that Arnold had received a letter some short time before, which had much confused him, since which he had disappeared. Colonel Hamilton, one of General Washington's aids, with some others were sent after him, but he having the start eluded the pursuit, took boat under pretence of a flag, and got on board the Vulture sloop of war lying in the North river; on which it may be truly said, that one vulture was receiving another. From on board this vessel he addressed a letter to General Washington, which, in whatever light it may be viewed, confirms him a finished villain.

The true character of Arnold is that of a desperado. His whole life has been a life of jobbs; and where either plunder or profit was the object, no danger deterred, no principle restrained him. In his person he was smart and active, somewhat diminutive, weak in his capacities and trifling in his conversation; and though gallant in the field, was defective in the talents necessary for command. The early convulsion of the times afforded him an introduction into life, to the elegance of which he was before a stranger, and the eagerness of the public, to reward and encourage enterprize, procured him at once both applause and promotion. His march to Quebec gave him fame, and the plunder of Montreal put the first stamp to his public character. His behaviour at Danbury and Saratoga once more covered over his crimes, which again broke forth in the plunder of Philadelphia, under pretence of supplying the army. From this time, the true spring of his conduct being known, he became both disregarded and disesteemed, and this last instance of his treachery has proved the public judgment right.

When we take a review of the history of former times, it will turn out to the honor of America, that, notwithstanding the trying variety of her situation, this is the only instance of defection in a general officer; and even in this case the unshaken honesty of those who detected him heightens the national character, to which his apostacy serves as a foil. From the nature of his crime, and his disposition to monopolize, it is reasonable to conclude he had few or no *direct* accomplices. His sole object was to make a monied bargain; and to be consistent with himself, he would as readily betray the side he has deserted to, as that he deserted from.

But there is one reflection results from this black business, that deserves notice, which is, that it shows the declining power of the enemy. An attempt to bribe is a sacrifice of military fame, and a confession of inability to conquer; as a proud people they ought to be above it, and as soldiers to despise it; and however they may feel on the occasion, the world at large will despise them for it, and consider America superior to their arms.

C. S.

Public Good

Being an Examination
Into the Claim of Virginia
to the Vacant Western Territory,
and
of the Right of
The United States to the Same.

To Which Is Added,
Proposals For Laying Off a New State,
To Be Applied as a Fund
for Carrying on the War,
or Redeeming the National Debt.

December 30, 1780

THE PREFACE.

The following pages are on a subject hitherto little understood, but highly interesting to the United States.

They contain an investigation of the claims of Virginia to the vacant western territory, and of the right of the United States to the same; with some outlines of a plan for laying out a new state, to be applied as a fund, for carrying on the war, or redeeming the national debt.

The reader, in the course of this publication, will find it studiously plain, and, as far as I can judge, perfectly candid. What materials I could get at I have endeavoured to place in a clear line, and deduce such arguments therefrom as the subject required. In the prosecution of it, I have considered myself as an advocate for the right of the states, and taken no other liberty with the subject than what a counsel would, and ought to do, in behalf of a client.

I freely confess that the respect I had conceived, and still preserve, for the character of Virginia, was a constant check upon those sallies of imagination, which are fairly and advantageously indulged against an enemy, but ungenerous when against a friend.

If there is any thing I have omitted or mistaken, to the injury of the intentions of Virginia or her claims, I shall gladly rectify it; or if there is any thing yet to add, should the subject require it, I shall as chearfully undertake it; being fully convinced, that to have matters fairly discussed, and properly understood, is a principal means of preserving harmony and perpetuating friendship.

THE AUTHOR.

PUBLIC GOOD, &c.

WHEN we take into view the mutual happiness and united interests of the states of America, and consider the important consequences to arise from a strict attention of each, and of all, to every thing which is just, reasonable and honourable; or the evils that will follow from an inattention to those principles; there cannot, and ought not, to remain a doubt, but that the governing rule of *right* and mutual good must in all public cases finally preside.

The hand of providence has cast us into one common lot, and accomplished the independence of America, by the unanimous consent of the several parts, concurring at once in time, manner and circumstances. No superiority of interest, at the expence of the rest, induced the one, more than the other, into the measure. Virginia and Maryland, it is true, might foresee, that their staple commodity, tobacco, by being no longer monopolized by Britain, would bring them a better price abroad: for as the tax on it in England was treble its first purchase from the planter, and they being now no longer compelled to send it under that obligation, and in the restricted manner they formerly were; it is easy to see, that the article, from the alteration of the circumstances of trade, will, and daily does, turn out to them with additional advantages.

But this being a natural consequence, produced by that common freedom and independence of which all are partakers, is therefore an advantage they are intitled to, and on which the rest of the states can congratulate them without feeling a wish to lessen, but rather to extend it. To contribute to the encreased prosperity of another, by the same means which occasion our own, is an agreeable reflection; and the more valuable any article of export becomes, the more riches will be introduced into and spread over the continent.

Yet this is an advantage which those two states derive from the independence of America superior to the local circumstances of the rest; and of the two it more particularly belongs to Virginia than Maryland, because the staple commodity of a considerable part of Maryland is flour, which, as it is an article that is the growth of Europe as well as of America, cannot obtain a foreign market but by under selling, or at least by limiting it to the current price abroad. But tobacco commands its own price. It is not a plant of almost universal growth, like wheat. There are but few soils and climes that produce it to advantage, and before the cultivation of it in Virginia and Maryland, the price was from four to sixteen shillings sterling a pound in England.*

But the condition of the vacant western territory of America makes a very different case to that of the circumstances of trade in any of the states. Those very lands, formed, in contemplation, the fund by which the debt of America would in a course of years be redeemed. They were considered as the common right of all; and it is only till lately that any pretension of claims has been made to the contrary.

That difficulties and differences will arise in communities ought always to be looked for. The opposition of interests, real or supposed; the variety of judgments; the contrariety of temper; and, in short, the whole composition of man, in his individual capacity, is tinctured with a disposition to contend; but in his social capacity there is either a right which, being proved, terminates the dispute, or a reasonableness in the measure, where no direct right can be made out, which decides or compromises the matter.

As I shall have frequent occasion to mention the word *right*, I wish to be clearly understood in my definition of it. There are various senses in which this term is used, and custom has, in many of them, afforded it an introduction contrary to its true meaning. We are so naturally inclined to give

---

*See sir Dalby Thomas's historical account of the rise and growth of the West-India colonies.

the utmost degree of force to our own case, that we call every pretension, however founded, *a right*; and by this means the term frequently stands opposed to justice and reason.

After Theodore was elected king of Corsica, not many years ago, by the meer choice of the natives, for their own convenience in opposing the Genoese, he went over into England, run himself into debt, got himself into jail, and on his release therefrom by the benefit of an act of insolvency, he surrendered up, what he called, *his* kingdom of Corsica, as a part of his personal property, for the use of his creditors; some of whom may hereafter call this a charter, or by any other name more fashionable, and ground thereon what they may term a *right* to the sovereignty and property of Corsica. But does not justice abhor such an action, both in him and them, under the prostituted name of a *right*, and must not laughter be excited where ever it is told.

A right, to be truly so, must be right in itself; yet many things have obtained the name of rights, which are originally founded in wrong. Of this kind are all rights by meer conquest, power or violence. In the cool moments of reflection we are obliged to allow, that the mode by which such right is obtained, is not the best suited to that spirit of universal justice which ought to preside equally over all mankind. There is something in the establishment of such a right that we wish to flip over as easily as possible, and say as little about as can be. But in the case of a *right founded in right* the mind is carried chearfully into the subject, feels no compunction, suffers no distress, subjects its sensations to no violences, nor sees any thing in its way which requires an artificial smoothing.

From this introduction I proceed to examine into the claims of Virginia; first as to the right, secondly as to the reasonableness, and lastly as to the consequences.

The name, *Virginia*, originally bore a different meaning to what it does now. It stood in the place of the word North-America, and seems to have been intended as a name comprehensive of all the English settlements or colonies on the continent, and not descriptive of any one as distinguishing it from the rest. All to the southward of Chesapeak, as low as the Gulf of Mexico, was called South-Virginia, and all to the northward North-Virginia, in a similar line of distinction, as we now call the whole continent North and South-America.*

The first character or patent was to sir Walter Rawleigh by Queen Elizabeth, of England, in the year 1583, and had neither name nor bounds. Upon sir Walter's return, the name *Virginia*, was given to the whole country, including the now United States. Consequently the present Virginia, either as a province or a state, can sit up no exclusive claim to the western territory under this patent, and that for two reasons; first, because the words of the patent run *to sir Walter Rawleigh, and such persons as he should nominate, themselves and their successors*; which is a line of succession Virginia does not pretend to stand in; and secondly, because a prior question would arise, namely, who are to be understood by Virginians under this patent? and the answer would be, all the inhabitants of America, from New-England to Florida.

This patent, therefore, would destroy their exclusive claim, and invest the right collectively in the thirteen states.

But it unfortunately happened, that the settlers under this patent, partly from misconduct, the opposition of the Indians, and other calamities, discontinued the process, and the patent became extinct.

After this James the first, who, in the year 1602, succeeded Elizabeth, issued a new patent, which I come next to describe.

This patent differed from the former in this essential point, that it had limits, whereas the other had none: the former was intended to promote discoveries where ever they could be made, which accounts why no limits were affixed, and this to settle discoveries already made, which likewise assigns a reason why limits should be described.

In this patent were incorporated two companies, called the South-Virginia company, and the North-Virginia company, and sometimes the London company, and the Plymouth company.

The South-Virginia or London company was composed chiefly of London adventurers; the North-Virginia or Ply-

---

*Oldmixon's history of Virginia.

mouth company was made up of adventurers from Plymouth in Devonshire, and other persons of the western parts of England.

Tho' they were not to fix together, yet they were allowed to chuse their places of settlement any where on the coast of America, then called Virginia, between the latitudes of 34 and 45 degrees, which was a range of 760 miles: the south company was not to go below 34 degrees, nor the north company above 45 degrees. But the patent expressed, that as soon as they had made their choice, each was to become limited to 50 miles each way on the coast, and 100 up the country; so that the grant to each company was a square of 100 miles, and no more. The North-Virginia or Plymouth company settled to the eastward, and in the year 1614 changed the name, and called that part New-England. The South-Virginia or London company settled near cape Henry.

This then cannot be the patent of boundless extent, and that for two reasons; first, because the limits are described, namely, a square of 100 miles; and secondly, because there were two companies of equal rights included in the same patent.

Three years after this, that is, in the year 1609, the South-Virginia company applied for new powers from the Crown of England, which were granted them in a new patent, and the boundaries of the grant enlarged; and this is the charter or patent on which some of the present Virginians ground their pretension to boundless territory.

The first reflection that presents itself on this enlargement of the grant is, that it must be supposed to bear some intended degree of reasonable comparison to that which it superceded. The former could not be greater than a square of one hundred miles; and this new one being granted in the lieu of that, and that within the space of three years, and by the same person, James the first, who was never famed either for profusion or generosity, cannot, on a review of the time and circumstances of the grant, be supposed a very extravagant or very extraordinary one. If a square of one hundred miles was not sufficiently large, twice that quantity was as much as could well be expected or solicited: but to suppose that he, who had caution enough to confine the first grant within moderate bounds, should in so short a space as three years, supercede it by another grant of many million times greater content, is, on the face of the affair, a circumstantial nullity.

Whether this patent of charter was in existence or not at the time the revolution commenced, is a matter I shall hereafter speak to, and confine myself in this place to the limits which the said patent or charter lays down.

The words are as follows:

"Beginning from the cape or point of land called cape or point Comfort, thence all along the sea coast to the NORTHWARD 200 miles; and from the said point or cape Comfort all along the sea coast to the *southward* 200 miles; and all that space or circuit of land lying from the sea coast of the precinct aforesaid up into the land throughout, from sea to sea, WEST and *north-west*."

The first remark I shall offer on the words of this grant is, that they are uncertain, obscure and unintelligible, and may be construed into such a variety of contradictory meanings as to leave at last no meaning at all.

Whether the 200 miles each way, from cape Comfort, were to be on a *straight* line, or ascertained by following the indented *line of the coast*, that is, *"all along the sea coast,"* in and out as the coast lay, cannot now be fully determined; because, as either will admit of supposition, and nothing but supposition can be produced, therefore neither can be taken as positive. Thus far may be said, that had it been intended to be a straight line, the word *straight* ought to have been inserted, which would have made the matter clear; but as no inference can well be drawn to the advantage of that which does *not appear* against that which *does*, therefore the omission implies negatively in favour of the coast indented line, or that the 400 miles were to be traced on the windings of the coast that is *"all along the sea coast."*

But what is meant by the words *"west and north-west"* is still more unintelligible. Whether they mean a west line and a north-west line, or whether they apply to the general lying of the land from the Atlantic, without regard to lines, cannot again be determined. But if they are supposed to mean lines to be run, then a new difficulty of more magnitude than all the rest arises; namely, From which end of the extent on the coast is the west line and the north-west line to be set off; as the difference in the content of the grant, occasioned by transposing them is many hundred million of acres; and either includes or excludes a far greater quantity of land than the whole thirteen United States contain?

In short, there is not a boundary in this grant that is clear, fixt and defined. The coast line is uncertain, and that being the base on which the others are to be formed, renders the whole uncertain. But even if this line was admitted, in either shape, the other boundaries would still be on supposition, till it might be said there is no boundary at all, and consequently no charter; for words which describe nothing can give nothing.

The advocates for the Virginia claim, laying hold of these ambiguities, have explained the grant thus:

Four hundred miles on the sea coast, and from the south point a west line to the great south sea, and from the north point a north-west line to the said south sea. The figure which these lines produce will be thus:

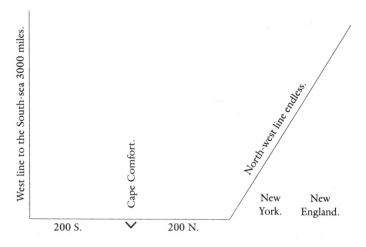

But why, I ask, must the west land line be set off from the south point, any more than from the north point? The grant or patent does not say from which it shall be, neither is it clear that a line is the thing intended by the words: but admitting it is, on what grounds do the claimants proceed in making this choice? the answer, I presume, is easily given, namely, because it is the most beneficial explanation to themselves they can possibly make; as it takes in many thousand times more extent of country than any other explanation would. But this, tho' it be a very good reason to them, is a very bad reason to us; and tho' it may do for the claimants to hope upon, will not answer to plead upon; especially to the very people, who, to confirm the partiality of the claimants choice, must relinquish their own right and interest.

Why not set off the west land line from the north end of the coast line, and the north-west line from the south end of the same? there is some reason why this should be the construction and none why the other should.

First, because, if the line of two hundred miles each way from cape Comfort, be traced by following the indented line of the coast, which seems to be the implied intention of the words, and a west line be set off from the north end, and a north-west line from the south end, these lines will all unite, (which the other construction never can) and form a compleat triangle, the content of which will be about twenty nine or thirty millions of acres, or something larger than Pennsylvania: and

Secondly, because this construction is following the order of the lines as expressed in the grant; for the *first* mentioned *coast* line, which is that to the *northward* of cape Comfort, and the *first* mentioned *land* line, which is the *west* line, have a numerical relation, being the *first mentioned of each*; and implies, that the *west* line was to be set off from the *north* point and *not* from the south point: and consequently the two *last* mentioned of each have the same numerical relation, and again implies that the *north-west* line was to be set off from the *south* point, and *not* from the *north* point. But why the claimants should break thro' the order of the lines, and, contrary to implication, join the *first* mentioned of the *one*, to the *last* mentioned of the *other*, and thereby produce a shapeless monster, for which there is no name nor any parallel in the world, either as to extent of soil or sovereignty, is a construction that cannot be supported.

The figure produced by following the order of the lines is as under.

N. B.   If the reader will cast his eye again over the words of the patent on page 259 he will perceive the numerical relation alluded to, by observing, that the first mentioned coast line and the first mentioned land line are distinguished by CAPITALS. And the last mentioned of each by *italics*, which I have chosen to do to illustrate the explanation.

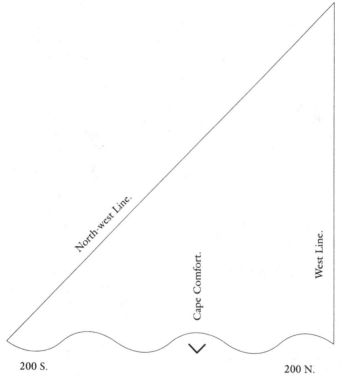

200 S.

200 N.

I presume that if four hundred miles be traced by following the inflexes of any sea shore, that the two extremes will not be more than three hundred miles distant from each other, on a straight line. Therefore to find the content of a triangle whose base is three hundred miles, multiply the length of the base into half the perpendicular, which, in this case is the west line, and the product will be the answer:

300 miles length of the base.
  150 half the perpendicular (supposing a right angled triangle)
_____
15000
300
_____
45,000 contents of the grant in square miles.
  640 acres in a square mile.
_____
1800000
270000
_____
28,800,000 contents in square acres.

Now will any one undertake to say, that this explanation is not as fairly drawn, (if not more so) from the words themselves, as any other that can be offered, because it is not only justified by the exact words of the patent, grant, or charter, or any other name by which it may be called, but by their implied meaning; and is likewise of such a content, as may be supposed to have been intended; whereas the claimants explanation is without bounds, and beyond every thing that is reasonable. Yet after all, who can say what were the precise meaning of terms and expressions so loosely formed, and capable of such a variety of contradictory interpretations!

Had the order of the lines been otherwise than they are in the patent, the reasonableness of the thing must have directed the manner in which they should be connected: but as the claim is founded in unreasonableness, and that unreasonableness endeavoured to be supported by a transposition of the lines, there remains no pretence for the claim to stand on.

Perhaps those who are interested in the claimants explanation will say, that as the south sea is spoken of, the lines must be as they explain them, in order to reach it.

To this I reply; first, that no man then knew how far it was from the Atlantic to the south sea, as I shall presently show, but believed it to be but a short distance: and,

Secondly, that the uncertain and ambiguous manner in which the south sea is alluded to, (for it is not mentioned by name, but only *"from sea to sea"*) serves to perplex the patent, and not to explain it: and as no right can be founded on an ambiguity, but on some proof cleared of ambiguity, therefore the allusive introduction of "sea to sea," can yield no service to the claim.

There is likewise an ambiguous mention made of *two lands* in this patent, as well as of two *seas*, viz. "and all that *space or circuit of land* lying from the sea coast of the precinct afore-said up into the *land throughout from sea to sea.*"

On which I remark, that the two *lands* here mentioned have the appearance of a major and a minor, or the greater out of which the less is to be taken: and the term from *"sea to sea"* may be said to apply descriptively to the *land throughout*, and not to the *space or circuit of land patented to the company*: in a similar manner that the former patent described a major of 760 miles extent, out of which the minor, or square of one hundred miles, was to be chosen.

But to suppose, that because the south sea is darkly alluded to, it must therefore, (at whatever distance it might be, which then nobody knew, or for whatever purpose it might be introduced) be made a certain boundary, and that without regard to the reasonableness of the matter, or the order in which the lines are arranged, which is the only implication the patent gives for setting off the land lines, is a supposition that contradicts every thing which is reasonable.

The figure produced by following the order of the lines will be compleat in itself, let the distance to the south sea be more or less: because, if the *land throughout from sea to sea* had not been sufficiently extensive to admit the west land line and the north west land line to close, the south sea, in that case, would have eventually become a boundary: but if the extent of the *land throughout from sea to sea,* was so great, that the lines closed without reaching the said south sea, the figure was compleat without it.

Wherefore, as the order of the lines, when raised on the indented coast line, produces a regular figure of reasonable dimensions, and of about the same content, tho' not of the same shape, which Virginia now holds within the Allegany Mountains; and by transposing them another figure is produced, for which there is no name, and cannot be compleated, as I shall presently explain, and of an extent greater than one half of Europe, it is needless to offer any other arguments to shew that the order of the lines must be the rule, if any rule can be drawn from the words, for ascertaining from which point the west line and north-west line were to be set off. Neither is it possible to suppose any other rule could be followed; because a north-west line set off two hundred miles above cape Comfort, would not only never touch the south sea, but would form a spiral line of infinite windings round the globe, and after passing over the northern parts of America and the frozen ocean, and then into the northern parts of Asia, would, when eternity should end and not before, terminate in the north pole.

This is the only manner in which I can express the effect of a north-west line, set off as above; because as its direction must always be between the north and the west, it consequently can never get into the pole nor yet come to a rest; and on the principle, that matter or space is capable of being eternally divided, must proceed on for ever.

But it was a prevailing opinion, at the time this patent was obtained, that the South sea was at no great distance from the Atlantic, and therefore it was needless, under that supposition, to regard which way the lines should be run; neither need we wonder at this error in the English government respecting America then, when we see so many and such glaring ones now, for which there are less excuse.

Some circumstances favoured this mistake. Admiral sir Francis Drake not long before this, had, from the top of a mountain in the Isthmus of Darien, which is the center of North and South America, seen both the South sea and the Atlantic; the width of the part of the continent where he then was, not being above 70 miles, whereas its width opposite Chesapeak bay is as great, if not greater, than in any other part, being from *sea to sea*, about the distance it is from America to England. But this could not then be known, because only two voyages had been made across the South sea; the one by the ship in which Magellan sailed, who died in his passage, and which was the first ship that sailed round the world, and the other by sir Francis Drake: but as neither of these sailed into a northern latitude in that ocean, high enough to fix the longitude of the western coast of America from the eastern, the distance across was intirely on supposition, and the errors they then ran into appear laughable to us who now know what the distance is.

That the company expected to come at the South sea without much trouble or travelling, and that the great body of land which intervened, so far from being their view in obtaining the charter, became their disappointment, may be collected from a circumstance mentioned in Stith's history of Virginia.

He relates, that, in the year 1608, which was at the time the company were soliciting this patent, they fitted up in England "a barge for captain Newport," (who was afterwards one of the joint deputy governors under the very charter we are now treating of) "which, for convenience of carriage, might be taken into five pieces, and with which he and his company were instructed to go up James River as far as the falls thereof, to discover the country of the Monakins, and from thence they were to proceed, *carrying their barge beyond the falls to convey them to the south sea;* being ordered not to return without a lump of gold, or a certainty of the said sea."

And Hutchinson, in his history of New England, which was called North-Virginia at the time this patent was obtained, says, "the geography of this part of America was less understood than at present. A line to the Spanish settlements was imagined much shorter than it really was. Some of Champlain's people, in the beginning of the last century, who had been but a few days march from Quebec, returned with great joy, supposing that from the top of a high mountain they had *discovered the South-Sea.*"

From these matters, which are evidences on record, it appears that the adventurers had no knowledge of the distance it was to the South-Sea, but supposed it to be no great way from the Atlantic; and also, that great extent of territory was not their object, but a short communication with the southern ocean, by which they might get into the neighbourhood of the Gold Coast, and likewise carry on a commerce with the East Indies.

Having thus shewn the confused and various interpretations this charter is subject to, and that it may be made to mean any thing and nothing; I now proceed to show, that, let the limits of it be more or less, the present Virginia does not, and cannot, as a matter of right, inherit under it.

I shall open this part of the subject by putting the following case:

Either Virginia stands in succession to the London company, to whom the charter was granted, or to the Crown of England. If to the London company, then it becomes her, as an outset in the matter, to shew who they were, and likewise that they were in possession at the commencement of the revolution.—If to the Crown, then the charter is of consequence superseded; because the Crown did not posses territories by charter, but by prerogative without charter. The notion of the Crown chartering to itself is a nullity; and in this case, the unpossessed lands, be they little or much, are in the same condition as if they never had been chartered at all; and the sovereignty of them devolves to the sovereignty of the United States.

The charter or patent of 1609 as well as that of 1606 was to Sir Thomas Gates, Sir George Summers, the reverend Richard Hackluit, prebend of Westminster, and others; and the government was then proprietary. Those proprietors, by virtue of the charter of 1609, chose Lord Delaware for their governor, and Sir Thomas Gates, Sir George Summers, and captain Newport, (the person who was to go with a boat to the South sea,) joint deputy governors.

Was this the form of government either as to soil or constitution at the time the present revolution commenced? if not, the charter was not in *being*; for it matters not to us how it came to be *out of being*, so long as the present Virginians, or their ancestors, neither are nor were sufferers by the change then made.

But suppose it could be proved to be in being, which it cannot, because *being* in a charter is power, it would only prove a right in behalf of the London company of adventurers, but how that right is to be disposed of is another question. We are not defending the right of the London company deceased 150 years ago, but taking up the matter at the place where we found it, and so far as the authority of the Crown of England was exercised when the revolution commenced.

The charter was a contract between the Crown of England

and those adventurers for their own emolument, and not between the Crown and the people of Virginia; and whatever
was the occasion of the contract becoming void, or surrendered up, or superceded, makes no part of the question now.
It is sufficient that when the United States succeeded to sovereignty they found no such contract in existence or even in
litigation. They found Virginia under the authority of the
Crown of England, both as to soil and government, subject
to quit-rents to the Crown and not to the company, and had
been so for upwards of 150 years: and that an instrument or
deed of writing, of a private nature, as all proprietary contracts are so far as land is concerned, and which is now only
historically known, and in which Virginia was no party, and to
which no succession in any line can be proved, and have
ceased for 150 years, should now be raked from oblivion and
held up as a charter whereon to assume a right to boundless
territory, and that by a perversion of the order of it, is something very singular and extraordinary.

If there was any innovation on the part of the crown, the
contest rested between the crown and the proprietors, the
London company, and not between Virginia and the said
crown. It was not her charter; it was the company's charter,
and the only parties in the case were the crown and the
company.

But why, if Virginia contends for the immutability of charters, has she selected this in preference to the two former
ones? All her arguments arising from this principle must go to
the first charter and not to the last; but by placing them to
the last, instead of the first, she admits a fact against her principle; because, in order to establish the last, she proves the
first to be vacated by the second in the space of 23 years, the
second to be vacated by the third in the space of 3 years; and
why the third should not be vacated by the fourth form of
government, issuing from the same power with the former
two, and which took place about 25 years after, and continued
in being for 150 years since, and under which all her public
and private business was transacted, her purchases made, her
warrants for survey and patents for land obtained, is too mysterious to account for.

Either the re-assumption of the London company's charter

into the hands of the crown was an usurpation, or it was not. If it was, then, strictly speaking, is every thing which Virginia has done under that usurpation illegal, and she may be said to have lived in the most curious species of rebellion ever known; rebellion against the London company of adventurers. For if the charter to the company (for it was not to the Virginians) ought to be in being now, it ought to have been in being then; and why she should admit its vacation then, and reject it now, is unaccountable; or why she should esteem her purchases of lands good which were *then* made contrary to this charter, and now contend for the operation of the same charter to possess new territory by, are circumstances which cannot be reconciled.

But whether the charter, as it is called, ought to be extinct or not, cannot make a question with us. All the parties concerned in it are deceased, and no successors, in any regular line of succession, appear to claim. Neither the London company of adventurers, their heirs or assigns, were in possession of the exercise of this charter at the commencement of the revolution; and therefore the state of Virginia does not, in point of fact, succeed to and inherit from the company.

But say they, we succeed to and inherit from the Crown of England, which was the immediate possessor of the sovereignty at the time we entered, and had been so for 150 years.

To say this, is to say there is no charter at all. A charter is an assurance from one party to another, and cannot be from the same party to itself.

But before I enter further on this case I shall concisely state how this charter came to be re-assumed by the power which granted it, the Crown of England.

I have already stated that it was a proprietary charter, or grant, to sir Thomas Gates and others, who were called the London company, and sometimes the South-Virginia company, to distinguish them from those who settled to the eastward (now New-England) and were then called the North-Virginia or Plymouth company.

Oldmixon's history of Virginia (in his account of the British empire in America) published in the year 1708, gives a concise progress of the affair. He attributes it to the misconduct, contentions and mismanagement of the proprietors, and their innovations upon the Indians, which had so exasperated them, that they fell on the settlers and destroyed at one time 334 men, women, and children.

"Some time after this massacre, says he, several gentlemen in England procured grants of land from the company, and others came over on their private accounts to make settlements; among the former was one captain Martin, who was named to be of the council. This man raised so many differences among them, that new distractions followed, which the Indians observing, took heart and once more fell upon the settlers on the borders, destroying, without pitying either age, sex, or condition.

"These and other calamities, being chiefly imputed to the mismanagement of the proprietors, whose losses had so discouraged most of their best members, that they sold their shares, and Charles the first on his accession to the throne dissolved the company, and took the colony into his own immediate direction. He appointed the governor and council himself, ordered all patents and process to issue in his own name, and reserved a quit-rent of two shillings sterling for every hundred acres."

Thus far our author. Now it is impossible for us at this distance of time to say what were all the exact causes of the change; neither have we any business with it. The company might surrender it, or they might not, or they might forfeit it by not fulfilling conditions, or they might sell it, or the Crown might, as far as we know, take it from them. But what are either of these cases to Virginia, or any other which can be produced. She was not a party in the matter. It was not her charter, neither can she ingraft any right upon it or suffer any injury under it.

If the charter was vacated it must have been by the London company; if it was surrendered it must be by the same; If it was sold nobody else could sell it, and if it was taken from them nobody else could lose it; and yet Virginia calls this her charter, which it was not within her power to hold, to sell, to vacate, or to lose.

But if she puts her right upon the ground that it never was sold, surrendered, lost, or vacated, by the London company, she admits that if they *had* sold, surrendered, lost, or vacated it, that it would have become extinct, and to her no charter at all. And in this case, the only thing to prove is the fact, which is, Has this charter been the rule of government, and of purchasing or procuring unappropriated lands in Virginia, from the time it was granted to the time of the revolution? Answer, the charter has not been the rule of government, nor of purchasing or procuring lands, neither has any lands been purchased or procured under its sanction or authority for upwards of 150 years.

But if she goes a step further, and says that they could not vacate, surrender, sell, or lose it, by any act they could do, so neither could they vacate, surrender, sell, or lose that of 1606, which was three years prior to this; and this argument, so far from establishing the charter of 1609, would destroy it; and in its stead confirm the preceding one which limited the company to a square of 100 miles. And if she still goes back to that of sir Walter Rawleigh, *that* only places her in the light of Americans in common with all.

The only fact that can be clearly proved, is, that the Crown of England exercised the power of dominion and government of Virginia, and of the disposal of the lands, and that the charter had neither been the rule of government or purchasing lands for upwards of 150 years, and this places Virginia in succession to the Crown and not to the Company. Consequently it proves a lapse of the charter into the hands of the crown by some means or other.

Now to suppose that the charter could return into the hands of the crown and yet remain in force, is to suppose that a man could be bound by a bond of obligation to himself.

Its very *being* in the hands of the crown from which it issued is a cessation of its existence; and an effectual unchartering all that part of the Grant which was not before disposed of. And consequently the state of Virginia standing thus in succession to the crown, can be intitled to no more extent of country as a state under the union, than what it possessed as a province under the crown. And all lands exterior to these bounds as well of Virginia as the rest of the states, devolve, in the order of succession to the sovereignty of the United States for the benefit of all.

And this brings the case to what were the limits of Virginia as a province under the crown of England.

Charter it had none. It's limits then rested at the discretion of the authority to which it was subject. Maryland and Pennsylvania became it's boundary to the eastward and northward and North-Carolina to the southward, therefore the boundary to the westward was the only principal line to be ascertained.

As Virginia from a proprietary soil and government was become what then bore the name of a royal one, the extent of the province, as the order of things then stood (for something must always be admitted whereon to form a beginning) was wholly at the disposal of the crown of England, who might enlarge, or diminish, or erect new governments to the westward, by the same authoritative right that Virginia now can divide a county into two; if too large, or too inconvenient.

To say, as has been said, that Pennsylvania, Maryland and North-Carolina, were taken out of Virginia, is no more than to say, they were taken out of America; because Virginia was the common name of all the country, north and south: and to say they were taken out of the chartered limits of Virginia, is likewise to say nothing; because after the dissolution or extinction of the proprietary company, there was nobody to whom any provincial limits became chartered. The extinction of the company was the extinction of the chartered limits. The patent could not survive the company, because it was to them a right, which, when they expired ceased to be any body's else in their stead.

But to return to the western boundary of Virginia at the commencement of the revolution.

Charters, like proclamations, were the sole act of the crown, and if the former were adequate to fix limits to the lands which it gave away, sold, or otherways disposed of, the latter were equally adequate to fix limits or divisions to those which it retained; and therefore, the western limits of Virginia, as the proprietary company was extinct and consequently the patent with it, must be looked for in the line of proclamations.

I am not fond of quoting these old remains of former arrogance, but as we must begin somewhere, and as the states have agreed to regulate the right of each state to territory, by the condition each stood in with the crown of England at the commencement of the revolution, we have no other rule to go by; and any rule which can be agreed on is better than none.

From the proclamation then of 1763, the western limits of Virginia, as a province under the crown of England, are described so as not to extend beyond the heads of any of the rivers which empty themselves into the Atlantic, and consequently the limits did not pass over the Allegany Mountain.

Extract from the proclamation of 1763 so far as respects boundary:

"AND WHEREAS it is *just* and *reasonable*, and *essential to our interest*, and the security of our colonies, that the several nations or tribes of Indians, with whom we are connected, and who live under our protection, should not be molested or disturbed in the possession of such parts of our dominions and territories, *as, not having been ceded to, or purchased by us, are reserved to them or any of them as their hunting grounds;* we do therefore, with the advice of our privy council, declare it to be our royal will and pleasure, that no governor, or commander in chief, in any of our colonies of Quebec, east Florida, or west Florida, do presume, upon any pretence whatever, to grant warrants of survey, or pass any patents for lands beyond the bounds of their respective governments, as described in their commissions: As ALSO that no governor or commander in chief of our other colonies or plantations in America, do presume, for the present, and until our further pleasure be known, to grant warrants of survey, or pass patents for any lands *beyond the heads or sources of any of the rivers which fall into the Atlantic ocean from the west or north-west,* or upon any lands whatever, *which not having been ceded to, or purchased by us, as aforesaid, are reserved unto the said Indians or any of them.*

"And we do further declare it to be our royal will and pleasure, for the present, as aforesaid, to reserve under our sovereignty, protection, and dominion, *for the use of the said Indians all the lands and territories,* not included within the limits of our said three new governments, or within the limits of the territory granted to the Hudson's-Bay company; as also, *all the lands and territories lying to the westward of the sources of the rivers, which fall into the sea from the west and north-west as aforesaid*; and we do hereby strictly forbid, on pain of our displeasure, all our loving subjects from making any purchases or settlements whatever, or taking possession of any of the lands above reserved, without our especial leave and licence for that purpose first obtained:

"And we do further strictly enjoin and require all persons whatever, who have either wilfully or inadvertently seated themselves upon any lands within the countries above described, or upon any other lands, *which, not having been ceded to, or purchased by us*, are still reserved to the said Indians, as aforesaid, forthwith to remove themselves from such settlements."

It is easy for us to understand, that the frequent and plausible mention of the Indians was only speciousness to create an idea of the humanity of government. The object and intention of the proclamation was the western boundary, which is here signified not to extend beyond the heads of the rivers: and these, then, are the western limits which Virginia had as a province under the crown.

And agreeable to the intention of this proclamation and the limits described thereby, lord Hilsborough, then secretary of state in England, addressed an official letter of the 31st of July, 1770, to lord Bottetourt, at that time governor of Virginia, which letter was laid before the council of Virginia by Mr. president Nelson, and by him answered on the 18th of October in the same year, of which the following are extracts:

"On the evening of the day your lordship's letter to the governor was delivered to me, and as it contains matters of great variety and importance, it was read in council, and, together with the several papers inclosed, it hath been maturely considered, and I now trouble your lordship with theirs as well as my own opinion upon the subject of them.

"We do not presume to say to whom our gracious sovereign shall grant his vacant lands," and "with respect to the establishment of a *new colony on the back of Virginia*, it is a subject of too great political importance for me to presume to give an opinion upon, however, permit me, my lord, to observe, that when that part of the country shall become sufficiently populated it may be a wise and prudent measure."

On the death of lord Bottetourt, lord Dunmore was appointed to the government, and he, either from ignorance of the subject, or other motives, made a grant of some lands on the Ohio to certain of his friends and favorites, which produced the following letter from lord Dartmouth, who succeeded lord Hilsborough as secretary of state:

"I think fit to inclose your lordship a copy of lord Hilsborough's letter to lord Bottetourt, of the 31st of July, 1770, the receipt of which was acknowledged by Mr. president Nelson, a few days after lord Bottetourt's death, and appears by his answer to it, to have been laid before the council. That board, therefore, could not be ignorant of what has passed here upon Mr. Walpole's application, nor of the king's express command, contained in lord Hilsborough's letter, that no lands should be granted beyond the limits of the royal proclamation of 1763, until the king's further pleasure was signified; and I have only to observe, that it must have been a very extraordinary neglect in them not to have informed your lordship of that letter and those orders."

On these documents I shall make no remarks. They are their own evidence, and shew what the limits of Virginia were while a British province; and as there was then no other authority by which they could be fixed, and as the grant to the London company could not be a grant to any but themselves, and of consequence ceased to be when they ceased to exist, it remained a matter of choice in the crown, on its reassumption of the lands, to limit or divide them into separate governments, as it judged best, and from which there was not, and could not in the order of government, be any appeal. Neither was Virginia, as a province, affected by it, because the monies, in any case, arising from the sale of lands, did not go into her treasury; and whether to the crown or to the proprietors was to her indifferent. And it is likewise evident, from the secretary's letter, and the president's answer, that it was in contemplation to lay out a new colony on the *back* of Virginia, between the Allegany Mountains and the Ohio.

Having thus gone thro' the several charters, or grants, and their relation to each other, and shewn that Virginia cannot stand in succession to a private Grant, which has been extinct for upwards of 150 years; and that the western limits of Virginia, at the commencement of the revolution, were at the heads of the rivers emptying themselves into the Atlantic, none of which are beyond the Allegany Mountains; I now proceed to the second part, namely,

The reasonableness of her claims:

Virginia, as a British province, stood in a different situation with the crown of England to any of the other provinces, because she had no ascertained limits, but such as arose from the laying off new provinces and the proclamation of 1763. For the name, Virginia, as I have before mentioned, was the general name of all the country, and the dominion out of which the several governments were laid off: and in strict propriety, conformable to the origin of names, the province of Virginia was taken out of the dominion of Virginia. For the term, *dominion*, could not appertain to the province, which retained the name of Virginia, but to the crown, and from thence was applied to the whole country, and signified its being an appendage to the crown of England, as they now say *"our dominion of Wales."*

It is not possible to suppose there could exist an idea, that Virginia, as a British province, was to be extended to the south sea at the distance of three thousand miles. The dominion, as appertaining at that time to the crown, might be claimed to extend so far, but as a province the thought was not conceiveable, nor the practice possible. And it is more than probable, that the deception made use of to obtain the patent of 1609, by representing the south sea to be near where the Allegany Mountains are, was one cause of its becoming extinct; and it is worthy of remarking, that no history (at least that I have met with) mentions any dispute or litigation, between the crown and the company in consequence of the extinction of the patent, and the re-assumption of the lands; and therefore the negative evidence corroborating with the positive, make it, as certain as such a case can possibly be, that either the company received a compensation for the patent, or quitted it quietly, ashamed of the imposition they had acted, and their subsequent mal-administration. Men are not inclined to give up a claim where there is any ground to contend on, and the silence in which the patent expired is a presumptive proof that its fate, from whatever cause, was just.

There is one general policy which seems to have prevailed with the English in laying off new governments, which was, not to make them larger than their own country, that they might the easier hold them manageable: this was the case with every one except Canada, the extension of whose limits was for the political purpose of recognizing new acquisition of territory, not immediately convenient for colonization.

But, in order to give this matter a chance thro' all its cases, I will admit what no man can suppose, which is, that there is an English charter that fixes Virginia to extend from the Atlantic to the south sea, and contained within a due west line, set off two hundred miles below cape Comfort, and a north west line, set off two hundred miles above it. Her side, then, on the Atlantic (according to an explanation given in Mr. Bradford's Paper of September 29th, 1779, by an advocate for the Virginia claims) will be four hundred miles; her side to the south three thousand; her side to the west four thousand; and her north-west line about five thousand; and the quantity of land contained within these dimensions will be almost 4,000,000,000, that is, four thousand million of acres, which is more than ten times the quantity contained within the present United States, and above an hundred times greater than the kingdom of England.

To reason on a case like this is such a waste of time, and such an excess of folly that it ought not to be reasoned upon. It is impossible to suppose that any patent to private persons could be so intentionally absurd, and the claim grounded thereon is as wild as any thing the imagination of man ever conceived.

But if, as I before mentioned, there was a charter which bore such an explanation, and that Virginia stood in succession to it, what would that be to us any more than the will of Alexander, had he taken it in his head to have bequeathed away the world? Such a charter or grant must have been obtained by imposition and a false representation of the country, or granted in error, or both; and in any of, or all, these cases, the United States must reject the matter as something they can know nothing of, for the merits will not bear an argument, and the pretention of right stands upon no better ground.

Our case is an original one; and many matters attending it must be determined on their own merits and reasonableness. The territory of the rest of the states is in general, within known bounds of moderate extent, and the quota which each state is to furnish towards the expence and service of the war, must be ascertained upon some rule of comparison. The number of inhabitants of each state formed the first rule; and it was naturally supposed that those numbers bore nearly the same proportion to each other, which the territory of each state did. Virginia, on this scale, would be about one fifth larger than Pennsylvania, which would be as much dominion as any state could manage with happiness and convenience.

When I first began this subject, my intention was to be extensive on the merits, and concise on the matter of right; instead of which, I have been extensive on the matter of right, and concise on the merits or reasonableness: and this alteration in my design arose, consequentially, from the nature of the subject; for as a reasonable thing the claim can be supported by no argument, and therefore needs none to refute it; but as there is a strange propensity in mankind to shelter themselves under the sanction of a right, however unreasonable that supposed right may be, I found it most conducive to the interest of the case, to shew, that the right stands upon no better grounds than the reason. And shall therefore proceed to make some observations on,

The consequences of the claim.

The claim being unreasonable in itself and standing on no ground of right, but such as, if true, must from the quarter it is drawn be offensive, has a tendency to create disgust and sour the minds of the rest of the states. Those lands are capable, under the management of the United States, of repaying the charges of the war, and some of them, as I shall hereafter show, may, I presume, be made an immediate advantage of.

I distinguish three different descriptions of lands in America at the commencement of the revolution. Proprietary or chartered lands, as was the case in Pennsylvania. Crown lands, within the described limits of any of the crown governments; and crown residuary lands that were without, or beyond, the limits of any province; and those last were held in reserve whereon to erect new governments and lay out new provinces; as appears to have been the design by lord Hillsborough's letter and the president's answer, wherein he says "with respect to the establishment of a *new* colony on the *back* of Virginia, it is a subject of too great political importance for me to presume to give an opinion upon; however, permit me, my lord, to observe, that when that part of the country shall become populated it may be a wise and prudent measure."

The expression is a *"new colony* on the *back* of Virginia"; and referred to lands between the heads of the rivers and the Ohio. This is a proof that those lands were not considered within, but beyond, the limits of Virginia as a colony; and the other expression in the letter is equally descriptive, namely, *"We do not presume to say to whom our gracious sovereign shall grant his vacant lands"*. Certainly then, the same right, which, at that time, rested in the crown, rests now in the more supreme authority of the United States; and therefore, addressing the president's letter to the circumstances of the revolution it will run thus,

"We do not presume to say to whom the *sovereign United States* shall grant their vacant lands, and with respect to the settlement of a *new colony* on the *back* of Virginia, it is a matter of too much political importance for me to give an opinion upon; however, permit me to observe, that when that part of the country shall become populated it may be a wise and prudent measure."

It must occur to every person, on reflection, that those lands are too distant to be within the government of any of the present states; and, I may presume to suppose, that were a calculation justly made, Virginia has lost more by the decrease of taxables, than she has gained by what lands she has made sale of; therefore, she is not only doing the rest of the states wrong in point of equity, but herself and them an injury in point of strength, service and revenue.

It is only the United States, and not any single State, that can lay off new states and incorporate them in the union by representation; therefore, the situation which the settlers on those lands will be in, under the assumed right of Virginia, will be hazardous and distressing, and they will feel themselves at last like aliens to the common wealth of Israel, their habitations unsafe and their title precarious.

And when men reflect on that peace, harmony, quietude, and security, which is necessary to prosperity, especially in making new settlements, and think that when the war shall be ended, their happiness and safety will depend on a union with the states, and not a scattered people, unconnected with, and politically unknown to, the rest, they will feel but little inclination to put themselves in a situation, which, however solitary and recluse, it may appear, at present, will then be uncertain and unsafe, and their troubles will have to begin where those of the United States shall end.

It is probable that some of the inhabitants of Virginia may be inclined to suppose, that the writer of this, by taking up the subject in the manner he has done, is arguing unfriendly against their interest. To this he wishes to reply;

That the most extraordinary part of the whole is, that Virginia should countenance such a claim. For it is worthy of observing, that, from the beginning of the contest with Britain, and long after, there was not a people in America who discovered, thro' all the variety and multiplicity of public business, a greater fund of true wisdom, fortitude, and disinterestedness, than the then colony of Virginia. They were loved—They were reverenced. Their investigation of the assumed rights of Britain had a sagacity which was uncommon. Their reasonings were piercing, difficult to be equalled and impossible to be refuted, and their public spirit was exceeded by none. But since this unfortunate land scheme has taken place, their powers seem to be absorbed. A Torpor has overshaded them, and every one asks what is become of Virginia?

It seldom happens that the romantic schemes of extensive dominion are of any service to a government, and never to a people. They assuredly end at last in loss, trouble, division, and disappointment. And was even the title of Virginia good, and the claim admissible, she would derive more lasting and real benefit by participating it, than by attempting the management of an object so infinitely beyond her reach. Her share with the rest, under the supremacy of the United States, which is the only authority adequate to the purpose, would be worth more to her, than what the whole would produce under the management of herself alone, and that for several reasons.

First, because her claim not being admissible nor yet manageable, she cannot make a good title to the purchasers, and consequently can get but little for the lands.

Secondly, because the distance the settlers will be at from her, will immediately put them out of all government and protection, so far, at least, as relates to Virginia: and by this means she will render her frontiers a refuge to desperadoes, and a hiding place from justice; and the consequence will be perpetual unsafety to her own peace and that of the neighbouring states.

Thirdly, Because her quota of expence for carrying on the war, admitting her to engross such an immensity of territory, would be greater than she can either support or supply, and could not be less, upon a reasonable rule of proportion, than nine tenths of the whole. And

Lastly, because she must sooner or later relinquish them, and therefore to see her own interest wisely at first, is preferable to the alternative of finding it out by misfortune at last.

I have now gone thro' my examination of the claims of Virginia in every case which I proposed; and for several reasons wish the lot had fallen to another person.

But as this is a most important matter, in which all are interested, and the substantial good of Virginia not injured but promoted, and as few men have leisure, and still fewer have inclination, to go into intricate investigation, I have at last ventured on the subject.

The succession of the United States to the vacant western territory is a right they originally sat out upon, and in the pamphlet, *Common Sense*, I frequently mentioned those lands as a national fund for the benefit of all; therefore, resuming the subject, where I then left off, I shall conclude with concisely reducing to system what I then only hinted.

In my last piece, the *Crisis Extraordinary*, I estimated the annual amount of the charge of the war and the support of the several governments at two millions pounds sterling, and the peace establishment at three quarters of a million, and, by a comparison of the taxes of this country with those of England, proved that the whole yearly expence to us, to defend the country, is but a third of what Britain would have drawn from us by taxes, had she succeeded in her attempt to conquer; and our peace establishment only an eighth part; and likewise shewed, that it was within the ability of the states to carry on the whole of the war by taxation without having recourse to any other modes or funds. To have a clear idea of taxation is necessary to every country, and the more funds we can discover and organize the less will be the hope of the enemy, and the readier their disposition to peace, which it is now *their* interest more than *ours* to promote.

I have already remarked that only the United States and not any particular state can lay off new states and incorporate them in the union by representation; keeping, therefore, this idea in view, I ask, might not a substantial fund be quickly created by laying off a new state, so as to contain between twenty and thirty million of acres, and opening a land office in all the countries in Europe for hard money, and in this country for supplies in kind at a certain price.

The tract of land that seems best adapted to answer this purpose is contained between the Allegany Mountain and the river Ohio, as far north as the Pennsylvania line, thence extending down the said river to the falls thereof, thence due south into the latitude of the North-Carolina line, and thence east to the Allegany Mountain aforesaid—I, the more readily, mention this tract, because it is fighting the enemy at their own weapons, as it includes the same ground on which a new colony would have been erected, for the emolument of the crown of England, as appears by lord Hilsborough's and Dartmouth's letters, had not the revolution prevented its being carried into execution.

It is probable there may be some spots of private property within this tract, but to incorporate them into some government will render them more profitable to the owners, and the condition of the scattered settlers more eligible and happy than at present.

If twenty millions of acres of this new state be patented and sold at twenty pounds sterling per hundred acres, they will produce four million pounds sterling, which, if applied to continental expences only, will support the war for three years, should Britain be so unwise to herself to prosecute it against her own direct interest and against the interest and policy of all Europe. The several states will then have to raise taxes for their internal government only, and the continental taxes as soon as the fund begins to operate, will lessen, and if sufficiently productive will cease.

Lands are the real riches of all the habitable world and the natural funds of America. The funds of other countries are, in general, artificially constructed; the creatures of necessity and contrivance; dependent upon credit, and always exposed to hazard and uncertainty. But lands can neither be annihilated nor lose their value; on the contrary, they universally rise with population, and rapidly so, when under the security of effectual government. But this it is impossible for Virginia to give, and, therefore, that which is capable of defraying the expences of the empire, will, under the management of any single state, produce only a fugitive support to wandring individuals.

I shall now enquire into the effects which the laying out a new state, under the authority of the United States, will have upon Virginia.

It is the very circumstance she ought to, and must, wish for, when she examines the matter thro' all its case and consequences.

The present settlers being beyond her reach, and her supposed authority over them remaining in herself, they will appear to her as revolters, and she to them as oppressors; and this will produce such a spirit of mutual dislike, that in a little time a total disagreement will take place, to the disadvantage of both.

But under the authority of the United States the matter is

manageable, and Virginia will be eased of a disagreeable consequence.

Besides this, a sale of the lands, continentally, for the purpose of supporting the expence of the war, will save her a greater share of taxes, than what the small sale she could make herself, and the small price she could get for them, would produce.

She would likewise have two advantages which no other state in the union enjoys, first, a frontier state for her defence against the incursions of the Indians; and the second is, that the laying out and peopling a new state on the back of an old one, situated as she is, is doubling the quantity of its trade.

The new state, which is here proposed to be laid out, may send its exports down the Missisippi, but its imports must come thro' Chesapeak Bay, and consequently Virginia will become the market for the new state; because, tho' there is a navigation from it, there is none into it, on account of the rapidity of the Missisippi.

There are certain circumstances that will produce certain events whether men think of them or not. The events do not depend upon thinking, but are the natural consequence of acting; and according to the system which Virginia has gone upon, the issue will be, that she will get involved with the back settlers in a contention about *rights* till they dispute with her own claims, and, soured by the contention, will go to any other state for their commerce; both of which may be prevented, a perfect harmony established, the strength of the states encreased, and the expences of the war defrayed, by settling the matter now on the plan of a general right; and every day it is delayed the difficulty will be encreased and the advantages lessened.

But if it should happen, as it possibly may that the war should end before the money which the new state may produce be expended, the remainder of the lands therein may be set apart to reimburse those, whose houses have been burnt by the enemy, as this is a species of suffering which it was impossible to prevent, because houses are not moveable property: and it ought not to be, that because we cannot do every thing, that we ought not to do what we can.

Having said thus much on the subject, I think it necessary to remark, that the prospect of a new fund, so far from abating our endeavours in making every immediate provision for the supply of the army, ought to quicken us therein; for should the states see it expedient to go upon the measure, it will be at least a year before it can be productive. I the more freely mention this, because, there is a dangerous species of popularity, which, I fear, some men are seeking from their constituents by giving them grounds to believe, that if they are elected they will lighten the taxes; a measure, which, in the present state of things, cannot be done without exposing the country to the ravages of the enemy by disabling the army from defending it.

Where knowledge is a duty ignorance is a crime; and if any man whose duty it was to know better has encouraged such an expectation, he has either deceived himself or them: besides, no country can be defended without expence, and let any man compare his portion of temporary inconveniences arising from taxations, with the real distresses of the army for the want of supplies, and the difference is not only sufficient to strike him dumb, but make him thankful that worse consequences have not followed.

In advancing this doctrine, I speak with an honest freedom to the country; for as it is their good to be defended, so it is their interest to provide that defence, at least, till other funds can be organized.

As the laying out new states will some time or other be the business of the country, and as it is yet a new business to us; and as the influence of the war has scarcely afforded leisure for reflecting on distant circumstances, I shall throw together a few hints for facilitating that measure, whenever it may be proper for adopting it.

The United States now standing on the line of sovereignty, the vacant territory is their property collectively, but the persons by whom it may hereafter be peopled will have an equal right with ourselves; and therefore, as new states shall be laid off and incorporated with the present, they will become partakers of the remaining territory with us who are already in possession. And this consideration ought to heighten the value of lands to new emigrants; because, in making purchases, they not only gain an immediate property, but become initiated into the right and heirship of the states to a property in reserve, which is an additional advantage to what any purchasers under the late government of England enjoyed.

The setting off the boundary of any new state will naturally be the first step, and as it must be supposed not to be peopled at the time it is laid off, a constitution must be formed, by the United States, as the rule of government in any new state, for a certain term of years, (perhaps ten) or until the state become peopled to a certain number of inhabitants; after which, the whole and sole right of modelling their government to rest with themselves.

A question may arise, whether a new state should immediately possess an equal right with the present ones in all cases which may come before Congress.

This, experience will best determine; but at first view of the matter it appears thus; That it ought to be immediately incorporated into the union on the ground of a family right, such a state standing in the line of a younger child of the same stock; but as new emigrants will have something to learn when they first come to America, and a new state requiring aid rather than capable of giving it, it might be most convenient to admit its immediate representation into Congress, there to sit, hear, and debate, on all questions and matters, but not to vote on any till after the expiration of seven years.

I shall in this place take the opportunity of renewing a hint which I formerly threw out in the pamphlet *Common Sense*, and which the several states will, sooner or later, see the convenience, if not the necessity, of adopting; which is, that of electing a Continental Convention, for the purpose of forming a Continental Constitution, defining and describing the powers and authority of Congress.

Those of entering into treaties, and making peace, they naturally possess, in behalf of the states, for their separate as well as their united good: but the internal control and dictatorial powers of Congress are not sufficiently defined, and appear to be too much in some cases, and too little in others; and therefore, to have them marked legally out will give additional energy to the whole, and new confidence to the several parts.

Common Sense, on the King of England's Speech

February 19 and 28, 1782

OF all the innocent passions which actuate the human mind, there is none more universally prevalent than curiosity. It reaches all mankind, and in matters which concern us, or concern us not, it alike provokes in us a desire to know.

Altho' the situation of America, superior to every effort to enslave her, and daily rising into importance and oppulence hath placed her above the region of anxiety, it still left her within the circle of curiosity; and her fancy to see the speech of a man who had proudly threatened to bring her at his feet, was visibly marked with that tranquil confidence which cared nothing about its contents. It was enquired after with a smile, read with a laugh, and dismissed with disdain.

But, as justice is due, even to an enemy, it is right to say, that the speech is as well managed as the embarrassed condition of their affairs could well admit of; and though scarce a line of it is true, except the mournful story of Cornwallis, it may serve to amuse the deluded commons and people of England, for whom it was calculated.

"The war," says the speech, "is still unhappily prolonged by that restless ambition which first excited our enemies to commence it, and which still continues to disappoint my earnest wishes and diligent exertions to restore the public tranquility."

How easy is it to abuse truth and language, when men, by habitual wickedness, have learned to set justice at defiance. That the very man who began the war, who, with the most sullen insolence refused to answer, and even to hear the humblest of all petitions, who hath encouraged his officers and his army in the most savage cruelties, and the most scandalous plunderings, who hath stirred up the Indians on one side, and the Negroes on the other, and invoked every aid of Hell in his behalf, should now with an air of affected pity turn the tables from himself, and charge on another the wickedness that is his own, can only be equalled by the baseness of the heart that spoke it.

TO BE NOBLY WRONG IS MORE MANLY THAN TO BE MEANLY RIGHT, is an expression I once used on a former occasion, and it is equally applicable now. We feel something like respect for consistency even in error. We lament the virtue that is debauched into a vice, but the vice that affects a virtue becomes the more detestable: and amongst the various assumptions of character, which hypocrisy has taught, and men have practised, there is none that raises a higher relish of disgust, than to see disappointed inveteracy twisting itself, by the most visible falshoods, into an appearance of piety it has no pretentions to.

"But I should not," continues the speech, "answer the trust committed to the sovereign of a FREE PEOPLE, nor make a suitable return to my subjects for their constant, zealous, and affectionate attachment to my person, family and government, if I consented to sacrifice, either to my own desire of peace, or to their temporary ease and relief, THOSE ESSENTIAL RIGHTS AND PERMANENT INTERESTS, upon the maintainance and preservation of which, the future strength and security of this country must principally depend."

That the man whose ignorance and obstinacy first involved and still continues the nation in the most hopeless and expensive of all wars, should now meanly flatter them with the name of a FREE PEOPLE, and make a merit of his crime, under the disguise of their essential rights and permanent interests, is something which disgraces even the character of perverseness. Is he afraid they will send him to Hanover, or what does he fear? Why is the sycophant thus added to the hypocrite, and the man who pretends to govern, sunk into the humble and submissive memorialist?

What those essential rights and permanent interests are, on which the future strength and security of England must principally DEPEND, are not so much as alluded to. They are words which impress nothing but the ear, and are calculated only for the sound.

But if they have any reference to America, then do they amount to the disgraceful confession, that England, who once assumed to be her protectress, is now become her

DEPENDENT. The British king and ministry are constantly holding up the vast importance which America is of to England, in order to allure the nation to carry on the war: now whatever ground there is for this idea, it ought to have operated as a reason for not beginning it; and therefore they support their present measures at their own disgrace, because the arguments they now use, are a direct reflection on their former policy.

"The favourable appearance of affairs," continues the speech "in the East Indies and the safe arrival of the numerous commercial fleets of my kingdom must have given you satisfaction."

That things are not QUITE so bad every where as in America may be some cause of consolation, but can be none for triumph. One broken leg is better than two, but still it is not joy: and let the appearance of affairs in the East-Indies be ever so favourable, they are nevertheless worse than at first, without a prospect of their ever being better. But the mournful story of Cornwallis was yet to be told, and it was necessary to give it the softest introduction possible.

"But in the course of this year," continues the speech "my assiduous endeavours to guard the extensive dominions of my crown, have not been attended with success equal to the justice and uprightness of my views"—what justice and uprightness there was in beginning a war with America the world will judge of, and the unequalled barbarity with which it has been conducted is not to be worn from the memory by the cant of snivelling hypocrisy.

"And it is with GREAT CONCERN that I inform you that the events of war have been very unfortunate to my arms in Virginia, having ended in the loss of my forces in that province."—And OUR great concern is that they are not all served in the same manner.

"No endeavours have been wanting on my part" says the speech "to extinguish that spirit of rebellion which our enemies have found means to foment and maintain in the colonies; and to restore to my DELUDED SUBJECTS in America that happy and prosperous condition which they formerly derived from a due obedience to the laws."

The expression of DELUDED SUBJECTS is become so hacknied and contemptable, and the more so when we see them making prisoners of whole armies at a time, that the pride of not being laughed at would induce a man of common sense to leave it off. But the most offensive falshood in the paragraph, is the attributing the prosperity of America to a wrong cause. It was the unremitted industry of the settlers and their descendants, the hard labour and toil of persevering fortitude that were the true causes of the prosperity of America. The former tyranny of England served to people it, and the virtue of the adventurers to improve it. Ask the man who with his axe hath cleared a way in the wilderness and now possesses an estate, what made him rich, and he will tell you the labour of his hands, the sweat of his brow and the blessing of heaven. Let Britain but leave America to herself and she asks no more. She has risen into greatness without the knowlege and against the will of England, and has a right to the unmolested enjoyment of her own created wealth.

"I will order" says the speech "the estimates of the ensuing year to be laid before you. I rely on your wisdom and public spirit for such supplies as the circumstances of our affairs shall be found to require. Among the many ill consequences which attend the continuation of the present war, I must sincerely regret the additional burthens which it must unavoidably bring upon my faithful subjects."

Strange! That a nation must run thro' such a labyrinth of trouble, and expend such a mass of wealth to gain the wisdom which an hour's reflection might have taught. The final superiority of America over every attempt which an island might make to conquer her, was as naturally marked in the constitution of things, as the future ability of a giant over a dwarf is delineated in his features while an infant. How far Providence, to accomplish purposes, which no human wisdom could foresee, permitted such extraordinary errors, will be believed by some and doubted by others, and still a secret in the womb of time, must rest till futurity shall give it birth.

"In the prosecution of this great and important contest," says the speech, "in which we are engaged, I retain a firm confidence in the PROTECTION OF DIVINE PROVIDENCE, and a perfect conviction in the justice of my cause, and I have no doubt, but, that by the concurrence and support of my parliament, by the valour of my fleets and armies, and by a vigorous, animated, and united exertion of the faculties and resources of my people, I shall be enabled to restore the blessings of a safe and honorable peace to all my dominions."

The king of England is one of the readiest believers in the world. In the beginning of the contest he passed an act to put America out of the protection of the crown of England, and though Providence, for seven years together hath put him out of HER protection, still the man has no doubt. Like Pharoah on the edge of the Red sea, he sees not the plunge he is making, and precipitately drives across the flood that is closing over his head.

I think it is a reasonable supposition, that this part of the speech was composed before the arrival of the news of the capture of Cornwallis; for it certainly has no relation to their condition at the time it was spoken. But, be this as it may, it is nothing to us. Our line is fixt. Our lot is cast. And America, the child of fate, is arriving at maturity. We have nothing to do but by a spirited and quick exertion, to stand prepared for war or peace. Too great to yield, and too noble to insult; superior to misfortune, and generous in success, let us untaintedly preserve the character we have gained, and show to future ages, an example of unequalled magnanimity. There is something in the cause and consequence of America that has drawn on her the attention of all mankind. The world has seen her brave. Her love of liberty; her ardour in supporting it; the justice of her claims, and the constancy of her fortitude has won her the esteem of Europe, and attached to her interest the first power of that country.

Her situation now is such, that to whatever point, past, present or to come she cast her eyes, new matter rises to convince her she is right. In her conduct towards her enemy, no reproachful sentiment lurks in secret. No sense of injustice is left upon the mind. Untainted with ambition and a stranger to revenge, her progress hath been marked by providence, and she, in every stage of the conflict has blest her with success.

But let not America wrap herself up in delusive hope and suppose the business done. The least remissness in preparation, the least relax in execution, will only serve to prolong the war and increase expences. If our enemies can draw consolation from misfortune, and exert themselves upon dispair, how much more ought we, who are to win a continent by the conquest and have already an earnest of success.

[To be continued in a future paper.]

[Continued from our Paper of the 19th Instant.]
Having in the preceding part made my remarks on the several matters which the speech contains, I shall now make my remarks on what it does not contain.

There is not a syllable in it respecting alliances. Either the injustice of Britain is too glaring, or her condition too desperate, or both, for any neighbouring power to come to her support. In the beginning of the contest, when she had only America to contend with, she hired assistance from Hesse and other smaller States of Germany, and for nearly three years did America, young, raw, undisciplined and unprovided, stand against the power of Britain, aided by twenty thousand foreign troops, and made a compleat conquest of one entire army. The remembrance of those things ought to inspire us with confidence and greatness of mind, and carry us through every remaining difficulty with content and chearfulness. What are the little sufferings of the present day, compared with the hardships that are past. There was a time, when we had neither house nor home in safety; when every hour was the hour of alarm and danger; when the mind, tortured with anxiety, knew no repose, and every thing but hope and fortitude was bidding us farewel.

It is of use to look back upon these things; to call to mind the times of trouble and the scenes of complicated anguish that are past and gone. Then every expence was cheap, compared with the dread of conquest and the misery of submission. We did not stand debating upon trifles, nor contending about the necessary and unavoidable charges of defence. Every one bore his lot of suffering, and looked forward to happier days and scenes of rest.

Perhaps one of the greatest dangers which any country can be exposed to arises from a kind of trifling, which sometimes steals upon the mind when it supposes the danger past; and this unsafe situation marks at this time the peculiar crisis of America. What would she once have given, to have known that her condition at this day should be what it now is? and yet we do not seem to place a proper value upon it, nor vigorously pursue the necessary measures to secure it. We know we cannot be defended, nor yet defend ourselves, without trouble and expence. We have no right to expect it; neither ought we even to look for it. We are a people, who, in our situation, differ from all the world. We form one common floor of public good and, whatever is our charge, it is paid for our own interest and upon our own account.

Misfortune and experience have now taught us system and method; and the arrangements for carrying on the war are reduced to rule and order. The quota of the several States are ascertained, and I intend in a future publication to shew what they are, and the necessity as well as the advantages of vigorously providing them.

In the mean time, I shall conclude this paper with an instance of *British clemency*, from Smollet's History of England, volume the 11th, page 239, printed in London. It will serve to show how dismal is the situation of a conquered people, and that the only security is in effectual defence.

We all know that the Stuart family and the House of Hanover opposed each other for the Crown of England. The Stuart family stood first in the line of succession, but the other was the most successful.

In July, 1745, Charles, the son of the exiled king, landed in Scotland, collected a small force, at no time exceeding five or six thousand men, and made some attempts to re-establish his claim. The late Duke of Cumberland, uncle to the present King of England, was sent against him, and on the sixteenth of April following Charles was totally defeated at Culloden, in Scotland. Success and power are the only situations in which clemency can be shewn, and those who are cruel, because they are victorious, can, with the same facility, act any other degenerate characters.

"Immediately after the decisive action at Culloden, the Duke of Cumberland took possession of Inverness; where six and thirty deserters, convicted by a court-martial, were ordered to be executed: then he detached several parties to ravage the country. One of these apprehended the lady Mackintosh, who was sent prisoner to Inverness, plundered her house, and drove away her cattle, though her husband was actually in the service of the government. The castle of lord Lovat was destroyed. The French prisoners were sent to Carlisle and Penrith: Kilmarnock, Balmerino, Cromartie, and his son the lord Macleod, were conveyed by sea to London; and those of an inferior rank were confined in different prisons. The marquis of Tullibardine, together with a brother of the earl of Dunmore, and Murray the pretender's secretary, were seized and transported to the Tower of London, to which the earl of Traquair had been committed on suspicion; and the eldest son of lord Lovat was imprisoned in the castle of Edinburgh. In a word, all the goals of Great-Britain, from the capital northwards, were filled with those unfortunate captives; and great numbers of them were crowded together in the holds of ships, where they perished in the most deplorable manner, for want of air and exercise. Some rebel chiefs escaped in two French frigates that arrived on the coast of Lochaber about the end of April, and engaged three vessels belonging to his Britannic majesty, which they obliged to retire. Others embarked on board of a ship on the coast of Buchan, and were conveyed to Norway, from whence they travelled to Sweden. In the month of May, the duke of Cumberland advanced with the army into the Highlands, as far as Fort-Augustus, where he encamped; and sent off detachments on all hands, to hunt down the fugitives, and lay waste the country with fire and sword. The castles of Glengary and Lochiel were plundered and burned; every house, hutt, or habitation, met with the same fate, without distinction; and all the cattle and provision were carried off; the men were either shot upon the mountains, like wild beasts, or put to death in cold blood, without form of trial; the women, after having seen their husbands and fathers murdered, were subjected to brutal violation, and then turned out naked, with their children, to starve on the barren heaths. One whole family was inclosed in a barn, and consumed to ashes. Those ministers of vengeance were so alert in the execution of their office, that in a few days there was neither house, cottage, man, nor beast, to be seen within the compass of fifty miles; all was ruin, silence and desolation."

I have here presented the reader with one of the most shocking instances of cruelty ever practised, and I leave it to rest on his mind, that he may be fully impressed with a sense of the destruction he has escaped in case Britain had conquered America; and likewise, that he may see and feel the necessity, as well for his own personal safety, as for the honor, the interest, the happiness of the whole community, to omit or delay no one preparation necessary to secure the ground we so happily stand upon.

Common Sense, on Financing the War

March 5, 1782

TO THE PEOPLE OF AMERICA.

ON THE EXPENCES, ARRANGEMENTS AND DISBURSEMENTS FOR CARRYING ON THE WAR, AND FINISHING IT WITH HONOUR AND ADVANTAGE.

WHEN any necessity or occasion has pointed out the convenience of addressing the public, I have never made it a consideration whether the subject was popular or unpopular, but whether it was right or wrong; for that which is right will become popular, and that which is wrong, though by mistake it may obtain the cry or fashion of the day, will soon lose the power of delusion, and sink into disesteem.

A remarkable instance of this happened in the case of Silas Deane; and I mention this circumstance with the greater ease, because the poison of his hypocrisy spread over the whole country, and every man, almost without exception, thought me wrong in opposing him. The best friends I then had, except Mr. Laurens, stood at a distance, and this tribute, which is due to his constancy, I pay to him with respect, and that the readier, because he is not here to hear it. If it reaches him in his imprisonment, it will afford him an agreeable reflection.

"As he rose like a rocket, he would fall like the stick," is a metaphor which I applied to Mr. Deane in the first piece which I published respecting him, and he has exactly fulfilled the description. The credit he so unjustly obtained from the public, he lost in almost as short a time. The delusion perished as it fell, and he soon saw himself stripped of popular support. His more intimate acquaintance began to doubt and to desert him long before he left America, and at his departure he saw himself the object of general suspicion. When arrived in France, he endeavoured to effect by treason what he had failed to accomplish by fraud. His plans, schemes and projects, together with his expectation of being sent to Holland to negociate a loan of money, had all miscarried. He then began traducing and accusing America of every crime,

which could injure her reputation. "That she was a ruined country; that she only meant to make a tool of France, to get what money she could out of her, and then to leave her, and accommodate with Britain." Of all which, and much more, Colonel Laurens and myself, when in France, informed Dr. Franklin, who had not before heard of it. And to compleat the character of a traitor, he has, by letters to this country since, some of which, in his own hand writing, are now in the possession of Congress, used every expression and argument in his power to injure the reputation of France, and to advise America to renounce her alliance, and surrender up her independence.* Thus, in France, he abuses America, and in his letters to America he abuses France; and is endeavouring to create disunion between the two countries, by the same arts of double-dealing by which he caused dissensions among the Commissioners in Paris, and distractions in America. But his life has been fraud, and his character is that of a plodding, plotting, cringing mercenary, capable of any disguise that suited his purpose. His final detection has very happily cleared up those mistakes, and removed those uneasinesses, which his unprincipled conduct occasioned. Every one now sees him in the same light; for towards friends or enemies he acted with the same deception and injustice, and his name, like that of *Arnold*, ought now to be forgotten among us. As this is the first time I have mentioned him since my return from France, it is my intention it shall be the last.—From this digression, which for several reasons I thought necessary to give, I now proceed to the purport of my address.

I consider the war of America against Britain as the country's war, the public's war, or the war of the people in their own behalf, for the security of their natural rights, and the protection of their own property. It is not the war of Congress, the war of the Assemblies, or the war of Govern-

*Mr. William Marshal, of this city, formerly a pilot, who had been taken at sea and carried to England, and got from thence to France, brought over letters from Mr. Deane to America, one of which was directed to *"Robert Morris, Esq."* Mr. Morris sent it unopened to Congress, and advised Mr. Marshal to deliver the others there, which he did. The letters were of the same purport with those which have been already published under the signature of *S. Deane*, to which they had frequent reference.

ment, in any line whatever. The country first, by a mutual compact, resolved to defend their rights and maintain their independance, *at the hazard of their lives and fortunes.* They elected their Representatives, by whom they appointed their members to Congress, and said, *act you for us, and we will support you.* This is the true ground and principle of the war on the part of America, and, consequently, there remains nothing to do, but for every one to fulfil his obligation.

It was next to impossible that a new country, engaged in a new undertaking, could set off systematically right at first. She saw not the extent of the struggle she was involved in, neither could she avoid the beginning. She supposed every step she took, and every resolution she formed, would bring her enemy to reason, and close the contest. Those failing, she was forced into new measures; and these, like the former, being fitted to her expectations, and failing in their turn, left her continually unprovided and without system. The enemy likewise was induced to prosecute the war, from the temporary expedients we adopted for carrying it on. We were continually expecting to see their credit exhausted, and they were looking to see our currency fail; and thus, between their watching us and we them, the hopes of both have been deceived, and the childishness of the expectation has served to encrease the expence.

Yet who, through this wilderness of error, has been to blame? where is the man who can say, the fault has not in part been his? They were the natural unavoidable errors of the day. They were the errors of a whole country, which nothing but experience could detect, and time remove. Neither could the circumstances of America admit of system, till either the paper currency was fixed or laid aside. No calculation of finance could be made on a medium falling without reason, and fluctuating without rule.

But there is one error which might have been prevented, and was not; and as it is not my custom to flatter, but to serve mankind, I will speak it freely. It certainly was the duty of every assembly on the continent to have known, at all times, what was the condition of its treasury, and to have ascertained at every period of depreciation, how much the real worth of the taxes fell short of their nominal value. This knowledge, which might have been easily gained, would have enabled them to have kept their constituents well informed, which is one of the greatest duties of representation. They ought to have studied and calculated the expences of the war, the quota of each State, and the consequent proportion that would fall on each man's property for his defence; and this must easily have shewn to them, that a tax of an hundred pounds could not be paid by a bushel of apples or an hundred of flour, which was often the case two or three years ago. But instead of this, which would have been plain and upright dealing, the little line of temporary popularity, the feather of an hour's duration, was too much pursued; and in this involved condition of things, every State, for the want of a little thinking, or a little information, supposed that it supported the whole expences of the war, when in fact it fell, by the time the tax was levied and collected, above three fourths short of its own quota.

Impressed with a sense of the danger to which the country was exposed by this lax method of doing business, and the prevailing errors of the day, I published, last October was a twelvemonth, *The Crisis Extraordinary*, on the revenues of America, and the yearly expence of carrying on the war. My estimation of the latter, together with the civil list of Congress, and the civil list of the several States, was Two Million Pounds sterling, which is very nearly Nine Millions of Dollars.

Since that time, Congress have gone into a calculation, and have estimated the expences of the war department and the civil list of Congress (exclusive of the civil list of the several governments) at Eight Millions of Dollars; and as the remaining million will be fully sufficient for the civil list of the several States, the two calculations are exceedingly near each other.

This sum of Eight Millions of Dollars they have called upon the States to furnish, and their quotas are as follows, which I shall preface with the resolution itself.

By the United States in Congress assembled,
October 30th, 1781.

RESOLVED,

THAT the respective States be called upon to furnish the Treasury of the United States with their quotas of eight millions of dollars, for the war department and civil list for the ensuing year, to be paid quarterly, in equal proportions, the first payment to be made on the first day of April next.

Resolved, That a Committee, consisting of a member from each State, be appointed to apportion to the several States the quota of the above sum.

November 2d.

The Committee, appointed to ascertain the proportions of the several States of the monies to be raised for the expences of the ensuing year, report the following resolutions:

That the sum of Eight Millions of Dollars, as required to be raised by the resolutions of the 30th of October last, be paid by the States in the following proportion.

New-Hampshire	373,598
Massachusetts.	1,307,596
Rhode-Island	216,684
Connecticut	747,196
New-York.	373,598
New-Jersey	485,679
Pennsylvania	1,120,794
Delaware	112,085
Maryland	933,996
Virginia.	1,307,594
North-Carolina.	622,677
South-Carolina	373,598
Georgia.	24,905
	8,000,000 Dollars

Resolved,

That it be recommended to the several States to lay taxes for raising their quotas of money for the United States, separate from those laid for their own particular use.

On these resolutions I shall offer several remarks.

First. On the sum itself, and the ability of the country.

Secondly. On the several quotas, and the nature of a union. And

Thirdly. On the manner of collection and expenditure.

First. On the sum itself, and the ability of the country. As I know my own calculation is as low as possible, and as the sum called for by Congress, according to their calculation, agrees very nearly therewith, I am sensible it cannot possibly be lower. Neither can it be done for that, unless there is ready money to go to market with; and even in that case, it is only by the utmost management and œconomy that it can be made to do.

By the accounts which were laid before the British parliament last spring, it appeared that the charge of only subsisting, that is feeding, their army in America, cost annually Four Millions Pounds sterling, which is very nearly Eighteen Millions of Dollars. Now if, for Eight Millions, we can feed, clothe, arm, provide for and pay an army sufficient for our defence, the very comparison shows that the money must be well laid out.

It may be of some use, either in debate or conversation, to attend to the progress of the expences of an army, because it will enable us to see on what part any deficiency will fall.

The first thing is, to feed them and provide for the sick.

Secondly, to clothe them.

Thirdly, to arm and furnish them.

Fourthly, to provide means for removing them from place to place. And,

Fifthly, to pay them.

The first and second are absolutely necessary to them as men. The third and fourth are equally as necessary to them as an army. And the fifth is their just due. Now if the sum which shall be raised should fall short, either by the several acts of the States for raising it, or by the manner of collecting it, the deficiency will fall on the fifth head, the soldiers pay, which would be defrauding them, and eternally disgracing ourselves. It would be a blot on the Councils, the country, and the revolution of America, and a man would hereafter be ashamed to own he had any hand in it.

But if the deficiency should be still shorter, it would next fall on the fourth head, *the means of removing the army from place to place*; and in this case, the army must either stand still where it can be of no use, or seize on horses, carts, waggons, or any means of transportation it can lay hold of; and in this instance the country suffers. In short, every attempt to do a thing for less than it can be done for, is sure to become at last both a loss and a dishonour.

But the country cannot bear it say some. This has been the most expensive doctrine that ever was held out, and cost America millions of money for nothing. Can the country bear to be over-run, ravaged and ruined by an enemy, which will immediately follow where defence is wanting, and defence will ever be wanting where sufficient revenues are not provided. But this is only one part of the folly. The second is, that when the danger comes, invited in part by our not preparing against it, we have been obliged, in a number of instances, to expend double the sums, to do that which at first might have been done for half the money. But this is not all. A third mischief has been, that grain of all sorts, flour, beef, fodder, horses, carts, waggons, or whatever was absolutely or immediately wanted, have been taken without pay. Now, I ask, why was all this done, but from that extremely weak and expensive doctrine, *that the country could not bear it?* that is, that she could not bear, in the first instance, that which would have saved her twice as much at last; or, in proverbial language, that she could not bear to pay a penny to save a pound; the consequence of which has been, that she has paid a pound for a penny. Why are there so many unpaid certificates in almost every man's hands, but from the parsimony of not providing sufficient revenues? Besides, the doctrine contradicts itself; because, if the whole country cannot bear it, how is it possible that a part should; and yet this has been the case. For those things have been had, and they must be had; but the misfortune is, they have been had in a very unequal manner and upon expensive credit, whereas with ready money they might have been purchased for half the price, and no body distressed.

But there is another thought which ought to strike us, which is,—How is the army to bear the want of food, cloathing and other necessaries? The man who is at home can turn himself a thousand ways, and find as many means of ease, convenience or relief: But a soldier's life admits of none of those: Their wants cannot be supplied from themselves: For an army, though it is the defence of a State, is at the same time the child of a country, and must be provided for in every thing.

And lastly, The doctrine is false. There are not three millions of people, in any part of the universe, who live so well, or have such a fund of ability as in America. The income of a common labourer, who is industrious, is equal to that of the generality of tradesmen in England. In the mercantile line, I have not heard of one who could be said to be a bankrupt since the war began, and in England they have been without number. In America almost every farmer lives on his own lands, and in England not one in a hundred does. In short, it seems as if the poverty of that country had made them furious, and they were determined to risk all to recover all.

Yet, notwithstanding those advantages on the part of America, true it is, that had it not been for the operation of taxes for our necessary defence, we had sunk into a state of sloth and poverty: For there was more wealth lost by neglecting to till the earth in the years 1776, 77 and 78, than the quota of the tax amounts to. That which is lost by neglect of this kind, is lost for ever; whereas that which is paid, and continues in the country, returns to us again; and at the same time that it provides us with defence, it operates not only as a spur but as a premium to our industry.

I shall now proceed to the second head, viz. ON THE SEVERAL QUOTAS, AND THE NATURE OF A UNION.

There was a time when America had no other bond of union, than that of common interest and affection. The whole country flew to the relief of Boston, and, making her cause their own, participated her cares and administred to her wants. The fate of war, since that day, has carried the calamity in a ten-fold proportion to the southward; but in the mean time the union has been strengthened by a legal compact of the States, jointly and severally ratified, and that which before was choice, or the duty of affection, is now likewise the duty of legal obligation.

The union of America is the foundation-stone of her independence; the rock on which it is built; and is something so sacred in her constitution, that we ought to watch every word we speak, and every thought we think, that we injure it not, even by mistake. When a multitude, extended, or rather scattered, over a continent, in the manner we are, mutually agree to form one common centre whereon the whole shall move, to accomplish a particular purpose, all parts must act together and alike, or act not at all, and a stoppage in any one is a stoppage of the whole, at least for a time.

Thus the several States have sent Representatives to assemble together in Congress, and they have empowered that body, which thus becomes their centre, and are no other than themselves in representation, to conduct and manage the war, while their constituents at home attend to the domestic cares of the country, their internal legislation, their farms, professions or employments: For it is only by reducing complicated things to method and orderly connection that they can be understood with advantage, or pursued with success. — Congress, by virtue of this delegation, estimates the expence, and apportions it out to the several parts of the empire according to their several abilities; and here the debate must end, because each State has already had its voice, and the matter has undergone its whole portion of argument, and can no more be altered by any particular State, than a law of any State, after it has passed, can be altered by an individual. For with respect to those things which immediately concern the union, and for which the union was purposely established and is intended to secure, each State is to the United States what each individual is to the State he lives in. And it is on this grand point, this movement upon one centre, that our existence as a nation, our happiness as a people, and our safety as individuals, depend.

It may happen that some State or other may be somewhat over or under rated, but this cannot be much. The experience which has been had upon the matter has nearly ascertained their several abilities. But even in this case, it can only admit of an appeal to the United States, but cannot authorise any State to make the alteration itself, any more than our internal government can admit an individual to do so in the case of an act of assembly; for if one State can do it, then may another do the same, and the instant this is done the whole is undone.

Neither is it supposeable that any single State can be a judge of all the comparative reasons which may influence the collective body in quoating out the continent. The circumstances of the several States are frequently varying, occasioned by the accidents of war and commerce, and it will often fall upon some to help others, rather beyond what their exact proportion at another time might be; but even this assistance is as naturally and politically included in the idea of a union, as that of any particular assigned proportion; because we know not whose turn it may be next to want assistance; for which reason, that is the wisest State which sets the best example.

Though in matters of bounden duty and reciprocal affection, it is rather a degeneracy from the honesty and ardour of the heart to admit any thing selfish to partake in the government of our conduct, yet in cases where our duty, our affections, and our interest all coincide, it may be of some use to observe their union. The United States will become heir to an extensive quantity of vacant land, and their several titles to shares and quotas thereof will naturally be adjusted according to their relative quotas during the war, exclusive of that inability which may unfortunately arise to any State by the enemy holding possession of a part; but as this is a cold matter of interest, I pass it by, and proceed to my third head, viz,

ON THE MANNER OF COLLECTION AND EXPENDITURE.

It hath been our error, as well as our misfortune, to blend the affairs of each State, especially in money matters, with those of the United States; whereas it is to our case, convenience and interest to keep them separate. The expences of the United States for carrying on the war, and the expences of each State for its own domestic government, are distinct things, and to involve them is a source of perplexity and a cloak for fraud. I love method, because I see and am convinced of its beauty and advantage. It is that which makes all business easy and understood, and without which every thing becomes embarrassed and difficult.

There are certain powers which the people of each State have delegated to their legislative and executive bodies, and there are other powers which the people of every State have delegated to Congress, among which is that of conducting the war, and, consequently, of managing the expences attending it; for how else can that be managed, which concerns every State, but by a delegation from each. When a State has furnished its quota, it has an undoubted right to know how it has been applied, and it is as much the duty of Congress to inform the State of the one, as it is the duty of the State to provide the other.

In the resolution of Congress already recited, it is recommended to the several States *to lay taxes for raising their quotas of money for the United States, separate from those laid for their own particular use.*

This is a most necessary point to be observed, and the distinction should follow all the way through. They should be levied, paid and collected separately, and kept separate in every instance. Neither have the civil officers of any State, or the government of that State, the least right to touch that money which the people pay for the support of their army and the war, any more than Congress has to touch that which each State raises for its own use.

This distinction will naturally be followed by another. It will occasion every State to examine nicely into the expences of its civil list, and to regulate, reduce and bring it into better order than it has hitherto been; because the money for that purpose must be raised apart, and accounted for to the public separately. But while the monies of both were blended, the necessary nicety was not observed, and the poor soldier, who ought to have been the first, was the last who was thought of.

Another convenience will be, that the people, by paying the taxes separately, will know what they are for; and will likewise know that those which are for the defence of the country will cease with the war, or soon after. For although, as I have before observed, the war is their own, and for the support of their own rights and the protection of their own property, yet they have the same right to know that they have to pay, and it is the want of not knowing that is often the cause of dissatisfaction.

This regulation of keeping the taxes separate has given rise to a regulation in the office of finance, by which it is directed,

"That the receivers shall, at the end of every month, make out an exact account of the monies received by them respectively, during such month, specifying therein the names of the persons from whom the same shall have been received, the dates and the sums; which account they shall respectively cause to be published in one of the newspapers of the State; to the end that every citizen may know how much of the monies collected from him, in taxes, is transmitted to the treasury of the United States for the support of the war; and also, that it may be known what monies have been at the order of the Superintendant of Finance. It being proper and necessary, that in a free country the people should be as fully informed of the administration of their affairs as the nature of things will admit."

It is an agreeable thing to see a spirit of order and œconomy taking place, after such a series of errors and difficulties. A government or an administration, who means and acts honestly, has nothing to fear, and consequently has nothing to conceal; and it would be of use if a monthly or quarterly account was to be published, as well of the expenditures as of the receipts. Eight millions of dollars must be husbanded with an exceeding deal of care to make it do, and therefore, as the management must be reputable, the publication would be serviceable.

I have heard of petitions which have been presented to the Assembly of this State (and probably the same may have happened in other States) praying to have the taxes lowered. Now the only way to keep taxes low is, for the United States to have ready money to go to market with; and tho' the taxes to be raised for the present year will fall heavy, and there will naturally be some difficulty in paying them, yet the difficulty, in proportion as money spreads about the country, will every day grow less, and in the end we shall save some millions of dollars by it. We see what a bitter, revengeful enemy we have to deal with, and any expence is cheap compared to their merciless paw. We have seen the unfortunate Carolineans hunted like partridges on the mountains, and it is only by providing means for our defence that we shall not be in the same condition. When we think or talk about taxes, we ought to recollect that we lie down in peace, and sleep in safety; that we can follow our farms or stores, or other occupations, in prosperous tranquility; and that these inestimable blessings are procured to us by the taxes that we pay. In this view, our taxes are properly our insurance-money; they are what we pay to be

made safe, and in strict policy are the best money we can lay
out.

It was my intention to offer some remarks on the impost
law of *five per cent.* recommended by Congress, and to be
established as a fund for the payment of the loan-office certificates and other debts of the United States; but I have already
extended my piece beyond my intention. And as this fund will
make our system of finance compleat, and is strictly just, and
consequently requires nothing but honesty to do it, there
needs but little to be said upon it.

C. S.

Philad. March 5, 1782.

[As this is on an interesting subject, the author requests the
several printers throughout the United States to give it a place
in their papers, without dividing it.]

The Necessity of Taxation

April 4, 1782

TO THE PEOPLE OF AMERICA.

CASTING my eye over a former publication (the Crisis, No. 9) on the loss of Charlestown, I was tempted to introduce this address by a quotation from the first paragraph of that number, as it appeared to me exceedingly applicable to the present circumstances of the country.

"Had America pursued her advantages with half the spirit she resisted her misfortunes, she would before now have been a conquering and a peaceful people; but lulled in the lap of soft tranquility, she rested on her hopes, and adversity only could convulse her into action."

This hath been the character of America in every part, and in every state and stage of the contest. Warmed by a love of liberty, and provoked by a sense of injuries, she encountered danger without fear, and misfortune without despondency: But no sooner was the point accomplished, than she returned with folded arms to rest, and seemed to wait with patience for new disasters.—Yet there is one reflection to be drawn from this character and conduct that is worth attending to, which is, that it is the sign and the natural effect of right principles, but not of right policy. Misfortune ever separates men in a bad cause, and unites them in a good one. The former are industrious only while they are prosperous, the latter while they are distressed. The one acts from impulse, the other from contrivance; and the whole mode and progress of their conduct, and their times of rest and action, are the reverse of each other.

But as we have learned knowledge from misfortune, let us likewise learn it from mistake; and wisely add for once, if we never do it again, the ardour of adversity to the strength of victory. Let us combine the glowing powers of resolute resistance with the tranquil advantages which conquest bestows; and render the present year as superior in system, as the latter was splendid in success.

The progress and revolution of our domestic circumstances are as extraordinary as the revolution itself. We began with paper, and we end with gold and silver. We sat out with parties, and we are approaching to unity. The strength, the property, and even the fashion of the country, are confederated in her support. Like robust and healthy youth, she hath shook off the agues of the winter, and steps forward with constitutional bloom and vigour. By suffering distresses, she hath learned both to bear and to prevent them; and the experience of every day, whether drawn from good fortune or from bad, whether from wisdom or mistake, hath added something to her cause, and much to her judgment.

From this general state of circumstances I shall proceed to more particular matters.

In my last publication I stated the yearly expence of the war, namely, eight millions of dollars; the nature of the union by which the States are bound together; and the propriety of keeping the taxes for the defence of the country separate from the expences of government; the right of the people to be regularly informed of the monies received and expended; and the duty of the country to provide its several quotas. — Government and the people do not in America constitute distinct bodies. They are one, and their interest the same. Members of Congress, members of Assembly, or Council, or by any other name they may be called, are only a selected part of the people. They are the representatives of majesty, but not majesty itself. That dignity exists inherently in the universal multitude, and, though it may be delegated, cannot be alienated. Their estates and property are subject to the same taxation with those they represent, and there is nothing they can do, that will not equally affect themselves as well as others. If they call for supplies, they call on themselves in common with the country. Their situation enables them to know the more secret circumstances of things, and that such or such revenues are necessary for the security and defence of their constituents, and the accomplishment of the great object for which they are chosen. And here the distinction ends.

The furnishing ourselves with right ideas, and the accustoming ourselves to right habits of thinking, have a powerful effect in strengthening and cementing the mind of the country and freeing it from the danger of partial or mistaken notions. It is not all the ardour which the love of liberty can inspire, nor the utmost fortitude which the most heroic virtue can create, that will of themselves make us successful conquerors. We must come down to order, system and method, and go through the cool and judicious, as well as the animating and elevated parts of patriotism. Method is to natural power, what slight is to human strength, without which a giant would lose his labour, and a country waste its force.

At the commencement of the war much political wisdom was not absolutely necessary. The high spirit of the country in a great measure supplied its place, and the printing-presses furnished the means. They became our Peru and Mexico, and as we wanted we drew them forth. Any body of men might at that time have carried on the war, who had resolution enough to proceed; because the difficulties of finance were then unknown, and the money came created to their hands. But those times are changed, and there is now a call on the wisdom and judgment, as well as on the firmness and patriotism of the country. Our situation is such, that the more it is understood the better it will appear; and with the means in our power, we want nothing but the united disposition to employ them.

When America resolved on independance, and determined to be free, she naturally included within that resolution all the means, whether of men or money, necessary to effect it. She had laid herself out for greater sufferings, and more expence and loss, than she has hitherto experienced, except in Carolina and Georgia. The idea of getting rich had not in those days an existance. All she expected was to live, and all she hoped for was to be free. She had resolved to abandon her habitations, to desert her towns, and to form new settlements in the wilderness, rather than submit. There was no condition to which her imagination could extend, that was not preferable to the oppressions that threatened her; and the experience of several years has shewn her opinion just, and proved her resolution firm.

Yet while the war was carried on by the mass of general opposition, the business of the country got deranged. Agriculture, trade and commerce became neglected, and something like poverty began to appear. Yet the resolution suffered no abatement, and their losses served to provoke them the higher. But experience has shewn that the way to enrich a country, and render it systematically formidable, is to give every possible rest to the inhabitants, that they may follow their various occupations undisturbed. A man who is harrassed about, either by the inroads of the enemy, or by marching to oppose them, soon suffers more by loss of time and the neglect of his affairs, than what a portion of taxes sufficient for his defence would amount to. And therefore it is to the good of the whole, as well as to the interest of the individual, that every one, who can, sets himself down to his business, and contributes his quota of taxes as one of the first duties he owes to his family, to himself, and to his country. Every amusement ought to be dispenced with, every indulgence curtailed, and every possible œconomy practiced, both public and private, until a revenue sufficient for the protection and good of the country is obtained, and the debt to public justice satisfied.

I have no idea of that kind of policy which ends in expence, disappointment and disgrace; and those have ever been and ever will be the consequence of deficient and unequal revenues. America has resolved to defend herself, and to support her independance at all hazards and events. Every man's portion of that charge becomes his debt of honour, interest and happiness; and to see any one indulging himself at home while that portion is unpaid, and the soldier who defends him suffering in the field, is the highest dishonour a man can undergo.

It is pity but some other word beside taxation had been devised for so noble and extraordinary an occasion, as the protection of liberty and the establishment of an independant world. We have given to a popular subject an unpopular name, and injured the service by a wrong assemblage of ideas. A man would be ashamed to be told that he signed a petition, praying that he might pay *less* than his share of the public expence, or that those who had trusted the public might never receive their money; yet he does the same thing when he petitions against taxation, and the only difference is, that by taking shelter under the name, he seems to conceal the meanness he would otherwise blush at. Is it popular to pay our debts, to do justice, to defend an injured and insulted country, to protect the aged and the infant, and to give to Liberty a land to live in? then must taxation, as the means by which those things are to be done, be popular likewise.

But to take a more local view of matters. Why has the back country been ravaged by the repeated incursions of the enemy and the Indians, but from the inability of the revenue to provide means for their protection? And yet the inhabitants of those countries were among the first to petition against taxation. In so doing, they eventually prayed for their own destruction, and, unhappily for them, their prayer was answered. Their quota of taxes would have been trifling, compared with their losses, and, what is still worse, their domestic sorrows. Alas! how unwisely, how unfeelingly, does a man argue, when he puts the safety of his family in competition with his tax.

There is so much of the honour, interest and independance of America staked upon taxation, that the subject must to every reflective mind make a strong impression. As we are now circumstanced, it is the criterion of public spirit; the touchstone of our good affections; and he who pays it the instant it is called for, does more for his country's good than the loudest talker in America. In vain are all our huzzas for liberty, without accompanying them with solid support. They will neither fill the soldier's belly, nor cloathe his back, they will neither pay the public creditors, nor purchase our supplies. They are well enough in their places, and though they are the effusion of our hearts, they are no part of our substance.

The Assembly of this State, Pennsylvania, have unanimously gone through the bill for raising the sum of 1,120,000 Dollars, being their quota for the year: And, as an example worthy both of notice and imitation, the oppressed and distressed State of South-Carolina, notwithstanding the severity of its fate, has already done the same. Those people know, by woeful experience, the value of defence, and that the inconvenience of struggling with a tax for the protection of the country is not to be named, in competition with the losses they have borne, and the sorrows and sufferings they have undergone.

However inconvenient the tax may be, we know it can last but for a time. Our expences will cease with the war, and our taxation in consequence. But while the war continues, and so great a part of every thing that is near and valuable to a country depends upon her revenue, I shall consider and treat taxation as a popular good. When the war shall be over, the case will be totally altered, and my language, if I then speak at all, will be entirely different. Besides, America is a new character in the universe. She started with a cause divinely right, and struck at an object vast and valuable. Her reputation for political integrity, perseverance, fortitude, and all the manly excellencies, stands high in the world, and it would be a thousand pities that, with those happy introductions into life, she suffered the least spot or blot to fall upon her *moral* fame. Never let it be said, that the country who could do what America has done, defrauded the widow and the orphan of their property, and the soldier of his pay.

The tax will be attended with some inconvenience; but what is inconvenience, when compared with distress and the ruin and plunderings of an enemy. How many things of far greater inconvenience has America already undergone, nay, even flourished in the midst of, which she once thought impossible to be borne. I hold taxation, which is to be applied to her own defence and her own good, one of the lightest of her difficulties, when considered with those which were occasioned by the want of it. We have several times been on the crisis of destruction by the insufficiency of our public revenues, and the heart of America would have ached with concern and sorrow, could she at all times have known what her exact situation has been. It is now the only point we have to attend to, nay it is the only one that is worth attending to; for let us accomplish this, and the rest will follow; and that consolation which every man's mind will feel, at knowing that the public Treasury is furnished with an ability of providing for the defence of the country, will amply recompence the difficulties he may go through, and the endeavours he may make, in paying in his allotted share. We shall be freed from the just murmurs of the suffering soldier; our eyes and ears will be no longer shocked with tales of slighted faith and suspected credit; and the face of our public, and of consequence of our private affairs, will wear a new and satisfied countenance. The idea, *that the country cannot bear it,* is a reproach upon her honour and firmness. She has borne ten times as much. Her fortitude and her principles have been tried in a thousand instances of severer fortune; and it is a paradox not to be explained, and which ought to be exploded, that the people whom no force or misfortune could conquer, no temptation seduce, should, at the summit of success, trepan themselves into destruction by an ignoble and impolitic covetousness.

Let us be, in every respect, such a nation as we ought to be, and shew to the enemy that it is no more in her power to conquer us by system than by arms. The purse of America, with œconomy, is longer than that of Britain, managed as it is by corruption and extravagance. The people of America are not a poor people, why should they appear so. We hurt our credit, our honour, our reputation in the world, by proclaiming ourselves what we are not, and give encouragement to the enemy to prolong the war, by holding out an idea of our want of money to carry it on. It is easy to see by the complexion of the New-York papers, that the present spirited exertions of the country to keep her public treasury supplied have wounded the last hopes of the enemy. It is a blow they never expected America to give, and their astonishment is as great as their despair.

It is a remark, worth making, that the people have always been a step forwarder than their representatives. There never was a backwardness in the country to do its part, when the part to be done became known and understood. National money matters are naturally attended with a degree of intricacy, which renders them not so easily comprehended as those which are more simple and obvious. Those of America have, from the fluctuating state of the former currency, been involved in new and original difficulties, and it required much judicious management to bring them right, and a vigorous exertion in the country afterwards to keep them so.

The present condition of our money matters, as concisely as they can be stated, is as follows:

There is a large sum due to persons who have lent their money to the Loan-Office, and to those who have otherwise trusted the public. Those debts are to be ascertained and proved, and the money arising from the impost duty of five per cent. on all imported goods is to be applied as a fund for the payment of the interest and principal, until the whole of them shall be discharged. This is the provision made for our debts already contracted, and when once the interest on them shall be regularly drawn, and the principal put into a train for payment, they will become as valuable as bond debts.

The sum of eight millions of dollars, which is apportioned out to be raised by the United States, is for the maintenance and other expences of the army, and to defray the government charges of the continent. If this sum is compared with the immense expence which Britain is at, the difference will appear exceedingly striking. She is obliged to raise upwards of ninety millions of dollars in taxes and loans every year, to do what we can accomplish, with ready money and frugality, for eight millions. So great is the contrast between a country sunk in corruption and extravagance, and one whose object is founded in just principles, and her plans regulated by good management.

But the difference may be carried still further. When the war shall cease with us, our taxes for that purpose will cease with it. We know they cannot now last for any long time; whereas the taxes of Britain being laid on only for the purpose of paying the interest, and never the principal of her debts, must continue for ever.

The publishing the sums of money received from each State, and expended on their united account, will be attended with several good effects. It will give satisfaction, which is a necessary object in national concerns. It will create emulation, and detect delinquency. The opener and fairer public business is transacted, the better it succeeds. Where no fraud is intended, there can be no occasion for concealment, and it is not only necessary that measures should be just, but that every body should know them to be so.

A few days will now carry us to the period of seven years war, and so extraordinary is the case, that instead of the country becoming poor and exhausted, she is grown rich and plentiful. There has been a singular fate attended all our wants, for whenever we imagined we should be ruined, by not having something which could not be done without, it arrived, as if of itself, just time enough to prevent the mischief. The last remarkable instance was in the influx of hard money, almost at the very moment when the paper currency failed, by which the circumstances of public and private business are so materially improved, that matters cannot go wrong, if we set heartily about what is right.

COMMON SENSE.

Response to an Accusation of Bribery

May 1, 1782

FOR THE FREEMAN'S JOURNAL.

THO' I do not think it worth while altogether on my own account, to take notice of a piece in the last Freeman's Journal, in which a very unwise and unkind allusion is made to a publication of mine in the latter end of the year 1780, entitled, PUBLIC GOOD, yet as that allusion is connected with a public measure, I shall for that reason, more than for myself, give it an answer.

The piece I refer to in the Freeman's Journal is signed *"Caractacus"* and the writer introduces it with the following paragraphs, viz.

"The public may be imposed on, when the condition and intention of the author is concealed, but when this is discovered, we may easily see the influence of twelve thousand acres of land, in causing a man to use all his talents to defraud the United States of their landed property, and at the same time unjustly incense them against a sister state.

"Few knew that the design of publishing a pamphlet, intitled Public Good, was to wrest out of the hands of the United States, a tract of land called Indiana, and appropriate it to the use of a sett of men, who can scarcely be called friends to the United States, excepting a few characters: but the design was evident to some, before the bribe was incautiously published. Through a prospect of receiving no opposition, the company committed a little blunder in being rather premature in the publication of their present."

If Caractacus is really an honest man and sincerely means to support the right of the United States, to the vacant western territory, against all encroachments either from Virginia or else where, he will gladly make himself known to me, because I can and will assist him; but if he is privately interested in the encroachments which Virginia has made, and is only making use of the name of the *United States* as a cover, he will conceal himself from me.

It certainly can be nothing to Caractacus, or even to the public (only as a matter of curiosity) how I came by the facts and materials which enabled me to write the pamphlet *Public Good*. It is sufficient to the public that I obtained them, and made use of them to prove their right to the western lands by, and that without putting them to any expence. But as I never do any thing that I wish to conceal, I shall relate the whole transaction, and all the material circumstances belonging to it.

In the pamphlet *Common Sense* published in January 1776, I mentioned the vacant western lands, as a fund which at the end of the war would redeem the expences of it. And in the arguments used in Congress in favour of independence, those very lands were pointed out for the same purpose. But to the astonishment of every reasonable man the state of Virginia set up a wild unfounded claim to the best part, and opened an office for the sale of them. By which means she has exhausted and weakened herself, and done much injustice to all her sister states, without even performing her quota of duty.

But it was impossible for me to pursue the subject, from the want of materials and information. I was struck with the general magnitude of the wrong done to the states, but could not enter as an advocate on their behalf, because, as I have already stated, the papers and proofs necessary to proceed upon were not in my possession, neither did I know where to obtain them. Another difficulty I found, or rather felt, was, the disagreeableness of taking up a subject of controversy against any state in the union, and particularly against Virginia, whose character I had, on every former occasion accustomed myself to esteem, and with many of whose principal citizens I continued on terms of intimacy, and friendship. And this nicety carried me so far as to decline a proposal, from the executive council of Pennsylvania, or some of them, in the year 1779 to attend on the commission for settling the boundary line between this state and Virginia; *because I would not interfere between two states. But the interest of the United States makes another question.*

Some time in the summer 1779, major Trent and other gentlemen of the Indiana Company came to me and stated the exceeding injuries they were likely to sustain, and the distress which several families were exposed to by the unkind conduct of Virginia, in endeavouring to wrest from them a tract of land which had been ceded to them by the Indians as a compensation for injuries which they, or some of their tribes, had committed, and to obtain a ratification of which, the company had been put to very great expences. They asked me for my assistance in behalf of the sufferers, and offered me any compensation I would require. Private justice is undoubtedly due to all men, and where that fails, public justice can have but a slender foundation.

However I might be inclined to wish them redress, my answer was short and decisive, which was, *that I never had nor ever would have any thing to do in private affairs.* And here the conference ended.

In the latter end of the year 1780, col. George Morgan and other gentlemen came again to me and endeavoured to make me understand, that whatever might be the event of the company's affairs, they were in possession of certain papers, which might be rendered exceedingly useful to the public, and proposed leaving them in my hands for perusal, which they did.

Here I got the very materials I had long wished for. The industry of the company, in prosecuting their own affairs, had collected together papers and documents in which the public, or in other words the United States, were exceedingly interested. I saw by those papers that the claim of Virginia to the western territory was ill founded either in right or reason, and that I could render a very essential service to the country by disentangling the matter from the obscurity in which it was then involved.

On a second interview I informed the gentlemen of my opinion respecting the papers they had left with me, and that I could make a very good use of them for the public interest; but that I would on *no account* mix the matter with any thing relative to the private affairs of the company, which as they were then before Congress would likewise be improper. They agreed to my proposition, and left them in my hands to do as I pleased with. From these papers and materials I compiled and finished the pamphlet PUBLIC GOOD, in which there is not a line or syllable respecting the company and every argument in it is in support of the public right of the United

States. I was glad to get at the papers, and I made the same use of them as if there had been no such body as the Indiana Company. But if the public have derived any service from the publication, and have acquired by it a better knowledge of their rights than they had before, they undoubtedly are under some obligation to the company for lending the materials, as well as to me for making use of them. And altho' the pamphlet has been published above a year and a half, it has never yet been answered by the advocates for the Virginia claims. I know it cannot be answered with success. I have ever kept a clear head and an upright heart, and am not afraid of being replied to. I never took up a matter without fully believing it to be right, and never yet failed in proving it so. But in this case I am the friend of Virginia as well as of the United States; because it is evident from her present circumstances, that her claims and her conduct have tended to impoverish her.

That the pamphlet was of service to the company is certain; but this is a natural consequence. The encroachment of Virginia extended over the company's lands as well as over those of the United States; and the company and the public standing thus in the same predicament with respect to Virginia, were reciprocally benefited by the endeavours of either to detect and eject her encroachments; and it was because the interest of the company was thus bound up with that of the United states, that made the acceptance of their present agreeable to me.

Caractacus says that "The design of publishing the pamphlet entitled PUBLIC GOOD was to wrest out of the hands of the *United States* a tract of land called Indiana."

Let the pamphlet speak for itself. There are yet some remaining copies which may be had at Mr. Claypoole's Printing office in Market street. The design of the pamphlet was to wrest, if I may copy the expression, the whole western territory from the unjust and enormous claims of Virginia. But Caractacus has I believe confessed more than he was aware of, for when he says that it was to wrest Indiana out of the *hands of the United States*, the declaration goes to prove that Indiana *is within* the *dominion of the United States and not within that of Virginia*. And consequently all the other western territory must be in the same situation. This is the very fact which the company are labouring to establish, and they certainly must be right, because their opposers cannot avoid occasionally declaring the same thing.

Thus much for the pamphlet. Now for the twelve thousand acres of land.

As soon as the pamphlet was published I returned the materials which the company had put into my hands, and they unanimously ordered a deed to be made out to me for what they call a voters share, which is, I suppose about the quantity mentioned. But so little effect or influence had this upon me, that I set off for France without ever applying for the deed, and returned again, without ever thinking about it, or taking the least notice of it, and it was not until the matter was mentioned to me again about three weeks or a month ago, that I gave myself any concern respecting it. And as to the paragraph in the newspapers which Caractacus refers to, of the company presenting me with a quantity of land, it was my own proposition that it should be made known, and I think it a reputation to the company that they have done that which those who were infinitely more obliged and indebted to me have neglected to do. From me the states have received the unremitted service of seven years, and to them I have not been the expence of a private soldier. I have done every thing *of* myself and *from* myself. The interest of the heart alone has carried me through a thousand things which others would have failed in or staggered at; and therefore the less Caractacus says upon this matter the less dishonor he will bring to light.

But as it ever was my disposition to acknowledge any return of kindness or friendship, from whatever quarter it came, I shall, in this place take the opportunity of mentioning a circumstance respecting the disposition of the present house of assembly of this state.

When the office of register of wills (a place worth six or seven hundred pounds a year) was likely to be vacant, and which has since happened, the speaker of the house, the hon F. A. Muhlenberg, informed me, that, from the knowledge he had of the house, the members had often expressed a wish of shewing me some instance of their respect, and that if I thought the office of register would be convenient to me, he would mention it in the house and he believed they would present me with it, without any application on my part.

I expressed to the speaker my sense of his friendship and of the good intentions of the house, and at the same time signified to him, that the necessary attendance on an office, or being any way charged with the duties of one, would unavoidably ingross my attention and take me out of the only line of service in which I could be generally useful, and therefore declined giving him the trouble of mentioning me on the occasion. I at the same time acquainted him with the present the Indiana company had made me.

Yet after this and several other instances I could mention, comes some unknown person sheltered under the machinery of a printer, and tells the public, that because the Indiana company, of their own accord had presented me with a quantity of land, and which I desired might be made known, and which was made known by all the papers of this city, about a week before the deed was made out, that I had accepted a *bribe*; when if there is any one circumstance in my character which distinguishes itself from the rest, it is *personal disinterestedness*, and an anxiety to serve a public cause in preference to myself. I never sought place, office, nor reward, since I have been in America; nor ever suffered resentment or disgust, nor the ins and outs of parties to warp me from the line of public good. And I have the pleasure of seeing, by the experience of every day, that the consistency of my character and the disinterestedness of my conduct have made almost every man my friend.

As to Caractacus I ought to be obliged to him for forcing me into the opportunity of saying what otherwise would not have been known, and I am persuaded that a thousand such little and unjustifiable insinuations will answer no other purpose than to procure me as many new friends. I have stood through too many tryals to be affected now either in fame or feeling by anonymous hints and insignificant falshoods; and perfectly satisfied that the public are satisfied with me, nay even that they conceive themselves obliged to me, and that among other things for the pamphlet in question, I shall take my farewel of Caractacus, and leave him to pursue at pleasure or at random whatever he likes best, for I have something of more consequence to attend to than minding either him or his squibs. I would not give a farthing to know who he is, nor care whether he writes or holds his tongue. And I farther assure him, that so far as justice goes, I shall endeavour to assist the company in any thing which I conceive to be right, and no farther. For it would be very extraordinary, that I should serve a whole country seven years for nothing, and refuse it to those who have served me.

COMMON SENSE.

The Crisis

May 11, 1782

ON THE PRESENT STATE OF NEWS.

SINCE the arrival of two, if not three packets, in quick succession, at New York from England, a variety of unconnected news has circulated through the country, and afforded as great a variety of speculation.

That something is the matter in the cabinet and councils of our enemies on the other side the water is certain; that they have run their length of madness, and are under a necessity of changing their measures may easily be seen into; but to what this change of measures may amount, or how far it may correspond with our interest, happiness and duty, is yet uncertain; and from what we have hitherto experienced, we have too much reason to suspect them in every thing.

I do not address this publication so much to the people of America as to the British ministry, whoever they may be, for if it is their intention to promote any kind of negociation, it is proper they should know before hand, that the United States have as much honour as bravery; that they are no more to be seduced from their alliance than their allegiance; that their line of politics is formed, and not dependant, like that of their enemy, on chance and accident.

On our part, in order to know, at any time, what the British government will do, we have only to find out what they ought NOT to do, and this last will be their conduct. For ever changing and for ever wrong; too distant from America to improve circumstances, and too unwise to foresee them; scheming without principle, and executing without probability, their whole line of management has hitherto been blunder and baseness. Every campaign has added to their loss, and every year to their disgrace; till unable to go on, and ashamed to go back, their politics have come to a halt, and all their fine prospects to the halter.

Could our affections forgive or humanity forget the

wounds of an infant country, we might, under the influence of a momentary oblivion, stand still and laugh. But they are engraven where no amusement can conceal them, and of a kind for which there is no recompence. Can ye restore to us the beloved dead? Can ye say to the grave give up the murdered? Can ye obliterate from our memories those who are no more? Think not then to tamper with our feelings by insidious contrivance, nor to suffocate our humanity by seducing us to dishonour.

In January 1780 I published part of the Crisis No. VIII in the Philadelphia news-papers, but did not conclude it in the following papers, and the remainder has lain by me to the present day.

There appeared about that time some disposition in the British cabinet to cease the further prosecution of the war, and as I had formed my opinion, that whenever such a design should take place, it would be accompanied with a dishonourable proposition to America respecting France; I had addressed the remainder of that number to expose the baseness of any such proposition. But the arrival of the next news from England declared her determination to go on with the war, and consequently as the political object I had then in view was not become a subject, it was unnecessary in me to bring it forward, which is the reason it was never published.

The matter which I allude to in the unpublished part I shall now make a quotation of, and apply it as the more enlarged state of things at this day shall make convenient or necessary. It is as follows.

"By the speeches which have appeared from the British parliament it is easy to perceive to what impolitic and imprudent excesses their passions and prejudices have in every instance carried them during the present war. Provoked at the upright and honourable treaty between America and France, they imagined nothing more was necessary to be done to prevent its final ratification, than to promise, through the agency of their commissioners (Carlisle, Eden and Johnstone) a repeal of their once offensive acts of parliament. The vanity of the conceit was as unpardonable as the experiment was impolitic. And so convinced am I of their wrong Ideas of America, that I shall not wonder, if in the last stage of political phrenzy, they propose to her to break her alliance with France and enter into one with them. Such a proposition, should it ever be made, and it has already been more than once hinted in parliament, would discover such a disposition to perfidiousness, and such disregard of honour and morals, as would add the finishing vice to national corruption. — I do not mention this to put America on the watch, but to put England on her guard, that she do not, in the looseness of her heart, envelop in disgrace every fragment of reputation." — Thus for the quotation.

By the complexion of some part of the news which have transpired through the New-York papers, it seems probable that this insidious era in the British politics is beginning to make its appearance. I wish it may not; for that which is a disgrace to human nature, throws something of a shade over all the human character, and the individual feels his share of the wound that is given to the whole.

The policy of Britain has ever been to divide America in some way or other. In the beginning of the dispute, she practised every art to prevent or destroy the union of the states, well knowing that could she once get them to stand singly she could conquer them unconditionally. Failing in this project in America she renewed it in Europe; and after the alliance had taken place, she made secret offers to France to induce her to give up America, and what is still more extraordinary, she at the same time made propositions to doctor Franklin then in Paris, the very court to which she was secretly applying, to draw off America from France. But this is not all.

On the 14th of September, 1778, the British court, through their secretary, lord Weymouth, made application to the marquis D'Almadovar the Spanish ambassador at London, to "ask the MEDIATION" for these were the words of the court of Spain for the purpose of negociating a peace with France, leaving America (as I shall hereafter show) out of the question. Spain readily offered her mediation, and likewise the city of Madrid as the place of conference, but withall, proposed that the United States of America should be invited to the treaty, and considered as independent during the time the business was negociating. But this was not the view of England. She wanted to draw France from the war, that she might uninterruptedly pour out all her force and fury upon America; and being disappointed in this plan, as well through the open and generous conduct of Spain, as the determination of France, she refused the mediation she had solicited.

I shall now give some extracts from the justifying memorial of the Spanish court, in which she has set the conduct and character of Britain, with respect to America, in a clear and striking point of light.

The memorial, speaking of the refusal of the British court to meet in conference with commissioners from the United States, who were to be considered as independent during the time of the conference, says,

"It is a thing very extraordinary and even ridiculous, that the court of London, who treats the colonies as independent, not only in acting, but of right, during the war, should have a repugnance to treat them as such, only in acting during a truce or suspension of hostilities. The convention of Saratoga; the reputing general Burgoyne as a lawful prisoner, in order to suspend his trial; the exchange and liberating other prisoners made from the colonies; the having named commissioners to go and supplicate the Americans, at their own doors, request peace of them, and treat with them and the Congress; and finally, by a thousand other acts of this sort, authorised by the court of London, which have been, and are true signs of the acknowledgment of their independence.

"In aggravation to all the foregoing, at the same time the British cabinet answered the King of Spain in the terms already mentioned; they were insinuating themselves at the court of France by means of secret emissaries, and making very great offers to her to abandon the colonies and make peace with England. But there is yet more: for at this same time the English ministry were treating by means of another certain emissary, with doctor Franklin, minister plenepotentiary from the colonies, residing at Paris, to whom they made various proposals to disunite them from France, and accommodate matters with England.

"From what has been observed it evidently follows, that the whole of the English politics was, to disunite the two courts of Paris and Madrid, by means of the suggestions and offers she separately made to them; and also to separate the colonies from their treaties and engagements entered into with France, and induce them to arm against the house of Bourbon, or MORE PROBABLY TO OPPRESS THEM WHEN THEY FOUND, FROM BREAKING THEIR ENGAGEMENTS, THEY STOOD ALONE AND WITHOUT PROTECTORS.

"This, therefore, is the net they laid for the American states; that is to say, to tempt them with flattering and very magnificent promises to come to an accommodation with them, exclusive of any intervention of Spain or France, that the British ministry might always remain the arbiters of the fate of the colonies.

"But the Catholic king, (the king of Spain) faithful on the one part to the engagements which bind him to the most Christian king, (the king of France) his nephew; just and upright on the other, to his own subjects whom he ought to protect and guard against so many insults; and finally, full of humanity and compassion for the Americans and other individuals who suffer in the present war; he is determined to pursue and prosecute it, and to make all the efforts in his power, until he can obtain a solid and permanent peace, with full and satisfactory securities that it shall be observed."

Thus far the memorial; a translation of which, into English, may be seen in full, under the head of STATE PAPERS, in the Annual Register for 1779, page 367.

The extracts I have here given, serve to shew the various endeavours and contrivances of the enemy to draw France from her connection with America, and to prevail on her to make a separate peace with England, leaving America totally out of the question and at the mercy of a merciless, unprincipled enemy. The opinion, likewise, which Spain has formed of the British cabinet character for meanness and perfidiousness, is so exactly the opinion of America, respecting it, that the memorial, in this instance, contains our own sentiments and language: for people, however remote, who think alike will unavoidably speak alike.

Thus we see the insidious use which Britain endeavoured to make of the propositions for a peace under the mediation of Spain.—I shall now proceed to the second propositions under the mediation of the emperor of Germany and the empress of Russia; the general outline of which was, that a congress of the several powers at war should meet at Vienna, in 1781, to settle preliminaries of peace.

I could wish myself at liberty to make use of all the information I am possessed of on this subject, but as there is a delicacy in the matter, I do not conceive it prudent, at least at present, to make references and quotations in the same manner as I have done with respect to the mediation of Spain, who published the whole proceedings herself; and, therefore, what comes from me, on this part of the business, must rest on my own credit with the public, assuring them, that when the whole proceedings, relating to the proposed congress at Vienna, shall appear, they will find my account not only true but studiously moderate.

We know that at the time this mediation was on the carpet, the expectations of the British king and ministry ran high with respect to the conquest of America. The English packet which was taken with the mail on board, and carried into l'Orient in France, contained letters from lord G. Germaine to sir Henry Clinton, which expressed in the fullest terms the ministerial idea of a total conquest. Copies of those letters were sent to congress and published in the News-papers of last year. Colonel Laurens brought over the originals, some of which, signed in the hand writing of the then secretary, Germaine, are now in my possession.

Filled with these high ideas, nothing could be more insolent towards America than the language of the British court on the proposed mediation. A peace with France and Spain she anxiously solicited; but America, as before, should be left to her mercy, neither would she hear any proposition for admitting an agent from the United States into the congress of Vienna.

On the other hand, France with an open, noble and manly determination, and the fidelity of a good ally, would hear no proposition for a separate peace, nor even meet in congress at Vienna, without an agent from America: and likewise that the independant character of the United States, represented by the agent, should be fully and unequivocally defined and settled before any conference should be entered on. The reasoning of the court of France on the several propositions of the two Imperial courts, which relate to us, is rather in the stile of an American than an ally; and she advocated the cause of America as if she had been America herself.—Thus the second mediation, like the first, proved ineffectual.

But since that time a reverse of fortune has overtaken the British arms, and all their high expectations are dashed to the ground. The noble exertions to the southward, under general Greene, the successful operations of the allied arms in the Chesepeak; the loss of most of their islands in the West-Indies and Minorca in the Mediterranean; the persevering spirit of Spain against Gibraltar; the expected capture of Jamaica; the failure of making a separate peace with Holland, and the expence of an hundred millions sterling, by which all these fine losses were obtained, have read them a loud lesson of disgraceful misfortune, and necessity has called on them to change their ground.

In this situation of confusion and despair their present councils have no fixt character. It is now the hurricane months of British politics. Every day seems to have a storm of its own, and they are scudding under the bare poles of hope. Beaten, but not humbled; condemned, but not penitent, they act like men trembling at fate and catching at a straw.—From this convulsion in the entrails of their politics, it is more than probable that the mountain groaning in labour, will bring forth a mouse as to its size, and a monster in its make. They will try on America the same insidious arts they tried on France and Spain.

We sometimes experience sensations to which language is not equal. The conception is too bulky to be born alive, and in the torture of thinking we stand dumb. Our feelings imprisoned by their magnitude, find no way out, and, in the struggle of expression, every finger tries to be a tongue. The machinery of the body seems too little for the mind and we look about for helps to shew our thoughts by.—Such must be the sensation of America, whenever Britain steaming with corruption, shall propose to her to sacrifice her faith.

But exclusive of the wickedness, there is a personal offence contained in every such attempt. It is calling us villains; for no man asks another to act the villain unless he believes him to be inclined to be one. No man attempts to seduce a truly modest woman. It is the supposed loseness of her mind that starts the thought of seduction, and he who offers it calls her a prostitute. Our pride is always hurt by the same propositions which offend our principles: for when we are shocked at the crime we are wounded by the supposition of our compliance.

Could I convey a thought that might serve to regulate the public mind, I would not make the interest of the alliance the basis of defending it. All the world are moved by interest, and it affords them nothing to boast of. But I would go a step higher and defend it on the ground of honour and principle. That our public affairs have flourished under the alliance, that it was wisely made and has been nobly executed, that by its assistance we are enabled to preserve our country from conquest and expel those who sought our destruction, that it is our true interest to maintain it unimpaired, and that while we do so no enemy can conquer us; are matters which experience has taught us, and the common good of ourselves, abstracted from principles of faith and honour, would lead us to maintain the connection.

But over and above the mere letter of the alliance, we have been nobly and generously treated, and have had the same respect and attention paid us, as if we had been an old established country. To oblige and be obliged is fair work among mankind, and we want an opportunity of showing to the world that we are a people sensible of kindness and worthy of confidence. Character is to us, in our present circumstances, of more importance than interest. We are a young nation just stepping upon the stage of public life, and the eye of the world is upon us to see how we act. We have an enemy that is watching to destroy our reputation, and who will go any length to gain some evidence against us, that may serve to render our conduct suspected and our character odious; because, could she accomplish this, wicked as it is, the world would withdraw from us, as from a people not to be trusted, and our task then would become difficult.

There is nothing sets the character of a nation in a higher or lower light with others, than the faithfully fulfilling, or perfidiously breaking of treaties. They are things not to be tampered with; and should Britain, which seems very probable, propose to seduce America into such an act of baseness, it would merit from her some mark of unusual detestation. It is one of these extraordinary instances in which we ought not to be contented with the bare negative of Congress, because it is an affront on the multitude as well as on the government. It goes on the supposition that the public are not honest men, and that they may be managed by contrivance tho' they cannot be conquered by arms. But, let the world and Britain know that we are neither to be bought nor sold. That our mind is great and fixt; our prospect clear: and that we will support our character as firmly as our independence.

But I will go still farther. General Conway who made the motion in the British parliament for discontinuing OFFENSIVE war in America, is a gentleman of an amiable character. We have no personal quarrel with him. But he feels not as we feel; he is not in our situation, and that alone, without any other explanation, is enough.

The British parliament supposes they have many friends in America, and that when all chance of conquest is over, they will be able to draw her from her alliance with France. Now, if I have any conception of the human heart, they will fail in this more than in any thing they have yet tried.

This part of the business is not a question of politics only but of honour and honesty; and the proposition will have in it something so visibly low and base that their partizans, if they have any, will be ashamed of it. Men are often hurt by a mean action who are not started at a wicked one, and this will be such a confession of inability, such a declaration of servile thinking, that the scandal of it will ruin all their hopes.

In short, we have nothing to do but to go on with vigour and determination. The enemy is yet in our country. They hold New York, Charlestown and Savannah, and the very being in those places is an offence, and a part of offensive war, and until they can be driven from them or captured in them, it would be folly in us to listen to an idle tale.—I take it for granted that the British ministry are sinking under the impossibility of carrying on the war. Let them then come to a fair and open peace with France, Spain, Holland and America in the manner they ought to do; but until then we can have nothing to say to them.

COMMON SENSE.

To Sir Guy Carleton

May 31, 1782

IT is the nature of compassion to associate with misfortune; and I address this to you in behalf even of an enemy, a captain in the British service now on his way to the Head Quarters of the American army, and unfortunately doomed to death for a crime not his own.—A sentence so extraordinary, an execution so repugnant to every human sensation, ought never to be told without the circumstances which produced it: and as the destined victim is yet in existence, and in your hands rest his life or death, I shall briefly state the case and the melancholy consequence.

Captain Huddy, of the Jersey militia, was attacked in a small fort on Tom's river, by a party of refugees in the British pay and service, was made prisoner together with his company, carried to New-York and lodged in the provost of that city; about three weeks after which, he was taken out of the provost down to the water side, put into a boat and brought again upon the Jersey shore, and there, contrary to the practice of all nations but savages, was hung up on a tree, and left hanging until found by our people, who took him down and buried him.

The inhabitants of that part of the country where the murder was committed, sent a deputation to general Washington with a full and certified state of the fact. Struck, as every human breast must be, with such brutish outrage, and determined both to punish and prevent it for the future, the general represented the case to general Clinton, who then commanded, and demanded that the refugee officer who ordered and attended the execution, and whose name is Lippencut, should be delivered up as a murderer: and in case of refusal, that the person of some British officer should suffer in his stead. The demand, though not refused, has not been complied with; and the melancholy lot (not by selection, but by casting lots) has fallen upon captain Asgil, of the guards, who, as I have already mentioned, is on his way from Lancaster to camp, a martyr to the general wickedness of the cause he engaged in, and the ingratitude of those he has served.

The first reflection which arises on this black business is, what sort of men must Englishmen be, and what sort of order and discipline do they preserve in their army, when, in the immediate place of their Head-Quarters, and under the eye and nose of their commander in chief, a prisoner can be taken at pleasure from his confinement and his death made a matter of sport.

The history of the most savage Indians does not produce instances exactly of this kind. They, at least, have a formality in their punishments. With them it is the horridness of revenge, but with your army it is the still greater crime, the horridness of diversion.

The British generals who have succeeded each other, from the time of general Gage to yourself, have all affected to speak in language they have no right to. In their proclamations, their addresses, their letters to general Washington and their supplications to congress (for they deserve no other name) they talk of British honour, British generosity and British clemency, as if those things were matters of fact; whereas, we whose eyes are open, who speak the same language with yourselves, many of whom were born on the same spot with you, and who can no more be mistaken in your words than in your actions, can declare to all the world, that so far as our knowledge goes, there is not a more detestable character, nor a meaner or more barbarous enemy than the present British one. With us you have forfeited all pretention to reputation, and it is only by holding you like a wild beast, afraid of your keepers, that you can be made manageable.—But to return to the point in question.

Tho' I can think no man innocent who has lent his hand to destroy the country which he did not plant, and to ruin those he could not inslave, yet abstracted from all Ideas of right or wrong on the original question, captain Asgil, in the present case, is not the guilty man. The villain and the victim are here separated characters. You hold the one and we the other. You disown or affect to disown and reprobate the conduct of Lippencut, yet you give him sanctuary; and by so doing you as effectually become the executioner of Asgil, as if you put the rope on his neck and dismissed him from the world.

Whatever your feelings on this extraordinary case may be

are best known to yourself. Within the grave of your own mind lies burried the fate of Asgil. He becomes the corpse of your will, or the survivor of your justice. Deliver up the one and you save the other; withhold the one and the other dies by your choice.

On our part the case is exceedingly plain; AN OFFICER HAS BEEN TAKEN FROM HIS CONFINEMENT AND MURDERED, AND THE MURDERER IS WITHIN YOUR LINES. Your army have been guilty of a thousand instances of equal cruelty, but they have been rendered equivocal and sheltered from personal detection. Here the crime is fixt; and is one of those extraordinary cases which can neither be denied nor paliated, and to which the custom of war does not apply; for it never could be supposed that such a brutal outrage would ever be committed. It is an original in the history of civilized barbarians, and is truly British.

On your part, you are accountable to us for the personal safety of the prisoners within your walls. Here can be no mistake; they can neither be spies nor suspected as such; your security is not endangered, nor your operations subjected to miscarriage, by men immurred within a dangeon. They differ in every circumstance from men in the field and leave no pretence for severity or punishment. But if to the dismal condition of captivity with you, must be added the constant apprehensions of death; if to be imprisoned is so nearly to be entombed; and, if after all, the murderers are to be protected and thereby the crime encouraged, wherein do you differ from Indians either in character or conduct.

We can have no idea of your honour or your justice in any future transaction, of what nature it may be, while you shelter within your lines an outrageous murderer and sacrifice in his stead an officer of your own. If you have no regard to us, at least spare the blood which it is your duty to save. Whether the punishment will be greater on he, who, in this case, innocently dies, or on he whom sad necessity forces to retaliate, is, in the nicety of sensation an undecided question? It rests with you to prevent the sufferings of both. You have nothing to do but to give up the murderer and the matter end.

But to protect him, be he who he may, is to patronize his crime, and to trifle it off by frivolous and unmeaning enquiries is to promote it. There is no declaration you can make, no promise you can give, that will obtain credit. It is the man and not the apology that is demanded.

You see yourself pressed on all sides to spare the life of your own officer, for die he will if you withhold justice. The murder of captain Huddy is an offence not to be borne with, and there is no security we can have that such actions or similar ones shall not be repeated, but by making the punishment fall upon yourselves. To destroy the last security of captivity, and to take the unarmed, the unresisting prisoner to private and sportive execution, is carrying barbarity too high for silence. The evil MUST be put an end to; and the choice of persons rests with you. But if your attachment to the guilty is stronger than to the innocent, you invent a crime that must destroy your character, and if the cause of your king needs to be so supported, forever cease, sir, to torture our remembrance with the wretched phrases of British honour, British generosity, and British clemency.

From this melancholy circumstance, learn, sir, a lesson of morality. The refugees are men whom your predecessors have instructed in wickedness the better to fit them to their master's purpose. To make them useful they have made them vile, and the consequence of their tutored villainy is now descending on the heads of their encouragers. They have been trained like hounds to the scent of blood and cherished in every species of dissolute barbarity. Their ideas of right and wrong are worn away in the constant habitude of repeated infamy, till like men practised in executions they feel not the value of another's life.

The task before you, tho' painful, is not difficult; give up the murderer, and save your officer, as the first outset of a necessary reformation.

COMMON SENSE.

Philadelphia, May 31, 1782.

To the Earl of Shelburne

October 29, 1782

A SPEECH which has been printed in several of the British and New-York News-papers, as coming from your Lordship, in answer to one from the Duke of Richmond of the 10th of July last, contains expressions and opinions so new and singular, and so enveloped in mysterious reasoning, that I address this publication to you, for the purpose of giving them a free and candid examination. The speech I allude to is in these words:

"His Lordship said it had been mentioned in another place, that he had been guilty of inconsistence. To clear himself of this, he asserted that he still held the same principles in respect to American independence, which he at first imbibed. He had been, and yet was of opinion, whenever the Parliament of Great-Britain acknowledges that point, the sun of England's glory is set for ever. Such were the sentiments he possessed on a former day, and such the sentiments he continued to hold at this hour. It was the opinion of Lord Chatham, and the opinion of many able statesmen. Other noble Lords, however, think differently; and as the majority of the cabinet support them, he acquiesced in the measure; dissenting from the idea, and the point is settled for bringing the matter into the full discussion of Parliament, where it will be candidly, fairly, and impartially debated. The independence of America would end in the ruin of England; and that a peace patched up with France would give that proud enemy the means of yet trampling on this country. The sun of England's glory he wished not to see set for ever; he looked for a spark at least to be left, which might in time light us up to a new day. But if independence was to be granted, if Parliament deemed that measure prudent, he foresaw in his own mind that England was undone. He wished to God that he had been deputed to Congress, that he might plead the cause of that country as well as of this, and that he might exercise whatever powers he possessed, as an orator, to save both from ruin, in a conviction to Congress, that, if their independence was signed, their liberties were gone for ever.

"Peace, his Lordship added, was a desirable object, but it must be an honourable peace, and not an humiliating one, dictated by France, or insisted on by America. It was very true this kingdom was not in a flourishing state, it was impoverished by war. But if we were not rich, it was evident that France was poor. If we were straitened in our finances, the enemy were exhausted in their resources. This was a great empire; it abounded with brave men, who were able and willing to fight in a common cause; the language of humiliation should not therefore be the language of Great-Britain. His Lordship said that he was not ashamed nor afraid of those expressions going to America. There were numbers, great numbers there, who were of the same way of thinking, in respect to that country being dependent on this, and who, with his Lordship, perceived ruin and independence linked together."

Thus far the speech, on which I remark,—That his Lordship is a total stranger to the mind and sentiments of America; that he has wrapped himself up in fond delusion that something less than independence may, under his administration, be accepted; and he wishes himself sent to Congress, to prove, the most extraordinary of all doctrines, which is, that independence, the sublimest of all human conditions, is loss of liberty.

In answer to which we may say, that in order to know what the contrary word DEPENDENCE means, we have only to look back to those years of severe humiliation, when the mildest of all petitions could obtain no other notice than the haughtiest of all insults; and when the base terms of unconditional submission were demanded, or undistinguishable destruction threatened. It is nothing to us that the Ministry have been changed, for they may be changed again. The guilt of government is the crime of a whole country; and the nation that can, though but for a moment, think and act as England has done, can never afterwards be believed or trusted. There are cases in which it is as impossible to restore character to life, as it is to recover the dead. It is a phœnix that can expire but once, and from whose ashes there is no resurrection. Some offences are of such a slight composition, that they reach no further than the temper, and are created or cured by a thought. But the sin of England has struck the heart of America, and nature has not left it in our power to say we can forgive.

Your Lordship wishes for an opportunity to plead before Congress *the cause of England and America, and to save, as you say, both from ruin.*

That the country, which, for more than seven years, has sought our destruction, should now cringe to solicit our protection, is adding the wretchedness of disgrace to the misery of disappointment; and if England has the least spark of supposed honor left, that spark must be darkened by asking, and extinguished by receiving, the smallest favor from America: For the criminal, who owes his life to the grace and mercy of the injured, is more executed by living than he who dies.

But a thousand pleadings, even from your Lordship, can have no effect. Honor, interest, and every sensation of the heart would plead against you. We are a people who think not as you think; and what is equally true, you cannot feel as we feel. The situation of the two countries are exceedingly different. We have been the seat of war. You have seen nothing of it. The most wanton destruction has been committed in our sight. The most insolent barbarity has been acted on our feelings. We can look round and see the remains of burnt and destroyed houses, once the fair fruit of hard industry, and now the striking monuments of British brutality. We walk over the dead whom we loved, in every part of America, and remember by whom they fell. There is scarcely a village but brings to life some melancholy thought, and reminds us of what we have suffered, and of those we have lost by the brutishness of Britain. A thousand images arise to us, which, from situation, you cannot see, and are accompanied by as many ideas which you cannot know, and therefore your supposed system of reasoning would apply to nothing, and all your expectations die of themselves.

The question whether England shall accede to the independence of America, and which your Lordship says is to undergo a parliamentary discussion, is so very simple, and composed of so few cases, that it scarcely needs a debate.

It is the only way out of an expensive and ruinous war,

which has now no object, and without which acknowledgment there can be no peace.

But your Lordship says, *"The sun of Great-Britain will be set whenever she acknowledge the independence of America."* Whereas the metaphor would have been strictly just to have left the sun wholly out of the figure, and have ascribed her not acknowledging it to the influence of the moon.

But the expression, if true, is the greatest confession of disgrace that could be made, and furnishes America with the highest notions of sovereign independent importance. Mr. Wedderburne, about the year 1776, made use of an idea of much the same kind, — *"Relinquish America!* says he. *What is it but to desire a Giant to shrink spontaneously into a dwarf."*

Alas! Are those people who call themselves Englishmen, of so little internal consequence, that when America is gone, or shuts her eyes upon them, their sun is set, they can shine no more, but grope about in obscurity and contract into insignificant animals. Was America, then, the giant of the empire, and England only her dwarf in waiting? Is the case so strangely altered, that those who once thought we could not live without them, now declare they cannot exist without us? Will they tell to the world, and that from their first Minister of State, that America is their all in all, that it is by her importance only they can live and breathe and have a being? Will they, who threatened to bring us at their feet, now cast themselves at ours, and own that without us they are not a nation? Are they become so unqualified to debate on independence, that they have lost all idea of it themselves, and are calling to the rocks and mountains of America to cover their insignificance? Or, if America is lost, is it manly to sob over it like a child for its rattle, and invite the laughter of the world, by declarations of disgrace. Surely the more consistent conduct would be to bear it without complaint, and to shew that England, without America, can preserve her independence and a suitable rank with other European powers. You were not contented while you had her, and to weep for her now is childish.

But Lord Shelburne thinks that something may yet be done. What that something is, or how it is to be accomplished, is a matter in obscurity. By arms there is no hope.

The experience of nearly eight years, with the expence of an hundred million pounds sterling, and the loss of two armies, must positively decide that point. Besides the British have lost their interest in America with the disaffected. Every part of it has been tried. There is no new scene left for delusion: And the thousands who have been ruined by adhering to them, and have now to quit the settlements they had acquired, and be conveyed like transports to cultivate the deserts of Augustine and Nova Scotia, has put an end to all further expectations of aid.

If you cast your eyes on the people of England, what have they to console themselves with for the millions expended, or what encouragement is there left to continue throwing good money after bad? America can carry on the war for ten years longer, and all the charges of government included, for less than you can defray the charges of war and government for one year. And I, who know both countries, know well that the people of America can afford to pay their share of the expence much better than the people of England can. Besides, it is their own estates and property, their own rights, liberties and government, they are defending, and were they not to do it, they would deserve to lose all, and none would pity them. The fault would be their own, and their punishment just.

The British army in America care not how long the war lasts. They enjoy an easy and indolent life. They fatten on the folly of one country and the spoils of another; and, between their plunder and their pay, may go home rich. But the case is very different with the labouring farmer, the working tradesman, and the necessitous poor in England, the sweat of whose brow goes day after day to feed, in prodigality and sloth, the army that is robbing both them and us. Removed from the eye of the country that supports them, and distant from the government that employs them, they cut and carve for themselves and there is none to call them to account.

But England will be ruined, says Lord Shelburne, if America is independent.

Then, I say, is England already ruined, for America is already independent: And if Lord Shelburne will not allow this, he immediately denies the fact which he infers. Besides, to make England the meer creature of America, is paying too great a compliment to us, and too little to himself.

But the declaration is a rhapsody of inconsistence. For to say, as Lord Shelburne has numberless times said, that the war against America is ruinous, and yet to continue the prosecution of that ruinous war for the purpose of avoiding ruin, is a language which cannot be understood. Neither is it possible to see how the independence of America is to accomplish the ruin of England after the war is over, and yet not effect it before. America cannot be more independent of her, nor a greater enemy to her, hereafter than she is now; nor England derive less advantages from her than at present: Why then is ruin to follow in the best state of the case, and not in the worst; and if not in the worst, why is it to follow at all.

That a nation is to be ruined by peace and commerce, and fourteen or fifteen millions a year less expences than before, is a new doctrine in politics. We have heard much clamour of national savings and œconomy, but surely the true œconomy would be to save the whole charge of a silly, foolish and headstrong war; because, compared with this, all other retrenchments are baubles and trifles.

But is it possible that Lord Shelburne can be serious in supposing the least advantage can be obtained by arms, or that any advantage can be equal to the expence, or the danger of attempting it. Will not the capture of one army after another satisfy him, but all must become prisoners? Must England ever be the sport of hope, and the dupe of delusion? Sometimes our currency was to fail; another time our army was to disband; then whole provinces were to revolt; such a General said this and that; another wrote so and so; Lord Chatham was of this opinion; and Lord somebody else of another: To-day 20,000 Russians and 20 Russian ships of the line were to come; to-morrow the Empress was abused without mercy or decency. Then the Emperor of Germany was to be bribed with a million of money, and the King of Prussia was to do wonderful things; at one time it was Lo here! and then it was Lo there! Sometimes this power, and sometimes that power, was to engage in the war, just as if the whole world was as mad and foolish as Britain. And thus, from year to year, has every straw been catched at, and every will-with-a-whisp led them a new dance.

This year a still newer folly is to take place. Lord Shelburne wishes to be sent to Congress, and he thinks that something may be done.

Are not the repeated answers which Congress has given and which all America supports, that they will not even hear any proposals whatever, until the unconditional and unequivocal independence of America is recognised, are not, I say, these declarations answer enough?

But for England to receive any thing from America now, after so many insults, injuries and outrages, acted towards us, would shew such a spirit of meanness in her, that we could not but despise her for accepting it. And so far from Lord Shelburne coming here to solicit it, it would be the greatest disgrace we could do them to offer it. England would appear a wretch indeed, at this time of day, to ask or owe any thing to the bounty of America. Has not the name of Englishman blots enough upon it, without inventing more. Even Lucifer would scorn to reign in Heaven by permission, and yet an Englishman can creep for only an entrance into America. Or has a land of liberty so many charms, that to be a door-keeper in it is better than to be an English Minister of State?

But what can this expected something be? or, if obtained, what can it amount to but new disgraces, contentions and quarrels. The people of America have for years accustomed themselves to think and speak so freely and contemptuously of English authority, and the inveteracy is so deeply rooted, that a person invested with any authority from that country, and attempting to exercise it here, would have the life of a toad under a harrow. They would look on him as an interloper, to whom their compassion permitted a residence. He would be no more than the Mungo of the farce, and if he disliked that, he must set off. It would be a station of degradation, debased by our pity, and despised by our pride, and would place England in a more contemptible situation than any she has yet suffered by the war. We have too high an opinion of ourselves, ever to think of yielding again the least obedience to outlandish authority; and for a thousand reasons, England would be the last country in the world to yield it to. She has been treacherous, and we know it. Her character is gone, and we have seen the funeral.

Surely she loves to fish in troubled waters, and drink the cup of contention, or she would not now think of mingling her affairs with those of America. It would be like a foolish dotard taking to his arms the bride that despises him, or who has placed on his head the ensigns of her disgust. It is kissing the hand that boxes his ears, and proposing to renew the exchange. The thought is as servile as the war was wicked, and shews the last scene of the drama as inconsistent as the first.

As America is gone, the only act of manhood is to *let her go*. Your Lordship had no hand in the separation, and you will gain no honor by temporising politics. Besides, there is something so exceedingly whimsical, unsteady, and even insincere in the present conduct of England, that she exhibits herself in most dishonorable colours.

On the second of August last General Carleton and Admiral Digby wrote to General Washington in these words:

"The resolutions of the House of Commons of the 27th of February last have been placed in your Excellency's hands, and intimations given at the same time, that further pacific measures were likely to follow. Since which, until the present time, we have had no direct communications from England; but a mail is now arrived, which brings us very important information. We are acquainted, Sir, *by authority*, that negotiations for a general peace have already commenced at Paris, and that Mr. Grenville is invested with full powers to treat with all the parties at war, and is now at Paris in the execution of his commission. And we are farther, Sir, made acquainted, *that his Majesty, in order to remove all obstacles to that peace which he so ardently wishes to restore, has commanded his Ministers to direct Mr. Grenville, that the Independence of the Thirteen Provinces should be proposed by him in the first instance, instead of making it a condition of a general treaty.*"

Now, taking your present measures into view, and comparing them with the declarations in this letter, pray what is the word of your King, or his Ministers, or the Parliament, good for? Must we not look upon you as a confederated body of faithless, treacherous men, whose assurances are fraud, and their language deceit? What opinion can we possibly form of you, but that you are a lost, abandoned, profligate nation, who sport even with your own character, and are to be held by nothing but the bayonet or the halter.

To say, after this, *that the sun of Great Britain will be set, whenever she acknowledges the independence of America*, when the not doing it is the unqualified lie of government, can be no other than the language of ridicule, the jargon of inconsistency. There were thousands in America who predicted the delusion, and looked upon it as a trick of treachery, to take us from our guard, and draw off our attention from the only system of finance, by which we can be called, or deserve to be called, a sovereign, independent people. The fraud, on your part, might be worth attempting, but the sacrifice to obtain it is too high.

There were others who credited the assurances, because they thought it impossible that men who had their characters to establish should begin it with a lie. The prosecution of the war by the former Ministry was savage and horrid, since which it has been mean, trickish and delusive. The one went greedily into the passion of revenge, the other into the subtilties of low contrivance, till, between the crimes of both, there is scarcely left a man in America, be he whig or tory, who does not despise or detest the conduct of Britain.

The management of Lord Shelburne, whatever may be his views, is a caution to us, and must be to the world, never to regard British assurances. A perfidy so notorious cannot be hid. It stands even in the public papers of New-York, with the names of Carleton and Digby affixed to it. It is a proclamation that the King of England is not to be believed: That the spirit of lying is the governing principle of the Ministry. It is holding up the character of the House of Commons to public infamy, and warning all men not to credit them. Such is the consequence which Lord Shelburne's management has brought upon his country.

After the authorised declarations contained in Carleton and Digby's letter, you ought, from every motive of honor, policy and prudence, to have fulfilled them, whatever might have been the event. It was the least attonement you could possibly make to America, and the greatest kindness you could do to yourselves; for you will save millions by a general peace, and you will lose as many by continuing the war.

COMMON SENSE.

Philadelphia, October 29, 1782.

P. S. The manuscript copy of this letter is sent your Lordship, by the way of our Head-Quarters, to New-York, inclosing a late pamphlet of mine, addressed to the Abbe Reynal, which will serve to give your Lordship some idea of the principles and sentiments of America.

C. S.

The Last Crisis

NUMBER XIII

April 19, 1783

"The times that tried mens souls," * are over—and the greatest and compleatest revolution the world ever knew is gloriously and happily accomplished.

But to pass from the extremes of danger to safety—from the tumult of war to the tranquility of peace, though sweet in contemplation, requires a gradual composure of the senses to receive it. Even calmness has the power of stunning when it opens too instantly upon us. The long and raging hurricane that should cease in a moment, would leave us in a state rather of wonder than enjoyment; and some moments of recollection must pass before we could be capable of tasting the full felicity of repose. There are but few instances, in which the mind is fitted for sudden transitions: it takes in its pleasures by reflection and comparison, and those must have time to act, before the relish for new scenes is compleat.

In the present case—the mighty magnitude of the object—the various uncertainties of fate it has undergone—the numerous and complicated dangers we have suffered or escaped—the eminence we now stand on, and the vast prospect before us, must all conspire to impress us with contemplation.

To see it in our power to make a world happy—to teach mankind the art of being so—to exhibit on the theatre of the universe a character hitherto unknown—and to have, as it were, a new creation entrusted to our hands, are honors that command reflection, and can neither be too highly estimated, nor too gratefully received.

In this pause then of recollection—while the storm is ceasing, and the long agitated mind vibrating to a rest, let us look back on the scenes we have passed, and learn from experience what is yet to be done.

Never, I say, had a country so many openings to happiness

*"These are the times that try mens souls." Crisis No. I. published December 19, 1776.

348

as this. Her sitting out into life, like the rising of a fair morning, was unclouded and promising. Her cause was good. Her principles just and liberal. Her temper serene and firm. Her conduct regulated by the nicest steps of order, and every thing about her wore the mark of honor.

It is not every country (perhaps there is not another in the world) that can boast so fair an origin. Even the first settlement of America corresponds with the character of the revolution. Rome, once the proud mistress of the universe, was originally a band of ruffians. Plunder and rapine made her rich, and her oppression of millions made her great. But America needs never be ashamed to tell her birth, nor relate the stages by which she rose to empire.

The remembrance, then, of what is past, if it operates rightly, must inspire her with the most laudable of all ambition, that of adding to the fair fame she began with. The world has seen her great in adversity. Struggling, without a thought of yielding, beneath accumulated difficulties. Bravely, nay proudly, encountering distress, and rising in resolution as the storm encreased. All this is justly due to her, for her fortitude has merited the character.—Let, then, the world see that she can bear prosperity; and that her honest virtue in time of peace, is equal to the bravest virtue in time of war.

She is now descending to the scenes of quiet and domestic life. Not beneath the cypress shade of disappointment, but to enjoy in her own land, and under her own vine, the sweets of her labours, and the reward of her toil.—In this situation, may she never forget, that a fair national reputation is of as much importance as independence. That it possesses a charm which wins upon the world, and makes even enemies civil. That it gives a dignity which is often superior to power, and commands a reverence where pomp and splendor fail.

It would be a circumstance ever to be lamented and never to be forgotten, were a single blot, from any cause whatever, suffered to fall on a revolution, which to the end of time must be an honor to the age that accomplished it: and which has contributed more to enlighten the world, and diffuse a spirit of freedom and liberality among mankind, than any human event (if this may be called one) that ever preceded it.

It is not among the least of the calamities of a long continued war, that it unhinges the mind from those nice sensations which at other times appear so amiable. The continual spectacle of woe blunts the finer feelings, and the necessity of bearing with the sight renders it familiar. In like manner, are many of the moral obligations of society weakened, till the custom of acting by necessity, becomes an apology where it is truly a crime. Yet let but a nation conceive rightly of its character, and it will be chastely just in protecting it. None ever began with a fairer than America, and none can be under a greater obligation to preserve it.

The debt which America has contracted, compared with the cause she has gained, and the advantages to flow from it, ought scarcely to be mentioned. She has it in her choice to do, and to live, as happily, as she pleases. The world is in her hands. She has now no foreign power to monopolize her commerce, perplex her legislation, or controul her prosperity. The struggle is over, which must one day have happened, and, perhaps, never could have happened at a better time*.

---

*That the revolution began at the exact period of time best fitted to the purpose, is sufficiently proved by the event.—But the great hinge on which the whole machine turned is the UNION OF THE STATES: and this union was naturally produced by the inability of any one state to support itself against a foreign enemy without the assistance of the rest.

Had the states severally been less able than they were when the war began, their united strength would not have been equal to the undertaking, and they must, in all human probability, have failed—And on the other hand, had they severally been more able, they might not have seen, or, what is more, might not have felt, the necessity of uniting; and either by attempting to stand alone, or in small confederacies, would have been separately conquered.

Now, as we cannot see a time (and many years must pass away before it can arrive) when the strength of any one state, or of several united, can be equal to the whole of the present united states, and as we have seen the extreme difficulty of collectively prosecuting the war to a successful issue, and preserving our national importance in the world, therefore, from the experience we have had, and the knowledge we have gained, we must, unless we make a waste of wisdom, be strongly impressed with the advantage, as well as the necessity, of strengthening that happy union which has been our salvation, and without which we should have been a ruined people.

While I was writing this note, I cast my eye on the pamphlet COMMON SENSE, from which I shall make an extract, as it applies exactly to the case. It is as follows.

'I have never met with a man, either in England or America, who hath not confessed his opinion that a separation between the countries would take

And instead of a domineering master, she has gained an Ally, whose exemplary greatness, and universal liberality, have extorted a confession even from her enemies.

With the blessings of peace, independence, and an universal commerce, the states, individually and collectively, will have leisure and opportunity to regulate and establish their domestic concerns, and to put it beyond the power of calumny to throw the least reflection on their honor. Character is much easier kept than recovered, and that man, if any such there be, who, from any sinister views, or littleness of soul, lends unseen his hand to injure it, contrives a wound it will never be in his power to heal.

As we have established an inheritance for posterity, let that inheritance descend with every mark of an honorable conveyance. The little it will cost, compared with the worth of the states, the greatness of the object, and the value of national character, will be a profitable exchange.

But that which must more forcibly strike a thoughtful penetrating mind, and which includes and renders easy all inferior concerns, is the UNION OF THE STATES. On this, our great national character depends. It is this which must give us importance abroad and security at home. It is through this only that we are, or can be nationally known in the world. It is the flag of the united states which renders our ships and commerce safe on the seas, or in a foreign port. Our Mediterranean passes must be obtained under the same stile. All our treaties, whether of alliance, peace, or commerce, are formed

---

place one time or other: And there is no instance in which we have shewn less judgment, than in endeavouring to describe, what we call, the ripeness or fitness of the continent for independence.

'As all men allow the measure, and differ only in their opinion of the time, let us, in order to remove mistakes, take a general survey of things, and endeavour, if possible, to find out the VERY TIME. But we need not go far, the enquiry ceases at once, for, THE TIME HATH FOUND US. The general concurrence, the glorious union of all things prove the fact.

'It is not in numbers, but in a union, that our great strength lies. The continent is just arrived at that pitch of strength, in which no single colony is able to support itself, and the whole, when united, can accomplish the matter; and either more or less than this, might be fatal in its effects.'
PAMPHLET COMMON SENSE.

under the sovereignty of the united states, and Europe knows us by no other name or title.

The division of the empire into states is for our own convenience, but abroad this distinction ceases. The affairs of each state are local. They can go no farther than to itself. And were the whole worth of even the richest of them expended in revenue, it would not be sufficient to support sovereignty against a foreign attack. In short, we have no other national sovereignty than as united states. It would even be fatal for us if we had—too expensive to be maintained, and impossible to be supported. Individuals or individual states may call themselves what they please; but the world, and especially the world of enemies, is not to be held in awe by the whistling of a name. Sovereignty must have power to protect all the parts that compose and constitute it: and as UNITED STATES we are equal to the importance of the title, but otherwise we are not. Our union well and wisely regulated and cemented, is the cheapest way of being great—the easiest way of being powerful, and the happiest invention in government which the circumstances of America can admit of.—Because it collects from each state, that, which, by being inadequate, can be of no use to it, and forms an aggregate that serves for all.

The states of Holland are an unfortunate instance of the effects of individual sovereignty. Their disjointed condition exposes them to numerous intrigues, losses, calamities, and enemies; and the almost impossibility of bringing their measures to a decision, and that decision into execution, is to them, and would be to us, a source of endless misfortune.

It is with confederate states as with individuals in society; something must be yielded up to make the whole secure. In this view of things we gain by what we give, and draw an annual interest greater than the capital.—I ever feel myself hurt when I hear the union, that great palladium of our liberty and safety, the least irreverently spoken of. It is the most sacred thing in the constitution of America, and that which every man should be the most proud and tender of. Our citizenship in the united states is our national character. Our citizenship in any particular state is only our local distinction. By the latter we are known at home, by the former to the

world. Our great title is, AMERICANS; our inferior one varies
with the place.

So far as my endeavours could go, they have all been directed to conciliate the affections, unite the interests, and
draw and keep the mind of the country together; and the
better to assist in this foundation work of the revolution, I
have avoided all places of profit or office, either in the state I
live in, or in the united states; kept myself at a distance from
all parties and party connections, and even disregarded all private and inferior concerns: and when we take into view the
great work we have gone through, and feel, as we ought to
feel, the just importance of it, we shall then see, that the little
wranglings and indecent contentions of personal party, are as
dishonorable to our characters, as they are injurious to our
repose.

It was the cause of America that made me an author. The
force with which it struck my mind, and the dangerous condition the country appeared to me in, by courting an impossible and unnatural reconciliation with those who were
determined to reduce her, instead of striking out into the
only line that could cement and save her, A DECLARATION OF
INDEPENDENCE, made it impossible for me, feeling as I did,
to be silent: and if, in the course of more than seven years, I
have rendered her any service, I have likewise added something to the reputation of literature, by freely and disinterest-
edly employing it in the great cause of mankind, and shewing
there may be genius without prostitution.

Independence always appeared to me practicable and probable; provided the sentiment of the country could be formed
and held to the object: and there is no instance in the world,
where a people so extended, and wedded to former habits of
thinking, and under such a variety of circumstances, were so
instantly and effectually pervaded, by a turn in politics, as in
the case of independence, and who supported their opinion,
undiminished, through such a succession of good and ill fortune, till they crowned it with success.

But as the scenes of war are closed, and every man preparing for home and happier times, I therefore take my leave of
the subject. I have most sincerely followed it from beginning
to end, and through all its turns and windings: and whatever

country I may hereafter be in, I shall always feel an honest pride at the part I have taken and acted, and a gratitude to Nature and Providence for putting it in my power to be of some use to mankind.

COMMON SENSE.

Philadelphia, April 19, 1783.

Commerce with Britain and the Necessity of Union

December 9, 1783

TO THE PEOPLE OF AMERICA.

In *"Rivington's New-York Gazette,"* of Dec. 6th, is a publication, under the appearance of a letter from London, dated Sept. 30th; and is on a subject which demands the attention of the United States.

The Public will remember, that a Treaty of Commerce between the United States and England was set on foot last Spring, and that until the said Treaty could be compleated, a Bill was brought into the British Parliament, by the then Chancellor of the Exchequer, Mr. Pitt, to admit and legalize (as the case then required) the Commerce of the United States into the British ports and dominions. But neither the one nor the other has been compleated. The Commercial Treaty is either broken off, or remains as it began; and the Bill in Parliament has been thrown aside. And in lieu thereof, a selfish system of English politics has started up, calculated to fetter the Commerce of America, by engrossing to England the carrying trade of the American produce to the West India Islands.

Among the advocates for this last measure, is Lord Sheffield, a member of the British Parliament, who has published a Pamphlet, entitled, *"Observations on the Commerce of the American States."* The pamphlet has two objects; the one is, to allure the Americans to purchase British manufactures; and the other, to spirit up the British Parliament to prohibit the Citizens of the United States from trading to the West-India Islands.

Viewed in this light, the pamphlet, though in some parts dextrously written, is an absurdity. It offends, in the very act of endeavouring to ingratiate; and his Lordship, as a politician, ought not to have suffered the two objects to have appeared together. The letter alluded to contains extracts from the pamphlet, with high encomiums on Lord Sheffield, for

355

laboriously endeavouring (as the letter stiles it) "to shew the mighty advantages of retaining the carrying trade."

Since the publication of this pamphlet in England, the Commerce of the United States to the West-Indies, in American vessels, has been prohibited; and all intercourse, except in British bottoms, the property of, and navigated by British subjects, cut off.

That a country has a right to be as foolish as it pleases, has been proved by the practice of England for many years past: In her island-situation, sequestered from the world, she forgets that her whispers are heard by other nations; and in her plans of politics and commerce, she seems not to know, that other votes are necessary besides her own. America would be equally as foolish as Britain, were she to suffer so great a degradation on her flag, and such a stroke on the freedom of her Commerce, to pass without a balance.

We admit the right of any nation to prohibit the Commerce of another into its own dominions, where there are no treaties to the contrary; but as this right belongs to one side, as well as to the other, there is always a way left to bring avarice and insolence to reason.

But the ground of security which Lord Sheffield has chosen to erect his policy upon, is of a nature which ought, and I think must awaken, in every American, a just and strong sense of national dignity. Lord Sheffield appears to be sensible that in advising the British Nation and Parliament to engross to themselves so great a part of the Carrying Trade of America, he is attempting a measure which cannot succeed, if the Politics of the United States be properly directed to counteract the assumption.

But, says he, in his Pamphlet, *"It will be a long time before the American States can be brought to act as a Nation, neither are they to be feared as such by us."*

What is this more or less than to tell us, that while we have no National System of Commerce, the British will govern our trade by their own Laws and Proclamations as they please. The quotation discloses a truth too serious to be overlooked, and too mischievous not to be remedied.

Among other circumstances which led them to this discovery, none could operate so effectually, as, the injudicious, uncandid, and indecent opposition made by sundry persons in a certain State, to the recommendations of Congress last Winter, for an import duty of five per cent. It could not but explain to the British a weakness in the National Power of America, and encourage them to attempt restrictions on her trade, which otherwise they would not have dared to hazard. Neither is there any State in the Union, whose policy was more mis-directed to its interest than the State I allude to, because her principal support is the Carrying Trade, which Britain, induced by the want of a well-centered Power in the United States to protect and secure, is now attempting to take away. It fortunately happened (and to no state in the Union more than the State in question) that the Terms of peace were agreed on before the Opposition appeared, otherwise, there needs not a doubt, that if the same idea of the diminished authority of America, had occurred to them at that time as has occurred to them since, but they would have made the same grasp at the Fisheries, as they have done at the Carrying Trade.

It is surprising that an authority which can be supported with so much ease, and so little expence, and capable of such extensive advantages to the country, should be cavelled at by those whose duty it is to watch over it, and whose existance, as a people depends upon it. But this, perhaps, will ever be the case, till some misfortune awaken us into reason, and the instance now before us is but a gentle beginning of what America must expect, unless she guards her Union with nicer care and stricter honour. United, she is formidable, and that with the least possible charge, a Nation can be so: Separated, she is a medley of individual nothings, subject to the sport of foreign Nations.

It is very probable that the ingenuity of Commerce may have found out a method to evade and supercede the intentions of the British in interdicting the Trade with the West-India Islands. The language of both being the same, and their customs well understood, the vessels of one country may, by deception, pass for those of another. But this would be a practice too debasing for a Sovereign people to stoop to, and too profligate not to be discountenanced. An illicit Trade, under any shape it can be placed, cannot be carried on without a violation of truth. America is now Sovereign and Independent, and ought to act all her affairs in a regular stile of character. She has the same right to say that no British vessel shall enter her ports, or that no British manufactures shall be imported but in American bottoms, the property of, and navigated by American subjects, as Britain has to say the same thing respecting the West-Indies. Or she may lay a duty of ten, fifteen, or twenty shillings per ton, (exclusive of other duties) on every British vessel coming from any port of the West-Indies where she is not admitted to trade, the said tonnage to continue as long on her side as the prohibition continues on the other.

But it is only by acting in Union, that the usurpations of foreign Nations on the freedom of trade, can be counteracted, and security extended to the Commerce of America. And when we view a Flag, which to the eye is beautiful, and to contemplate its rise and origin, inspires a sensation of sublime delight, our National Honour must unite with our Interest to prevent injury to the one, or insult to the other.

COMMON SENSE.

New-York, Dec. 9, 1783.

On the Affairs of Pennsylvania

September 15, 1786

AT the commencement of the present constitution, it was strongly opposed, and as strongly contended for. This gave existence to two parties, which have since maintained nearly an equal contest, sometimes the one, and sometimes the other, prevailing at elections.

Among those who at that time opposed the alteration of the constitution, I bore my share, in a number of publications, entitled "A serious address to the people of Pennsylvania on the present state of their affairs."

Whether a single legislative Assembly, or a legislature composed of two branches, is best suited to support the just principles of equal liberty, is a point I never touched upon in any of those publications. My aim was to quiet the dispute, and prevent it from entangling the country, at a time when the utmost harmony of its powers was necessary to its safety. The constitution was upon experiment, and the manner in which a single House would use such an abundance of power would best determine whether it ought to be trusted with it.—Besides this, the constitution very prudently held out, in the forty-seventh section, the probability of its own defects, by appointing the means (by a convention) at the period of every seven years, of adding new articles or amending defective ones. The words in the said section are:— "The Council of Censors shall also have power to call a convention, to meet within two years after their sitting, if there appears to them an absolute necessity of amending any article of the constitution which may be defective, explaining such as may be thought not clearly expressed, and the adding such as are necessary for the preservation of the rights and happiness of the people." Therefore, any alteration which experience or circumstances shall prove necessary or proper is consistent with the constitution itself.

But the causes or reasons which then operated for not altering the constitution, could not be conclusively taken as causes or reasons for confirming it. When many people, those reasons went no further than to give the constitution a fair trial, or, rather, to give a single legislature a sufficient opportunity to shew with what degree of wisdom and prudence, impartiality and moderation, it would act. With others, the attempt to alter appeared to be ill-timed. And there were many who held an opinion, that has always prevailed among the political part of mankind, which is, that the form of government best calculated for preserving liberty in time of peace, is not the best form for conducting the operations of war; and that as the government of a single house had a considerable resemblance to the government of a single person, the present form, on account of the quickness of its execution, was preferable during the war to the proposed alterations.

There is, however, one fact very clearly deduced from the experience had, which is, that a single legislature, into the hands of whatever party it may fall, is capable of being made a compleat aristocracy for the time it exists: And that when the majority of a single house is made upon the ground of party prejudice, or fitted to be the dupes thereof, that its government, instead of comprehending the good of the whole dispassionately and impartially, will be that of party favor and oppression. To have established the present form as the best, it was absolutely necessary that the prejudices of party should have no operation within the walls of the legislature; for when it descends to this, a single legislature, on account of the superabundance of its power, and the uncontrouled rapidity of its execution, becomes as dangerous to the principles of liberty as that of a despotic monarchy. The present form was well intended, but the abuse of its power operates to its destruction. It withstood the opposition of its enemies, and will fall through the misconduct of its friends.

At the commencement of the revolution, it was supposed that what is called the executive part of a government was the only dangerous part; but we now see that quite as much mischief, if not more, may be done, and as much arbitrary conduct acted, by a legislature. In establishing the Executive Council, the constitution took care to prevent its being subject to inconsistent and contradictory conduct, and sudden convulsions. This is done by providing, that the periods of their elections shall not all expire at once. By this means, says the nineteenth section of the constitution, "there will in every subsequent year be found in the council a number of persons acquainted with the proceedings of the foregoing years, whereby the business will be more consistently conducted, and, moreover, the danger of establishing an inconvenient aristocracy be effectually prevented."

The council are as much the choice and representatives of the people as the assembly are, and have the same common interest in the community; and if it is necessary to guard against such events in the council, it is equally so in the legislature; and this would undoubtedly have been the case, could the convention have foreseen the capricious and inconsistent conduct of assemblies.

By the whole legislative power being entrusted to a single body of men, and that body expiring all at once, the state is subject to the perpetual convulsions of imperfect measures and rash proceedings; as by this means it may happen (as it has happened already) that a number of men, suddenly collected, unexperienced in business, and unacquainted with the grounds, reasons and principles, which former assemblies proceeded on in passing certain acts, and without seeking to inform themselves thereof, may precipitate the state into disorder by a confused medley of doing and undoing, and make the grievances they pretend to remove.

Of this kind was the attack made by a late assembly on that most useful and beneficial institution, incorporated by a former assembly, *The Bank of North-America*. The proceedings on this business are a stain to the national reputation of the state. They exhibit a train of little and envious thinking, a scene of passion of arbitrary principles and unconstitutional conduct; and the disgrace is filled up by assigning an untruth (which themselves have since acknowledged to) in the preamble to the act for annulling the charter of the Bank, as a cause for doing it. Such a disreputable circumstance in government could scarcely have happened, but from the cause I have already stated. For the Assembly which did it was newly formed, and elected on one of those sudden caprices which often happens in a free country, and there was not one man amongst them fully acquainted with the nature of the business they were going upon.

Public Banks are reckoned among the honors, privileges and advantages of a free people, and are never found among those under a despotic government. It is the confidence which people have in the measures and principles of government, and the strict observance of faith and honor on the part of government, which encourage people to put their money into circulation by means of a public Bank. A faithless or arbitrary government cannot be trusted, and therefore in free countries only are Banks established. In this state it has been the means of restoring that credit and confidence among individuals, which for many years was lost, and without which, agriculture, commerce, and every species of business, must decline and languish.

As gold and silver are not the natural products of Pennsylvania, we have no other hard money than what the produce of the country exported to foreign parts brings in. This being the case, the interest of the farmer and the merchant, the one being employed to raise the produce and the other to export it, are as naturally connected, as that of sowing the grain is connected with reaping the harvest; and any man must be held an enemy to the public prosperity, who endeavours to create a difference, or dissolve the mutual interest existing between them. The Plough and the Sail are the Arms of the state of Pennsylvania, and their connection should be held in remembrance by all good citizens.

As blood, tho' taken from the arm, is nevertheless taken from the whole body, so the attempt to destroy the Bank eventually operated to distress the farmer as well as the merchant; for if the one is prevented in the means of buying the produce of the country, the other, of consequence, is deprived of the opportunities of selling.

I shall conclude this paper with remarking, that so long as it shall be the choice of the people to continue the legislature in a single house, the circumstances of the country and the importance of the trust (being greater than that committed to any single body of men in any state in the union) evidently require, that the persons to be elected thereto be men freed from the bigotry and shackles of party, of liberal minds, and conversant in the means of increasing the riches of the state, and cultivating and extending the prosperity thereof.

COMMON SENSE.

Philad. Sept. 15, 1786.

Attack on Paper Money Laws

November 3, 1786

PAPER Money, Paper Money, and Paper Money! is now, in several of the states, both the bubble and the iniquity of the day. That there are some bad people concerned in schemes of this kind cannot be doubted, but the far greater part are misled. People are got so bewildered upon the subject that they put and mistake one thing for another. They say Paper Money has improved the country—Paper Money carried on the war, and Paper Money did a great many other fine things.

Not one syllable of this is truth; it is all error from beginning to end. It was CREDIT which did these things, and that credit has failed, by non-performance, and by the country being involved in debt and the levity and instability of government measures.

We have so far mistaken the matter that we have even mistaken the name. The name is not Paper Money, but Bills of Credit: But it seems as if we were ashamed to use the name, knowing how much we have abused the thing. All emissions of paper for government purposes is not making of money, but making use of credit to run into debt by. It is anticipating or forestalling the revenue of future years, and throwing the burden of redemption on future assemblies. It is like a man mortgaging his estate and leaving his successors to pay it off. But this is not the worst of it, it leaves us at last in the lurch by banishing the hard money, diminishing the value of the revenue, and filling up its place with paper, that may be like something to-day and to-morrow nothing.

So far as regards Pennsylvania, she cannot emit bills of credit, because the assembly which makes such an emission cannot bind future assemblies either to redeem them or receive them in taxes. The precedent of revoking the charter of the bank, established by a former assembly, is a precedent for any assembly to undo what another has done. It circumscribes the power of any assembly to the year in which it sits; that is, it cannot engage for the performance of any thing beyond that time. And as an assembly cannot issue bills of credit and redeem them within the year, and as it cannot by that precedent bind a future assembly so to do, it therefore cannot with the necessary security do it at all; because people will not put confidence in the paper promises or paper emissions of those who can neither perform the engagement within the time their own power exist nor compel the performance after that time is past. The politicians of the project for revoking the bank charter (and it was besides most wantonly done), to use a trite saying, aimed at the pidgeon and shot the crew—they fired at the bank and hit their own paper.

As to making those bills what is called legal tenders, we have no such thing in this state, which is one reason they have not depreciated more: But as it is a matter which engrosses the attention of some other states, I shall offer a few remarks on it.

The abuse of any power always operates to call the right of that power in question. To judge of the right or power of any assembly in America to make those bills a legal tender, we must have recourse to the principles on which civil government is founded; for if such an act is not compatible with those principles, the assembly which assumes such a power, assumes a power unknown in civil government, and commits treason against its principles.

The fundamental principles of civil government are security of our rights and persons as freeman, and security of property. A tender law, therefore, cannot stand on the principles of civil government, because it operates to take away a man's share of civil and natural freedom, and to render property insecure.

If a man had a hundred silver dollars in his possession, as his own property, it would be a strange law that should oblige him to deliver them up to any one who could discover that he possessed them, and take a hundred paper dollars in exchange. Now the case, in effect, is exactly the same; if he has lent a hundred hard dollars to his friend, and is compelled to take a hundred paper ones for them. The exchange is against his consent, and to his injury, and the principles of civil government provides for the protection, and not for the violation of his rights and property. The state, therefore, that is under the operation of such an act, is not in a state of civil government, and consequently the people cannot be bound to obey a law which abets and encourages treason against the first principles on which civil government is founded.

The principles of civil government extend in their operation to compel the exact performance of engagements entered into between man and man. The only kind of legal tenders that can exist in a country under a civil government is the particular thing expressed and specified in those engagements or contracts. That particular thing constitutes the legal tender. If a man engages to sell and deliver a quantity of wheat, he is not to deliver rye, any more than he who contracts to pay in hard money is at liberty to pay in paper or in any thing else. Those contracts or bargains have expressed the legal tender on both sides, and no assumed or presumptuous authority of any assembly can dissolve or alter them.

Another branch of this principle of civil government is, that it disowns the practice of retrospective laws. An assembly or legislature cannot punish a man by any new law made after the crime is committed; he can only be punished by the law which existed at the time he committed the crime. This principle of civil government extends to property as well as to life; for a law made after the time that any bargain or contract was entered into between individuals can no more become the law for deciding that contract, than, in the other case, it can become the law for punishing the crime; both of those cases must be referred to the laws existing at the time the crime was done or the bargain made. Each party then knew the relative situation they stood in with each other, and on that law and on that knowledge they acted, and by no other can they be adjudged—Therefore all tender laws which apply to the alteration of past contracts, by making them dischargable on either side, different to what was the law at the time they were made, is of the same nature as that law which inflicts a punishment different to what was the law at the time the crime was committed: For in all cases of civil government the law must be before the fact.

But was there no illegality in tender laws, they are naturally defective on another consideration. They cannot bind all and every interest in the state, because they cannot bind the state itself. They are, therefore, compulsive where they ought to be free; that is, between man and man, and are naturally free where, if at all, they ought to be compulsive: for in all cases where the state reserves to itself the right of freeing itself, it cannot bind the individual, because the right of the one stands on as good ground as that of the other.

COMMON SENSE.

Philadelphia, Nov. 3, 1786.

To Thomas Jefferson

February? 1788

AFTER I got home, being alone and wanting amusement I sat down to explain to myself (for there is such a thing) my Ideas of natural and civil rights and the distinction between them. I send them to you to see how nearly we agree.

Suppose 20 persons, strangers to each other, to meet in a Country not before inhabited. Each would be a sovereign in his own natural right. His will would be his Law, but his power, in many cases, inadequate to his right, and the consequence would be that each might be exposed, not only to each other, but to the other nineteen.

It would then occur to them that their condition would be much improved, if a way could be devised to exchange that quantity of danger into so much protection, so that each individual should possess the strength of the whole number.

As all their rights, in the first case, are natural rights, and the exercise of those rights supported only by their own natural individual power, they would begin by distinguishing between these rights they could individually exercise fully and perfectly and those they could not.

Of the first kind are the rights of thinking, speaking, forming and giving opinions, and perhaps all those which can be fully exercised by the individual without the aid of exterior assistance, or in other words, rights of personal competency. Of the second kind are those of personal protection of acquiring and possessing property, in the exercise of which the individual natural power is less than the natural right.

Having drawn this line they agree to retain individually the first Class of Rights or those of personal Competency; and to detach from their personal possession the second Class, or those of defective power and to accept in lieu thereof a right to the whole power produced by a condensation of all the parts. These I conceive to be civil rights or rights of Compact, and are distinguishable from Natural rights, because in the one we act wholly in our own person, in the other we agree not to do so, but act under the guarantee of society.

It therefore follows that the more of those imperfect natural rights, or rights of imperfect power we give up and thus exchange the more security we possess, and as the word liberty is often mistakenly put for security Mr. Wilson has confused his Argument by confounding the terms.

But it does not follow that the more natural rights of *every kind* we resign the more security we possess, because if we resign those of the first class we may suffer much by the exchange, for where the right and the power are equal with each other in the individual naturally they ought to rest there.

Mr. Wilson must have some allusion to this distinction or his position would be subject to the inference you draw from it.

I consider the individual sovereignty of the states retained under the Act of Confederation to be of the second class of rights. It becomes dangerous because it is defective in the power necessary to support it. It answers the pride and purpose of a few Men in each State, but the State collectively is injured by it.

To George Washington

My Dear Sir   London Octr 16th 1789

I need not tell you how much I rejoice at the prosperous accounts from America, or how happy I feel that you have relinquished the temptations of quiet retirement for the busy scenes of Public Good. Had the opportunity of your coming once more forward not have offered itself you might have injoyed retirement with serenity; but retirement would have lost its felicity, had it been haunted, as would have been the case, with the impression of having declined, for the sake of ease, a station in which you could be so publicly useful. I am certain you will feel the happier for this sacrifice, because to be perfectly so the mind must justify itself in every thing.

Mr Mappa the Gentleman who will present you this is an exiled Hollander, and, as I am informed, very capital in his line which is that of a letter-founder—I have given him a letter to Dr Franklin, the proper Patron of his Art, and as it is a branch in which improvement is wanted in America, I hope his coming will benifit both the Country and himself.

Mr Jefferson who, I expect, will arrive as soon as this letter, will inform you of my proceedings here—I am constructing a Bridge of one Arch in Partnership with the Walkers of Rother-ham Yorkshire—The Arch is 110 feet Span and five feet high from the Cord line—We began it in July and I expect it in London about the Middle of Novr—In the mean time I am going over to France—A Share in two revolutions is living to some purpose—I shall be exceedingly happy to see a line from you, which if addressed to the Care of Benjn Vaughn Esqr.—Jeffries Square London will find me any where. With every Wish for your happiness and Mrs Washington's—I am—my Dear Sir your most affectiona. obedient Humble Servant

THOMAS PAINE

Please to remember me among the Circle of my friends.

To Benjamin Rush

Dear Friend   Paris March 16th 1790

As I do not expect this letter will come to hand of a considerable time I shall not enter into any details of news or
circumstances.—My principal intention in writing it is to introduce a friend of mine and yourself, to the corresponding
acquaintance of each other—Among the few intimates I have
made on this side the water, I have met with none more con-
genial than the Gentleman I am writing of, M. Christie, and it
is by his desire that I undertake this office—As it is probable
your future acquaintance, with the Atlantic between you, may
continue a long time, I will leave you, in the outset, nothing
to guess at that may be convenient to know in an acquaintance of this kind—M. Christie's Father is a Banker at Mon-
trose, Scotland, he has studied Physic as if he were to practice
it, but his intention is to settle in London in the Banking
line—He is passing some at Paris as a Man of observation
before he undertakes, Atlas-like, the world on his own shoulders—He has made himself acquainted with as many subjects, and as many literary characters ancient and Modern as
any one I have met with of his age—and is in confidence with
several of our friends Dr. Price, Priestly and your friend Dr.
Purcival of Manchester—by whom he was introduced a few
days ago, by letter, to Mrs. Neckar and I have taken him with
me to the Duke de la Rochefoucaut—the Marquis de la Fayette and others of my friends here.

I leave this Place in company with M. Rutlege tomorrow
for London—I go expressly for the purpose of erecting an
Iron Bridge which Mss. Walker's of Rotherham, Yorkshire, and
I have already constructed, and is now ready for putting together. It is an Arch of 110 feet span, and five feet high, from
the Cord line—It is as portable as common Bars of Iron, and
can be put up and taken down at pleasure and is in fact rendering Bridges a portable manufacture—Sir Joseph Banks,
after paying me some compliments by letter on this novel
construction says—"I expect many similar improvements
from your Countrymen, who think with vigour, and are in a
great measure free from those Shackles of Theory which are

imposed on the Minds of our people even before they are capable of exerting their mental faculties to advantage."

With respect to the French Revolution be assured that every thing is going on right—little inconveniences, the necessary consequence of pulling down and building up, may arise, but even those are much less than ought to have been expected. Our friend the Marquis is, like his Great Patron and Master, General Washington acting a great Part—I take over with me to London the Key of the Bastile which the Marquis entrusts to my Care as his present to General Washington and which I shall send by the first American Vessel to N. York—It will be yet some months before the New Constitution will be completed at which time there is to be procession, and I am engaged to return to Paris to carry the American flag—

In England, the Ministerial party oppose every Iota of Reformation—the high Benificed Clergy and Bishops, cry out that the Church is in danger and all those who are interested in the remains of the feudal System join the Clamour—I see very clearly that the conduct of the British Government by opposing reformations will detach great Numbers from the Political interest of that Country, and that France thro the influence of principles and the divine Right of Men to freedom will have a stronger party in England than she ever had thro the Jacobite bug-bear of the divine Right of Kings in the Stuart line—

I see by the papers that you have had a Convention to re-Model the Constitution—I very soon saw that the Constitutionalists would overthrow the Constitution by rashly using that power which was entrusted to their moderation—The spirit of the Constitution required prudence, and the Actors substituted temper and party in the room of it and thereby subjected the legislation of every year to the caprice of an election day—

I wish most anxiously to see my much loved America—it is the Country from whence all reformations must originally spring—I despair of seeing an Abolition of the infernal trafic in Negroes—we must push that matter further on your side the water—I wish that a few well instructed Negroes could be sent among their Brethren in Bondage, for until they are enabled to take their own part nothing will be done—

I hope this Summer will terminate all my prospects in Europe—but at any rate I will not exceed the spring Vessels of next year—Present me with much affection to all my friend —as I pride myself on having many I particularize none—

I am with many wishes for your happiness and your family & connections

Your affectionate friend,
THOMAS PAINE.

To George Washington

Sir   London May 1st 1790

Our very good Friend the Marquis de la Fayette has entrusted to my care the Key of the Bastile and a drawing, handsomely framed, representing the demolition of that detestible prison, as a present to your Excellency, of which his letter will more particularly inform. I feel myself happy in being the person thro' whom the Marquis has conveyed this early trophy of the Spoils of Despotism and the first ripe fruits of American principles transplanted into Europe to his great Master and Patron. When he mentioned to me the present he intended you my heart leaped with Joy—It is something so truly in character that no remarks can illustrate it, and is more happily expressive of his remembrance of his American friends than any letters can convey. That the principles of America opened the Bastile is not to be doubted, and therefore the Key comes to the right place.

I beg leave to suggest to your Excellency the propriety of congratulating the King and Queen of France (for they have been our friends) and the National assembly on the happy example they are giving to Europe. You will see by the King's Speech, which I inclose that he prides himself on being at the head of the Revolution, and I am certain that such a congratulation will be well received and have a good effect.

I should rejoice to be the direct bearer of the Marquis's present to your Excellency but I doubt I shall not be able to see my much loved America till next spring. I shall therefore send it by some *American* Vessel to New York. I have permitted no drawing to be taken here, tho' it has been often requested, as I think there is a propriety that it should first be presented. But Mr West wishes Mr Trumbull to make a painting of the presentation of the Key to you.

I returned from France to London about five Weeks ago—and I am engaged to return to Paris when the Constitution shall be proclaimed and to carry the American Flag in the procession—I have not the least doubt of the final and compleat success of the French Revolution—Little Ebbings and flowings, for and against, the natural companions of revolutions, sometimes appear, but the full current of it, is, in my opinion, as fixed as the Gulph Stream.

I have manufactured a Bridge (a Single arch) of one hundred & ten feet Span, and five feet high from the Cord of the Arch—It is now on board a vessel coming from Yorkshire to London, where it is to be erected—I see nothing yet to dissappoint my hopes of its being advantageous to me—it is this only which keeps me Europe—and happy shall I be when I shall have it in my power to return to America. I have not heard of Mr Jefferson since he sailed except of his arrival. As I have always indulged the belief of having many friends in America, or rather no Enemies, I have nothing else particularly to mention—but my affectionate remembrances to all— and am, Sir, with the greatest Respect your much obliged and Obedient Humble servant

THOMAS PAINE

If any of my Friends are disposed to favour me with a letter, it will come to hand by addressing it to the care of Benjn Vaughn Esqr. Jeffries Square London.

To Samuel Adams

January 1, 1803

FOR THE NATIONAL INTELLIGENCER.

TOWARDS the latter end of last December I received a letter from a venerable patriot, Samuel Adams, dated Boston, Nov. 30. It came by a private hand, which I suppose was the cause of the delay. I wrote Mr. Adams an answer dated Jan. 1st, and that I might be certain of his receiving it, and also that I might know of that reception, I desired a friend of mine at Washington to put it under cover to some friend of his at Boston, and desire him to present it to Mr. Adams. The letter was accordingly put under cover while I was present and given to one of the clerks of the Post-Office to seal and put in the mail. The clerk put it in his pocket-book, and either forgot to put it in the mail, or supposed he had done so among other letters. The Post-master General, on learning this mistake, informed me of it last Saturday, and as the cover was then out of date, the letter was put under a new cover with the same request and forwarded by the post. I felt concern at this accident, lest Mr. Adams should conclude I was unmindful of his attention to me; and therefore, lest any further accident should prevent or delay his receiving it, as well as to relieve myself from that concern, I give the letter the opportunity of reaching him by the news-papers. I am the more induced to do this, because some manuscript copies have been taken of both letters, and therefore, there is a possibility of imperfect copies getting into print; and besides this, if some of the federal printers, (for I hope they are not all base alike) could get hold of a copy they would make no scruple of altering it and publishing it as mine. I therefore send you the original letter of Mr. Adams and my own copy of the answer.

THOMAS PAINE.

Federal City, Jan. 22, 1803.

BOSTON, Nov. 30th, 1802.

SIR,

I have frequently with pleasure reflected on your services to my native, and your adopted country. Your Common Sense, and your Crisis unquestionably awakened the public mind, and led the people loudly to call for a declaration of our national independence. I therefore esteemed you as a warm friend to the liberty, & lasting welfare of the human race. But when I heard, that you had turned your mind to a defence of infidelity, I felt myself much astonished, and more grieved, that you had attempted a measure so injurious to the feelings, and so repugnant to the true interest of so great a part of the citizens of the United States. The people of New-England, if you will allow me to use a Scripture phrase, are fast returning to their first love. Will you excite among them the spirit of angry controversy, at a time, when they are hastning to unity and peace? I am told that some of our news-papers have announced your intention to publish an additional pamphlet upon the principles of your Age of Reason. Do you think, that *your pen*, or the pen of any other man can unchristianize the mass of our citizens, or have you hopes of converting a few of them to assist you in so bad a cause? We ought to think ourselves happy in the enjoyment of opinion without the danger of persecution by civil or ecclesiastical law.

Our friend, the present President of the United States, has been calumniated for his liberal sentiments by men, who have attributed that liberality to a latent design to promote the cause of infidelity. This, and all other slanders have been made without a shadow of proof. Neither religion, nor liberty can long subsist in the tumult of altercation, and amidst the noise and violence of faction.

Felix qui cautus.
Adieu.
SAMUEL ADAMS.

Mr. Thomas Paine.

TO SAMUEL ADAMS

My dear and venerable friend,

I received with great pleasure your friendly and affectionate letter of Nov. 30th and I thank you also for the frankness of it. Between men in pursuit of truth, and whose object is the happiness of man both here and hereafter, there ought to be no reserve. Even error has a claim to indulgence, if not to respect, when it is believed to be truth. I am obliged to you for your affectionate remembrance of what you stile my services in awakening the public mind to a declaration of independence and supporting it after it was declared. I also, like you, have often looked back on those times, and have thought that if independence had not been declared at the time it was the public mind could not have been brought up to it afterwards. It will immediately occur to you, who were so intimately acquainted with the situation of things at that time, that I allude to the black times of *Seventy six*; for though I know, and you my friend also know, they were no other than the natural consequences of the military blunders of that campaign, the country might have viewed them as proceeding from a natural inability to support its cause against the enemy, and have sunk under the despondency of that misconceived idea. This was the impression against which it was necessary the country should be strongly animated.

I now come to the second part of your letter, on which I shall be as frank with you as you are with me. "But, (say you) when I *heard* you had turned your mind to a defence of *infidelity*, I felt myself much astonished, &c." What, my good friend, do you call believing in God *infidelity*? for that is the great point maintained in the *Age of Reason* against all divided beliefs and *allegorical* divinities. The bishop of Landaff (Doctor Watson) not only acknowleges this, but pays me some compliments upon it in his answer to the second part of that work. *"There is,* (says he) *a philosophical sublimity in some of your ideas when speaking of the Creator of the Universe."*

What then, (my much esteemed friend for I do not respect

you the less because we differ, and that perhaps not much, in religious sentiments) what I ask is this thing called *infidelity?* If we go back to your ancestors and mine, three or four hundred years ago, for we must have had fathers and grandfathers or we should not be here, we shall find them praying to saints and virgins, and believing in purgatory and transubstantiation, and therefore all of us are infidels according to our forefathers belief. If we go back to times more ancient we shall again be infidels according to the belief of some other fore fathers.

The case, my friend, is, that the world has been over-run with fable and creeds of human invention, with Sectaries of whole nations, against other nations, and sectaries of those sectaries in each of them against each other. Every sectary, except the quakers, has been a persecutor. Those who fled from persecution persecuted in their turn, and it is this confusion of creeds that has filled the world with persecution and deluged it with blood. Even the depredation on your commerce by the Barbary powers, sprang from the crusades of the church against those powers. It was a war of creed against creed, each boasting of God for its author, and reviling each other with the name of infidel. If I do not believe as you believe, it proves that you do not believe as I believe, and this is all that it proves.

There is however one point of union wherein all religions meet, and that is in the first article of every man's creed, and of every nation's creed, that has any creed at all. *I believe in God.* Those who rest here, and there are millions who do, cannot be wrong as far as their creed goes. Those who chuse to go further *may be wrong,* for it is impossible that all can be right since there is so much contradiction among them. The first, therefore, are in my opinion on the safest side.

I presume you are so far acquainted with ecclesiastical history as to know, and the bishop who has answered me has been obliged to acknowlege the fact, that the books that compose the New Testament were voted by *yeas* and *nays* to be the word of God as you now vote a law, by the popish councils of Nice and Laodocia, about 1450 years ago. With respect to the fact there is no dispute, neither do I mention it for the sake of controversy. This vote may appear authority enough to some, and not authority enough to others. It is proper however that every body should know the fact.

With respect to the *Age of Reason* which you so much condemn, and that I believe without having read it, for you say only that you *heard* of it, I will inform you of a circumstance because you cannot know it by other means.

I have said in the first page of the first part of that work, that it had long been my intention to publish my thoughts upon religion, but that I had reserved it to a later time of life. I have now to inform you why I wrote it and published it at the time I did.

In the first place, I saw my life in continual danger. My friends were falling as fast the guilliotine could cut their heads off, and as I every day expected the same fate, I resolved to begin my work. I appeared to myself to be on my death bed, for death was on every side of me, and I had no time to lose. This accounts for my writing at the time I did; and so nicely did the time and the intention meet, that I had not finished the first part of that work more than six hours before I was arrested and taken to prison. Joel Barlow was with me, and knows the fact.

In the second place, the people of France were running headlong into Atheism, and I had the work translated and published in their own language, to stop them in that career, and fix them to the first article (as I have before said) of every man's creed who has any creed at all, *I believe in God*. I endangered my own life, in the first place, by opposing in the convention the execution of the king, and labouring to shew they were trying the monarchy, and not the man, and that the crimes imputed to him were the crimes of the monarchical system; and I endangered it a second time by opposing Atheism, and yet *some* of your priests, for I do not believe that all are perverse, cry out, in the *war whoop* of monarchical priestcraft, What an infidel! What a wicked man is Thomas Paine! They might as well add, for he believes in God, and is against shedding blood.

But all this *war whoop* of the pulpit has some concealed object. Religion is not the cause, but is the stalking horse. They put it forward to conceal themselves behind it. It is not a secret that there has been a party composed of the leaders of the Federalists, for I do not include all Federalists with their leaders, who have been working by various means for several years past, to overturn the Federal constitution established on the representative system, and place government in the new world on the corrupt system of the old. To accomplish this a large standing army was necessary, and as a pretence for such an army, the danger of a foreign invasion must be bellowed forth, from the pulpit, from the press, and by their public orators.

I am not of a disposition inclined to suspicion. It is in its nature a mean and cowardly passion, and upon the whole, even admitting error into the case, it is better, I am sure it is more generous, to be wrong on the side of confidence, than on the side of suspicion. But I know as a fact, that the English government distributes annually fifteen hundred pounds ster-ling among the Presbyterian ministers in England, and one thousand among those of Ireland, and when I hear of the strange discourses of some of your ministers and professors of colleges, I cannot, as the quakers say, find freedom in my mind to acquit them. Their anti-revolutionary doctrines invite suspicion even against one's will, and in spite of one's charity to believe well of them.

As you have given me one scripture phrase I will give you another for those ministers. It is said in Exodus, chapter 22, verse 28, *"Thou shalt not revile the gods nor curse the ruler of thy people."* But those ministers, such I mean as Dr. Emmons, curse ruler and people both, for the majority are, politically, the people, and it is those who have chosen the ruler whom they curse. As to the first part of the verse, that of *not reviling the gods*, it makes no part of my scripture. I have but one God.

Since I began this letter, for I write it by piece-meals, as I have leisure, I have seen the four letters that passed between you and John Adams. In your first letter you say, "let divines and philosophers, statesmen and patriots, unite their endeav-ours to *renovate the age* by inculcating in the minds of youth *the fear and love of the Deity, and universal philanthropy.*" Why, my dear friend, this is exactly *my* religion, and is the whole of it. That you may have an idea that the *Age of Reason* (for I believe you have not read it) inculcates this reverential fear and love of the Deity, I will give you a paragraph from it:

"Do we want to contemplate his power? We see it in the immensity of the creation. Do we want to contemplate his wisdom? We see it in the unchangeable order by which the incomprehensible whole is governed. Do we want to contemplate his munificence? We see it in the abundance with which he fills the earth. Do we want to contemplate his mercy? We see it in his not withholding that abundance even from the unthankful."

As I am fully with you in your first part, that respecting the deity, so am I in your second, that of *universal philanthropy*, by which I do not mean merely the sentimental benevolence of wishing well, but the practical benevolence of doing good. We cannot serve the Deity in the manner we serve those who cannot do without that service. He needs no service from us. We can add nothing to eternity. But it is in our power to render a service *acceptable* to him, and that is not by praying, but by endeavouring to make his creatures happy. A man does not serve God when he prays, for it is himself he is trying to serve, and as to hiring or paying men to pray, as if the Deity needed instruction, it is in my opinion an abomination. One good School Master is of more use and of more value than a load of such persons as Dr. Emmons and some others.

You, my dear and much respected friend, are now far in the vale of years; I have yet, I believe, some years in store, for I have a good state of health and a happy mind, and I take care of both, by nourishing the first with temperance and the latter with abundance.

This, I believe, you will allow to be the true philosophy of life. You will see by my third letter to the citizens of the United States, that I have been exposed to, and preserved through, many dangers, but instead of buffetting the Deity with prayers as if I distrusted him or must dictate to him, I reposed myself on his protection; and you, my friend, will find, even in your last moments, more consolation in the silence of resignation than in the murmuring wish of prayer.

In every thing which you say in your second letter to John Adams respecting our rights as men and citizens in this world I am perfectly with you. On other points we have to answer to our creator and not to each other. The key of heaven is not in the keeping of any sect, nor ought the road to it to be obstructed by any. Our relation to each other in this world is as men, and the man who is a friend to man and to his rights, let his religious opinions be what they may, is a good citizen, to whom I can give, as I ought to do, and as every other ought, the right hand of fellowship, and to none with more hearty good will, my dear friend, than to you.

THOMAS PAINE.

Federal City, Jan.ʳʸ 1, 1803.

The Construction of Iron Bridges

June 13, 1803

As bridges, and the method of constructing them, are becoming objects of great importance throughout the United States, and as there are at this time proposals for a bridge over the Delaware, and also a bridge beginning to be erected over the Schuylkill at Philadelphia, I present the public with some account of the construction of Iron bridges.

The following memoir on that subject, written last winter at the federal city, was intended to be presented to congress. But as the session would necessarily be short, and as several of its members would be replaced by new elections on the ensuing session, it was judged better to let it lie over. In the mean time, on account of the bridges now in contemplation, or began, I give the memoir the opportunity of appearing before the public and the persons concerned in those works.

THOMAS PAINE.

Bordentown on the Delaware,
New Jersey, June 13, 1803.

TO THE CONGRESS OF THE UNITED STATES.

I have deposited in the office of the secretary of state, and under the care of the patent office, two models of iron bridges; the one in paste board, the other cast in metal. As they will shew by inspection the manner of constructing iron bridges, I shall not take up the time of congress with a description by words.

My intention in presenting this memoir to congress is to put the country in possession of the means and of the right of making use of the construction freely; As I do not intend to take any patent right for it.

As America abounds in rivers that interrupt the land communication, and as by the violence of floods, and the breaking up of the ice in the spring, the bridges, depending for support

384

from the bottom of the river, are frequently carried away. I turned my attention, after the revolutionary war was over, to find a method of constructing an arch, that might, without rendering the height inconvenient or the ascent difficult, extend at once from shore to shore, over rivers of three, four, or five hundred feet and probably more.

The principle I took to begin with, and work upon, was that the small segment of a large circle was preferable to the great segment of a small circle. The appearance of such arches and the manner of forging and putting the parts together admit of many varieties, but the principle will be the same in all. The bridge architects I conversed with in England denied the principle, but it was generally supported by mathematicians, and experiment has now established the fact.

In 1786 I made three models, partly at Philadelphia, but mostly at Bordentown in the state of Jersey. One model was in wood, one in cast iron, and one in wrought iron connected with blocks of wood, representing cast iron blocks, but all on the same principle that of the small segment of a large circle.

I took the last mentioned one with me to France in 1787, and presented it to the academy of sciences at Paris for their opinion of it. The academy appointed a committee of three of their own body—Mons. Le Roy, and Abbe Bossou, and Mons. Borda. The first was an acquaintance of Dr. Franklin, and of Mr. Jefferson, then minister at Paris. The two others were celebrated as mathematicians. I presented it as a model for a bridge of a single arch of 400 feet span over the river Schuylkill at Philadelphia. The committee brought in a report which the academy adopted—that an arch on the principle and construction of the model, might, in their opinion, be extended 400 feet, the extent proposed.

In September of the same year, I sent the model to Sir Joseph Banks, President of the Royal Society in England, and soon after went there myself.

In order to ascertain the truth of the principle on a larger scale than could be shewn by a portable model of five or six feet in length, I went to the iron foundery of Messrs. Walkers, at Rotherham in the county of Yorkshire in England, and had a compleat Rib of 90 feet span, and 5 feet of height from the cord-line to the centre of the arch, manufactured and erected.

It was a segment of a circle of 410 feet diameter; and until this was done, no experiment on a circle of such an extensive diameter had ever been made in architecture, or the practicability of it supposed.

The Rib was erected between a wall of a furnace belonging to the iron-works, and the gable end of a brick building, which served as butments. The weight of iron in the Rib was three tons, and we loaded it with double its weight in pig iron. I wrote to Mr. Jefferson, who was then at Paris, an account of this experiment; and also Sir Joseph Banks in London, who in his answer to me says—"I look for many other bold improvements from your countrymen, the Americans, who think with vigour, and are not fettered with the trammels of science, before they are capable of exerting their mental faculties to advantage."

On the success of this experiment, I entered into an agreement with the iron founders at Rotherham to cast and manufacture a compleat bridge, to be composed of five ribs of 110 feet span, and 5 feet of height from the cord-line, being a segment of a circle of 610 feet diameter, and to send it to London to be erected as a specimen for establishing a manufactory of iron bridges to be sent to any part of the world.

The bridge was erected at the village of Paddington near London, but being in a plain field where no advantage could be taken of butments without the expence of building them, as in the former case, it served only as a specimen of the practicability of a manufactory of iron bridges. It was brought by sea, packed in the hold of a vessel, from the place where it was made; and after standing a year was taken down without injury to any of its parts, and might be erected any where else.

At this time my bridge operations became suspended. Mr. Edmund Burke published his attack on the French revolution and the system of representative government, and in defence of government by hereditary sucession, a thing which is in its nature an absurdity because it is impossible to make wisdom hereditary; and therefore, so far as wisdom is necessary in a government, it must be looked for where it can be found. Sometimes in one family; sometimes in another. History informs us that the son of Solomon was a fool. He lost ten tribes out of twelve.* There are those in later times who lost thirteen.

The publication of this work of Mr. Burke, absurd in its principles and outrageous in its manner, drew me, as I have said, from my bridge operations, and my time became employed in defending a system then established and operating in America and which I wished to see peaceably adopted in Europe — I therefore ceased my work on the bridge to employ myself on the more necessary work, *Rights of Man*, in answer to Mr. Burke.

In 1792 a convention was elected in France for the express purpose of forming a constitution on the authority of the people, as had been done in America, of which convention I was elected a member. I was at that time in England, and knew nothing of my being elected till the arrival of the person who was sent officially to inform me of it.

During my residence in France, which was from 1792 to 1802, an iron bridge of 236 feet span and 34 of height from the cord line was erected over the river Wear at the town of Sunderland in the county of Durham in England. It was done chiefly at the expence of the two members in parliament for that county, Milbanke and Burdon.

It happened that a very intimate friend of mine sir Robert Smyth (who was also an acquaintance of Mr. Monroe the American minister and since of Mr. Livingston) was then at Paris. He had been colleague in parliament with Milbanke, and supposing that the persons who constructed the iron bridge at Sunderland had made free with my model, which was at the iron works where the Sunderland bridge was cast, he wrote to Milbanke on the subject, and the following is that gentleman's answer.

With respect to the bridge over the river Wear at Sunderland, it certainly is a work well deserving admiration both for its structure and utility, and I have good grounds for saying, that the first idea was suggested by Mr. Paine's bridge exhibited at Paddington. What difference there may be in some part of the structure, or in the proportion of wrought and cast iron, I cannot pretend to say, Burdon

*2 Chron. Chap. 10.

having undertaken to build the bridge, in consequence of his having taken upon himself whatever the expence might be beyond between three and four thousand pounds (sterling) subscribed by myself and some other gentlemen. But whatever the mechanism might be it did not supercede the necessity of a center* [The writer has here confounded a center with a scaffolding] which center [continues the writer] was esteemed a very ingenious piece of workmanship, and taken from a plan sketched out by Mr. Nash an architect of great merit who had been consulted in the outset of the business, when a bridge of stone was in contemplation.

With respect therefore to any gratuity to Mr. Paine, though ever so desirous of rewarding the labours of an ingenious man, I do not feel, how, under the circumstances already described I have it in my power, having had nothing to do with the bridge after the payment of my subscription, Mr. Burdon then becoming accountable for the whole.—But if you can point out any mode, according to which it should be in my power to be instrumental in procuring him any compensation for the advantages the public may have derived from his ingenious model, from which certainly the outline of the bridge at Sunderland was taken, be assured it will afford me very great satisfaction†.   RA. MILBANKE.

The year before I left France the government of that country had it in contemplation to erect an iron bridge over the river Seine at Paris. As all edifices of public construction came under the cognizance of the minister of the interior, (and as their plan was to erect a bridge of five iron arches of one hundred feet span each, instead of passing the river with a single arch, and which was going backward in practice, instead of forward, as there was already an iron arch of 236 feet in existence) I wrote the minister of the interior, the citizen Chaptal, a memoir on the construction of iron bridges. The following is his answer.

The minister of the interior to the citizen Thomas Paine.

I have received, citizen, the observations that you have been so good as to address to me upon the construction of iron bridges. They will be of the greatest utility to us in a moment when this new

*It is the technical term, meaning the boards and timbers which form the arch upon which the permanent materials are laid: when a bridge is finished, the workmen they say are ready to strike centre, that is to take down the scaffolding.

†The original is in my possession.

kind of construction goes to be executed for the first time. I see with pleasure, citizen, that you have rights of more than of one kind to the thankfulness of nations, and I give you, cordially, the particular expression of my esteem*. CHAPTAL.

A short time before I left France a person came to me from London with plans and drawings for an iron bridge of one arch over the river Thames at London, of 600 feet span, and sixty feet of height from the cord line. The subject was then before a committee of the house of commons, but I know not the proceedings thereon.

As this new construction of an arch for bridges, and the principles on which it is founded, originated in America, as the documents I have produced sufficiently prove, and is becoming an object of importance to the world, and to no part of it more than our own, on account of its numerous rivers, and as no experiment has been made in America to bring it into practice, further than on the models I have executed myself, and at my own expence, I beg leave to submit a proposal to Congress on the subject, which is,

To erect an experiment rib of about 400 feet span, to be the segment of a circle of at least 1000 feet diameter, and to let it remain exposed to public view, that the method of constructing such arches may be generally known.

It is an advantage peculiar to the construction of iron bridges, that the success of an arch of given extent and height, can be ascertained without being at the expence of building the bridge; which is, by the method I propose, that of erecting an experiment rib on the ground where advantage can be taken of two hills for butments.

I began in this manner with the rib of 90 feet span, and five feet of height, being a segment of a circle of 410 feet diameter. The undertakers of the Sunderland bridge began in the same manner. They contracted with the iron founders for a single rib, and finding it to answer, had five more manufactured like it, and erected into a bridge consisting of six ribs, the experiment rib being one. But the Sunderland bridge does not carry the principle much further into practice than had been done by the rib of 90 feet span and five feet in

*The original in French is in my possession.

height, being, as before said, a segment of a circle of 410 feet diameter. The Sunderland bridge being 206 feet span and 34 feet of height, gives the diameter of the circle of which it is a segment, to be 444 feet, within a few inches, which is but a larger segment of a circle of 34 feet more diameter.

The construction of those bridges does not come within the line of any established practice of business. The stone architect can derive but little from the theory or practice of his art that enters into the construction of an iron bridge; and the iron founder, though he may be expert in moulding and casting the parts, when the models are given him, would be at a loss to proportion them unless he was acquainted with all the lines and properties belonging to a circle.

If it should appear to Congress that the construction of iron bridges will be of utility to the country, and they should direct that an experiment rib be made for that purpose, I will furnish the proportions for the several parts of the work, and give my attendance to superintend the erection of it freely.

But, in any case, I have to request that this memoir may be put on the Journals of Congress, as an evidence hereafter, that this new construction of bridges originated in America.

THOMAS PAINE.

Federal City, Jan. 3, 1803.

N. B. The two models mentioned in the memoire, will, I expect, arrive at Philadelphia by the next packet from the federal city, and will remain for some time in Mr. Peale's Museum.

Of the Term
"Liberty of the Press"

October 20, 1806

THE writer of this remembers a remark made to him by Mr. Jefferson concerning the English Newspapers which at that time, 1787, while Mr. Jefferson was Minister at Paris, were most vulgarly abusive. The remark applies with equal force to the Federal papers of America. The remark was, that "the licentiousness of the press produces the same effect as the restraint of the press was intended to do. The restraint, said he, was to prevent things being told, and the licentiousness of the press prevents things being believed when they are told." We have in this state an evidence of the truth of this remark. The number of federal papers in the city and state of New-York are more than five to one to the number of republican papers, yet the majority of the elections go always against the federal papers, which is demonstrative evidence that the licentiousness of those papers are destitute of credit.

Whoever has made observation on the characters of nations will find it generally true, that the manners of a nation, or of a party, can be better ascertained from the character of its press than from any other public circumstance. If its press is licentious, its manners are not good. Nobody believes a common liar, or a common defamer.

Nothing is more common with printers, especially of Newspapers, than the continual cry of the *liberty of the press*, as if because they are Printers they are to have more privileges than other people. As the term *"liberty of the press"* is adopted in this country without being understood I will state the origin of it and shew what it means. The term comes from England, and the case was as follows.

Prior to what is called in England *the revolution*, which was in 1688, no work could be published in that country without first obtaining the permission of an officer appointed by the government for inspecting works intended for publication. The same was the case in France, except that in France there were forty who were called *censors*, and in England there was but one, called Impremateur.

At the revolution the office of Impremateur was abolished and as works could then be published without first obtaining the permission of the government officer, the press was, in consequence of that abolition, said to be free, and it was from this circumstance that the term *liberty of the press* arose. The press, which is a tongue to the eye, was then put exactly in the case of the human tongue. A man does not ask liberty before hand to say something he has a mind to say, but he becomes answerable afterwards for the atrocities he may utter. In like manner, if a man makes the press utter attrocious things he becomes as answerable for them as if he had uttered them by word of mouth. Mr. Jefferson has said in his inaugural speech, that *"error of opinion might be tolerated when reason was left free to combat it."* This is sound philosophy in cases of error. But there is a difference between error and licentiousness.

Some lawyers in defending their clients, (for the generality of lawyers like Swiss soldiers will fight on either side) have often given their opinion of what they defined the liberty of the press to be. One said it was this; another said it was that, and so on, according the case they were pleading. Now these men ought to have known that the term, *liberty of the press,* arose from a FACT, the abolition of the office of Imprimateur, and that opinion has nothing to do in the case. The term refers to the fact of Printing *free from prior restraint,* and not at all to the matter Printed whether good or bad. The public at large, or in case of prosecution, a jury of the country will be the judges of the matter.

COMMON SENSE.

CHRONOLOGY

NOTE ON THE TEXTS

NOTES

INDEX

Chronology

1737   Born January 29 in Thetford, Norfolk, England, the son of Joseph Pain and Frances Cocke Pain. (Joseph Pain, born 1708, a Quaker, was a corsetmaker who also worked a small farm. In 1734 he married Frances Cocke, born c. 1697, an Anglican and the daughter of a Thetford attorney.) Christened Thomas Pain and baptized in the Church of England (will later be confirmed in the Church of England, although he will frequently attend Quaker meetings with father).

1738   Sister Elizabeth born August 29. She dies in infancy.

1743   Begins attending grammar school in Thetford. Enjoys studying history, mathematics, and science.

1750   Leaves school to begin apprenticeship as a corsetmaker in his father's shop.

1756   Enlists on privateer *Terrible*, but is persuaded not to sail by father.

1757   Serves on privateer *King of Prussia* for six months of the Seven Years War. Works in London for a master corsetmaker. Attends philosophical and scientific lectures given by Benjamin Martin and James Ferguson, and becomes acquainted with astronomer John Bevis.

1758   Moves to Dover, Kent, where he continues working as a journeyman corsetmaker.

1759   Becomes master corsetmaker, opening his own shop in Sandwich, Kent, in April. Marries Mary Lambert, an orphan who works as a maid, on September 27. They move to Margate, Kent.

1760   Wife dies.

1761   Abandons corsetmaking and returns to Thetford to study for position in the excise service.

1762–63   Appointed to excise service as a supernumerary officer on December 1, 1762, through the patronage of Frederic Falkland. Assigned to Grantham, Lincolnshire, where he gauges brewers' casks.

1764   Appointed on August 8 as a permanent excise officer, with annual salary of £50, and assigned to the Alford Out-Ride, coastal district in Lincolnshire.

1765   Dismissed from excise service on August 29 for clearing consignment of merchandise without inspecting the goods, an offense commonly committed by excise officers. Returns to corsetmaking in Diss, Norfolk.

1766   Moves to London and teaches in private academy at Goodman's Fields for £25 a year. Successfully petitions in July for reinstatement as an excise officer, but is unable to find a vacant position.

1767   Begins teaching at school in Kensington in January.

1768   Appointed to excise position in Lewes, Sussex, in February. Lodges in the home of Samuel Ollive, a tobacconist and one of the town's leading citizens. Becomes involved in town and parish affairs and joins a social club that meets in the White Hart Inn. Writes poems and political satires from a Whig viewpoint.

1769–70   Moves to new lodgings after Samuel Ollive dies in July 1769. Begins running tobacco shop with Ollive's widow while continuing his excise duties.

1771   Marries the Ollives' daughter, Elizabeth (b. 1749), on March 26.

1772–73   Joins other excise officers in petitioning Parliament for higher salaries. Begins work on pamphlet *The Case of the Officers of Excise* during summer 1772, and has 4,000 copies printed (costs are paid by subscription of excise officers). Spends winter 1772–73 in London distributing pamphlet to members of Parliament, and presents copy to playwright Oliver Goldsmith. Parliament takes no action on petition.

1774   Dismissed from excise service on April 8 for being absent from his post without permission. Tobacco shop fails, and on April 14 Pain sells his household possessions and shop stock at public auction to pay his debts. Signs formal separation agreement with wife on June 4 and receives £35 in return for renouncing future claims against her property. Goes to London, where his friend George Lewis Scott, a scientist and member of the excise board, introduces him to Benjamin Franklin. Pain sails for Philadelphia in early October, carrying letter of introduction from Franklin to his son-in-law, Richard Bache. Falls ill, possibly with typhus, during voyage. Lands on November 30 and is cared for by Dr. John Kearsley, a friend of Franklin.

1775   Writes essay for the January number of *The Pennsylvania Magazine; or American Monthly Museum*, published by printer Robert Aitken, then becomes its editor in February. Contributes poems and articles on science and politics to the magazine under pseudonyms and publishes other writers, including John Witherspoon and Francis Hopkinson (there is no evidence that Pain wrote essay condemning slavery that appeared in the *Pennsylvania Journal* in March, although it is often attributed to him). Revolutionary War begins with fighting between Massachusetts militia and British troops at Lexington and Concord on April 19. Becomes friends with several Philadelphia advocates of the American cause, including Dr. Benjamin Rush, mathematician and astronomer David Rittenhouse, retired druggist Christopher Marshall, former brewer Timothy Matlack, Dr. Thomas Young, and teacher James Cannon. Meets John Adams. Leaves editorship of *Pennsylvania Magazine* in September. Writes newspaper articles with Thomas Pryor encouraging the home manufacture of saltpeter (potassium nitrate), a gunpowder ingredient.

1776   Publishes *Common Sense*, a pamphlet calling for the creation of an independent American republic, in Philadelphia on January 10 (pamphlet is attributed to "an Englishman"). Directs that his share of the profits from its sale be used to buy mittens for American troops in Quebec. Begins spelling his name "Paine." Expanded second edition of *Common Sense* is published on February 14; the pamphlet is read throughout the colonies and sells tens of thousands of copies (Paine later estimates that

150,000 copies were sold in 1776). Using pseudonym
"The Forester," Paine publishes series of letters in the
Pennsylvania press in April and May defending American
independence and republicanism and attacking critics of
Common Sense. Shortly after Congress adopts Declaration
of Independence on July 4, Paine joins the Associators, a
Pennsylvania militia, and becomes secretary to General
Daniel Roberdeau. Serves with the "Flying Camp," a mi-
litia force defending Perth Amboy, New Jersey, against
possible British seaborne attack; when it disbands in September, becomes aide-de-camp to General Nathanael
Greene at Fort Lee, New Jersey. Writes reports on the
war for the Pennsylvania press. British forces cross the
Hudson River on November 20, forcing evacuation of
Fort Lee. Paine joins American troops under George
Washington in their retreat across New Jersey, then leaves
the army at Trenton and returns to Philadelphia in early
December to write. Pamphlet *The American Crisis, Number I*, intended to rally American morale after series of
defeats in New York and New Jersey, published in Phila-
delphia on December 19. Encouraged by victory of
Washington's army at Trenton on December 26.

1777   Publishes *The American Crisis, Number II* in January,
continuing series championing the American cause (pamphlets are signed "Common Sense"; Paine's authorship of
series becomes widely known). Appointed secretary to
commission sent by Congress to negotiate with several
Indian tribes and meets with them at Easton, Pennsylvania, in late January. Elected to the Committee of Correspondence of the Whig Society of Philadelphia on April 1.
Publishes *The American Crisis, Number III* in April.
Congress creates Committee for Foreign Affairs on April
17; on nomination of John Adams, Paine is appointed as
its secretary at salary of $70 a month. Plans to write his-
tory of the American Revolution. Publishes *The American
Crisis, Number IV* in September as British army approaches Philadelphia, then flees the city. Pennsylvania
executive council appoints Paine as its observer with
Washington's army on October 10; Paine frequently visits
the army at its camps in Pennsylvania, including Valley
Forge. Spends the remainder of the year at the Bordentown, New Jersey, home of his friend Joseph Kirkbride.

1778   France and the United States sign treaties of alliance and
            commerce on February 6 (news reaches Congress on May
            2). Paine travels to Lancaster, Pennsylvania, in February to
            resume duties as secretary to the Committee for Foreign
            Affairs (Congress is meeting in nearby York). Publishes
            fifth *Crisis* in March. Returns to Philadelphia with Con-
            gress in early July after the British army leaves the city.
            Publishes sixth *Crisis* in October and seventh in Novem-
            ber. Writes four articles defending the 1776 Pennsylvania
            state constitution, which had created a unicameral legisla-
            ture, replaced the governor with an executive council, and
            extended the vote to all male taxpayers (constitution con-
            tinues to be subject of intense struggle within the state).
            In December Paine becomes involved in factional contro-
            versy surrounding the conduct of Silas Deane, a Con-
            necticut merchant sent by Congress to France in 1776 to
            purchase war supplies, now under suspicion of improperly
            profiting from his mission (Deane's supporters include
            John Jay, Gouverneur Morris, and leading Philadelphia
            merchant Robert Morris, who is a business partner of
            Deane; among his opponents are Samuel Adams, Richard
            Henry Lee, and Paine's friend Henry Laurens). After
            Deane publicly accuses his critics in Congress of unfair
            treatment, Paine writes series of articles attacking Deane
            for making unfounded charges and for failing to account
            for his financial dealings in France.

1779   Paine publishes more articles on Deane in which he refers
            to secret diplomatic correspondence proving that military
            supplies sent to America from France before treaty of alli-
            ance were gifts from the French government, not pur-
            chases made by Deane. Conrad Alexandre Gérard, French
            minister to the United States, writes to Congress protest-
            ing Paine's articles (disclosure of covert aid to the U.S.
            while France was at peace with Britain is potentially em-
            barrassing to Louis XVI). Paine asks for opportunity to
            defend himself before Congress against charge of indis-
            cretion; when his request is denied, he resigns as secretary
            of the Committee for Foreign Affairs on January 8. Con-
            gress adopts resolution on January 12 disavowing Paine's
            articles and declaring that Louis XVI had not sent aid to
            the United States before the treaty of alliance was signed.
            Paine refuses offer from Gérard to become paid writer of

material promoting close American ties with France. Publishes series of articles and letters defending his conduct in Deane affair, which has angered Deane's influential supporters. Takes low-paying position as a clerk with merchant Owen Biddle in April. Becomes increasingly involved in effort to control prices in Pennsylvania as inflation worsens. On May 25 Paine is elected to two extra-legal citizens' committees, one charged with regulating the price of staple goods, the other with investigating the affairs of Robert Morris, who is accused of profiting excessively from his dealings in military supplies. Publishes three articles in June and July urging Congress to make the securing of American fishing rights off Newfoundland a condition of peace with Britain and warning against excessive deference to French interests. After a series of hostile articles appear in press questioning Paine's loyalty to the American cause, a mass meeting held in Philadelphia on July 27 adopts resolution in his support. By late September refusal of merchants and farmers to sell goods at regulated prices causes collapse of efforts to implement price controls; Paine becomes opponent of price regulation and advocate of currency reform as means of controlling inflation. Seeks financial support for his writing from the Pennsylvania executive council. Appointed clerk of the Pennsylvania assembly on November 2.

1780   Publishes *The Crisis, No. VIII* in February and *The Crisis, No. IX* in June. Proposes system of voluntary private contributions to support American troops; idea is successfully implemented by Robert Morris. Receives an honorary master's degree from the newly created University of Pennsylvania on July 4. Paine writes in September to Joseph Reed, president of the Pennsylvania executive council, proposing that the state secretly send him to England to publish articles advocating peace with an independent America; Reed rejects the plan as too dangerous. Publishes pamphlet *The Crisis Extraordinary* in October, calling for the states to levy and collect taxes to finance the war. Resigns position as clerk of the assembly in November. Meets Marquis de Lafayette and Marquis de Chastellux. Using documents supplied by the Indiana Company, a land-speculation company, Paine writes *Public Good*, pamphlet published December 30, contesting Virginia's claim to territory northwest of the Ohio River and urging cession of the claim to Congress. (Dispute over western land claims had caused Maryland to withhold ratification of the Articles of Confederation; in 1781 the Virginia legislature conditionally cedes its western lands to Congress, and Maryland ratifies the Articles.)

1781 Accompanies Colonel John Laurens, an aide to George Washington and son of Henry Laurens, to France on mission to obtain further loans and supplies. Travels at his own expense after opposition in Congress prevents him from serving as Laurens' official secretary. Sails from Boston on February 11 and lands in France on March 9. Sees Franklin, now serving as American minister to France (Franklin plays major role in securing further aid from French government). Disillusioned by his treatment in the United States, Paine considers staying in Europe, but decides to return to America. Sails with Laurens on June 1 and arrives in Boston on August 25. Returns to Philadelphia in severe financial hardship. Surrender of Lord Cornwallis at Yorktown, Virginia, on October 19 ends major fighting in the Revolutionary War. Silas Deane is discredited by publication of letters urging reconciliation with Britain. Paine discusses with Robert Morris, now superintendent of finance, the possibility of his writing public letters and articles in support of measures to finance the war and restore national credit.

1782 In February Paine, Washington, secretary for foreign affairs Robert R. Livingston, and Robert Morris make clandestine agreement under which Paine will receive $800 a year from a secret fund controlled by Morris in return for writing in support of new financial measures. Publishes articles on taxation in March and April after showing them to Morris. Paid 1,530 livres (about $300) by the Chevalier de la Luzerne, Gérard's successor as French minister to the United States, for writing in *The Crisis, No. XI* in May that the United States and France should jointly negotiate peace with Britain. In response to Abbé Guillaume Raynal's *The Revolution of America*, Paine publishes *Letter Addressed to the Abbé Raynal* in August, insisting on the unique nature of the American Revolution and praising the American alliance with France. Sends copies to France for distribution and receives 50 guineas from La Luzerne. Writes series of public letters urging Rhode Island to grant Congress power to levy a 5 percent impost on imports (Rhode Island legislature had rejected measure, which requires unanimous consent of the states, after 11 other states had approved it). Travels to Providence, Rhode Island, in December to work for the impost.

1783   Publishes additional letters in the Rhode Island press, then returns to Philadelphia in February after Virginia's repeal of its earlier ratification of the impost causes the measure to lapse. Paine's visit is denounced by advocates of state sovereignty, who accuse Congress of improperly attempting to influence Rhode Island's decision. Congress ratifies preliminary peace treaty with Britain on April 15. Paine publishes *The Last Crisis, No. XIII* on April 19, the eighth anniversary of the battles of Lexington and Concord. Appeals to Congress in June for remuneration for his contribution to the Revolution. Spends summer in Bordentown with the Kirkbride family. Goes to New York in December, where he appeals to the state legislature for compensation. Writes public letter urging American states to form a closer union in response to British exclusion of American ships from the West Indies.

1784   Returns to Philadelphia in January, then goes in February to Bordentown, where he now owns a house and five acres of land. New York legislature approves compensation for Paine in April, and in June he receives the confiscated estate of a Tory in New Rochelle. Despite support from Washington, Thomas Jefferson, and James Madison, bill to award Paine a land grant is rejected by the Virginia legislature in June; its defeat is ascribed to resentment against Paine for challenging Virginia land claims in *Public Good*.

1785   Elected to American Philosophical Society in January. Awarded £500 by the Pennsylvania assembly in April and $3,000 by Congress in October for his services during the Revolution (may never have received the money from Pennsylvania). Works on series of inventions, including smokeless candles and innovative design for a single-arch iron bridge using principles of stone vaulting (Paine writes that design was inspired by pattern of spider's web). Hires mechanic John Hall in November as workshop assistant. Publishes letter in December criticizing recent decision of the Pennsylvania assembly to repeal state charter of the Bank of North America, founded in 1782 by Robert Morris and his associates.

1786   Publishes widely circulated pamphlet *Dissertations on Government; the Affairs of the Bank; and Paper Money* in February, arguing in favor of rechartering the bank and opposing the issue of paper money not backed by specie. (Pennsylvania assembly had issued £150,000 in paper money in March 1785, and the bank's refusal to accept it at face value had contributed to the revocation of its charter in September 1785.) Discusses steamboat development with inventor John Fitch in March. Continues writing public letters in defense of the bank during the spring and is criticized by its opponents, including assemblyman John Smilie, who accuses Paine of writing for hire. Exhibits wooden and cast-iron models of single-arch bridge in the garden of Franklin's house in June. Publishes letter in September arguing that party prejudice has made unicameral legislature established by the 1776 Pennsylvania constitution dangerous to liberty. Works in the fall on a wrought-iron bridge model. Denounces paper money in letter published in November. Shows new bridge model to Franklin and David Rittenhouse in late December.

1787   Exhibits wrought-iron bridge model in State House Yard in Philadelphia in January. Tries unsuccessfully to secure funding from the Pennsylvania assembly for building bridge across the Schuylkill River. Attends weekly meetings of the newly formed Society for Political Enquiries, whose members include Franklin, Gouverneur Morris, Benjamin Rush, and James Wilson. Hoping to gain endorsements for his iron bridge, Paine sails for France on April 26, carrying letters of introduction from Franklin to leading French scientific and political figures. Lands in France on May 26 and goes to Paris. Begins friendship with Jefferson, now serving as American minister to France, and sees Lafayette. Presents bridge model to the French Academy of Sciences in July and receives its endorsement in August. Travels to London in September, seeking endorsement of the Royal Society. Sees mother in Thetford and provides annuity for her (father died in 1786). Publishes pamphlet *Prospects on the Rubicon*, urging Britain not to go to war with France over the factional struggle in the Netherlands. Becomes friends with writer and member of Parliament Edmund Burke, who had supported American colonists in the 1770s; through Burke, Paine meets leaders of Whig opposition, including Charles James Fox and the Duke of Portland. Meets painters John Trumbull and Benjamin West. Made honorary member of the Society for Constitutional Information, English political reform group whose leading members include John Frost, Thomas Hollis, John Cartwright, Thomas Holcraft, and John Horne Tooke. Returns to Paris in December to pursue plans for bridging the Seine.

1788   Paine, Jefferson, and Lafayette follow ratification controversy over the proposed United States constitution and debate the constitution among themselves. Returns to London in June to seek investors for bridge. Sends reports on British politics to Jefferson (position of American minister to Britain has been vacant since John Adams returned to the U.S. in the spring). Goes to ironworks at Rotherham, Yorkshire, in fall to supervise construction of 90-foot bridge arch.

1789   Continues working on bridge, moving between London and Rotherham. Tours English factories. Tests weight-bearing capacity of bridge in April and begins planning construction of 110-foot span. Continues correspondence with Jefferson, sending reports on British politics and receiving accounts of events in France. Estates General convene at Versailles on May 5 after being summoned by Louis XVI to address worsening financial and political situation in France. On June 17 the Third Estate declares itself to be a National Assembly, and after a majority of the clergy join them, the members of the Assembly vow on June 20 not to disperse until France has been given a written constitution. Alarmed by royalist troop movements, Paris crowd storms the Bastille, fortress used as a prison, on July 14. In August the National Assembly abolishes feudal system and adopts the Declaration of the Rights of Man and Citizen, drafted in part by Lafayette. Paine travels to Paris in November and sees Lafayette, now commander of the Paris National Guard.

1790   Corresponds with Edmund Burke on French Revolution in January. Burke gives speech in Parliament in February denouncing the Revolution and begins writing *Reflections on the Revolution in France*. Paine returns to England in March. Sees Gouverneur Morris, now in London as President Washington's personal envoy. Writes to Lafayette, urging French support for Spain in its confrontation with Britain over Nootka Sound (France remains neutral, and Spain avoids war by making concessions). Bridge components are shipped to London in May; Paine hires workers and begins supervising assembly of demonstration span in field near village of Paddington. Writes essay on establishing a mint in the United States. Bridge assembly is completed in fall; despite praise from members of the Royal Society, Paine is unable to find a buyer. *Reflections on the Revolution in France* is published November 1 and sells 12,000 copies within a month.

1791   *Rights of Man: Being an Answer to Mr. Burke's Attack on the French Revolution* published by Paine in London on February 22 and then withdrawn, possibly due to printer Joseph Johnson's fear of government prosecution. Pamphlet is reissued by printer J. Jordan on March 16 and sells tens of thousands of copies in several editions, including cheap editions authorized by Paine, for which he receives no royalties. Paine returns to Paris in the spring. After unsuccessful attempt by Louis XVI and Marie Antoinette to flee the country, June 20–22, Paine joins with Etienne Claivière, the Marquis de Condorcet, Jacques Pierre Brissot de Warville, and Achille François Duchastelet to form the Republican Club. Writes broadside manifesto calling for Louis XVI to be deposed; it is translated by Duchastelet and distributed on July 1. First number of *Le Républicain*, journal of the Republican Club, appears July 2 with article by Paine. Continues his advocacy of a republican government for France in public letter to Abbé Sieyès, published on July 9 (Paine's publications are among earliest calling for overthrow of the monarchy). Returns to London in mid-July. *Life of Thomas Pain*, hostile biography subsidized by the Pitt ministry and written by George Chalmers under the pseudonym "Francis Oldys," is published July 19, making public details of Paine's early life, including his two marriages. Paine attends meetings of the Society for Constitutional Information and other political reform groups. On September 14 Louis XVI agrees to first written French constitution,

instituting a limited monarchy. In London, Paine sees
American poet Joel Barlow, John Horne Tooke, writer
and political thinker William Godwin, and woman's
rights advocate Mary Wollstonecraft, author of *A Vindi-
cation of the Rights of Men*, an earlier response to Burke.
Proposes toast to the "Revolution of the World" at dinner held November 4 to commemorate the Glorious
Revolution of 1688. Experimental bridge arch in Paddington is disassembled when Paine is unable to find a buyer
or investors. (Paine's design is further developed by Row-
land Burdon, who builds 236-foot single-arch iron bridge
over the Wear at Sunderland, England, in 1793–96, the
longest bridge of its kind yet built. Ironwork for Sunderland Bridge is cast at Rotherham under supervision of
foreman William Yates, who had earlier worked with
Paine on his demonstration span. Although Paine holds
patent on his design, he receives no compensation for the
Wear bridge.)

1792   Paine publishes *Rights of Man, Part the Second, Combin-
ing Principle and Practice* in London on February 16.
Pamphlet discusses possible forms of republican government and proposes government programs to alleviate
plight of the poor; it goes through four printings within two weeks, and sales of both parts of *Rights of Man*
exceed 200,000 copies by end of 1792. France declares
war on Austria on April 20 (Prussia enters war as Aus-
trian ally early in summer). Paine receives summons on
May 21 to stand trial on June 8 for misdemeanor offense
of seditious libel; Pitt ministry also issues proclamation
ordering magistrates to investigate writers and printers
of seditious literature. Home secretary Henry Dundas
tells Parliament on May 25 that proclamation is directed
against *Rights of Man*, which Dundas links to increasing
agitation by reform and workingmen's societies. Paine
responds in public letter to Dundas, praising American example of representative government. Trial is postponed until December. Paine stays in London with
Thomas (Clio) Rickman, a friend from Lewes. Insurrection in Paris on August 10 leads to final overthrow of the
monarchy and summoning of National Convention.
Lafayette, a supporter of constitutional monarchy, flees
France (captured by the Austrians, he is imprisoned until
1797). National Assembly confers honorary French citi-

zenship on Paine and 16 other foreigners on August 26. Electoral assembly in Pas-de-Calais elects Paine to the National Convention on September 6 (he is also elected by three other departments). Paine finishes pamphlet *Letter Addressed to the Addressers on the Late Proclamation*, in which he calls for the election by universal manhood suffrage of a national convention to establish a new constitution in Britain. Accepts Convention seat and arrives in Calais to enthusiastic welcome on September 13. Travels to Paris and votes with the Convention on September 21 to formally abolish the monarchy and proclaim the French Republic. Follows sessions and speaks in the Convention through an interpreter (Paine never becomes proficient in spoken French). Opposes proposal by Danton to allow election of judges regardless of their lack of legal training. Appointed on October 11 to nine-man committee charged with drafting new republican constitution (only Paine and two other members of the committee survive the Terror of 1793–94). Lives at White's Hotel in Paris and associates almost exclusively with people who speak English. Sees Joel Barlow, Gouverneur Morris (now American minister to France), Condorcet, Brissot, Clavière, Jean-Marie and Manon Roland, Edmond Genêt (who becomes French minister to the U.S. in 1793), printer Nicolas de Bonneville, and François Xavier Lanthenas; most of his close associates in the Convention are leaders of the Girondin faction, who favor spreading the Revolution throughout Europe. Paine meets in October with Irish revolutionary Lord Edward Fitzgerald and recommends that France financially support an insurrection in Ireland. Supports trial of Louis XVI for treason (proceedings begin December 11). Loyalist crowds in Britain hang and burn Paine in effigy and government supporters circulate hostile tracts and broadsides. On December 18 Paine is convicted in absentia of seditious libel and is outlawed for failing to stand trial (outlawry makes him subject to indefinite imprisonment and the forfeiture of his property). Pitt ministry begins prosecuting printers and sellers of *Rights of Man*.

1793 Convention debates fate of Louis XVI. Paine becomes leading opponent of his execution, arguing that Louis should be imprisoned for the duration of the war and then exiled to the United States. Convention approves death sentence on January 17. Paine speaks in support of granting a reprieve, but motion is defeated and Louis is guillotined on January 21. France declares war on Great Britain and the Netherlands on February 1 (President Washington proclaims American neutrality in the conflict on April 22). Paine moves into house on Faubourg St. Denis. Plays cards and chess with friends and sees Mary Wollstonecraft, Joel Barlow, and Clio Rickman, who had fled England to avoid prosecution for selling Paine's work. After Girondin leaders have Jean-Paul Marat indicted in April for inciting violence against members of the Convention, Paine helps Brissot attack Marat in the press and testifies against him at his trial. Marat is acquitted amid popular acclaim; episode discredits Girondins and increases influence of Jacobins. Paine writes pessimistically to Jefferson on April 20 about course of the French Revolution and warns Danton in letter of May 6 about "spirit of denunciation." Paris crowds force suspension of 22 leading Girondins from Convention on June 2. Paine avoids the Convention during the summer; begins to drink heavily. Meets with Jacobin leader Bertrand Barère in late August and advises him to send commissioners to the United States to strengthen Franco-American relations. Assists Barère in purchasing food from the United States. Brissot, and 9 other Girondins are guillotined on October 31 (Clavière and Duchastelet commit suicide later to avoid execution and Condorcet dies in prison in spring 1794, possibly after taking poison). Paine works during autumn on pamphlet *The Age of Reason*, deistic examination of religion. On December 25 Barère criticizes letting foreigners serve in the Convention; Paine is then denounced by name, and Convention expels him and its other foreign member, Prussian-born Anacharsis Cloots. Paine and Cloots are arrested on December 28 on orders of the Committee of General Security and imprisoned in the former Luxembourg Palace.

1794   *The Age of Reason; Being an Investigation of True and of Fabulous Theology* published in Paris in January. Paine appeals to Gouverneur Morris for help with his case. In February Morris writes to French foreign minister Deforgues that Paine is an American citizen and inquiring into the reasons for his arrest. Deforgues responds that Paine has made himself subject to French law by accepting

French citizenship and a seat in the Convention, and Morris does not pursue the matter (Morris writes to Jefferson that bringing attention to Paine's case would increase the likelihood of his execution). In prison Paine debates religion with Cloots, an atheist, until Cloots is guillotined on March 24. Sees Danton in prison before his execution on April 5. Falls seriously ill with fever in mid-June as executions in Paris rapidly increase. Robespierre is guillotined on July 28 along with many of his followers. Paine partially recovers from his illness and writes appeal to the Convention and to the Committee of Public Safety on August 6, but receives no response. Learns that James Monroe has replaced Morris as American minister in August. Appeals to Monroe in letter in which he describes Morris as "my inveterate enemy," and receives encouraging reply on October 4. Monroe formally petitions Committee of General Security on November 1, asserting Paine's American citizenship, praising his role in the American Revolution, and asking that he be either released or tried. Paine is released from prison on November 4, in poor health and suffering from abscess in his side; Monroe and his wife, Elizabeth, care for him in their home in Paris. Convention votes on December 8 to reinstate him as a member.

1795   Writes letter to Washington on February 22, reproaching the President for failing to aid him during his imprisonment, but at Monroe's urging does not send it. In June the Convention begins considering new constitution that establishes indirectly elected bicameral legislature and a five-man executive Directory, and limits voting to payers of direct taxes and soldiers who served under the Republic. Paine publishes *Dissertation on First Principles of Government*, pamphlet defending universal manhood suffrage, and appears before the Convention on July 7 for the first time since 1792 to oppose property qualifications for voting (suffrage limitation is not changed, and constitution is approved by Convention in August). In early August Paine finishes second part of *The Age of Reason*, containing detailed attack on the authority of the Bible (published in autumn). Falls dangerously ill in September with recurrence of abscess and is cared for by Elizabeth Monroe. Writes and sends letters in late September to Washington and to James Madison, now a leader of Republican opposition to the Federalist administration, accusing Washington of "treachery" for failing to aid him. Convention dissolves in October as new constitution takes effect (Paine does not seek election to new legislature). Continues to suffer from abscess. During the winter writes pamphlet *Agrarian Justice*, calling for the taxation of landed property and the creation of a public fund to compensate persons for their lost natural inheritance of land.

1796   Directory tells Monroe that it considers restrictive definition of neutral maritime rights contained in Jay's Treaty, the Anglo-American agreement negotiated in 1794 and ratified in 1795, to be hostile to France. In April Paine publishes *The Decline and Fall of the English System of Finance*, predicting that the cost of war against France will cause the Bank of England to collapse. Directory pays for pamphlet to be translated and printed throughout Europe. Relations between Paine and Monroe are strained by Paine's open hostility toward Washington's administration and his ties to Jean-François Reubell and other members of the Directory. Paine moves out of Monroe's house during spring and into rooms in Paris suburb of Suresnes. Writes lengthy public letter to Washington, accusing him of treachery and hypocrisy, criticizing his generalship in the Revolution, and denouncing Jay's Treaty as a betrayal of American interests and a breach of faith with France. Completes letter on July 30 and sends it to Benjamin Franklin Bache, Franklin's grandson and publisher of the Philadelphia *Aurora*, who prints excerpts in October and November (letter is published as pamphlet in February 1797). Washington administration recalls Monroe and sends Charles Cotesworth Pinckney to replace him. Directory authorizes seizure of American ships trading with Britain and refuses to receive Pinckney as new American minister.

1797   Paine joins French deists in newly organized Society of Theophilanthropists in January. Meets Irish revolutionary Theobald Wolfe Tone. Leaves Paris in March and goes to Le Havre intending to return to America, but does not sail for fear of capture by British frigates blockading the port. Pamphlet *Agrarian Justice, Opposed to Agrarian Law, and to Agrarian Monopoly* published. Paine returns to Paris in May and moves in with printer Nicolas de Bonneville, his wife, Marguerite, and their children. Writes articles for Bonneville's paper, *Bien Informé*. In response to increasingly frequent French seizures of American ships, President John Adams appoints three commissioners to negotiate with the Directory. Paine writes public letter in September protesting printer Thomas Williams' conviction for blasphemy for selling *The Age of Reason* in England. American commissioners arrive in Paris in October. Paine advises French foreign minister Talleyrand and the commissioners to work for international agreement on neutral maritime rights. Publishes pamphlet in November defending the Directory's use of the army on September 4 to purge the legislature of royalist members. Writes articles in December proposing construction of fleet of shallow-draft gunboats to be used in an invasion of England.

1798   Continues advocating invasion scheme, hoping that it will lead to revolution in England; sends detailed memorandum on plan to General Napoleon Bonaparte. Becomes friends with American inventor Robert Fulton. Assists British and American citizens living in France in their dealings with the government. Writes to Directory in June advocating French assistance to revolutionary uprising in Ireland (Directory sends several small expeditions, which are defeated; Tone is captured and commits suicide to avoid being hanged). Publication in the United States of dispatches from American commissioners revealing that three French diplomatic agents had solicited them for $240,000 bribe as precondition for negotiation ("XYZ Affair") causes public furor, and during the summer United States begins waging undeclared naval war against France. Talleyrand and the Directory distance themselves from Paine, who is intensely disliked by the Adams administration.

1799   Works on essays on international commerce. Bonaparte overthrows Directory in coup d'etat on November 9. Paine spends winter in Bruges, Belgium, with Joseph Vanhuele, one of his cellmates in Luxembourg prison. *Bien Informé* is suppressed after it compares Bonaparte to Oliver Cromwell.

1800   Paine returns to Paris in spring and resumes living with
            Bonneville family. Tells Oliver Ellsworth, member of new
            commission sent by President Adams, that Jay's Treaty
            and the recall of Monroe have made negotiating a
            Franco-American agreement extremely difficult. French
            authorities warn Paine that he will be deported if he
            continues to behave "irregularly." Speaks critically of
            Bonaparte in conversations with British and American
            friends. Publishes *Pacte Maritime*, essays on international
            commerce and neutral maritime rights. Builds five-foot-
            long bridge models and writes proposal for linking re-
            gions of France through series of canals and iron bridges.
            American commissioners sign treaty on September 30
            ending naval conflict with France. Encouraged by news of
            Jefferson's presidential candidacy, Paine writes to him in
            October, enclosing copies of trade essays (published in
            1801 as *Compact Maritime*) and expressing wish to return
            to the United States.

1801   Jefferson, now president, writes to Paine in March, offer-
            ing him passage on an American warship returning from
            France (Paine continues to fear capture by the Royal
            Navy). Paine decides to wait for ship bearing Robert R.
            Livingston, the new American minister to France.
            Jefferson's offer becomes public and is denounced by the
            Federalist press. Paine works on inventions, including a
            crane and a planing machine. Sees Livingston when he
            arrives in December.

1802   Britain and France sign armistice in March, suspending
            British blockade. Paine sails from Le Havre in early Sep-
            tember and lands in Baltimore on October 30. Federalist
            press widely attacks him as an infidel and a drunkard.
            Goes to Washington, D.C., where Jefferson receives him
            at the executive mansion. Publishes series of letters "To
            the Citizens of the United States" in the Republican
            press, in which he bitterly attacks Washington and John
            Adams. After port of New Orleans is closed to American
            navigation, Paine writes to Jefferson proposing that the
            United States purchase Louisiana Territory from France
            with the consent of its inhabitants (Jefferson is already
            considering purchasing New Orleans). Receives letter
            from Samuel Adams, who writes that he is "grieved" by
            Paine's "defence of infidelity."

1803 Writes and publishes a response to Adams defending his religious beliefs. Travels in February to Philadelphia; Benjamin Rush, angered by *The Age of Reason*, refuses to see him. Goes to Bordentown, where he sees Joseph Kirkbride for the last time (Kirkbride dies in autumn). Encounters hostile reception from pro-Federalist crowd in Trenton. Travels to New York in early March and sees Monroe, who is about to sail for France as a special envoy with instructions to purchase New Orleans and the Floridas (Monroe and Livingston are unexpectedly offered entire Louisiana Territory by the French, and sign treaty for its purchase on May 2). Attends dinner for 70 people held in his honor on March 18. Returns to Bordentown. Marguerite de Bonneville and her three sons arrive in Bordentown (Nicolas de Bonneville, who is under surveillance by the French police, is unable to leave France). Writes public letter criticizing Federalist proposals to seize New Orleans by force. Corresponds with Jefferson on constitutional implications of Louisiana Purchase. Travels to Stonington, Connecticut, to visit Nathan Haley, a sea captain he had known in France. Discusses current events with neighboring farmers and fishermen. Goes to his New Rochelle farm in autumn, but falls ill and lodges in village.

1804 Returns to New York in January. Marguerite de Bonneville, unhappy in Bordentown, comes to New York with her sons, and Paine assumes responsibility for their schooling. Paine becomes friends with physician Nicholas Romaine, philanthropist John Pintard, auctioneer John Fellows (who had published *The Age of Reason* in the United States), veterinarian and blacksmith William Carver, and deist Elihu Palmer, publisher of *The Prospect, or View of the Moral World*. Writes frequently for *The Prospect*, mainly on religious subjects. Publishes article predicting successful invasion of England by Bonaparte. Returns to cottage on New Rochelle farm in spring. Sells 60 acres of farm for $4,020 to pay his debts. Writes article in September denying right of Louisiana's inhabitants to immediate statehood and to continue importing slaves.

1805 Recommends to Jefferson that the United States mediate between France and the rebels in Haiti. Begins collecting his works for projected five-volume edition. Goes to New

York in January and stays with William Carver until April, when he returns to New Rochelle. Contributes pieces to *The American Citizen*, Republican newspaper edited by English political exile James Cheetham, including last in series of letters "To the Citizens of the United States," criticizing Federalist hostility toward France. Publishes pamphlet *Constitutions, Governments, and Charters* in June, advocating new procedures for legislative grants of state charters. Writes three-part letter to the *Aurora*, criticizing the gubernatorial veto established by the 1790 Pennsylvania state constitution and calling for extensive legal reform, including use of arbitration wherever possible in civil cases. Begins to drink heavily as health declines.

1806   Angered when New Rochelle election officials question his American citizenship and refuse to count his ballot. Moves in spring into home of William Carver at 36 Cedar Street in New York. Writes widely reprinted essay attributing yellow fever to putrid air rising from stagnant mud and recommending rebuilding of wharves as a preventive measure. Becomes friends with Irish exile Thomas Addis Emmet, brother of executed revolutionary leader Robert Emmet. Suffers apoplectic fit on July 25 and is confined to bed for weeks. Moves in November into home of portrait painter John Wesley Jarvis at 85 Church Street. Becomes friends with Jarvis. Quarrels with Carver over boarding bill.

1807   Writes series of articles advocating construction of a gunboat fleet to defend American coasts. Quarrels with Cheetham and begins publishing his writing in *Public Advertiser*, Republican paper printed by Jacob Frank. Moves in April to home of baker Zakarias Hitt on Broome Street. Builds model gunboats and sends them along with written proposal to Jefferson in September. Writes articles attacking Cheetham and Chief Justice John Marshall.

1808   Moves to cheap tavern at 63 Partition (later Fulton) Street after Hitt raises rent to $7 a week in January. Friends persuade him to sell house and land in Bordentown, and in July he begins boarding in house on Herring Street (now 293 Bleecker Street) in Greenwich Village, north of the city. Loses use of his legs. Last known published piece, attack on Cheetham and the Federalists, appears on August 25.

1809   Makes out will on January 18, leaving most of estate to Marguerite de Bonneville and her sons (Benjamin Bonneville later becomes an army officer, western explorer, and subject of an 1837 book by Washington Irving). Requires constant care as his condition worsens. Develops severe swelling and painful skin sores in March. Society of Friends denies his request to be buried in a Quaker cemetery, claiming that Paine's followers might try to build a monument, which Quaker rules forbid. Visited by Secretary of the Treasury Albert Gallatin. Carried on May 4 to nearby house (now site of 59 Grove Street) rented by Bonneville family. Refuses entreaties that he recant deism and accept Christianity. Dies on morning of June 8. Buried on New Rochelle farm on June 9. (In 1819 English journalist William Cobbett has Paine's remains exhumed and sent to England, intending to build a memorial to him; the plan fails and remains are eventually lost.)

Note on the Texts

This volume contains a selection of pamphlets, articles, addresses, and letters written by Thomas Paine, arranged chronologically. The texts of the items published during Paine's lifetime are taken from their original sources, whether pamphlet, newspaper, or book. Because Paine's writings were often immediately reprinted by others, many of the pieces included have a complex printing history, and extensive research, therefore, underlies the discovery of the facts of that history and the determination of the best choice of texts for inclusion in this volume. Letters not published during Paine's lifetime are taken from the best modern texts. The articles that make up what became known as *The American Crisis* are not grouped together; because they appeared sporadically from 1776 to 1783, they are presented in this volume according to the date of their first publication. The specific texts of the works included here are described in the following annotated list (which also identifies the descriptive titles supplied in this volume for some of the pieces).

Common Sense was first published by Richard Bell on January 10, 1776. An expanded edition, prepared by Paine, was published by William and Thomas Bradford on February 14, 1776. Because of the huge demand for the pamphlet, the Bradfords gave the work to two printing firms, the shop of Melchior Styner and Charles Cist, and the shop of Benjamin Towne. Collation shows that the work of Towne is more accurate, and the text of that version is printed here.

The four numbered Forester letters were published in more than one Philadelphia newspaper. The texts of the letters here are from the first printings: "Letter I. To Cato," *Pennsylvania Packet*, April 1, 1776; "Letter II. To Cato," *Pennsylvania Gazette*, April 10, 1776; "Letter III. To Cato," *Pennsylvania Packet*, April 22, 1776; "Letter IV," *Pennsylvania Journal*, May 8, 1776. The text of one other letter, unnumbered and untitled (here given the title "Reply to Cato's Eighth Letter"), comes from the *Pennsylvania Evening Post*, April 30, 1776, its only appearance.

The American Crisis comprises a group of articles published and numbered by Paine over a period of seven years. After publishing articles numbered I–IX, Paine did not assign number X, though in its place he published *The Crisis Extraordinary*, which was followed by number XI. He skipped number XII, and he called the final article in the series *The Last Crisis, Number XIII* (published on the anniversary of the Lexington-Concord battle, April 19, and perhaps numbered in honor of the thirteen states). Without Paine's authorization, James Carey of Philadelphia published in 1797 an edition of Paine's collected works, in which he grouped together various articles under the heading "The American Crisis"; besides including the numbered pieces, he combined three articles under the number X, chose another to be labeled XII, and added others under the titles "Supernumerary Crisis I" and "Supernumerary Crisis II." Later editors adopted this classification, but since it did not originate with Paine it is not adopted here.

The first publication of *The American Crisis, Number I* was in a pamphlet printed by Styner and Cist in Philadelphia on December 19, 1776; a second printing, bearing this date on the last page, followed soon after. Publication in newspapers followed. Though for many years it was thought that the first appearance was in the *Philadelphia Journal* on December 19, 1776, that paper had temporarily suspended its publication. Paine himself wrote in a letter to Henry Laurens on January 14, 1779, that he gave "that piece to the printer gratis, and confined him to the price of two coppers, which was sufficient to defray his charges." His statement confirms that the first publication of the work was as a pamphlet. The text presented here is that of the first printing.

The American Crisis, Number II was published in pamphlet form by Styner and Cist in Philadelphia on January 17, 1777, before it appeared in any newspapers. The text of that edition is printed here.

The American Crisis, Number III was published in pamphlet form by Styner and Cist in Philadelphia on April 25, 1777. No newspaper versions are known to have appeared. The text printed here is of the first edition.

The American Crisis, Number IV was published in pamphlet form by Styner and Cist in Philadelphia on September 13, 1777, and on the same day in the *Pennsylvania Evening Post*. The text of the pamphlet version is printed here.

The American Crisis, Number V was published as a pamphlet by John Dunlap on March 23, 1778, in Lancaster, Pennsylvania, where Paine had gone during the British occupation of Philadelphia. No newspaper publication has been located. The text of the first edition is printed here.

"Prospects for War Between Britain and France" (the descriptive title supplied here for an item headed only "To the People of America"), appeared in the *Pennsylvania Gazette,* June 10, 1778, published in York Town (York, Pennsylvania) during the British occupation of Philadelphia; that text is printed here.

"The Crisis, Number VI" appeared first in the *Pennsylvania Packet*, published by John Dunlap, in Philadelphia on October 22, 1778, and that text is printed here.

"The Crisis, Number VII" was published in the *Pennsylvania Packet* on November 12, 1778, and that text is printed here.

"Portion of a Letter to Henry Laurens" (1778?) appeared untitled in the New York *Public Advertiser* on May 30, 1807 (Paine contributed articles to this journal during this period). That text is printed here.

"Response to *Observations on the American Revolution*" appeared under the heading "For the *Pennsylvania Packet*" and was published in that paper on March 20, 1779. That text is printed here.

"Response to the Riot Outside James Wilson's House" appeared under the heading "To the printer of the *Pennsylvania Packet*," and was published there on October 16, 1779. That text is printed here.

"The Crisis, Number VIII" appeared in the *Pennsylvania Packet* on February 26, 1780; a line at the end stated: "To be concluded in a subsequent paper," but no subsequent installment was published. That text is printed here.

"The Crisis, No IX" was first published in the *Pennsylvania Packet* on June 10, 1780, but a corrected version was published there on June 13, 1780, with a note apologizing for the errors of the earlier version. The text printed here is that of the June 13, 1780, printing.

The Crisis Extraordinary was published as a pamphlet by William Harris in Philadelphia on October 7, 1780. Other pamphlet versions later appeared, as well as newspaper texts. The text printed here is that of the first edition.

Public Good, Being an Examination Into the Claim of Virginia to the Vacant Western Territory, and Of the Right of The United States to the Same. To which is added, Proposals for laying off a new State, to be applied as a fund for carrying on the war, or redeeming the national debt. By the author of Common Sense was published as a pamphlet by John Dunlap in Philadelphia on December 30, 1780. That text is printed here.

"Common Sense, on the King of England's Speech," appeared in two installments. The first was printed in the *Pennsylvania Packet* on February 19, 1782, ending with the note "To be continued in a future paper." The second part was printed in the *Pennsylvania Gazette*, February 27, 1782. The printings of the *Gazette* and *Packet* are from the same typesetting (the *Gazette* printing of the first part appeared on February 20, and the second part appeared in the *Pennsylvania Packet* on February 28). Other newspaper appearances are derived from these two. The texts printed here are those of the *Pennsylvania Packet* and *Pennsylvania Gazette*, February 19 and February 27, 1782.

"Common Sense, on Financing the War" was published in the *Pennsylvania Gazette* and the *Pennsylvania Journal* on March 6, 1782 (the text which appeared in the *Pennsylvania Packet* on March 7 is from the same typesetting as that of the *Gazette*). The *Journal* version omits most of Paine's quotation from the congressional resolution. The article was carried by other papers, but the earliest and most complete printings are those of the *Gazette* and the *Packet*. The text printed here is that of the *Pennsylvania Gazette*. (Paine's three articles, published on February 19, 27, and March 6, 1782, were gathered together and titled "Crisis X," without his authorization, by James Carey in *The Works of Thomas Paine*, published in 1797.)

"The Necessity of Taxation" appeared in the *Pennsylvania Gazette* and the *Pennsylvania Journal* on April 3, 1782 (it appeared in the *Packet* on April 4, 1782, printed from the same typesetting as the *Gazette*). Because the text of the *Gazette* seems more accurate than that of the *Journal,* that text is printed here.

"Response to an Accusation of Bribery," written for the *Freeman's Journal,* was published in that newspaper on May 1, 1782, and does not seem to have appeared elsewhere; that text is printed here.

"The Crisis, No. XI" was first published in the *Pennsylvania Packet* and the *Pennsylvania Journal* on May 11, 1782 (other newspaper versions are derived from them). There are very few variants between the *Packet* and the *Journal* texts. The text printed here is that of the *Pennsylvania Packet*.

"To Sir Guy Carleton" was published in the *Pennsylvania Packet,* June 1, 1782, and was later reprinted in five other papers. (In Carey's 1797 edition of the *The Works of Thomas Paine,* this piece was retitled "Supernumerary Crisis I"; Paine himself had no part in preparing that collected edition.) The text printed here is that of the *Pennsylvania Packet*.

"To the Earl of Shelburne" was published in the *Pennsylvania Gazette* and in the *Pennsylvania Journal* on October 30; the *Pennsylvania Packet* version, published on October 31, is identical to that of the *Gazette*. The article was later printed in other papers. (Carey's collected edition prints this piece as "Crisis XII," but no contemporary version used that title.) The text printed here is that of the *Pennsylvania Gazette*.

"The Last Crisis, No. XIII," dated Philadelphia, April 19, 1783, was published in the *Pennsylvania Packet* and in the *Pennsylvania Journal* on that day (the *Gazette* and *Freeman's Journal* versions appeared on April 23). The text of the *Packet* seems the most accurate, and that text is printed here.

"Commerce with Britain and the Necessity of Union" was dated December 9, 1783, by Paine and published in *Rivington's New-York*

Gazette, under the title "To the People of America" on December 10, 1783. The letter was written in response to an article that had appeared in the *Gazette* on December 6, and it was later reprinted in other papers. (This letter was published as "The Supernumerary Crisis II" by Carey in his edition of *The Works of Thomas Paine.*) The text printed here is that of *Rivington's New-York Gazette.*

"On the Affairs of Pennsylvania," dated by Paine "Philad. Sept. 15, 1786," was published in the *Pennsylvania Gazette,* September 20, 1786, as the fifth in his series of articles defending the Bank of North America. It was also published in the *Pennsylvania Packet* on September 21, with no variants. The text printed here is that of the *Gazette.*

"Attack on Paper Money Laws," dated by Paine "Philadelphia, Nov. 3, 1786," is number VI in his series on the Bank. It was published in the *Pennsylvania Packet,* November 7, 1786, and on November 8 in the *Gazette.* The text printed here is that of the *Packet.*

"To Thomas Jefferson," February? 1788, was not published during Paine's lifetime. The text of the letter printed here is that of *The Papers of Thomas Jefferson,* vol. 13, edited by Julian P. Boyd, Princeton University Press, 1956. Used with permission.

"To George Washington," October 16, 1789, was not published during Paine's lifetime. The text of the letter printed here is that of *The Papers of George Washington, Presidential Series,* vol. 4, edited by W. W. Abbot and Dorothy Twohig, University Press of Virginia, 1993. Used with permission of the University Press of Virginia.

"To Benjamin Rush," March 16, 1790, was not published during Paine's lifetime. (A portion of the letter, addressed to "A Friend in Philadelphia," appeared in *Miscellaneous Letters and Essays on Various Subjects, by Thomas Paine,* published in London by R. Carlile in 1819.) The text printed here is that of the holograph manuscript in the Library of Congress.

"To George Washington," May 1, 1790, was not published during Paine's lifetime. The text of the letter printed here is that of the typescript transcription prepared by the staff of *The Papers of George Washington,* edited by W. W. Abbot and Dorothy Twohig, for a forthcoming volume in the *Presidential Series.* Used with permission of the University Press of Virginia.

"To Samuel Adams, January 1, 1803" includes an introduction by Paine, the letter from Samuel Adams, and Paine's reply, all published by Paine in *The National Intelligencer,* Washington, D.C., on January 26, 1803; that text is printed here.

"The Construction of Iron Bridges" was published in the *Aurora,* Philadelphia, June 17, 1803, and signed "Thomas Paine, Bordentown on the Delaware, June 13, 1803"; that text is printed here.

"Of the Term 'Liberty of the Press' " was published in *The American Citizen*, New York, October 20, 1806, and that text is printed here.

This volume presents the texts of the original printings (and in one case original holograph) chosen for inclusion here; it does not attempt to reproduce features of eighteenth-century typography and handwriting, such as the long letter "s" or the use of quotation marks at the beginning of every line of a quotation. The texts are printed without other changes, except for the correction of typographical errors. Spelling, punctuation, and capitalization are often expressive features, and they are not altered, even when inconsistent or irregular.

Notes

In the notes below, the reference numbers denote page and line of this volume (the line count includes headings). No note is made for material included in standard desk-reference books such as Webster's *Collegiate*, *Biographical*, and *Geographical* dictionaries. Footnotes in the text are Paine's own. Biblical quotations are keyed to the King James Version. Quotations from Shakespeare are keyed to *The Riverside Shakespeare*, ed. G. Blakemore Evans (Boston: Houghton Mifflin, 1974). For references to other studies and further biographical background, see Alfred Owen Aldridge, *Man of Reason: The Life of Thomas Paine* (Philadelphia: J. P. Lippincott, 1959); Audrey Williamson, *Thomas Paine, His Life, Work, and Times* (New York: St. Martin's Press, 1973); David Freeman Hawke, *Paine* (New York: Harper & Row, 1974); and Eric Foner, *Tom Paine and Revolutionary America* (New York: Oxford University Press, 1976).

5.4–6   Man . . . THOMSON.] James Thomson, *Liberty: A Poem* (1736), part IV, lines 636–37.

13.4   Gideon . . . prophet Samuel] Judges 6–8, especially 8:22–23; I Samuel 8:5–20, 12:17–19.

17.29   Saul . . . lot] I Samuel 10:17–24.

19.39–40   Sir William Meredith] Meredith (d. 1790) was a Whig Member of Parliament, 1754–80, and author of several pamphlets on British politics.

20.38   Mr. Pelham] Henry Pelham (1695?–1754), first lord of the treasury (prime minister) and chancellor of the exchequer from 1743 until his death.

22.29   miseries of Hanover] The German electorate of Hanover, whose ruling dynasty had also reigned in Britain since 1714, was invaded by the French during the Seven Years War (1756–63).

26.10   Boston] British troops had occupied Boston since June 1774. The city was besieged by American forces from April 19, 1775, until the British evacuation on March 17, 1776.

27.27–29   Milton . . . deep."] *Paradise Lost* (1667), Book IV, lines 98–99.

28.1–2   repeal . . . undeceived us]   Parliament repealed the Stamp Act in
March 1766 after widespread colonial resistance, but in 1767 again asserted its
right to tax the American colonies by enacting import duties on glass, lead,
paint, paper, and tea that had been proposed by chancellor of the exchequer
Charles Townshend. At the same time Parliament established an American
board of customs commissioners, based in Boston and answering to the British treasury board, which would become highly resented by the American
colonists.

28.40–29.2   temporary stoppage . . . acts]   In response to the Boston
Tea Party of 1773, Parliament passed four laws in spring 1774 that became
known in the American colonies as the Coercive, or Intolerable, Acts. The
acts closed Boston harbor until "obedience to the laws" was restored in the
town and the destroyed tea paid for, increased the Crown's power over Massachusetts government, permitted the trials of persons accused of committing
capital crimes while enforcing the law or collecting revenue in the colonies to
be removed to Britain or Nova Scotia, and allowed the quartering of troops
in occupied domestic dwellings throughout the colonies. Widespread opposition to the acts resulted in the meeting of the First Continental Congress in
Philadelphia on September 5, 1774, and the creation by Congress on October
18 of the Continental Association. The articles of the Association pledged the
colonies to discontinue the slave trade and cease importing goods from Great
Britain, Ireland, and the East and West Indies after December 1, 1774, to
cease consuming British goods after March 1, 1775, and, if necessary, to cease
all exports (excluding rice) to Britain, Ireland, and the West Indies after September 10, 1775. The Association was enforced by elected town, city, and
county committees, which punished violators by publicity and boycott.

34.19   *Dragonetti . . . rewards."*]   Giacinto Dragonetti (1738–1818),
Trattato delle virtù e dei premi (1765).

35.16   Indians and Negroes]   In 1775 Lord Dunmore, royal governor of
Virginia, attempted to enlist Indians from the northwest frontier as allies
against the American patriots. Dunmore also issued a proclamation in November 1775 offering to free slaves of rebel masters if they would fight with
British forces.

37.39   *Entic's naval history*]   John Entick, *A new naval history; or, Compleat view of the British marine* . . . (1757).

38.3   Mr. Burchett]   Josiah Burchett (1666?–1746), secretary of the Ad-
miralty, 1698–1742, and writer on British naval history.

38.27   bombs]   Small naval vessels used for shore bombardment.

39.12   Terrible . . . Death]   Captain William Death commanded the privateer *Terrible*, 26 guns, in its engagement with the French privateer *Vengeance*, 36 guns, at the western entrance to the English Channel on
December 27, 1756. After a battle lasting three hours, Captain Death was
fatally wounded and the *Terrible* surrendered. Paine later wrote in *Rights of*

Man that he had briefly enlisted onboard the *Terrible;* see 604.34–605.4 in this volume.

41.32–33   Pennsylvania . . . lands]   Royal charters granted to Connecticut colonists in 1662 and to William Penn in 1681 resulted in conflicting territorial jurisdiction over the Wyoming Valley in present-day northeastern Pennsylvania. In 1769 Connecticut settlers began moving into the valley, and in 1774–75 the Connecticut colonial government organized the region as a township, and then as a separate county, in Connecticut. After Pennsylvania militia unsuccessfully attempted to drive the Connecticut settlers from the valley late in 1775, the Continental Congress mediated an agreement allowing the settlers to remain for the duration of hostilities with Britain. A commission appointed by Congress awarded permanent jurisdiction to Pennsylvania in 1782.

44.3–5   Associators petition . . . twenty-eight]   A committee of privates serving in the Military Association (the Pennsylvania militia) submitted two petitions to the assembly in October 1775. The first called for the adoption of a law making militia service compulsory for all freemen; the second asserted that it would not violate liberty of conscience to levy fines on Quakers who refused to serve. On November 17, 1775, the assembly divided 14–14 on the question of requiring 20 days of compulsory militia drill a year. The speaker cast the deciding vote in the affirmative, and on November 25 the assembly passed a militia law that levied fines on "Non-Associators."

44.37–39   Mr. Cornwall . . . Assembly]   Charles Wolfram Cornwall (1735–89) was a junior lord of the treasury in the North government, 1774–80, and then Speaker of the House of Commons, 1780–89. The New York general assembly adopted a remonstrance to the House of Commons in early 1775 that protested several parliamentary measures, including the Declaratory, Coercive, and Quebec Acts (sees notes 91.15–16, 28.40–29.2, and 49.37). On May 15, 1775, the House of Commons debated the petition, and after voting 186–67 that it claimed rights inconsistent with the legislative authority of Parliament, refused it further consideration.

45.38   Burgh's political Disquisitions]   James Burgh (1714–75), British political writer whose *Political Disquisitions* (1774), criticizing the structure of government in Great Britain, was widely influential in the American colonies.

46.19–20   same day . . . Speech]   On January 10, 1776, copies of the speech delivered by George III at the opening of Parliament on October 26, 1775, reached Philadelphia.

47.19   Sir John Dalrymple]   Dalrymple (1726–1810) was the author of several works on historical and scientific subjects, including *The Address of the people of Great-Britain to the inhabitants of America* (1775), which reaffirmed Britain's political authority over the colonies.

49.37   unjust extention . . . Canada]   The Quebec Act of 1774 extended the boundaries of Quebec southward to the Ohio River, thereby including territory claimed by Virginia, Massachusetts, and Connecticut. It was also resented by many colonists for establishing civil government in Quebec without an elected legislature and for granting the Roman Catholic Church the right to collect tithes in the province.

51.12–13   letter . . . New-York papers] An extract from a letter "from a Gentleman in London, to his friend in this city, dated July 26, 1775" appeared in *Rivington's New-York Gazetteer* on October 12, 1775, and was reprinted in the *New-York Gazette and the Weekly Mercury* the following week. The letter described the North ministry as sincerely pursuing reconciliation with the colonists and urged Americans to negotiate a settlement with Britain that recognized parliamentary supremacy over the colonies. A reply printed in the *New York Journal* on November 14, 1775, attributed the letter to Dr. Myles Cooper (1737–85), a Loyalist clergymen who had served as president of King's College in New York from 1763 until May 1775, when he fled the city.

51.28   footing . . . sixty-three] Before the end of the Seven Years War in 1763, Britain had rarely imposed taxes on the American colonies, or enforced those legally in effect, which were designed primarily for the regulation of trade and not the raising of revenue.

54.20–24   "The ANCIENT . . . GENERAL."] The Quaker address, written by John Pemberton (1727–95), clerk of the Monthly Meeting of Philadelphia, was dated January 20, 1776.

60.4   CATO] Writing under the name "Cato," the Rev. Dr. William Smith (1727–1803), an Anglican clergyman and provost of the College of Philadelphia, published four letters in the Philadelphia press in March 1776 opposing American independence and criticizing *Common Sense*. Smith published four more "Cato" letters in April 1776.

61.20   *Cassandra*] An essay published under the name "Cassandra" had appeared in the Philadelphia press in late March 1776 criticizing "Cato's" arguments. It has been attributed to James Cannon, a mathematician, teacher, and friend of Paine.

62.1–2   Committee . . . Convention] The Philadelphia Committee of Inspection and Observation, an elected body established in 1774 to carry out the resolves of the First Continental Congress, called on February 28, 1776, for a provincial convention to take into consideration "the present state of the province," including the underrepresentation of the western counties in the assembly. In March the assembly agreed to add 13 new seats in the western counties and four in Philadelphia, and scheduled a special election for May 1, 1776.

62.26–27   body of M'Leod.] Captain Donald McLeod, a British officer killed at the battle of Moore's Creek Bridge in North Carolina on February 27, 1776, while leading Loyalist forces. He was reported to have been hit by nine musket balls and 24 pieces of shot.

63.21   Commissioners]   Under the Prohibitory Act passed by Parliament on December 22, 1775, George III was authorized to appoint commissioners with the power to grant pardons and restore the king's protection to regions of the colonies that had ceased to be in rebellion. On May 3, 1776, the king named Admiral Richard Howe, commander of the Royal Navy in America, and his brother, General William Howe, commander of the British Army in America, as commissioners.

65.13   thy soliloquy]   "Cato" had prefaced one of his letters with a ten-line parody of *Hamlet*, III.i.69–77, that contained the phrase ". . . Who would endure this Pain"; the mock soliloquy also referred to advocates of independence John Adams, Christopher Marshall, Thomas Young, James Cannon, and Benjamin Rush.

67.17–18   Gentleman . . . *principles*]   David Rittenhouse (1732–96), Philadelphia scientist and advocate of independence.

68.39–40   Oration . . . Montgomery]   *An Oration in memory of General Montgomery, and of the Officers who fell with him, December 31, 1775, before Quebec,* delivered on February 19, 1776, by the Rev. Dr. William Smith, the author of the "Cato" letters, and subsequently printed as a pamphlet.

69.27–30   *"my dear . . .* MacDonald's commission]   The Rev. Dr. William Smith was born in Aberdeen, Scotland. Lieutenant Colonel Donald MacDonald was sent to North Carolina in 1775 by General Gage to recruit immigrants from the Scottish Highlands for the king's service. MacDonald was later commissioned as a brigadier-general of militia by Josiah Martin, the royal governor of North Carolina, and assembled a force of 1,400 Loyalists, approximately two-thirds of whom were Highlanders. He was captured by Patriot forces after the battle of Moore's Creek Bridge, February 27, 1776.

69.31–32   *Plain Truth*]   *Plain Truth: addressed to the inhabitants of America, containing remarks on a late pamphlet, entitled Common sense . . . ,* published in Philadelphia in March 1776 under the name "Candidus." Although its authorship has been attributed by some to the Rev. Dr. William Smith, it is now believed to have been written by James Chalmers, a Maryland Loyalist.

72.33–34   act . . . pirates]   The Prohibitory Act of December 22, 1775, made ships involved in commerce with the American colonies subject to seizure by the Royal Navy.

75.17   *Allen*]   William Allen (1704–80), chief justice of Pennsylvania, 1750–74, and his son, Andrew (1740–1825), a Pennsylvania delegate to the Continental Congress, 1775–76, were both opponents of independence.

80.32   *Rosseau*]   Jean Jacques Rousseau, *Projet de paix perpétuelle* (1761).

81.15   The charter]   Magna Charta, signed by King John in 1215.

82.15   scripture . . . Ez 35.]   In his fifth letter, "Cato" criticized the use of scripture in *Common Sense,* and then wrote that the only modern king rejected by God in the Bible was "*Mounsier,* the King of *France,*" citing the prophecy concerning Mount Seir in Ezekiel 35. "Cato" interpreted Ezekiel 35 as a warning against Protestant America allying itself with Catholic France, and wrote that this "application is much more natural" than that which *Common Sense* had made of I Samuel 8.

83.27   *Common Man*]   "A Common Man" was the signature used in a letter addressed to "Cato, Cassandra, and All the Writers on the Independence Controversy" that appeared in the Philadelphia press in late March 1776. The letter called for the press debate on independence to be conducted with less personal acrimony and greater attention to the economic consequences of independence.

84.15–16   Gentleman . . . instructions]   John Dickinson (1732–1808) drafted instructions, adopted by the assembly on November 9, 1775, that enjoined Pennsylvania's delegates in Congress to "utterly reject" proposals for independence from Britain.

88.17   before . . . Quebec]   American troops besieged Quebec until the arrival of a British relief expedition on May 6, 1776.

89.9   Clymer and Allen]   George Clymer (1739–1813), the leading "Independent" candidate, and later a signer of the Declaration of Independence; Andrew Allen (1740–1825), Pennsylvania attorney general and delegate to Congress, who later swore allegiance to the king and emigrated to England. Samuel Howell and Alexander Wilcox, candidates on the "Dependent" or "Moderate" ticket with Allen, were also elected on May 1, receiving 941 and 921 votes respectively.

90.14–15   odium . . . Assembly]   In January 1775 the New York assembly refused to appoint delegates to the Second Continental Congress. The New York Committee of Sixty, formed in 1774 to enforce the nonimportation Association (see note 28.40–29.2), then called for the election of a provincial convention, which met on April 20, 1775, and appointed delegates to Congress. In May 1775 legislative power in New York passed to the newly elected provincial congress.

91.15–16   declared, . . . WHATSOEVER,"]   The Declaratory Act of 1766, passed after the repeal of the Stamp Act, reaffirmed Parliament's authority to legislate for the American colonies.

95.39   this city]   Philadelphia.

100.4   LORD HOWE]   Vice Admiral Richard Howe (1727–99), 4th Viscount Howe.

100.5–6   "What's . . . CHURCHILL.]   Cf. Charles Churchill (1731–64), "The Author," lines 113–14: "What's in this name of *Lord,* that I should fear / To bring their vices to the public ear?"

100.22–23   published a proclamation]   On November 30, 1776, the

Howe brothers offered pardons and papers of protection to colonists who would swear an oath of allegiance to the king within 60 days.

101.4–5   deceased brother's] George Augustus Howe (1724–58), older brother of Richard and William, had been killed fighting the French at Ticonderoga during the Seven Years War. The General Court (legislature) of Massachusetts appropriated £250 for a monument to him in Westminster Abbey.

102.7   14th . . . September] In their declaration of July 14, 1776, the Howes announced their authority to grant pardons. Their declaration of September 19, 1776, asserted that the king would "direct a revision" of royal instructions and "concur in the revisal" of parliamentary acts adverse to colonial interests if the Americans would cease fighting and renew their allegiance to the crown.

102.18   the gentlemen . . . business] Benjamin Franklin, John Adams, and Edward Rutledge were appointed by Congress on September 6, 1776, to confer with Lord Howe. They met with him on Staten Island, New York, on September 11.

106.9–10   Quakers . . . Pemberton,"] The address urged Quakers to resist military service, special taxes in support of the war, and oaths of loyalty to the new revolutionary governments. (For John Pemberton, see note 54.20–24 in this volume.)

107.21   Colonel Rohl's] Colonel Johann Gottlieb Rall (c. 1720–76), killed during Washington's surprise attack on the Hessian garrison at Trenton, New Jersey, December 26, 1776.

108.29–30   butcherly . . . St. Vincents] After gaining possession of St. Vincent from France in the peace treaty of 1763, Britain became the first European power to make a concerted effort to settle the island against the resistance of its Carib population. In 1797 the surviving Caribs were deported.

113.32–33   "We . . . back."] Cf. Luke 9:62.

114.10–11   Hugh Gaine's . . . paper] The New-York Gazette and the Weekly Mercury, a Loyalist newspaper.

114.29   duke of Gloucester] William Henry (1743–1805), Duke of Gloucester, younger brother of George III.

118.29–30   the Colonies . . . rebellion] George III proclaimed the colonies to be in rebellion on August 23, 1775.

118.32–34   FIRST. . . petitioned] In October 1774 the First Continental Congress adopted a resolution repudiating the Declaratory Act of 1766, a nonimportation agreement (see note 28.40–29.2), a petition to the king, and an address to the people of Great Britain.

123.21–23   Poland . . . French] In 1772 nearly 30 percent of Poland's territory was partitioned among Russia, Austria, and Prussia. Genoa sold Corsica to France in 1768.

123.28   treaty . . . Hessians]   Early in 1776 Britain concluded a treaty with the prince of Hesse-Kassel to hire mercenary soldiers for service in America. Eventually 30,000 mercenaries from six German states fought in the Revolutionary War, 17,000 of whom were from Hesse-Kassel. Over 7,500 German mercenaries were killed or died from disease, and another 5,000 deserted.

128.10   Lord North's motion]   Lord North proposed that Parliament refrain from laying revenue taxes upon the colonies if the colonial assemblies agreed to levy their own taxes to support imperial defense and colonial government. Parliament approved the proposal on February 27, 1775.

129.28   East-India . . . TEA]   In 1773 Parliament attempted to rescue the East India Company from bankruptcy by giving it a monopoly of the tea trade in the American colonies. The measure led to widespread colonial resistance, including the Boston Tea Party of December 16, 1773.

130.12   second petition]   The "Olive Branch" petition, drafted by John Dickinson, was adopted by Congress on July 5, 1775, and signed on July 8. It criticized the conduct of the ministry since 1763 and appealed to the king's "royal magnanimity and benevolence" in seeking reconciliation with Britain. George III refused to receive the petition when it reached London and, on August 23, 1775, proclaimed the colonies to be in rebellion.

133.14-15   charge . . . DRAYTON]   In his charge, delivered on April 23, 1776, Drayton (1742-79) reviewed the events leading to the adoption of a temporary constitution by the South Carolina provincial congress on March 26, 1776. Drayton said that both the recent actions of George III and those of James II in 1688 had broken "the original contract between king and people" by violating fundamental laws, and asserted that the American revolution was as justified as the 1688 revolution in England. He concluded his charge by declaring, "The Almighty created America to be independent of Britain."

133.16-17   ADDRESS . . . New-York]   *An Address of the Convention of the Representatives of the State of New-York, to their Constituents,* written by John Jay and printed in Fishkill, New York, on December 23, 1776.

133.39-40   sister . . . society]   George III was alleged to have secretly married Hannah Lightfoot, a Quaker woman, while he was Prince of Wales.

135.4   20th of November]   The Quaker address appeared December 20, 1776; see note 106.9-10.

152.13   Knight . . . Post]   A Knight of the Windmill is one who fights chimeras, from Cervantes' *Don Quixote* (1605-15), Part I, chapter 8, in which Quixote attacks a windmill that he has mistaken for a giant. A Knight of the Post was a person who earned a living as a perjurer, so named from the signposts outside court where such persons could be found waiting to be bribed. The term was also used as a variant of "Knight of the Whipping Post"—a swindler, cheat, or otherwise notorious person.

158.14   General Carleton . . . lakes.]   In October 1776, after encountering determined resistance on Lake Champlain from American naval forces led by Benedict Arnold, General Guy Carleton (1724–1808) decided to withdraw his troops into Canada.

162.10   attack . . . Mud-Island.]   Mud Island, on the Pennsylvania shore of the Delaware below the mouth of the Schuylkill, was the site of Fort Mifflin, which withstood British attack from September 26 to November 16, 1777.

162.12   fable of Bender]   After his defeat by the Russians at Poltava in 1709, Charles XII of Sweden sought refuge in Ottoman territory, eventually making his camp on the Dniester River at Bender (now Bendery, Moldova). For diplomatic reasons Sultan Ahmed III ordered Charles taken into custody, and on February 1, 1713, several thousand Janissaries attacked his encampment. For eight hours Charles and his personal guards fought the Turks from inside a stone house, fleeing only after the roof was set on fire. While running to another building, Charles fell and was captured (he returned to Swedish territory in 1714).

164.35–36   Charles of Sweden]   Presumably, Charles XII of Sweden (1682–1718).

168.11   My official situation]   In April 1777 Paine had been elected by Congress to the post of secretary to the Committee for Foreign Affairs.

177.16   treaty with France]   France and the United States concluded a treaty of alliance on February 6, 1778, in which France recognized the United States and promised, in the event of war between France and Britain, to fight with the United States until Britain accepted American independence.

179.27   burning . . . Mr. Borden's]   A British raiding party sailed up the Delaware to Bordentown, New Jersey, on May 8, 1778, and burned the house of Mr. Borden. The next day it burned the nearby house of Colonel Joseph Kirkbride, a friend of Paine.

181.4–5   CARLISLE . . . EDEN]   Frederick Howard, Earl of Carlisle, and William Eden were members of a British peace commission authorized by Parliament in March 1778; Sir Henry Clinton succeeded Sir William Howe as commander of the British Army in America in May 1778. The Carlisle commission was instructed to accede to nearly all American demands except independence, but Congress refused to meet with the commissioners and voted on April 22, 1778, not to negotiate with Britain unless it recognized American independence.

181.15   last proclamation]   The proclamation was issued in New York by Carlisle and Eden on October 3, 1778.

189.14   expedition to Egg-Harbour]   On October 14, 1778, British forces raided Little Egg Harbor, New Jersey, and burned several houses and ten privateering vessels. The next day they killed 50 men of Pulaski's Legion on nearby Minock Island before withdrawing.

198.4   Admiral Saunders]   Sir Charles Saunders (1713?–75) commander-in-chief of the Royal Navy in the Mediterranean, 1760–63 and 1773–75.

206.5   Mr.   Banks   and   Dr.   Solander]   Naturalists   Joseph   Banks (1743–1820) and Daniel Solander (1736–82) sailed aboard the *Endeavour* with Captain James Cook on his first voyage around the world, 1768–71.

208.33–36   "*yet . . . wither*]   Cf. Jonah 3:4–4:7.

216.18   *Admiral*]   While serving as president of the South Carolina provincial congress, Drayton was onboard the schooner *Defence* when it exchanged fire with the British vessels *Tamar* and *Cherokee* off Charleston on November 11, 1775. The South Carolina council of safety then appointed Drayton to command the ship *Prosper* on December 16, despite his lack of maritime experience. Drayton saw no action with the *Prosper,* but remained its commander until March 27, 1776, when he was elected chief justice of the state by the general assembly.

216.38–39   Mr. Deane's impositions]   For Paine's involvement in the controversy over Silas Deane's conduct, see Chronology, 1778 and 1779.

218.10   affair of the fourth]   A group of militiamen gathered in Philadelphia on October 4, 1779, for the purpose of driving from the city "disaffected persons and those who supported them." The militia expelled several opponents of extralegal price controls and then marched toward the house of James Wilson, a leading opponent of price controls and the 1776 state constitution, and a prominent legal defender of Tories accused of treason. Wilson had meanwhile gathered about 20 friends and political allies, including financier Robert Morris, inside his house. When the militia arrived outside shots were exchanged between the two groups. Four militiamen were killed, along with one man inside the house and an onlooker who had joined in the attack. The fighting ended when Joseph Reed, president of the Pennsylvania executive council, arrived with a mounted militia unit and dispersed the crowd. Although arrests were made, no one was ever tried for the shootings, and in March 1780 the executive council pardoned all persons involved in the "Fort Wilson Riot."

222.11–12   Confederated . . . Europe]   Spain declared war against Britain on June 21, 1779.

230.29   fate of Charlestown]   On May 12, 1780, the British captured over 5,000 prisoners when the American garrison at Charleston, South Carolina, surrendered.

235.1   *The Crisis Extraordinary*]   On May 28, 1780, George Washington sent a letter from his camp at Morristown, New Jersey, to Joseph Reed, president of the Pennsylvania executive council, describing the army's need for provisions and asking for help from the state authorities in obtaining supplies. In the letter, Washington wrote: "The crisis in every point of view is extraordinary and extraordinary expedients are necessary."

243.26   emissions stopt]   On September 1, 1779, Congress resolved to limit emissions of Continental paper money at $200 million, and on March 18, 1780, it approved a plan for retiring the existing Continental currency and replacing it with $10 million in new paper money.

246.2   forty to one]   The financial measures adopted by Congress valued the existing paper currency at 40–1 against specie.

246.26–27   pamphlet . . . Dalrymple]   See note 47.19.

253.3–7   VIRGINIA . . . UNITED STATES]   The draft Articles of Confederation submitted in July 1776 gave Congress power to set the boundaries of states, including those whose colonial charters claimed lands extending to the South Sea (Pacific Ocean). This provision was opposed by delegates from Virginia and other states with western land claims and was removed from the revised Articles approved by Congress on November 15, 1777, and submitted to the state legislatures for ratification (the Articles had to be ratified by all 13 states before they could take effect). By February 1779 ratification had been approved in every state except Maryland, whose legislature insisted on restoring to Congress power to set state boundaries (many prominent Maryland political leaders had made speculative land purchases in the western territory which they feared the Virginia legislature would invalidate). On January 2, 1781, the Virginia legislature offered to cede to Congress its lands northwest of the Ohio River on condition that new states be eventually formed out of the territory and that purchases made from the Indians by land companies be voided. Under pressure from the Chevalier de la Luzerne, French minister to the United States, the Maryland legislature approved the Articles of Confederation on February 2 and their ratification was completed on March 1, 1781.

255.39   sir Dalby . . . account]   *An historical account of the rise and growth of the West-India collonies, and of the great advantage they are to England, in respect to trade* (London, 1690).

257.38   Oldmixon's . . . Virginia.]   John Oldmixon (1673–1742), *The British Empire in America,* 2 vols. (1708).

259.10–11   cape . . . Comfort]   Located at the end of the peninsula between the York and James rivers, where Hampton Roads flows into Chesapeake Bay; later the site of Fort Monroe.

266.8–9   Stith's . . . Virginia.]   The Rev. William Stith (1707–55), *The History of the First Discovery and Settlement of Virginia* (Williamsburg, 1747).

266.21   Hutchinson . . . New England]   Thomas Hutchinson, *The History of the Province of Massachusetts Bay* (1764–67).

287.22   the speech]   In his speech at the opening of Parliament on

November 27, 1781, George III pledged to continue the war despite the surrender of British forces under Lord Cornwallis at Yorktown on October 19. News of the capitulation had reached London on November 25.

288.4   expression . . . used]   In the first "Forester" letter; see page 60 in this volume.

293.19   Smollet's . . . England]   Tobias George Smollett, *A Complete History of England* (1757–65).

297.5   Colonel . . . myself]   Paine and Colonel John Laurens traveled to France in 1781 and, with the help of Benjamin Franklin, obtained additional financial aid from the French government.

297.16   Commissioners in Paris]   Congress appointed Benjamin Franklin, Silas Deane, and Thomas Jefferson to serve as diplomatic commissioners in Europe on September 26, 1776. Jefferson declined the appointment and was replaced by Arthur Lee, who quarreled with Deane and accused him of misconduct.

315.20   New-York papers]   New York City remained under British occupation until November 1783.

319.37   major Trent]   William Trent (1715–1787) joined George Morgan (1743–1810) and other land speculators in unsuccessfully petitioning the Virginia legislature and Congress to validate their title to a northwestern land grant made by the Six Nations in 1768 as compensation for losses incurred by traders during the Pontiac Indian War of 1763–65.

325.9   cabinet and councils]   Lord George Germain, secretary of state for the American colonies since November 1775, resigned on February 11, 1782. On February 27 the House of Commons voted to cease offensive operations in America and on March 5 it authorized peace negotiations. Lord North resigned on March 20 and on March 22 the Marquis of Rockingham agreed to form a new ministry with the Earl of Shelburne serving as secretary for colonial affairs. The Rockingham administration then moved to negotiate peace with the United States while seeking to split the Franco-American alliance.

334.13–34   Huddy . . . Asgil]   Joshua Huddy, a militia artillery captain, was captured on March 24, 1782, by members of the Associated Loyalists and imprisoned on a British ship at New York. Captain Richard Lippencott of the Associated Loyalists removed Huddy from the ship under pretense of using him in a prisoner exchange and took him under guard to Middletown, New Jersey, where he was hanged on April 12. A placard placed on Huddy's body announced that his death was in retaliation for the alleged murder of New Jersey Loyalist Philip White on March 30 (Monmouth County patriots claimed White had been killed while trying to escape). Washington wrote to Clinton on April 21 demanding that Lippencott be surrendered to American authorities; Clinton, who had already ordered Lippencott court-martialed, replied on April 25 that he would try the person responsible for Huddy's death. Washington then ordered the selection of a British officer for possible retaliation, and on May 26 Charles Asgill, a 19-year-old officer who had surrendered at Yorktown in 1781, was chosen by lot.

337.31 murderer . . . officer] In August 1782 Carleton informed Washington that the court-martial had acquitted Lippencott on the grounds that he had executed Huddy under orders from William Franklin, commander of the Associated Loyalists and former royal governor of New Jersey (Franklin was a natural son of Benjamin Franklin). Washington referred the matter to Congress with the recommendation that Asgill not be hanged (executing Asgill would have violated the Yorktown capitulation agreement, which protected British prisoners against retaliatory measures). After learning that Louis XVI and Marie Antoinette hoped that Asgill would be spared, Congress ordered his release on November 7, 1782. Lippencott emigrated to Canada at the end of the war.

338.1 *Earl of Shelburne*] Following the death of the Marquis of Rockingham on July 1, 1782, the Earl of Shelburne had become first lord of the treasury (prime minister) in a new cabinet.

341.10–11 Mr. Wedderburne] Alexander Wedderburn (1733–1805) was solicitor general, 1771–78, and attorney general, 1778–80, in the North ministry.

342.8–9 Augustine] St. Augustine, capital of the British province of East Florida, 1763–83, and a refuge for Loyalists during the Revolution.

343.33 20,000 Russians] In 1775 the North ministry sought to hire Russian mercenaries to fight in America. After Empress Catherine II rejected the proposal, agreements were negotiated with several German princes; see note 123.28.

344.33 Mungo] A black slave and servant in *The Padlock* (1768), comic opera by Isaac Bickerstaffe (1733–?1808), music by Charles Dibdin (1745–1814).

345.17–18 Admiral Digby] Robert Digby (1732–1815), commander-in-chief of the Royal Navy in North America, 1781.

347.7 pamphlet . . . Reynal] *Letter addressed to the Abbe Raynal on the affairs of North-America. In which the mistakes in the abbe's account of the Revolution of America are corrected and cleared up* (Philadelphia, 1782) was Paine's reply to *Révolution de l'Amérique* (translation, *The Revolution of America*, Boston and New York, 1781) by l'Abbé Guillaume Thomas François Raynal (1713–96).

355.23–24 Lord Sheffield] John Baker Holroyd (1735–1821), Earl of Sheffield, whose *Observations on the commerce of the American states with Europe and the West Indies* was published in 1783.

357.2 certain State] Rhode Island.

357.18   the Fisheries] The peace treaty of 1783 secured American fishing rights off Newfoundland and Nova Scotia. In three articles published in Philadelphia, June–July 1779, Paine had urged Congress to protect the fisheries.

359.3–5   present constitution . . . parties] The Pennsylvania state constitution adopted on September 28, 1776, vested legislative powers in a unicameral general assembly, elected annually by all male taxpayers over 21 and by non-taxpaying sons of freeholders over 21 (this was the widest suffrage adopted by any state). Executive power was given to a 12-member council elected by the freemen; the council had no veto power. Supreme court judges were to serve for seven-year terms. After its adoption the constitution became the focus of a continuing political struggle within the state between its "Constitutionalist" supporters, who were strongest in the western counties, and its "Republican" or "Anti-Constitutionalist" opponents, who were led by Philadelphia commercial interests.

359.10–11   "A serious . . . affairs."] The piece appeared in the *Pennsylvania Packet* in four parts in early December 1778.

361.29–31   attack . . . *North-America*] On September 13, 1785, the Pennsylvania assembly repealed the charter it had granted to the Bank on April 1, 1782. The Bank was rechartered by the assembly in March 1787.

365.11–12   legal tenders . . . state] In March 1785 the Pennsylvania assembly issued £150,000 in bills of credit which could be used to buy land from, and to pay debts, taxes, and custom and import duties owed to, the state; the paper money was not, however, legal tender for paying private debts. By the end of 1786 paper money had been issued as full legal tender in North Carolina, Georgia, New Jersey, and Rhode Island.

368.2   February? 1788] This letter was probably written in February 1788, when Paine, Jefferson, and the marquis de Lafayette were meeting regularly in Paris to discuss the proposed federal constitution of the United States.

369.4   Mr. Wilson] Paine refers to James Wilson's speech at the Pennsylvania ratifying convention, November 24, 1787, subsequently issued as a pamphlet, *The Substance of a Speech Delivered by James Wilson, Esq. Explanatory of the General Principles of the Proposed Federal Constitution . . .* (1787).

370.22–23   Walkers . . . Yorkshire] The Walker brothers owned a large ironworks.

377.32   Felix qui cautus] Happy is he who is cautious.

381.26   Dr. Emmons] Nathanael Emmons (1745–1840), Massachusetts Congregational minister known for his support of the Federalist party. On April 9, 1801, he delivered a sermon comparing Jefferson to Jeroboam, the sinful ruler described in I Kings and II Chronicles.

381.32–33   four letters . . . Adams.] The letters, written between September 12 and November 20, 1790, discussed the nature of government; they were published as a pamphlet in 1802.

382.29–30   third . . . States]   Paine's letter appeared in the *National Intelligencer*, November 29, 1802, and described his imprisonment in Paris during the Jacobin Terror of 1793–94.

Index

☆☆☆ The Library of America

The contents of this Paperback Classic are drawn from *Thomas Paine: Collected Writings* (Eric Foner, editor), volume number 76 in the Library of America series, which also includes *Rights of Man* and *The Age of Reason*.

Created with seed funding from the National Endowment for the Humanities and the Ford Foundation, The Library of America is a nonprofit cultural institution that preserves our nation's literary heritage by publishing, and keeping permanently in print, authoritative editions of America's best and most significant writing. Hailed as "the most important book-publishing project in the nation's history" (*Newsweek*), this award-winning series maintains America's most treasured writers in "the finest-looking, longest-lasting edition ever made" (*The New Republic*).

Since 1982, over 250 hardcover volumes have been published in the Library of America series, each containing up to 1600 pages and including a number of works. In many cases, the complete works of a writer are collected in as few as three compact volumes. New volumes are added each year to make all the essential writings of America's foremost novelists, historians, poets, essayists, philosophers, playwrights, journalists, and statesmen part of The Library of America.

Each volume features: authoritative, unabridged texts • a chronology of the author's life, helpful notes, and a brief textual essay • a handsomely designed, easy-to-read page • high-quality, acid-free paper, bound in a cloth cover and sewn to lie flat when opened • a ribbon marker and printed end papers.

For more information, a complete list of titles, tables of contents, and to request a catalogue, please visit www.loa.org.

The Library of America Paperback Classics Series

American Speeches: Political Oratory from Patrick Henry to Barack Obama (various authors)
Edited and with an introduction by Ted Widmer
ISBN: 978-1-59853-094-0

The Education of Henry Adams by Henry Adams
With an introduction by Leon Wieseltier
ISBN: 978-1-59853-060-5

The Pioneers by James Fenimore Cooper
With an introduction by Alan Taylor
ISBN: 978-1-59853-155-8

The Red Badge of Courage by Stephen Crane
With an introduction by Robert Stone
ISBN: 978-1-59853-061-2

Narrative of the Life of Frederick Douglass, an American Slave
by Frederick Douglass
With an introduction by John Stauffer
ISBN: 978-1-59853-351-4

The Souls of Black Folk by W.E.B. Du Bois
With an introduction by John Edgar Wideman
ISBN: 978-1-59853-054-4

Essays: First and Second Series by Ralph Waldo Emerson
With an introduction by Douglas Crase
ISBN: 978-1-59853-084-1

The Autobiography by Benjamin Franklin
With an introduction by Daniel Aaron
ISBN: 978-1-59853-095-7

The Scarlet Letter by Nathaniel Hawthorne
With an introduction by Harold Bloom
ISBN: 978-1-59853-112-1

Indian Summer by William Dean Howells
With an introduction by John Updike
ISBN: 978-1-59853-156-5

The Varieties of Religious Experience by William James
With an introduction by Jaroslav Pelikan
ISBN: 978-1-59853-062-9

Selected Writings by Thomas Jefferson
With an introduction by Tom Wicker
ISBN: 978-1-59853-096-4

The Autobiography of an Ex-Colored Man by James Weldon Johnson
With an introduction by Charles Johnson
ISBN: 978-1-59853-113-8

Selected Speeches and Writings by Abraham Lincoln
With an introduction by Gore Vidal
ISBN: 978-1-59853-053-7

The Call of the Wild by Jack London
With an introduction by E. L. Doctorow
ISBN: 978-1-59853-058-2

Moby-Dick by Herman Melville
With an introduction by Edward Said
ISBN: 978-1-59853-085-8

Common Sense, The Crisis & Other Writings from the American Revolution by Thomas Paine
With an introduction by Eric Foner
ISBN: 978-1-59853-433-7

My First Summer in the Sierra and Selected Essays by John Muir
With an introduction by Bill McKibben
ISBN: 978-1-59853-111-4

Selected Tales, with The Narrative of Arthur Gordon Pym
by Edgar Allan Poe
With an introduction by Diane Johnson
ISBN: 978-1-59853-056-8

Uncle Tom's Cabin by Harriet Beecher Stowe
With an introduction by James M. McPherson
ISBN: 978-1-59853-086-5

Walden by Henry David Thoreau
With an introduction by Edward Hoagland
ISBN: 978-1-59853-063-6

Democracy in America by Alexis de Tocqueville
The Arthur Goldhammer Translation, in two volumes
Edited and with introductions by Olivier Zunz
Volume 1 — ISBN: 978-1-59853-151-0
Volume 2 — ISBN: 978-1-59853-152-7

The Adventures of Tom Sawyer by Mark Twain
With an introduction by Russell Baker
ISBN: 978-1-59853-087-2

Life on the Mississippi by Mark Twain
With an introduction by Jonathan Raban
ISBN: 978-1-59853-057-5

Selected Writings by George Washington
With an introduction by Ron Chernow
ISBN: 978-1-59853-110-7

The House of Mirth by Edith Wharton
With an introduction by Mary Gordon
ISBN: 978-1-59853-055-1

Leaves of Grass, The Complete 1855 and 1891–92 Editions by Walt Whitman
With an introduction by John Hollander
ISBN: 978-1-59853-097-1

For more information, please visit **www.loa.org/paperbackclassics/**